CW01511700

ALF FRANCIS—Racing Mechanic 1948–1958

Stirling Moss.   A. Francis

ALF FRANCIS
Racing Mechanic 1948–1958

His own story as told to
and written by

PETER LEWIS

Motor-Racing Correspondent of "The Observer" 1954–1960

FOREWORD

by

STIRLING MOSS

A **Foulis** Motoring Book

Original edition first published 1957.
Reprinted 1958 and 1959.

This edition, with new closing chapter,
first published 1991.

Published by:
Haynes Publishing Group
Sparkford, Nr Yeovil
Somerset BA22 7JJ, England

Haynes Publications Inc
861 Lawrence Drive, Newbury Park,
California 91320, USA

A catalogue record for this book is available
from the British Library

ISBN 0 85429 937 8

Library of Congress Catalog Card Number
91-76108

Printed in England by J H Haynes & Co Ltd.

FOREWORD

Behind the scenes of almost any public spectacle, there is a presiding genius, whose job it is to make sure that everything is organized down to the last detail to enable those in the public eye to give their best. In athletics he is the team coach ; in the theatre the stage director and in motor-racing he is the chief mechanic. His work is arduous and, especially during the season, almost unending, while his efforts are unsung and almost unknown to the outside world. But on him to a very large extent rests the responsibility of maintaining his drivers' reputation.

Such a man is Alf Francis, who spent some three years of his career as my own mechanic and who has now recorded in this book the reminis-ences of his crowded life around the circuits of Europe. I first worked with him in 1950 and 1951 when I was a team driver with the late John Heath's H.W.M. stable. Then following a season with Peter Whitehead Alf joined me in 1953. He saw me through the not-so-happy Cooper-Alta days, to the much more successful season of 1954 when I ran, and he looked after, my own Formula 1 Maserati. After that he stayed with me in 1955 and 1956, whilst I was with the Mercedes-Benz and Maserati works teams.

His book gives a graphic description of a racing mechanic's hectic life and has brought back for me many memories of forgotten times and incidents. He is very outspoken, but then Alf was never one to mince words. He would say exactly what he thought and felt, even if it hurt ! But at least he left you in no doubt of where you, or anyone else, stood in his estimation.

Above all, Alf Francis had an almost unbelievable amount of enthusiasm and drive ; the cars and getting them on to the grid in top condition came before everything else, especially food and sleep ! He was fanatically con-scientious and painstaking, but he liked to be left alone to do a job. In the workshop he was the boss, and his driver, or anyone else, nosing around inquisitively trying to tell him what he should do or how he should do it, could be certain of a very cool reception.

During the season, he could be relied upon to be on top of the situation, despite the strain and the time limits imposed by having to follow the " circus " round Britain and Europe week-end after week-end. Often there were hundreds of miles to be covered between circuits, and some of his adventures *en route* with his precious charge deserve to be recorded.

5

Alf aimed high and it was his obsession to beat the factory teams with a privately-entered car. Between us, we almost managed it with the Maserati in 1954, but eventually we were forced to the conclusion that it was impossible for two men and a car to take on the concentrated might of the works team organization, and win into the bargain. Even so, we got very near to it and a great deal of the credit for the showing we managed to put up is due to Alf Francis and his mechanical " green fingers."

After all, a racing car must go and keep going, before the driver can take it past the chequered flag. Keeping it going for me was Alf's responsibility—one that he fulfilled admirably.

STIRLING MOSS.

London, October, 1957.

Contents

Front cover of the original edition,
designed and sketched by
Sylvia Francis

List of Illustrations

ACKNOWLEDGEMENTS

This book would never have been written if I had not travelled from Oulton Park to London one Sunday morning in August 1954, sharing the driving cab of the Commer transporter with Alf Francis and Tony Robinson. It was during the journey that I worked out with Alf the contents of an article on Stirling Moss which later appeared under Alf's name in " Everybody's." What he told me during the journey about the life of a motor-racing mechanic convinced me that there was more than enough material for this book.

Therefore, it is thanks to Stirling Moss that the book came to be written—for he arranged for me to meet Alf at Oulton Park—and it is thanks again to Stirling for the Foreword. He not only read every single word of the manuscript at a time when his many and varied commitments left very little time for anything else but was more than helpful with comments and constructive suggestions.

Alf and I would also like to take this opportunity of thanking Douglas Armstrong—who was Associate Editor of " Motor Racing " at the time—for establishing the first contact between the authors and the Publisher and afterwards reading the book in manuscript form, with a very critical eye, and giving us the benefit of his valuable advice. Last but by no means least we should like to express our thanks to Alf's wife, Sylvia, who designed and painted the front cover and also drew the black and white sketches inside the book.

PETER LEWIS.

Pinner,
Middlesex.

INTRODUCTION

This is not only my story but the story of racing mechanics everywhere and of many other people behind the scenes whose contribution to the sport of motor-racing is invaluable but rarely publicized.

For nine years I have lived and worked in friendly rivalry with these people and in this book I have endeavoured to tell something of the hardships and frustrations that are part of this fascinating sport where success goes hand in hand with failure ; a sport which is a challenge not only to individuals, but to the motor-engineering capabilities of a nation.

I have felt for some time that such a story should be told and I hope that this book will be regarded as my tribute to those who like myself have chosen the hard yet sometimes satisfying life of a motor-racing mechanic, giving little consideration for their private life. People often ask me why I still go motor-racing. I tell them that I do so not just because I want to overcome the constant challenge of The Sport but because I want to help, and make some contribution however small, to the success story of British cars.

ALF FRANCIS.

Dorking, October, 1957.

CHAPTER 1

BITTEN BY THE " BUG "

The interview—My first race—Some notes on the G.P. Alta

One Saturday afternoon in April 1948 I found myself sitting in the offices of H.W. Motors Limited, being interviewed by John Heath and his partner, George Abecassis. I was there in answer to an advertisement : " Racing gentleman requires mechanic to maintain his Grand Prix car. Knowledge of Continent and languages an asset."

My answers to the questions put by Heath and Abecassis were short and to the point.

"Any previous experience of racing cars ? "

Answer : " No."

" Have you ever been to a motor-race ? "

Answer : " No."

And then—almost in desperation—came a final question.

" Have you ever seen a racing car ? "

Once again my answer was in the negative and, half apologetically, I mumbled something about my father having competed in rallies and trials in Poland before the war, adding that I knew the Continent fairly well and could speak several languages. Then I reached for my hat !

However, John Heath, who had been studying me closely, had other ideas.

" What we are looking for is a keen man who is conscientious and willing to learn." Then, to Abecassis : " How about giving him a trial ? "

If anyone was uncertain it was me, and I must have looked it, for Heath took me outside and showed me an E.R.A. and a Maserati. He tried to convince me that looking after racing cars was not at all difficult, but I don't mind admitting that as we stood there he had all the confidence. I had absolutely none at all.

* * * *

I had seen the H.W.M. advertisement in *The Autocar* the previous month and to this day I do not know what prompted me to look through the Classified Section, for I had no intention of buying a motor-car. However, it was not a car that attracted my attention but an invitation to write to a Box Number—an invitation that was to change my whole life.

My wife, Sylvia, came into the room and I handed *The Autocar* to her.

" Of course you have a chance," she replied in answer to my question. " You may not know anything about racing cars but you are a good mechanic, and you know the Continent well."

So I wrote to the Box Number and in due course received a reply. Could I be at Walton-on-Thames by 2.30 p.m. on Saturday, April 10th ?

I was then working at Furlongs Garage in Woolwich, where I had been employed since my demobilization from the 1st Polish Armoured Division at the end of the war. My father, a motor engineer, had a garage in Poland when I was a boy and I have been connected with motor-cars all my life. As a matter of fact I forged a driving licence when I was only seventeen so that I could get a job as a maintenance engineer with a bus transport company in Grudziadz, a small town near Danzig.

I started at Furlongs as an engine fitter. Then, when they handled the Perkins Diesel, I was put in charge of their Diesel Engineering Department. They treated me very well but I had been with them sixteen months and the prospects did not seem too promising.

I had no idea how to get to Walton ; just that it was on the other side of London from Woolwich. Grossly underestimating the time required to cross London I set off just after midday and arrived in Walton at 4 p.m., one-and-a-half hours late. Miserably I sat down to wait whilst other mechanics, who should have been interviewed after me, were called in before me.

When I arrived home in Woolwich I was quite frank with Sylvia.

" Well, I think they are going to give me a trial," I told her, " but for once I have taken on more than I can handle. I am really worried about leaving Furlongs."

Fortunately, I did not have to make a move straight away, for on April 19th I received the following letter from John Heath :

> " We are most anxious to choose for a member of our staff a person who has similar ideas to ourselves, and were wondering if the following proposition would meet with your approval. Would it be possible for you to obtain, shall we say, eight days' leave from your present employment to give you an opportunity to come to the forthcoming race at Jersey with us ? We would naturally pay your expenses in this matter, and it would, of course, give us an opportunity of gauging your abilities. If this interests you, please get in touch with the writer immediately upon receipt of this letter, as the lorry and mechanics depart from here on Friday, April 23rd, at 8 a.m. sharp."

And so, two weeks after the interview, I found myself on the way to Jersey, travelling in the lorry under the guise of a friend of Abecassis and supposedly on holiday.

Soon after arriving in Jersey we had clutch trouble on the recently acquired 6-cylinder Maserati that Abecassis was driving. It was really nothing to do with me but I thought I had the answer. It seemed to me that everyone in the *equipe* knew how to cure the clutch slip but no one was prepared to prove his theories. After the second day of practice I joined in the discussion about the clutch and offered to do the job myself.

I cured the trouble—admittedly with a little " bodging up "—and learned that improvisation can work with a Grand Prix car as well as with anything else. In theory, improvisation is not possible ; in fact, it is not only possible but widely used.

I met Duncan Hamilton in Jersey and my first impression was not very favourable. He was Pit Manager and I wondered how anyone could play the fool so much and yet go motor-racing seriously. Since then I have changed my ideas. Hamilton is the sort of man who can do things one would never expect him to do. There is absolutely nothing outwardly serious about him but when a real job of work has to be done, such as co-driving the winning Jaguar at Le Mans in 1953 with Tony Rolt, then Hamilton proves his real worth.

I suggested, and Hamilton agreed, that we organize an efficient fuel replenishment system and whilst he held the stopwatch I practised with the mechanics until we were changing two wheels on the Maserati and taking on fifteen gallons of fuel and two gallons of oil in thirty-one seconds.

I kept them and myself hard at it during Saturday evening and Sunday morning and in the race we carried out the drill in thirty-eight seconds. We were quicker than the mechanics on Reg Parnell's Maserati and consequently Abecassis moved up a place. The race was eventually won by Gerard (E.R.A.) and we were second. Parnell was third.

As the Maserati crossed the line, Hamilton caught me a terrific whack on the back, which left me breathless, and the rest of the team then proceeded to behave in an almost childish fashion. I thought they were crazy. In the evening there was a hectic party, the object of the exercise being to consume the maximum quantity of alcohol in the shortest possible time.

I had imagined motor-racing as a serious business but it had all been very easy-going during the race and I could not help feeling that the general atmosphere on the circuit and at the party afterwards was entirely a " good time " one. I could not see the sport offering me a secure future. How right I was.

On the way home from Jersey I thought to myself, " If this is motor-racing then I don't think I want any part of it," but I had to admit that I had been fascinated by the whole thing. Meeting people, making new friends, preparing the car and getting satisfaction out of curing the clutch trouble, and refuelling our Maserati quicker than Parnell's mechanics.

I did not remain with Furlongs much longer. The motor-racing " bug " had bitten me, my mind was not on my job, and I decided that the crazy atmosphere of a motor-racing *equipe* was preferable to the monotony of working in a Woolwich garage. I left Furlongs on friendly terms and have since visited them on many occasions. They are always pleased to see me and, I think, proud that one of their engine fitters eventually became chief mechanic to Stirling Moss.

I officially joined H.W. Motors Limited a week before the *equipe* left for the British Empire Trophy Race in the Isle of Man on May 25th. There was only one other mechanic—John Powell—working for the small *equipe*. He had been there a year and whilst not actually an apprentice was a real enthusiast. His job was to look after the streamlined Alta sports car, whilst mine was to look after the Grand Prix Alta which Geoffrey Taylor had just finished building for Abecassis. I was loaned to Taylor to help develop the car and gain experience and knowledge at the same time.

Abecassis was tremendously enthusiastic about this brand new project, the first car ever built in England specifically as a G.P. machine and the first with independent suspension on all four wheels. Often he would come into the workshop and sit in a corner for hours, pondering and watching the car take shape.

Personally, I enjoyed very much working on the G.P. Alta. I liked it and had great faith in its development. With such an advanced design we had a sporting chance against the foreign opposition. All the Alta lacked was reliability and I am sure this would have come from development. In 1948 we already possessed a car far ahead of its time, that compares favourably in certain aspects with G.P. machines designed in 1952 and 1953. At least we must acknowledge the fact that this country does not always lag behind in technical matters. I go so far as to say that in 1948 Geoffrey Taylor was certainly equal to and possibly *ahead* of the Continentals.

For instance, the design of the light alloy gearbox was very much akin to the normal current Colombo design, and a comparison of the Alta ratios with a Formula 1, 2½-litre Maserati is interesting. The first speed ratio of the four-speed box designed by Colombo is 2.4 to 1, whereas the Alta is lower—2.524 to 1. The second speed ratios are closer ; Colombo 1.45 to 1 and the Alta 1.56 to 1. The third speed ratio is 1.2 to 1 for Colombo and 1.248 to 1 for the Alta.

The ratios vary hardly at all, except on first gear, and the meshing of the gears and layout of the box itself is very little different, with the exception that the Alta employed synchromesh.

The rear drive consisted of two helical cut spur gears, incorporating the Alta Z.F. type differential unit. The final drive pinion was mounted on the gearbox layshaft, with one of the spur gears, and the main shaft input was turned through 90 deg. straight cut bevels.

Actually, the layout enabled Geoffrey Taylor to drop the pinion shaft 5½ inches below the level of the axle shaft centre, and here again the Alta design is very close to current Ferrari practice. In fact, if I had connected the gearbox with the rear axle the layout of the final drive would have been identical to Colombo's current design.

With the propeller shaft 5½ inches lower in the frame than the output shaft, a combined gearbox and back axle would have made a very nice unit. The entire rear axle assembly was bolted to the frame in a flexible mounting and it was a simple matter to remove the prop. shaft and the drive shafts of the rear hub assembly.

The suspension, of parallelogram type, was most interesting. The top wishbones operated Girling twin-piston shock-absorbers whilst the bottom ones incorporated rubber blocks of cylindrical form, mounted inside the chassis cross member, thus forming the actual springing of the car in canti-lever fashion. Shortening or lengthening the rubber blocks adjusted the tension for varying conditions.

In my opinion the pivoting of the wishbones was one of the weakest points in the Alta design. The bushes in the wishbones, of rubber silent bloc type, did not give a feeling of rigidity at high speeds. This was unfortunate because the chassis was light and exceptionally strong and stable. Even so we did not have any trouble with the suspension from the point of view of reliability, and I would like to experiment with the system again one day. I am sure it has possibilities but, so far as I am aware, no further development work has been carried out. As a spring medium it is lighter than coil springs or torsion bars and very reliable. It cannot break and does not become fatigued.

The steering geometry was also very advanced and can be compared with current Colombo design. A pull and push-rod operated from the steering box, which was mounted on the bell housing of the engine, on to a cantilever which again operated divided trackrods to a forward pointing steering arm. In those days such an arrangement caused considerable comment and criticism. Now it is quite normal.

CHAPTER 2

RACING THE ALTAS

Drama in the Isle of Man—My first " drive "—
Disaster in the Swiss G.P.—Rebuilding the G.P. car—
24 miserable hours at Spa—The French G.P. teaches me a lesson—
Sleepless nights at Zandvoort

Looking back, it seems that the Alta was fated from the start. In the Isle of Man a half-shaft worked loose during practice for the British Empire Trophy and badly damaged the hub. I don't mind admitting that we panicked. With the race next day what on earth could we do ?

I suggested to Abecassis and Taylor that we build up the hub again by electric welding. Taylor said it was impossible.

" Where are you going to find anyone at this time of night ? " he asked. "And who is going to turn it on the lathe ? "

Admittedly it was late but, forgetting the old saying that starts " Fools rush in," I replied that I would do the job—with a hammer, file and chisel.

Taylor laughed.

" You'll never get it running true."

I could feel the colour rising in my cheeks.

"All right," I replied, " I'll make a bet with you. If you leave me here alone and come back to-morrow morning the car will be ready and the hub *will* be running true."

I must say that, once my course of action had been agreed, Geoffrey Taylor did not attempt to interfere in any way. In fact, he had remained in the background during the preparation of the car and the practice session. This is a sensible and realistic approach. His job was finished and the last thing he wanted to do was to make a nuisance of himself.

I spent all night doing the job, working with a vice on a wooden box between my knees, smoking innumerable cigarettes provided by the Lodge Competition Manager, and very soon finding that I had committed myself to the most skilled job I had ever handled. Nevertheless, I persevered. I was determined to complete what I had set out to do and had no wish to admit failure to Geoffrey Taylor. I finished the job just in time for breakfast and, believe me, I would not dream of tackling such a job these days within the same time limit.

During the morning we took the car out on the circuit and all seemed well. An hour or so later, as I looked at the Alta on the starting line, I felt a thrill of pride that by working all night I had enabled it to get there. I had taken a great liking to the car. It looked equal to Parnell's 16 valve Maserati and, as far as I could see, was quite as stable on the road. I think, at this stage, Abecassis was still fond of the car as well. The only person who did not seem very interested was John Heath.

The opposition in this 140-mile race around the 3.88-mile Douglas circuit was formidable and included a number of E.R.A.s, Rolt's 8-cylinder, 8-carburetter Alfa-Romeo, and the 4.C.L. Maseratis of Parnell and R. E. Ansell.

In spite of the opposition everything about our own outfit seemed just as happy-go-lucky in the Isle of Man as in Jersey. There was very little pit control, other than John Heath himself, and my only responsibility was to look after the mechanical preparation of the car. I do not believe any special plan or race strategy was worked out.

Down went the flag and away went the Alta. One—two—three laps, and she did not come round. A spring had broken on the pressure release valve, and George Abecassis walked back to the pit under the mistaken impression that the engine had blown up. It was not, as reported, gearbox trouble although admittedly Abecassis had complained about difficult gear changes in practice, which in my opinion were entirely due to the use of the synchromesh box.

The thing that impressed me most in the Trophy Race was the magnificent driving of Parnell in the Maserati, particularly the way he cut past the pits. Every lap his wheels were within an inch of the low wall on which we were standing, and it was amazing to me how they passed repeatedly over exactly the same spot. Those of us who stood on the wall to give signals had to be very careful, and anyone who sat down and dangled his legs over the wall was running the risk of losing them !

Our signal station and pit was at the extreme end of the line. The cars used to leave the road on the notorious Governor's Bridge and, by the time they touched down again, were on the outside of the circuit and very, very close to the pits wall. From this point drivers had to take the correct line for the next corner, a sharp right-hand one, and unskilled drivers would frequently find themselves at a most awkward angle on touching down, due to the fact that whilst airborne and with no wheel adhesion they moved the steering wheel. It was most exciting to watch certain drivers reorientate themselves !

Parnell drove a wonderful race. He was the only man who looked to my inexperienced eye like a potential champion. His handling of the Maserati seemed head and shoulders above the other drivers and I could not see his equal in that race. I say he was the Stirling Moss of his day, although admittedly the Maserati was a hard car to beat.

His magnificent drive should have been rewarded with victory but fate stepped in on the last lap as the chequered flag was unfurled. The Maserati ran out of fuel and the auxiliary fuel tank feed failed, due, I believe, to there being no air supply to the tank.

As soon as the news came over the loudspeakers we all shouted at Parnell's mechanics : " Take some petrol out to him." They did so, encouraged by all and sundry to " Get a move on," but it was not possible to get the Maserati going and the E.R.A. of G. Ansell took the chequered flag.

I recall how disappointed and angry I was about the retirement of our car. I knew that the night before the race, whilst I had been filing the hub, there had been a terrific party. It was such a hectic one that certain residents of a particular hotel, seeking refuge, had to climb down sheets from their windows, whilst several characters were tossed into the swimming pool from the first floor. I was annoyed because I had been working on the car whilst all this was going on. I was also rather puzzled. It seemed a strange way to prepare for a race. After all, I thought to myself, drivers should be at their best at the wheel of a car capable of well over a hundred miles an hour. I was learning.

I did not realize that in those days motor-racing was an excuse for a good time and the serious business of the sport or the mechanical side of the car one raced was frequently of a secondary nature. People did not make sacrifices, as they do to-day, in order to go motor-racing. To the majority it was just an exciting sport for people who could afford it, with a cocktail bar or saloon bar background, and very little importance was placed on physical fitness.

I felt sorry for Geoffrey Taylor because it was the first outing of the G.P. Alta—a car designed and built entirely by Taylor himself—and its performance was not much reward for the years of thought and hard work spent on the project.

After the race I went out to the car with Geoffrey Taylor. We soon found the trouble, jammed the pressure relief valve on the manifold into position, and wired it up so that Geoffrey Taylor could proudly drive the car back to the hotel. I suppose it would have taken thirty seconds to mend that spring if the Alta had been brought into the pits during the race. It was the first unlucky incident with the ill-fated Alta and we took her back to England the following day.

We were not very happy about the stability of the car and it was decided to alter the setting of the rubber springing, using a different type of rubber and thus altering the tension of the shock-absorbers. This we did, afterwards taking the Alta to Odiham Airfield. I was full of enthusiasm ; in a few months and learning the hard way—in races—we would cure all our teething troubles and really make this British car go.

I shall never forget this trial run because it was the first time I had ever handled a racing car. It was a rainy day and after everyone else had driven the car and expressed satisfaction, Abecassis told me to take her out.

Off I went, very gingerly and keeping the revs well down. I changed into second at 2,000 and in fact the needle of the rev. counter never exceeded 2,000 in any gear. Abecassis called me in.

" For goodness' sake, Alf, don't drive it as though it's a Daimler or a Rolls-Royce and you are a chauffeur. It's a racing car—drive it like one."

It was at this precise moment that I abandoned all idea of ever racing a G.P. car. I had almost made up my mind on this point out on the slippery airfield perimeter, but even so was surprised to learn that I was *that* bad. I have never changed my views. I am not the sort of person who likes to handle a lot of horses and I much prefer to drive a small car, such as Stirling Moss' Standard, to its limit ; its speed is my limit.

Even to-day, nine years later, I do not consider that my inability to handle a G.P. car at speed is a serious disadvantage. Instead I use my imagination, mixing with the drivers and joining in their conversation. In this way I try to build up an impression of how I would feel in their shoes so far as a particular car is concerned.

Stirling Moss does not agree with me on this point. Many times, in the heat of the moment, he has said to me : " The whole trouble with you, Alf, is that you haven't got the guts to drive a racing car." Then, as the conversation has progressed, he has softened a little to the extent of saying : " Talking about drivers, there are only a very few good ones, and I count you as one. It is the way you make the lorry go because, touch wood, you have not had any accidents. The speeds you have to maintain and the distances you have to cover do not allow much of a safety margin."

It all adds up to the fact that driving a lorry or a small saloon car is much more in my line than racing a G.P. or sports machine.

We towed the Alta back to Walton behind John Heath's Citroen. Abecassis was driving and we touched 60 m.p.h. in places. That's when I learned how to hold a racing car on the road—behind Abecassis, on the end of a tow rope, and in driving rain !

Our next race was the Swiss Grand Prix at Berne, on the difficult and dangerous " drivers' " circuit of the Bremgarten. It was one of the annual classics and the European Grand Prix of 1948. I realize now how fortunate I was, not so many weeks after leaving my work bench at Furlongs, to see famous drivers and cars in action at such an important event. I decided that, whatever she might do in the race, the Alta was going to be prepared as well as any of the Continental team cars. And she was ; Varzi, Villoresi, Farina and Count Trossi all admired her turnout and the British car was almost as impressive in action. On the first day of practice Abecassis recorded fourth fastest time, behind two Type 158 Alfa-Romeos and a two-stage supercharged Maserati. This was no mean achievement, particularly as the Alfas—also with two-stage superchargers—were developing over 300 brake horse power.

I felt very new and not a little dubious for this was so different from Jersey and the Isle of Man. There I had been depressed because I felt people did not take the sport serious enough, but at Berne I was worried about my own capabilities because they took it so seriously. The team organization frightened me with its efficiency. This was the real motor-racing scene.

At the practice session I wondered whether I had taken on too much. There were the Alfa-Romeos of Wimille, Trossi, Sanesi and Varzi ; the Maseratis of Farina, Ascari, Villoresi and Fagioli ; the unsupercharged 6-cylinder Lago Talbots of Chiron and Rosier.

The atmosphere in the town was almost electric. Everywhere—in shops and restaurants—the talk was of the European Grand Prix. I felt I was up against something really big and this was only my second outing as a motor-racing mechanic.

Anyway, we were soon hard at work and there was no time to worry. I took the lorry on to the circuit and drove round slowly, making occasional notes. It has since become a habit and as soon as I arrive at a circuit— excepting the Nurburgring with its fourteen-and-a-half miles—I go round in the transporter. It seems to me that a heavy lorry, with its very high C. of G. and fully laden, gives a true impression of the angle of bends and condition of the surface. I am also able to " feel " gradients better.

Looking out from the comparatively high vantage point of the driving cab I can gain a more accurate impression than, for instance, from the front seat of a private car.   I have never been very much at fault with my assessment of a circuit and the information I obtain is invaluable when choosing axle ratios.

A funny thing happened at Berne. I had not spoken German for two years or so and that part of Switzerland is Swiss-German.   When we left the Alta in the garage it was necessary, in order to ensure a reliable performance from the supercharger, to drain off the alcohol fuel and run the engine on petroil for a few minutes so as to lubricate the inside of the supercharger.   It was then necessary to prime the carburetter with petrol in order to start the car again.

When we wanted to take part in the first practice session I asked the garage proprietor for two litres of petrol, forgetting that petrol is German for paraffin.   I actually wanted Benzin.

Naturally, with paraffin in the carburetter the car would not start. What a job we had towing it round the town.   I was desperate and just could not make it out.   Then I stopped and told myself not to panic.   There must be something very unusual going on.   I put my head under the bonnet, sniffed around the carburetter—and the mystery was solved.

The Alta, with Abecassis driving, was on the third row of the grid and the atmosphere before the start was tremendously impressive.   I watched as the Alfa-Romeos and Maseratis were pushed on to the grid and the electric starters wheeled into position and engaged.   The Alta was the only car without an electric starter and, ignoring the amused comments of some of the Italian mechanics, I produced that relic of a bygone age, a starting handle.

As the flag dropped, there was Abecassis trying unsuccessfully to get into first gear.   The synchromesh " box " made this very difficult, but eventually he got away, lying in twelfth place.   Every lap of the first four or five, going like a bomb, he managed to pull up a place and was just about to pass the last of the Talbots (which proves that the Alta was faster) when he was pushed off the road on to the grass verge and hit a telegraph pole.

That was the end of our European G.P.   Although the Alta did not catch fire, it hit the pole with its rear wheels, snapping it in half, and finished in a cornfield almost a total wreck.

Abecassis was not badly hurt and this was a great relief to me for Varzi had been killed in practice and Kautz had succumbed to his injuries after crashing on the second lap of the race.   My relief eventually gave way to disappointment for I was sure in my own mind that the Alta had been pushed too hard during the early stages.   I found myself sympathizing with the car, not the driver.   After all, it had gone so well during practice and so fast for a British project.

With the Alta wrecked I strolled behind the pits to watch the Alfa-Romeo mechanics at work.   I was there when their No. 3 car came in to refuel.   This was the slowest of the Alfas and I realized that it had been brought in first to give the pit personnel practice before the two faster cars were refuelled.   This was the first of many tactical moves I was to learn from our Continental rivals.

I was beginning to see the value of race strategy and tactics and at Berne I suddenly became completely absorbed in motor-racing. I wanted to race the way Alfas did (they had twenty-six mechanics at the European G.P. and it fascinated me to watch their efficient organization at work) and decided that, if I carried on, that was the way I would do it. I told myself that if one wants to motor-race, one must do it wholeheartedly and sacrifice oneself solely to that purpose.

When the No. 2 car came into the pit, I timed their refuelling routine and decided that the Alfa-Romeo mechanics were not setting an impossible pace. In fact, their time of 33 seconds seemed slow to me. I mentally resolved, there and then, not to take too much notice of the stories I had read and been told of " fantastic pit stops " and " amazing speed." It seemed to me then—and it still does—that the " independent " does not do too badly. Often, I think, a factory team is famous for its product and nothing ever goes wrong that cannot be glossed over in some way or other !

We could not tow the Alta but went out on to the circuit after the race with the Ford Thames van and lifted bodily into the lorry what was left of the car. It is a melancholy experience to go out on a circuit and tow in a crashed car. I have done it several times in my career. When it happens the first time, and you move off with a wrecked car in the back of the transporter, you suddenly realize that " It can happen to you."

It was depressing after we had prepared the Alta so carefully and she had gone so well in practice. But that is motor-racing. If you are connected with the sport you must be willing to work for days and nights with only a few hours' sleep and no proper food and then see all your work undone in a blow-up or a crash. Within a matter of hours you must be hard at work again, repairing the car for the next race—often in six days' time.

The following week we were racing John Heath's streamlined Alta sports car in the 24-hour race at Spa, whilst the G.P. Alta was due at the French G.P. at Rheims a week later. John Heath told me to take the G.P. car to Paris, strip it down in the garage of M. Bonnet (of D.B. Panhard fame) and rebuild it there. The necessary parts would be sent out from England and considerable shipping costs saved. As I drove through the night towards Paris, I told myself that Heath must have confidence to entrust me with such a task. I hummed an old Polish marching song. Life was good, even if there was a wrecked racing car in the back of the van.

John Powell and I arrived in Paris the morning following the Berne race and worked all day and most of the following night stripping down the car. It took two weeks to rebuild the G.P. Alta at M. Bonnet's garage— one week before the Spa race and one week afterwards. The whole of the rear end had been torn off in the crash at Berne ; the fuel tank, rear suspension carriers and wishbones, and the entire left-hand rear side of the chassis, complete with wheel. And yet the axle had not been harmed—although the inside drive shafts had been bent and the universals damaged.

The most difficult job was to straighten the actual chassis without the aid of jigs or data of any sort. I was guessing about the wheelbase to a certain extent for Geoffrey Taylor did not come over to Paris and I was not able to speak to him before starting work. He is strange in this way and it might appear that he lacks the initiative to supervise. But this is not so. He is a shy, reserved man whom you rarely, if ever, see on the circuits and he was quite happy to leave me in Paris on my own. I asked him later in the season why he did not come over to M. Bonnet's garage. I am not quite sure whether his reply was a compliment or not :"After the Isle of Man incident with the half-shaft, I was fully convinced that you were better left alone."

I put in some very long hours on the G.P. Alta, mostly on my own, working from early morning to late at night. The tools were almost primitive when I consider what I should need for a similar job to-day but M. Bonnet had a first-class welder who helped to straighten the chassis and make new suspension carriers. The cross-member holding the wish-bones had been completely destroyed.

When Heath and Abecassis arrived by air in Paris on their way to Spa they stayed just long enough to see how we had been getting on and then took the lorry, with John Powell, and set off for Spa. It was agreed that they would practise without me whilst I continued working on the G.P. car. I would then travel by train to Spa for the race.

The Belgian classic was described at the time as " one of the most dangerous motor races of recent years," because of the appalling weather conditions. It rained almost from start to finish, having rained for days before the race, and drivers had to cope with fog and mist as well on this fast, fatiguing Ardennes circuit, which rapidly became slippery and like a skating rink in parts.

There were at least seven crashes to my knowledge and one of them was the Alta. Nevertheless, it was an interesting race and I really enjoyed it in my capacity as Pit Manager. It was the only twenty-four hour race I have ever seen and, strange as it may seem, I have never been to Le Mans.

I think we could have won if only Abecassis had not tried to build up such a commanding lead. He was afraid of engine trouble and considered that we needed seventy minutes or so on the credit side to allow for pit stops. My view was that the Alta should keep up a steady pace and not be " pushed " to the front of the " field." I even went so far as to suggest that we change drivers every two hours during the night, instead of every three, particularly in view of the shocking weather conditions. I knew, having driven long-distance buses in Poland in 1938 and 1939 after my father died, that one goes much faster in the first two hours and loses rather a lot in the third hour when one is already tired, particularly at high speed.

We were leading when Heath came in at the end of the second " stint." The Alta was refuelled with petrol and oil (she was in a very good state and Heath had no complaints) and Abecassis went away, intent on increasing the lead in this twenty-four hour race. As I checked the green car past the pits at intervals of ten minutes or so on this fairly lengthy circuit of nine miles, I had a premonition that something was going to happen.

It did. An hour after Abecassis had taken over, the green Alta was missing. The minutes ticked by—three, four, five, six. I ran to Race Control. Yes, the Alta had run off the road. No, it was not on fire. The driver—who knows ?

The Alta was fortunately not very far from the pits. I broke into a jog-trot. Soon I was wiping the sweat out of my eyes with the back of my hand, and when I at last found the Alta, submerged in a ditch, I had almost run myself to a standstill. The rain was coming down in torrents and I was absolutely soaking wet.

As I gulped for breath, Abecassis told me that, as he was coming through this particular fast bend, the water shone in the lights and looked similar to the glistening wet circuit. He went straight on—and soon found himself going straight off—and into the ditch. It had been an optical illusion.

We decided to fish the car out and continue the race as we were still well placed. We tried to move the Alta. It was impossible. Then two marshals willingly gave a helping hand. Still the car would not budge an inch. With not very much confidence I suggested that we try to start the engine. Incredibly, it started and, after a jerk or two, Abecassis reversed out of the ditch.

I sat on the mudguard whilst Abecassis drove the car quickly back to the pits. Undoubtedly I was more relieved than he was when we eventually arrived. Whilst the sump oil was being changed (it was full of water) and I was trying to straighten the mudguard an official arrived on the scene.

" I regret to inform you," he said, " that you are disqualified."

When I had calmed down, I asked him the reason.

" You had outside assistance," he replied, " and secondly you are not allowed to make a longer stop than one hour, and it is already one hour and ten minutes since your car ran off the road."

That was that. Abecassis and Heath went back to the hotel for a change of clothing. I was left with the lorry in the paddock and, to say the least, most indignant. It occurred to me later that I could easily have caught pneumonia that night. After a few drinks, I settled down in the cab of the lorry. I had no choice for I could not get across the track and away from the circuit until the race finished in the morning.

On the way from Spa to Paris next day I let John Powell drive whilst I dozed contentedly in the cabin of the transporter. Like most continentals I enjoy my food and wine and had eaten well before leaving Spa.

This pleasant state of affairs did not last long. I was awakened by violent braking as we approached a level crossing which, like so many in France, made a sudden and disturbing appearance as we rounded a fast bend. Disturbing because a car was already on the crossing, coming from the opposite direction and well and truly in the middle of the road !

The transporter lurched as John pulled over and the Frenchman passed us with no more than the width of this book to spare. Then John and I looked at each other and swore roundly for a rumbling noise told us that all was not well inside the van.

We pulled up, well beyond the level crossing and, sure enough, there was the streamlined Alta with a most unstreamlined nose. When we had loaded the van there was no room for the Alta in the ground floor section and it had been loaded on the top set of runners. The car had come off the rails and badly damaged its nose.

This was a serious setback. I already had enough trouble in Paris with the G.P. Alta. Now I had the sports car to worry about as well.

Muttering darkly to myself about the meteoric driving methods of Frenchmen, and in a vile temper, I took the wheel.

In Paris, at M. Bonnet's works, we set about the task of finishing the G.P. Alta and straightening the nose of the streamliner. When the G.P. car was at last completed I asked M. Bonnet whether we should test it at Montlhery. He laughed.

" No, we will just try it out around the block."

" But what about a road licence ? " I asked.

" Sans faire rien," replied Bonnet. " We are on the outskirts of Paris and no one bothers about racing cars—taxed or untaxed."

I took the Alta round the block a few times and she seemed satisfactory, so I asked M. Bonnet whether he would like to try the car. Off he went. Five minutes passed and I listened for the car. Ten minutes—and I was getting worried. Fifteen—and I was frantic. I could see myself explaining to George Abecassis how the Alta had been interned by the authorities as an undesirable alien vehicle when it came into sight with a delighted, wind-ruffled M. Bonnet at the wheel. His verdict was sufficient reward for the time and energy spent on the Alta. Just one word—" Formidable."

Naturally I wanted to go out and celebrate but I was broke. This brings me to an important point concerning expenses. Whilst a mechanic does not have to worry about his board and lodging he rarely receives any spending money. I do not need to tell you that motor-racing is one sport where a full packet of twenty cigarettes and the ability to buy anything from a pint of bitter to a *coup* of champagne is vitally necessary. That is the way it is and I doubt whether it will ever change. I could write pages about friendships made over a glass or two of wine on the Continent and the good turns and help I have later received from those friends.

I think it is most important that mechanics have a daily allowance for personal expenses. Quite apart from anything else it is a psychological necessity. In many hotels all over Europe, with my board and lodging paid, I have not had enough money to buy a round of drinks at the bar. You may say that a mechanic's salary should be sufficient. I would advise you to travel round with the " circus " for one season as a mechanic and see what sort of salary you need—to get what you want, when you want it, and at the right price.

The next race for which the G.P. Alta had been entered was the French G.P. (July 18th) on the very fast four-and-a-half mile Rheims circuit. Once again there was the Grand Prix circus, the knowledgeable crowds, the pomp and ceremony of the military bands and the tense atmosphere. It was all becoming a vital part of my life.

I must admit I was bitterly disappointed at Rheims when John Heath told me he was driving the Alta instead of George Abecassis. Abecassis was not feeling too fit after the Spa crash but, selfishly, I did not acknowledge this fact.

I felt that all my time and hard work had been wasted, for I knew John Heath could not put up such a good performance as Abecassis To me, rebuilding the Alta had been a challenge and now I wanted to see the result of my work and particularly whether the car could triumph over the 4½-litre Lago-Talbots.

I knew we could not hope to beat the 1½-litre supercharged Alfa-Romeos (which Wimille, Sanesi and Ascari were to bring home to a 1, 2, 3 victory) but the Talbot was a different matter. The Alta, before the crash, had been superior at Berne and now I wanted to see how it would behave on the fast Rheims circuit which favours heavier cars such as the Talbots.

I had a feeling that John Heath was not too happy about driving the car and this may well have been the case. After all, I had more or less rebuilt it, having only been a few months with H.W.M., and at Rheims the Alta was reaching 140 m.p.h. on the straights.

Fifteen minutes before the start John Heath had not arrived. I could not imagine what had happened. I was beginning to think that it might be necessary for me to impersonate Heath to the extent of starting with the car, completing part of a lap, retiring on the " back leg " of the circuit and walking to the pits. After all we were being paid starting money !

It would have been a comparatively simple matter, as John Heath was not well known, and I could have disguised myself easily with goggles and a crash hat. This was a plan I could never have put into operation with such a well-known driver as Stirling Moss, even had it been necessary, which it never was.

With only ten minutes to go, Heath arrived and we pushed the car on to the rear of the grid. The Alta was the only British car, for the organizers had refused to allow the E.R.A.s of Bira and Brooke to start. They said the cars were too old and slow.

After only seven laps, Heath pulled into the pits and complained of clutch slip. I went under the car at once and felt the flywheel to see if it was unduly hot. I found it no warmer than the engine, indicating that there had not been undue friction.

However, I could not reassure Heath that the clutch was normal and when he got out of the cockpit I took his place. I started the engine, engaged first gear and revved up to 5,000 revs (the Alta peaked at 6,000 but the torque was excellent between 4,500 and 5,000), then let out the clutch and stalled the engine. When I checked the pedal movement I found it quite normal. From the cockpit I looked up at John Heath.

" You can carry on ; there's nothing wrong with the clutch."

However, Heath retired the car, giving clutch slip as the reason, and it does show how an incident such as the Berne crash can upset the morale of a team organization and undermine that vital element of mutual trust. Heath was, understandably, not quite sure of me or the Alta and the whole framework of our effort at Rheims dissolved around his hesitation.

I told myself that, before we could go motor-racing with a hundred per cent. team effort, I should have to inspire much more confidence in the drivers. For the first time I saw that there had to be a strong link, almost a sentimental one, between driver and mechanic, and that it was just as important to forge that personal link as to get the car to the " grid " in first-class condition. I still had a lot to learn about motor-racing.

Back at Walton we stripped down the Alta and sent the engine to Geoffrey Taylor so that it could be prepared for the Zandvoort races on

August 7th. We experienced trouble with one of the supercharger oil seals and the "blower" was not ready to fit on the car when we left for Harwich and the Hook of Holland. For the first, but certainly not the last time, I experienced the frustration and anxiety of travelling with a car to a circuit and not knowing whether I should have time to get it to the starting line in one hundred per cent. trim.

Fortunately, on the day before practice, Abecassis arrived with the "blower" and I spent all night fitting it. I hardly had time for a jug of coffee and hot rolls before getting the car out to the circuit. The Alta seemed in good trim and imagine my disappointment, after a sleepless night, when we ran into a spate of gearbox trouble.

The one-way helical gears were causing excessive pressure on the thrust washers and the resultant friction caused the washers and bushes to run very hot. One of the shafts and its bronze bushes seized solid on the gearshaft. The shaft itself was so badly scored that we could not possibly use it again.

We were faced with a formidable problem. Where could we find another shaft and gears. Fortunately, Geoffrey Taylor had a set in stock at Kingston and it was sent off by plane to Rotterdam and brought on to Zandvoort by an Army despatch rider.

Once again I worked all night, fitting the shaft and gears in time for the second practice session when Abecassis made second fastest time but in the process broke one of the gears in the gearbox. I knew that another sleepless night was on the cards and sure enough it took me all night to strip down the gearbox and reassemble a complete set of gears from the original box and the replacement sent by Geoffrey Taylor.

In the race, which marked the opening of the Zandvoort Circuit and was run in two heats and a final, the Alta shared the front row of the grid in Heat 1 with Rolt on the Dixon-tuned Alfa-Romeo and T. C. Harrison on a C-Type E.R.A. This was the meeting where B.R.D.C. provided all the cars and drivers.

On the very first lap the Alta was out of the race with bent valves. I felt utterly dejected and my only wish was to get away from the circuit and catch up on my sleep. The meeting held no further interest for me.

Abecassis walked back to the pits.

"There's no point in worrying," he said, "we may as well forget about it and enjoy ourselves this evening."

Well, I thought, that's one way of looking at it. However, I did worry for it seemed that the Alta was fated. This was its fourth appearance, and its fourth failure.

By 8.30 p.m. I was sound asleep in the Military Barracks where I had been billeted but it seemed I had only been in bed a few seconds when I felt someone shaking me.

"There is a taxi downstairs and the driver has been told to wait. He will not go away without you."

I dragged myself out of bed, washed and dressed. At least, whatever the cause of this midnight summons, it would not be anything to do with that pernicious piece of machinery in the transporter.

The taxi driver was crazy or else trying to impress me. I was bounced about like a pea in a pod and thrown from side to side in the most alarming fashion. I was scared stiff !

It transpired that Abecassis had sent the taxi and told the driver not to leave the barracks without me. He thought I would enjoy the prize-giving party, and for the third night I went without sleep. It was 6 a.m. before I returned to the barracks and at 10 a.m. I was taken on an official sightseeing tour of The Hague. Good intentions—but all I wanted was to be left alone to get some sleep.

CHAPTER 3

BUILDING THE H.W. ALTA

Birth of a project—Enthusiasm and common sense pays dividends—
Test day at Odiham airfield.

Towards the end of 1948 it was decided that we would build our own racing car for the new Formula 2, to be known as the H.W. Alta. The G.P. Alta had been an expensive car to race and we had been plagued with troubles.

Both Heath and Abecassis were in favour of the new project, the former because he had always been interested in building a car of his own shape and design, rather thinking in terms of a sports car that could also be used as a single-seater racer. Abecassis was interested because he had always preferred racing cars to sports cars, which was the reason he bought the Formula 1 G.P. Alta. Geoffrey Taylor was not in any way associated with the project.

However, there was a good deal of discussion and argument, for Abecassis was not entirely convinced that it was a feasible proposition, and this gave me the opportunity of putting forward a case for the G.P. Alta. I had grown to like her, and defended her merits stoutly in the hope that she would be given another chance. There was an indefinable air of sadness about the car as though she knew her days were numbered. Perhaps I was being sentimental but that is nothing to be ashamed of in motor-racing.

We argued for hours before a final decision was made. Abecassis saw the F.2 car as a very difficult problem and pointed out that we had no machine shop or welder. John Heath immediately volunteered to do all the welding himself, which meant he would have to work at night for during the day he had the H.W.M. garage and car sales business to look after with Abecassis. I was the only person available to work on the new car all day.

And so, with very little money but a great deal of enthusiasm and a willingness to work hard at all hours, we tackled the job of building what was, in fact, the guinea pig for the H.W.M. racing cars of 1950.

It was the first time H.W.M. had built any sort of car. Neither Heath nor I knew very much about it, and it was Abecassis, with his more practical experience of driving racing cars and his wide technical knowledge from the theoretical point of view, who was the " gaffer." Needless to say, I never referred to him in this way ! In fact, no one looks less like a " gaffer " than George Abecassis.

Our lack of knowledge was balanced to a certain extent by common sense, for a great deal can be achieved when one is really up against it by making a straightforward, down to earth, common-sense approach. Undoubtedly it frequently compensates for lack of knowledge.

The idea was to build a car that could be taxed and used as a sports car—with mudguards, doors and lights—or as a racing car in the new Formula 2. By incorporating as many production parts as possible we hoped to build it comparatively cheaply. With this view in mind we took the 2-litre, 4-cylinder twin O.H.C. Alta engine from Heath's streamliner and gave it an E.N.V. type preselector gearbox, which in those days could be bought for £5 or so. John Heath maintained that the E.N.V. " box " would save time in construction and, bearing in mind the troubles we had experienced with the synchromesh gears on the G.P. Alta, give us a more satisfactory " box " under racing conditions.

We used Citroen rack and pinion steering which was easily obtainable and the most suitable steering geometry for the transverse leaf springs. The back axle came from a Lagonda Rapier.

We had long and often heated arguments about the rear end. John Heath wanted to use quarter elliptic springs and two torque arms but this was impossible with a solid beam axle. It just would not work and I became so exasperated trying to demonstrate that the whole structure would lift both sides as a solid mass that I actually threatened to walk out.

It was Abecassis who calmed us down and acted as peacemaker. Often he used to break up arguments between Heath and myself, like a referee separating a couple of fighters. Sometimes he would appear on the scene when we were going at it hammer and tongs. Quietly he would break in : " Let's hear both sides again." At least the argument then became a discussion.

Heath finally agreed that the whole rear end should be re-designed and we finished up with one torque arm, and quarter eliptic springs a la Bugatti principle, to locate the axle laterally.

The chassis was a simple one, consisting of two large diameter tubes with three cross-members to ensure rigidity and constructed by Heath himself. It was built in such a way that it could accommodate a narrow two-seater body to comply with F.I.A. regulations.

Our biggest problem was the front suspension. I had no knowledge whatsoever of steering geometry and soon found out, talking to Heath and Abecassis, that they knew very little about it either. I spent hours in my digs, after leaving the " works," pondering the problem. I refused to admit defeat for I saw it as another challenge to my ingenuity.

At last I had the answer. Why not use a cross-member of box section type, constructed from steel taken from old air raid shelters of the type that stood under living-room tables during the war. Wishbones could be fabricated from the same source and designed to incorporate Standard 12 uprights, stub axles and transverse leaf springs.

It took us several months to build the H.W. Alta and I shall always remember this period for the tremendous enthusiasm that we all put into the project. Every evening there was a conference between Heath, Abecassis and myself to discuss what I should do the following day. In general I cut, filed and joined the chassis parts and Heath welded them at night. Not that he was left on his own by any means. We were all so enthusiastic that the workshop became our second home. Night after night we worked until the early hours.

I made a schedule of priority jobs that had to be completed before Christmas : (1) Finish plates for back axle assembly ; (2) Make distance pieces for back plates ; (3) Drill light holes in back plates ; (4) Assemble H pieces and stub axles ; (5) Assemble half-shafts ; (6) Make E.N.V. gearbox mounting ; (7) Make seat mountings ; (8) Make steering mounting.

I have a note in my diary : " December 23, 1948. Christmas Eve and I am finishing the back axle assembly of the Alta so that J. H. can weld it."

We had hoped the car would be ready for Christmas but the body held us up. They were so busy over at the Surbiton works of the Cooper Car Co. that it had to be built mostly on an overtime basis.

What a feeling of pride and satisfaction we had when N.P.A.5 was tested at Odiham Airfield soon after Christmas. Its behaviour was almost beyond criticism and in my opinion it was the best H.W.M. ever built from the point of view of road-holding. N.P.A.5 never sheared a stub axle or went off the road during her entire racing history.

It would be foolish to say that we were not surprised at the performance of the car. After all, there had been no brilliant designs on the drawing board, no brilliant technicians with slide rules. To all intents and purposes we were three amateurs (with a common-sense approach) who proved to themselves that they could build a racing car. Who can honestly say that there is not more satisfaction in a job well done than in almost anything else in life.

On the way back from Odiham I realized that I had found another reason for staying in this fascinating motor-racing game—even at £10 a week. Frankly, the actual construction of the car had given each one of us deep personal satisfaction. The question of pounds, shillings and pence did not enter into it. How many people I wonder can say that the nature of their work is more important than the monetary gain ?

And so, about to start my second season of motor-racing, I found myself absolutely " sold " on the idea of staying in the sport. There had been differences with Abecassis and Heath but nothing of a really serious nature. My work had been mainly for Abecassis, who left me to myself and gave me more of a free hand than Heath and thus more confidence.

I must admit that, if I think I am right, I will say so most emphatically. In the heat of an argument I sometimes forget to whom I am talking and this does not always go down too well. However, I think both Abecassis and Heath realized that my anger came from enthusiasm and a burning desire to " take the bull by the horns."

A corner of the H.W.M. workshops at Walton-on-Thames. John Heath and George Abecassis are watching the ill-fated G.P. Alta being prepared for the 1949 British G.P., a race that gave the car its day of glory. Propped against the wall is the template for the front suspension cross member of the H.W.-Alta (seen below) and on the bench itself is a differential casing made from sheet metal. As far back as 1940 H.W.M. planned a rear-engined car, with a Citroen gearbox behind the driver, and an Alta power unit.

John Heath on his way to victory in the 70-mile 1949 Manx Cup. He is driving the H.W.-Alta, guinea pig for the H.W.M. racing cars of 1950. The same car, running on normal fuel and with mudguards and a full electrical system, was second in the Grand Prix of the A.C.F. for sports cars at Comminges later in the season. The unorthodox driving position favoured by John Heath, which makes it appear that he is trying to get ahead of the car, is clearly shown.

Tooling up at the end of the 1949 season prior to building the team of four H.W.M.s, two-seaters with the driver sitting alongside the propeller shaft. The prototype is in the foreground whilst tubular chassis—checked and set aligned for welding and with the cross members in position —are in the background. The welder was only able to work in the evenings and on a part-time basis. The H.W.-Alta is in the far corner of the workshop.

Close-up of the prototype, showing the combined oil filter oil cooler. The Standard Twelve uprights and the transverse leaf spring are easily seen and it is interesting that the spring ran through the cross-member. At the rear is the triangular shaped cross-member incorporating the differential unit, which was fabricated from sixty-seven separate pieces of sheet metal. Above it is the rear transverse leaf spring.

CHAPTER 4

THE 1949 SEASON

*Success and disappointment at Goodwood—Dismal failure in Jersey of the
G.P. Alta—Silverstone and the greatest race of the G.P. car—
We meet Stirling Moss in the Isle of Man—Abecassis crashes at 100 m.p.h.—
Triumph of the H.W. Alta—Rheims, swan song of the G.P. car—
A bottle of " coke " at Comminges.*

The first public meeting of the 1949 Season, attended by some forty
thousand spectators, was at Goodwood on Easter Monday. It was a busy
one for me because we took three cars down there ; the G.P. Alta, the
H.W. Alta and a Cooper H.R.D. belonging to Abecassis which had been
built with a specially long wheelbase to accommodate his legs. Actually,
I did not have much to do with the H.W. Alta at Goodwood for John
Heath looked after it himself, with the assistance of John Powell, and my
main responsibility was the G.P. Alta.

A word or two about Abecassis and Heath as drivers. I would describe
Abecassis as one of the pre-war gentlemen drivers who has not acquired
his style of driving from anyone. He has his own style and on one of his
good days is a difficult driver to catch and a pleasure to watch in action.
He never panics. He will pull into the pit and calmly tell you what he
thinks is the trouble. He does not get excited nor throw fits of temperament.

You can often tell how good is a driver by watching his behaviour on
the starting line. A bad driver will find faults with the car—which are too
late to remedy in any case—and one knows at once that he is the worrying
sort. People of this nature do not get very far.

There is another type of driver who, even on the grid a few seconds
before the flag falls, will be wondering whether to use first or second gear
to get away, and whether to start the engine as agreed with his mechanics
or one minute earlier.

Abecassis is like Moss. Once on the starting line he might discuss a
pretty girl in the crowd but certainly not the car. That is of no importance
at this stage. With both Abecassis and Moss it was usually me who
asked the anxious questions.

During my motor-racing career there are two people with whom I
have particularly enjoyed working. One is Abecassis, the other Moss.
With these same two people I feel absolutely safe and confident when they
are driving on the public roads.

John Heath, in my opinion, was never meant to be a driver of fast
cars but forced himself to be one. I used to admire his guts—for that is
a quality Heath never lacked—but always at the back of my mind was a
feeling that he was driving at the absolute limit of his own capabilities.

He used to say to me : "Alf, you don't like me driving, do you ? " and I had to admit that he was right.

Heath was not an excitable driver, any more than Abecassis, but he had no particular style and never appeared brilliant on any circuit. In short, his abilities did not match his undoubted enthusiasm and courage.

At Goodwood the ill-fated G.P. car retired with gearbox trouble after only three laps of the Chichester Cup and came home sixth in the big race, the Richmond Trophy, after chronic misfiring.

During the winter Geoffrey Taylor had refused to consider any alternative to the synchromesh gearbox in spite of my frequent and often heated criticism. I am sure that a good " dog " engagement with plain cut gears would have been preferable on the G.P. Alta and far less troublesome. Personally, I cannot see what advantage there is in using synchromesh, for a " dog " engagement is as quick, if not quicker, with a high-revving engine. However, Geoffrey Taylor was adamant in his refusal to replace the synchromesh, and to make matters worse we had gearbox breathing trouble, with oil spilling all over the place.

Neither was the Alta engine at its best. The carburetters, mounted on the base of the supercharger, were flooding badly due to engine vibration, and the Alta was " losing " plugs. We had not experienced trouble of this nature during 1948 and this new problem was caused by Geoffrey Taylor seeking extra brake horse power, and finding it, during the winter months.

Increasing the b.h.p. had altered the vibration period to the detriment of the carburetters, and it is a good example of how one step forward in motor-racing can easily mean one or two steps back.

Another weak point of Alta engines, which certainly upset carburation at Goodwood, is the slow rate of draining oil from the camshaft drives. Oil accumulates in such quantities that it builds up around the valve stems, and whilst every engine has a tendency to draw oil past the stems, this is particularly so with the Alta. I have always found that, however weak the mixture, the plugs are invariably sooty. I have never seen an Alta engine with clean plugs—not even to-day—and it is a fault that should be cured, for too much oil in the combustion chambers results in a serious loss of power.

In the second Easter Handicap, Abecassis was third with the Cooper, in spite of clutch and carburation trouble. The race was won by nineteen-year-old Stirling Moss, also in a Cooper, and already people were talking about the boy as a " find." I must admit that at this time I saw Moss as a rather thrusting driver who tended to push his car and himself just a little too near the limit. How wrong I was.

The H.W. Alta delighted us all with its performance. John Heath brought the car home to fourth place in the Lavant Cup (won by Dudley Folland's 1,905-c.c. Ferrari) and to sixth place in the First Easter Handicap after a ding-dong struggle with Oscar Moore (O.B.M.). Not a bad day of racing for the first outing of the car.

We came away from Goodwood with mixed feelings for although Heath was jubilant about the performance of his sports car, Abecassis was most disappointed with the G.P. car. I remember thinking to myself : " It won't be long now. The G.P. car has had it ! ' '

The poor old car was in trouble again when we went over to Jersey for the road race on April 28th. After a practice run we removed the cylinder head to try and find the cause of misfiring, as these were signs of water on the plugs, and found that not only had the valve seats moved but the cylinder head was porous. Geoffrey Taylor was at this time developing a new type of head, incorporating an alteration to the angle of the valves, and this was flown out to us.

We worked all night fitting the new head and were so tired next day that I resolved to turn in early in order to be fresh for the race. It was not to be ; two of Reg Parnell's mechanics were staying in the same hotel and got me out of bed. To cut a long and sordid story short, I ended up asleep in a cupboard under the stairs, in my pyjamas. I still shudder when I think of the hangover I had next day.

This brings me to a point. Drinking before a race does not help either the driver or the people who control his movements from the pit. It just is not possible for people who want to go motor-racing with the maximum chance of success.

On the starting grid I leaned over Abecassis as he sat in the car.

" What do you reckon is the ' form ' here ? " he asked.

" Let's have a crack from the start," I replied. " The car is ' right ' and, if it goes, then it will go well. Don't hang about waiting to see what's going to happen with the others."

The starter's flag was raised. It slashed down and the field thundered away, all except the Alta which freewheeled slowly towards the pits Abecassis looked hard at me.

" The back axle's gone."

I nodded glumly for it was not an opportune moment for me to tell him that, with my monumental hangover, I could not have cared less.

The H.W. Alta put up a good performance in the same race to finish in twelfth place, at the rear of the field and behind much more potent machinery in the nature of E.R.A.s, Maseratis and a Ferrari. John Heath, crouched low over the Alta's wheel, put up a most determined fight in torrential rain and on a soaking wet circuit. His performance and the behaviour of this fine little sports car against Grand Prix machinery was some consolation for the retirement of Abecassis.

However, the G.P. car was to have its day of glory, and significantly enough—for I still think this car could have been developed as the most potent British challenger of its day in Formula 1—it was in the British G.P. at Silverstone on May 14th. As this was a race of full Grand Prix length a supplementary fuel tank had to be fitted underneath the driver's seat.

She was going well on the first day of practice, when Abecassis lapped in 2 minutes 19 seconds as against the fastest lap of the day set by Peter Walker (E.R.A.) in 2 minutes 13.2 seconds. At the second practice session Villoresi put up fastest time in his Maserati at 2 minutes 9.8 seconds, and Abecassis recorded ninth fastest time at 2 minutes 17.6 seconds.

The car was perfect in practice and for the first time we had a pre-race night unaccompanied by the usual panic about something or other.

Although we still had the original gearbox a suggestion of mine that we do away with synchromesh on first gear had been adopted and it was certainly easier to engage gear.

On race day Villoresi occupied " pole " position, whilst the rest of the front row consisted of Gerard (E.R.A.), de Graffenried (Maserati), Walker (E.R.A.) and Bira (Maserati). Abecassis started from the third row and in a field of twenty-five cars was lying fifth after ten laps. This was too good to be true. The car was going like a bomb and sounded more healthy than it had ever done. Abecassis was really enjoying himself, driving on top of his form.

Then, round about a third of the race distance, the green car drew into the pits. I whipped up the bonnet ; a pool of petrol was rapidly forming underneath the car ! With only a four-inch clearance between the body and the ground I could not get my head underneath to look up at the float chambers, so lay on my back and groped around. I soon found that one of the float chambers had come right off and was hanging at the end of a length of fuel feed piping.

I shouted to the pits for a $\frac{3}{8}$ in. pipe plug and then set about shutting off the fuel supply line. When the plug was handed to me I had great difficulty in plugging the carburetter body without crossing the threads for when the chamber broke off it had damaged them.

At last the job was finished and the Alta went away. The pit stop had taken four minutes, three seconds. I blame myself for the float chamber breaking because I should have inspected it before the race and had I done so would have found it cracked. It was just one of those unfortunate things which even the best organized *equipes* cannot guard against.

Meanwhile the Alta was fairly streaking round the circuit and pulling up, place by place, from the back of the field. The car was virtually running on one float chamber but she sounded in fine fettle and to our amazement the lap speeds increased. Abecassis was having the time of his life, responding nobly to our pit signals urging him on. Even when he lost part of the exhaust system this did not slow him down. However, after half distance the Alta had another pit stop—of forty seconds this time—when the remaining float chamber flooded.

Fortunately the broken exhaust was no problem. It had snapped off at its pivotal point behind the driver and there was no danger of Abecassis being overcome by exhaust fumes ; neither was there any danger of fire so no action was necessary.

Off he went again and we were all so excited about the prospects of the flying Alta getting to grips with the front end of the field that James Tilling (who was managing the pit) agreed with my suggestion to speed up Abecassis even more. This was the first time our pit had been really well organized and our code was a simple one : F. for faster.

Twice we showed the chalked message to Abecassis and then, much to the disgust of Mrs. Abecassis, I added the plus sign.

" Do you want to kill my husband ? " she said.

" Madame," I replied, " we are motor-racing."

Well, the Alta finished seventh and we won £50 prize money, having completed ninety-six of the hundred laps. The pit stops had cost us

4 minutes 43 seconds and the Alta had been lapping around the 2 minute 18 second mark. Without these two stops we might have finished fifth, behind the E.R.A. of D. Hampshire and B. Cotton with ninety-nine laps to its credit.

This was the greatest race of the G.P. Alta. We had overcome the gearbox, back axle and valve troubles, the car had been prepared with more care and interest by all concerned, and it had gone like a bomb ! We had, in fact, gone motor-racing really seriously for the first time and I had enjoyed the experience immensely.

Two weeks later, in the B.R.D.C. Isle of Man races, we came up against Stirling Moss with disastrous results. Most of us—drivers and mechanics—held the same views about the young man. We were sure that sooner or later he would overdo things and that once would be enough. Then he would slow down and we should not hear much more about him. That was the general opinion.

Abecassis had entered his Cooper in the Manx Cup and when the loud-speakers announced that he had made fastest time of the day in practice we proudly pushed the Cooper towards the lorry.

Shortly afterwards the loudspeakers crackled again. Moss had beaten the time by a fraction of a second. Abecassis turned to me.

" Let's get the Cooper out again. I am sure I can beat this."

Off went Abecassis and, sure enough, he beat Moss's time. There was great excitement in the Moss pit where Stirling's father was discussing with bystanders whether or not his son should try again.

They decided to do so and, as we were pushing the Cooper towards the paddock, Moss went off in a blare of sound. Once again he cut down the Abecassis time.

" Oh no," I thought to myself, as Abecassis turned to me, " not again."

Sure enough, he wanted the Cooper wheeled out on to the circuit and he also wanted something on which to brace his feet in the cockpit.

" I can go faster," said Abecassis, " if only I can brace myself, particularly at Governor's Bridge."

There was no quick means of modifying the cockpit and when Abecassis suggested wiring a piece of wood on to the floorboards underneath the pedals I told him I thought it would prove very dangerous. However, he insisted and with this peculiar modification went out on to the circuit.

On the first lap, as the car went over the Governor's Bridge, it became airborne and the piece of wood must have broken away from its fixing. I can only imagine that it settled on the pedals and the weight of Abecassis' feet kept it there. Anyway, it seemed that the Cooper came down on the road with its wheels locked and immediately darted off at a tangent and hit a tree head-on at over a hundred miles an hour.

Apprehensive of what we might find we ran to the car. There was Abecassis, sitting in the driving seat, but neither he nor the seat were still in the car ! I asked him how he was feeling. His reply : " Never mind. Just give me a cigarette." His injuries : bruises and abrasions !

The car was absolutely written off. I have never seen anything like it.

The Cooper was so bent that it was impossible to remove the engine (still in one piece) without cutting the chassis.

It was some consolation that John Heath won the eighteen-lap 70-mile Manx Cup in the H.W. Alta after Moss had retired with magneto trouble. I remember Tony Rolt helping me to hold the cup as it was filled with champagne. In the excitement I slipped and was smothered from head to foot in the precious liquid.

In spite of his phenomenal resistance to the shock of hitting the tree at such a speed, it was too much to expect Abecassis to drive the G.P. Alta in the British Empire Trophy. It was unfortunate, for Abecassis had lapped the four-mile circuit only seven seconds slower than Parnell's Maserati.

John Heath drove the car and we were all delighted with its performance. He was relegated to the back of the grid, as he had not practised, but nevertheless put up a first-class performance in a car he had only driven previously for a very short time. He finished tenth at an average speed of 64.98 m.p.h. (as against his average in the Manx Cup of 65.32 m.p.h.) and towards the end of the race was getting within six seconds cf the very fast lap times put up by Abecassis in the car. The race was won by Gerard (E.R.A.) at 71.06 m.p.h. for 1 hour 57 minutes 54 seconds.

That evening, for the first time, I was invited to a cocktail party for the drivers and the dinner that followed. I was not surprised to find George Abecassis there, in very good form and little the worse for his accident, for he had watched the victory of Heath in the Manx Cup from our pits, supported under the arms by a couple of brooms borrowed from the hotel. They made excellent crutches reversed in this way and it was regarded as quite normal when he turned up at the party with them.

Our next meeting was Rheims, and the French G.P., won by Louis Chiron in his 4½-litre Talbot. I shall always remember this race for the wonderful driving of Peter Whitehead who looked a certain winner until, only six laps from the end, his Ferrari developed gearbox trouble. The G.P. Alta suffered a similar fate but Abecassis was in good company because Fangio, with a broken throttle control on his Maserati, also failed to finish.

In the Coupe des Petites Cylindres, preceding the Grand Prix and won by Ascari's Formula 2 Ferrari, Abecassis drove his Cooper. It had been rebuilt since its crash in the Isle of Man in that Coopers had provided a new chassis and body and we had installed the engine. Abecassis retired with clutch trouble but John Heath in the H.W. Alta was more fortunate and had an absolutely trouble-free run, finishing fifth against formidable Formula 2 opposition.

Stirling Moss was unlucky to break the chain on his Cooper-J.A.P. and we all admired his pluck in pushing the car more than half a mile to the pits where his father was acting as chief mechanic. We watched whilst a new chain was fitted and I could not help feeling sorry for Moss when the Cooper refused to start. Stirling may not remember but this was the occasion he tried to push-start a car against the direction of the race, the pits at Rheims being situated on a slight gradient.

I shouted across to Mr. Moss : " Leave the car alone. We will give him a push."

However, the gradient and the reluctance of the Cooper to start almost beat us and it was only after several stops for breath that we managed to get Stirling away.

It was at Rheims that I learned how to straighten valve stems in a hurry. Oscar Moore over-revved his car in practice and bent the valves. I was amazed at the way he straightened them, on an anvil with a hammer, afterwards spinning them between the jaws of a vice to find whether the mushroom stems were running true. Anyway, it worked and on many occasions since the day I saw Oscar Moore do this in a French garage, I have repaired valves—when time was short—in the same way.

After Rheims, the Alta disappeared from the G.P. scene. I was very sorry for I had grown to like the car as much as everyone else had grown to dislike it. I still say we could have made this motor-car go. All it needed was time to develop the chassis and engine. Geoffrey Taylor's ideas were right and he will not mind my saying that he is a fine practical engineer but a little bit old-fashioned at times.

Taylor and Abecassis used to race at Brooklands and Crystal Palace before the war and it was Taylor's life ambition to build a G.P. car. The Alta was launched without vast sums of money behind it (certainly nothing like the hundreds of thousands of pounds that have been spent on the B.R.M.s), but by the personal sacrifice of Taylor himself.

The car did not deserve its fate. As soon as it had been assembled, it went straight to a circuit without a trial of any sort. Fate was against the G.P. Alta from the very start and circumstances stunted its development.

The performance of the Alta at Silverstone was a great encouragement to all of us and after the shock-absorbers had been stiffened at the rear end and the silent bloc bushes removed from the front suspension links the car lapped the Isle of Man circuit in practice in 3 minutes 13 seconds, third fastest time of the day.

Unfortunately, Abecassis crashed and was unable to drive in the British Empire Trophy. Had he done so I am sure he would have put up a good fight against opposition of the calibre of Parnell's Maserati and proved the capabilities of the Alta. Had Abecassis done well so soon after the Silverstone effort the resultant enthusiasm of driver and designer might well have ensured immediate and steady development.

As it was, the man who could have " pushed " the development of the car was unable to drive it for many weeks following his accident and the energies and resources of H.W.M. were concentrated on developing an entirely different type of car—the H.W. Alta sports car.

If ever the dice were loaded against a car it was so with the G.P. Alta and although the car was pushed into a corner at Walton, more or less in disgrace, I am proud to have been associated with the first real G.P. car ever to have been made in this country and with the man who designed and built it. One of my most treasured possessions is the single sheet of foolscap paper, with instructions how to maintain and service the Alta, which Geoffrey Taylor handed to me the day I collected the car from his " works."

Our next engagement was in August, at Comminges near Toulouse, where John Heath had entered the H.W. Alta for the Grand Prix of the A.C.F. for sports cars. The regulations specified 80 Octane commercial fuel and after Rheims, we fitted four Amal carburetters in place of the twin S.U. layout. Unfortunately, it was impossible to synchronize the Amals before the race ; we just could not get the engine running evenly and eventually reverted to two S.U.s.

The heat at Comminges was almost unbearable and when I tell you that we had no pits with awnings as at Silverstone or Goodwood, and that our pits were simply areas of pavement marked out with whitewash, you will appreciate our extreme discomfort. The cars came in for attention by running up a wooden ramp on to the pavement.

John Heath drove a really good race at Comminges for it was no mean achievement to cover 312 miles single-handed, in a cockpit almost red-hot from the heat and at a consistently fast pace that eventually resulted in second place in general classification and first place in the cars up to 2-litres.

In the pits we were almost roasted and when Harry Schell came in and had a bucket of water poured over him I almost wished I was a driver. Half-way through the race, Heath came in for a drink. I had prepared for this eventuality by laying in a stock of Coca-Cola, which I stood in what little shade our shadows threw on the pavement. However, the " Coke " was almost " on the boil " when I picked up a bottle and the contents actually began to bubble as he pulled into the pit. Heath took one pull at the Coca-Cola and promptly spat it back at me.

" You are so useless," he said, " you cannot even keep the drinks cool."

He then set off in such a temper and at such a pace that I was not at all surprised when he finished in second place. The Coca-Cola had done a good job !

Heath had quite a tussle with Chinetti (Ferrari) towards the end of the race and to our delight was able to hold him. He sat hard on the tail of the Italian car until Chinetti spun off and unwisely allowed spectators to push-start him. Our old friend Rene Bonnet saw it happen and lodged a complaint which resulted in the Italian being dropped to eighth place.

It was at Comminges that I returned late to the hotel to find that John Powell had been severely bitten by bed bugs. I ran downstairs and complained to the manager. Sympathetically he listened to what I had to say and then, gravely reaching under the counter, produced a type of flit gun.

" Mr. Francis," he said, " it is necessary from time to time to declare war on our visitors. To-night is just such a night and, as I am on my own, I ask you to make the campaign for me."

I was so disarmed that I meekly went upstairs, sprayed John whilst he slept, and then sprayed myself.

After Comminges, we moved on to Lausanne for the Formula 2 race where the H.W. Alta retired with a porous cylinder head, having completed forty-eight of the sixty laps. I cannot remember the details but the retirement was the cause of a fairly heated argument between John Heath and myself, during which I asked for and was granted a week off.

Back in England I decided to take a " busman's holiday " and to visit the September Goodwood Meeting as a spectator. It was the last appearance of the H.W. Alta and I remember riding down to Goodwood on my motor-cycle, paying ten shillings to get in and watching the racing from Madgwick Corner. Abecassis drove the car and was fourth in the Madgwick Cup, whilst John Heath careered off the course at Woodcote Corner in a handicap race and had to retire.

I had to admit to myself, chugging back to Woolwich on my motor-cycle, that a week was just about long enough to be away from motor-racing. Naturally, I did not express this sentiment to my wife who, in a little over fifteen months, had become a " motor-racing widow."

She has been one ever since and I don't think many wives would have put up with it as she has done. In a busy continental season I am away from home more or less from April to September. There is not much home life for a motor-racing mechanic.

CHAPTER 5

ENTER THE H.W.M.s

A formidable task—The plan materializes—
Moss joins H.W.M.—Six-day weeks, 14-hour days—
Testing the prototype—Bad luck at Goodwood.

For several weeks after the Goodwood September meeting all was quiet on the Walton front. I must admit that as we neared the end of October I began to wonder about the future for it was obvious that the G.P. Alta would not race again and that left only the H.W. Alta, which was not my responsibility.

It was about this time that John Powell, who had decided there was no future in motor-racing, applied for a transfer from the racing department to the garage and John Heath agreed. This left me on my own and Heath suggested that we build a rear-engined car. I was most enthusiastic—on the basis of trying anything once—but George Abecassis was not convinced.

" The Auto-Union did not stay on the road," he pointed out. " How on earth do you think we can build a rear-engined racing car with any more chance of success ? "

Logic won the day and the project was abandoned.

However, very soon we were to have far more work than we could handle in a seven-day week. One evening John Heath came into the workshop in a very good mood.

" You know, Alf," he said, " I have decided to give you ten shillings a week rise because of your work last year."

I must have looked rather glum for he asked what was the matter.

" Well," I replied, " I'm afraid ten shillings won't save me. Living in digs at Walton and keeping my home going at Woolwich has reduced to nothing what little capital I had when I joined H.W.M. In fact, I am ' in the red.' "

I should mention here that when I first joined H.W.M. they found me " digs " and paid two-thirds of the cost. As employers, Heath and Abecassis were nice people.

Heath was quick to appreciate my point and suggested that it might be possible for H.W.M. to buy a house for me in Walton.

" You see," he went on, " we are thinking of building a team of two-seater sports cars, based on the successful design of the H.W. Alta. Peter Clark of H.R.G. has an entry at Le Mans and we plan to run them there."

This was wonderful news and something I had never expected. All thoughts of financial worries vanished and I listened whilst Heath talked about the scheme and explained how one of the oil companies would finance us to a considerable extent.

" Even that will not be sufficient," he said, " and I am selling some of my private property."

I was walking on air when I went back to my digs that night but what a formidable task we had set ourselves in planning to build a " works " team of four cars in little more than four months !

In the best traditions of the motor-racing game, conference after conference was held in the workshop. There was never any question of sitting round a table in a clean office. Oil, grease, petrol fumes ; it was all an essential part of our planning.

It was agreed that the design would be as simple as possible and that production components would be used wherever practical in order to keep down costs. The power unit would be basically the same as that used in the H.W. Alta but, as we only had one of these engines, four more were ordered from Geoffrey Taylor.

Heath explained that we would build a prototype and four team cars more or less at the same time.

" We will press on with the team cars," he explained, " without waiting until the prototype has been track-tested. The prototype will be more in the nature of a workshop guinea pig than anything else. . . . We must get these cars ready for the start of the 1950 season in March," he continued, " so that they can be raced prior to Le Mans. And time is desperately short."

There was not a great deal of difficulty from the technical point of view, proceeding with the four team cars at the same time as the prototype, because so much preliminary work of a prototype nature had been carried out by the H.W. Alta. We were fortunate in having the sports car as a basis for the H.W.M. design, fortunate because it had behaved so well and had absolutely no vices at all. We had no hesitation in using its front suspension system on the H.W.M. but, at the rear end, John Heath decided on transverse leaf springs and two wishbones in parallelogram form, similar to John Cooper's design on the successful 500's.

The H.W.M. differed very little from the H.W. Alta and it would be true to say that the only major difference was in the design of the back axle itself, where independent suspension and a transverse leaf spring was used in place of a solid beam axle. The differential unit was a simple, straightforward type of E.N.V. design, with no self-locking devices and with a straight cut crown wheel and pinion.

John Heath decided to change from the E.N.V.-type gearbox to the Armstrong Siddeley preselector box, as it was not possible to obtain the E.N.V. boxes in sufficient numbers and, furthermore, spares were difficult. Heath purchased five or six gearboxes from Armstrong Siddeley and Geoffrey Taylor designed a special bell-housing so that they could be incorporated.

It was necessary to have more personnel and two new mechanics joined us—Tom O'Hara and Rex Woodgate. O'Hara came from the Monaco Motor and Engineering Co., Limited, where he had been one of John Wyer's foremen, and was serious, hard-working and conscientious. In his early forties, he was older than me, which could have created bad feeling but, I am happy to say, never did. He was married and living at home and as our working day grew longer and longer, poor Tom became more and more unpopular with his wife.

Rex Woodgate was a much younger man and joined us from Stirling Moss. He was inclined to be temperamental and highly-strung but, for all that, proved himself very clever, with considerable technical knowledge. He was the ideal man for work on the prototype and had some excellent ideas.

I wonder whether Rex remembers the day he arrived at Walton and the outcome of our first meeting. He came into the workshop and introduced himself.

" Alf, I am supposed to work with you here."

" Very pleased to meet you," I replied. " Where are your tools ? "

" I have none," replied Rex.

" Well," I said, " we have a tradition in motor-racing . . . we like people to bring their own tools."

I don't think Rex ever forgave me, and understandably so, for he had to sell his precious O.M., which he was running at the time, for a " song " in order to buy a set of tools. But what a set ! I have never seen such a beautiful collection of chromium plated tools except maybe the Vanwall outfits.

It was at this time that Stirling Moss, following his successful season with the Cooper-J.A.P., was invited to try the H.W. Alta at Odiham airfield. Stirling was only twenty at the time but had impressed the motor-racing world with his ability to keep up with more powerful machinery driven by more experienced drivers.

I well remember that dull, December day at Odiham. I could see that Stirling was a little uneasy for it was the first time he had handled anything more powerful than the Cooper. However, he put the H.W. Alta through its paces most convincingly and we were all impressed.

I thought he looked rather sheepish as he drove back to where we were standing. When he got out of the car he said miserably :

" Sorry, but I think I've cracked the sump. Ran over one of those half submerged landing lights on the runway."

I thought John Heath would explode and Stirling has since told me that he fully expected to be turned down on the spot. However, we all realized that here was a youngster who could really handle a fast car. He obviously had the instinct, the natural sense of balance that tells a racing driver by " feel " just how much he can safely do. It is not surprising when one appreciates that his dentist father was himself a well-known Brooklands driver and his mother a rally driver.

And so the boy who at the age of seventeen—a year after leaving school —made up his mind to become a professional racing driver was signed on with H.W.M. less than three years later.

With our driver problem solved, to the extent that Moss would make up a team of three with Heath and Abecassis, and with the obvious enthusiasm of O'Hara and Woodgate to back me up, I set about organizing the " shop." The first step was to make the necessary jigs. One must have them when building four or five chassis at the same time and we made our own. Once there was a " jig " for a particular part it only remained to saw and weld material for the other cars.

One of our main concerns was to find a welder so that there would be no delay in the production programme. It was quite out of the question for John Heath—who had welded the H.W. Alta chassis more or less "after office hours"—to do the work. We were all going to be far too busy on the constructional and design side to worry about welding and Jack Tolly, the welder from Cooper Cars at Surbiton, came over to Walton in his spare time.

John Heath and I spent every evening hard at work on the prototype. He explained to me what he wanted to do, and as soon as the practicability of a part was agreed and it had been incorporated in the prototype, we went ahead at once with identical parts for the team cars. It was as near as we could get to mass-production and the four H.W.M.s were rarely more than four or five days behind the prototype.

We came up against a problem when, in line with our policy of keeping down production costs, we endeavoured to use a Triumph Mayflower chassis. When an effort was made to incorporate our own suspension units so much work was involved removing brackets and generally modifying the chassis to suit our purpose that we found it quicker to make our own.

The facilities at H.W.M. were not entirely adequate. Admittedly, the drive shafts and transmission parts were machined by Frank Green at a small engineering works outside Walton owned by John Heath, but all the steel required for the construction of the cars was hand-cut by us and afterwards welded and filed. All we had to help us of a mechanical nature was a small guillotine which never cut more than $\frac{1}{8}$ in. strip steel. We also had an old lathe and drill. The latter was very useful for lightening the chassis, and we used it to drill and cut holes in the cross members.

It was a period of hard work, so much so that I would never have thought it possible for a small group of people—three mechanics and John Heath—to be kept so busy that their thoughts were constantly of the cars and the various problems connected with them. We never thought or talked of anything else, not even on those rare occasions when there was time to sit down and have a quiet cup of tea. Looking back it seems to me now that we completed an almost impossible task.

The work was undertaken by us all with such energy and enthusiasm that by Christmas the chassis were almost in a mobile state—on wheels but without the body structure. When I tell you that we worked six days a week until 10 or 11 o'clock, having started at 8 o'clock in the morning, and that no overtime was paid, you will appreciate that our enthusiasm for the project was such that financial considerations did not matter.

We were quite happy to be employed on a flat rate basis and no one ever complained of being underpaid. Quite frankly—and you can believe this of all of us—money just did not matter when we were building the H.W.M.s.

Admittedly, after a few weeks I asked John Heath whether he would allow us half-a-crown an evening to buy a cup of coffee and something to eat. Our breaks were hurried ones, as well as being few and far between, and there was certainly no time to get home for a snack. If circumstances had not forced us to spend our own money in this way I should not have bothered to ask for the extra half-a-crown.

I also arranged with Heath that Tuesday evening was our night off.

We found ourselves getting on each other's nerves and it was essential to get away from the workshop, even if our thoughts remained there ! Nevertheless, we worked something like a 65-hour week and I wonder how many people to-day, outside motor-racing, would be prepared to do that. I know people in the game who work like this, and always will, because they have discovered that working hard at the job you like is worth far more than earning overtime in a job you do not like.

I particularly admired Tom O'Hara. At his age, and with his experience, he could have earned far more for his working day at several other garages. Even an unskilled man, on an overtime basis, could have earned more than we did.

Of the two partners John Heath was the driving force. Abecassis very rarely appeared in the Competition Section and it seemed to me that, after laying up the G.P. Alta, he did not have the same enthusiasm for any other project.

Moss was a frequent visitor to Walton. He came over once or twice a week to see how we were getting on and proudly displayed the odd black eye—received in a boxing bout in the gymnasium—or some choice bruises from the rugby field. It was obvious he was trying to convince us (and he did) how well he, for his part, was preparing for the 1950 season.

We admired him, too, for his interest in the mechanical side. He did not know a great deal but in his usual thorough manner spent a lot of time with Ray Martin, who was building a Kieft 500 for him, learning how to weld and gleaning what information he could about the engine. We all appreciated his sincere interest in *our* job and it has since become one of his most likeable characteristics. It makes for a fine team spirit.

His theories about power to weight ratios were very sound indeed. Many times, during a brief lull and over a cigarette, he would comment on these lines : " Why should we use this gauge steel ? Why not a thinner gauge ? The power to weight ratio would be improved and I consider it vitally important."

I must admit that, in those days, he knew more about power to weight ratios than I did. It was a new line of thought to me and at the time I did not believe in such extremes.

At last the day arrived for testing the prototype at Odiham. The other cars were either at the bodybuilders (the Leacroft Sheet Metal Works at Egham) or having their frames completed in the workshop.

I am proud to say I had the honour of being the first person to drive the H.W.M. Naturally, I was not able to comment on its high speed behaviour but as I drove round the airfield perimeter I felt instinctively that she was " right." I only had a limited knowledge of how the car should feel in the hands of a racing driver but she seemed to respond so well and the engine was remarkably " sweet."

Then John Heath took out the H.W.M. and came back in jubilant mood. As Abecassis went away, Heath congratulated us on our achievement. We had practically no trouble with the car, just a spot of carburation bother which we had expected on the first outing, and this was soon put right.

Before we started work on the carburetters I took off the bonnet and put it behind Geoffrey Taylor's car. Unfortunately, somebody decided to reverse the car, with dire consequences to the bonnet. The main problem then was to soften the wrath of John Heath and quickly we lifted the damaged bonnet and put it behind his Citroen. Then I went over to Heath and said to him :

" You are a fine one. You must have backed the Citroen on to the H.W.M. bonnet."

He gave me a real old-fashioned look but could not very well question my statement. Often it was policy with John Heath to take the bull by the horns in this way.

The Alta engine behaved very well and this pleased me because I had spent a lot of time with Geoffrey Taylor on the bench, trying to improve the tune of the engine. At first we were getting between 110 and 115 b.h.p. and we tried to obtain more power by running a four-branch exhaust system. The engine was put on a test bed with three exhaust pipes running into a silencer. The other remained in the open whilst we experimented with it, trying to establish the correct length. Suddenly, we found ourselves getting 130 b.h.p. with only this single exhaust pipe in the open ! Further tuning was abandoned and we set about modifying the other three exhaust pipes to the length of the single one, expecting to get even more power from the engine. As it turned out we were disappointed.

Although the prototype had behaved so well and required very little in the way of modification we were not yet ready to go motor-racing with the team cars. The bodywork was not complete in all cases and the engines were not yet assembled, one of them still being under test on the bench at Geoffrey Taylor's works. The cars were only a few days behind the prototype but, strictly speaking, it was the cars minus their power units.

Nevertheless, we felt rather lost. The Odiham trials might have taken a very different course and then it would have been another session of fourteen-hour days to modify and test in time for Goodwood. As it was we almost felt unemployed. What luxury it was to be able to relax—not too much of course—and to work without an unrelenting time factor.

The first appearance of the H.W.M.s was at the Goodwood Easter Meeting. We took two cars and had a lot of bad luck, although Heath was fourth fastest in practice on the Saturday, recording 1 minute 43 seconds as against Parnell's lap (fastest in practice) with the Maserati in 1 minute 40.4 seconds.

In the five-lap scratch race for the Lavant Cup Abecassis retired with a punctured carburetter float, after circulating quite rapidly, and Heath dropped himself almost to the back of the field with a spin.

There was some doubt whether Moss would be able to drive at Goodwood as his licence had been temporarily suspended by the Civil Court following a piece of brisk cornering in his Morris Minor, and the conviction prevented him holding a competition licence. However, the organizers and R.A.C. Stewards allowed him to compete in the Chichester Cup (five laps Formula Libre), the second H.W.M. being handled by Abecassis. Both cars finished some way down the field, Abecassis having lost time by running off the road, and the race was won by Bira (1,490 c.c. Maserati). Baring then took over Abecassis' car for a handicap race and finished at the end of the field.

In the big race of the day, the Richmond Trophy, Abecassis was lying fifth—handicapped as were other drivers by torrential rain and wind of gale force—when he retired, not because of trouble with the car but because he was soaking wet and most uncomfortable and did not realize he was so well placed. It was almost a tropical downpour.

It remained for Moss, driving Heath's H.W.M. in the Third Easter Handicap, to put up our best performance of the day. He got away well, with Duncan Hamilton (1,496-c.c. supercharged Maserati), from the 40-second mark and although passed by Hamilton on the second lap was nevertheless only 2.2 seconds behind him at the finish. Scratch man Bira came home third, some way back.

I remember how, after the last race, Charles Cooper of Cooper Cars, came over and slapped me on the back.

" Now, how about these famous H.W.M.s of yours ? " he said.

I am sure Charles did not mean to be unkind but naturally he was pleased that we had not done too well as he had a sports car of his own design under construction.

I must admit that I was a little depressed and when I had loaded the cars on the transporter went over to the bar for a drink. John Heath was there, obviously not very happy about the performance of the H.W.M.s either. He told me so in no uncertain manner.

" Well," I replied, " one thing I will promise you. We will not be defeated by one meeting. We are going to fight back—and that goes for all of us. If we all work together for H.W.M., whatever the problems, we can be the most successful team in Britain."

Heath nodded, not entirely convinced but nevertheless impressed by my sincerity.

All the way back to Walton I pondered over this question of setbacks as a stepping-stone to success, for it was obviously linked closely with morale, and I decided that the correct mental approach was to accept the fact that proficiency could only be acquired by considerable experience.

I have since found that through experience one gets to know a car so well that eventually one is able to extract the last ounce of efficiency from it. One can only truly learn from setbacks and experience, for there is no harder school, and it is not possible to improve a motor-car unless you accept this fact. I cannot help thinking that, had we raced the G.P. Alta on more occasions, we would have learned more in less time.

The only way to iron out troubles is to compete as frequently as possible. A test drive, similar to those when British G.P. cars cover some three hundred miles on a circuit such as Oulton Park, does not to my mind prove anything conclusively ; it does not tell anyone how that car will behave against opposition and with all the various race factors in operation, in a grande epreuve. The only successful way of developing a racing car is to put in the maximum number of racing hours.

The hardest test ground of all is the actual race. It is because we in this country did not go motor-racing on a big scale until the 1957 season—when the Vanwalls put out a formidable challenge in World Championship events—that we failed to develop British cars fast enough to keep up with the opposition and to stay the distance.

The prototype of the 1950 cars used a 1960-cc. Alta engine specially built for John Heath by Geoffrey Taylor. The four Grand Prix Amal carburetters, used with two large S.U. float chambers, gave excellent results on the bench but track tests at Montlhery were unsatisfactory and the Amals were never used in a race ; their main fault was that they did not provide sufficient power low down. At the rear of the camshaft cover can be seen the troublesome, gear-type fuel pump.

The four branch exhaust system of the prototype improved the power output of the engine on the bench but was liable to break off under racing conditions. This layout was used for half the 1950 season and the frequent breakages caused several retirements. The double-decker Ford Thames transporter is in the background.

Frontal view of the prototype of the 1950 cars. The brake back-plate, fabricated from sheet metal and lightened by the inclusion of cooling holes, can clearly be seen. Each back-plate took at least twenty-five hours to make, mainly because of the dished shape. Standard production back-plates were not sufficiently dished to allow the drums themselves to project into the air stream.

The cockpit layout showing the cutaway door to conform with F.I.A. regulations for sports cars. Brackets welded to the chassis would have permitted the fitting of a passenger seat but as the team H.W.M.s were never raced as sports cars the extra seats were never fitted. The E.N.V. gearbox, with selector on the steering column, can be clearly seen and also the well laid out instrument panel which had an ammeter and a light switch in the top left-hand corner.

CHAPTER 6

THE H.W.M.s INVADE EUROPE

Testing at Montlhery—The G.P. de Paris—
Some notes on race organization—Shambles at Roubaix—
Vegetable oil solves a problem—Panic at Mons—
Cream cakes lose a race—The F.2 race at Berne—
Trouble with the Swiss polizei.

The Secretary to H.W. Motors, Mrs. O. M. Vaughan, surely breathed a sigh of relief when she learned that the H.W.M. " Circus " was safely on foreign soil. Those of you who have completed a set of car papers will be able to appreciate the work involved in making a declaration covering a team of racing cars and all their equipment, and Mrs. Vaughan made all the arrangements for getting us over to the Continent for the series of continental engagements that started on April 30th with the Formula 1 Grand Prix de Paris at Montlhery.

Once across the Channel it was my responsibility to accommodate the mechanics, find a garage near each circuit where we could work on the cars, pay all the bills and keep the accounts. I was, in fact, the " Cooks·representative " with the team as well as being chief mechanic.

I had problems of my own and one of the first entries in my diary for 1950 reads : "April 26th—Went to London and collected French and Swiss Visas." At this time I was still a Polish subject and could not leave the United Kingdom without a visa. My British naturalization papers had not come through and it was not easy to obtain the visas as I had only travel documents instead of a British passport.

I must mention here the kindness of Det.-Sgt. G. Davies of Scotland Yard who interviewed me in connection with my naturalization. He was most sympathetic and it was more than a pleasure to deal with the British police force after certain unpleasant experiences with the German Gestapo when Poland was invaded.

On my return from London with the visas we loaded the lorry for the Continent, and I collected £15 from the petty cash and twenty petrol coupons. This was it. I could hardly believe I was about to start a continental season with a full team of cars, less than two years after leaving Furlongs Garage in Woolwich. I saw Sylvia for a few minutes during the evening. She was naturally upset that I was going abroad but neither she nor I had any idea of the fantastic season of motor-racing that lay ahead, or that we should not see each other for at least four months.

The lorry left Walton at 8.30 a.m. on Thursday the 27th, driven by Rex Woodgate, and at ten o'clock I went to the bank to collect £100-worth of Travellers' Cheques. It was my responsibility to take charge of all the documents connected with the journey, such as shipping papers, tickets vehicle log books, etc. I had even been told to look after the laundry so that the team mechanics were always turned out in a clean suit of overalls !

George Abecassis took me to Dover in the Citroen, where we found that we could not get the lorry on the Ostend boat as it was fully booked. Not a very good start !

So we had to wait for the 9 p.m. Dunkirk Ferry, which was annoying to say the least because it meant that we should disembark at the unearthly hour of 5 a.m. I don't mind admitting that I have never liked getting up early in the morning.

We arrived in Paris later than planned, not feeling on top of the world by any means, and after a hurried meal went straight out to Montlhery. We had not track-tested the cars since Goodwood and were anxious to put in as much time as possible at the circuit before the race.

This was the first time I had seen the famous permanent competition and test track. It is some fourteen miles south-west of Paris and is a fairly lengthy circuit of nearly eight miles, which can be adapted to different race distances and is banked in parts. For a medium fast circuit the surface is bad.

We carried a stock of four axle ratios per car (3.7, 4.0, 4.5 and 4.8), which in those days was quite ambitious. It was possible to change the complete axle unit in an hour-and-a-half. It was not too difficult, just a matter of disconnecting the drive shaft from the outer housing. The nose pieces were completely interchangeable and saved us the trouble of changing crown wheels and pinions. There was no meshing of gears to worry about.

We were not very pleased with the results of our first practice session. There was chronic misfiring on the Abecassis car. It was similar to the trouble we had experienced with the G.P. Alta, when the plugs oiled up due to oil being sucked past the valve stems, and Abecassis was losing a lot of power.

Moss was also losing revs and could not get nearer than 5,500 to the maximum of 6,000 revs. He did not have the same trouble as Abecassis and we cured the power loss, to a certain extent, by removing the air filters which gave him another 200 revs.

In the final practice session Abecassis was faster than Moss, lapping the road circuit in quite an impressive manner for our first outing on the Continent. We were far from downhearted. We had never expected to make such good time against the Formula 1 cars, and Abecassis did very well to record fourth fastest.

Unfortunately, Moss broke his rear offside spring carrier and I had to telephone Walton for the necessary material to make up a new one. We also decided to replace the drive shafts on both cars with larger diameter ones, at 9/16-in., as it was doubtful whether the smaller ones would stand up to the race distance of nearly two hundred miles.

This was not all. The Abecassis car was oiling up on No. 1 plug. It was persistent and I was convinced the piston was sucking oil past the inlet valve guides but no one would agree with me that it was anything to do with oil ; everyone else maintained the carburetter was flooding, due to faulty carburation. Anyhow, I had my way, and it was agreed that the engine would be modified to the extent of employing another drain on the camshaft chamber.

We had not experienced this oiling up trouble to the same extent with the H.W. Alta, for the simple reason that it was a different design of engine. The 2-litre engines for the H.W.M.s had been specially manufactured by Geoffrey Taylor, whereas the H.W. Alta power unit was a modified $1\frac{1}{2}$-litre engine.

The material for the spring carrier arrived by air and we then worked all night on the two cars. Paris was wide awake by the time we had finished but at least the team was ready to go to the starting grid.

A word now about our pit organization. At this stage H.W.M. was much more of an amateur outfit than a professional one and the pits passed information to the drivers—such as their position and the number of laps covered—rather than attempt to direct them as a team. Rex and I looked after the pit whilst Mr. and Mrs. Moss remained interested but unemployed spectators.

What little knowledge I had of pit work came from the 1948 and 1949 seasons. Rex and I worked out various drills to cover refuelling and tyre changes before leaving England because by this time I fully realized that to knock a second off a lap-time is very difficult but to save ten seconds in the pits is often very easy.

We kept all our spares in the pit, such as tyres, wheels, fuel, oil, carburetter parts and spare magnetos, and very little else in the way of equipment was carried in the lorry from circuit to circuit. We naturally had spare axle ratios, a spare gearbox and a certain amount of raw material for modifications to suspension links or wishbones on the spot but it was not a very well organized workshop when one considers our programme of racing a team of cars almost every week-end.

I refused to carry a welding plant. From what I had seen in previous seasons the owner rarely uses it. The plant is borrowed day and night by everyone else and is a dead loss to the " parent company."

In the Montlhery race Abecassis was delayed on the start line. There was one warming-up lap, followed almost immediately by the start, and although I advised both drivers not to stop their engines after the preliminary lap Abecassis not only switched off his motor but got out of the car as well, thinking he had the usual four or five minutes in hand before the " off." Just as he did so the starter raised his flag, dropped it almost immediately, and there was the H.W.M. still on the grid. Fortunately, Moss got away with the rest.

We lost valuable seconds push-starting the Abecassis car, whilst the French officials shouted, gesticulated and panicked as only they know how. At last, he went away in a blare of sound and it was not long before he was lying fifth, behind Moss. Unfortunately, although the new draining channel had helped to cure the misfiring, a broken exhaust pipe forced him to retire.

Moss was more fortunate and completed twenty-four laps—driving magnificently and impressing the crowd with his skill—until a connecting rod broke and he retired. The race, our first Continental appearance with the H.W.M.s, was won by Grignard (Lago-Talbot).

It was at Montlhery that I had an argument with Mr. Moss. After

Abecassis retired I considered it was up to me to do something about getting the No. 1 driver into the remaining car. I felt that Abecassis, as team-leader, would want us all—particularly the drivers—to work as a team rather than as individuals. With this in mind I decided to " arrange " a change of drivers when Moss came in for fuel.

I regarded Abecassis as the No. 1 driver. He had put up a faster time in practice than Moss, who was a newcomer to the *equipe* and No. 2 driver. The fact that during the race Moss was quicker than Abecassis did not alter my assessment of the team set-up.

As Rex and I would be fully engaged in refuelling the car I asked Mr. Moss to suggest to Stirling that he offer his car to Abecassis. Mr. Moss was very upset :

" The boy has done well and is lying second. Why change drivers now ? "

It was only natural that Alfred Moss, who was delighted with his son's performance, should feel like this but I considered that Abecassis—with more practical experience than Moss—should be in the car. To me the team was all that mattered and I was not interested in personalities.

Mr. Moss would still not agree with me so, reluctantly, I had to tell him : " I will not refuel the car unless Stirling offers his ' drive ' to Abecassis."

Shortly afterwards we called in the car for fuel and waited to see what would happen. It took place so quickly that the spectators certainly were unaware of the drama. A quick exchange of words between Moss senior and junior was followed by Stirling jumping out of the car and saying something to Abecassis who replied at once :

" Never mind, Stirling, you have done well so far—get on with it."

I did not regret the action I had taken for, in my opinion, when a driver or mechanic starts motor-racing he is an apprentice and has to learn to respect those who have more experience than himself. Unless one learns at the start it is often too late and swollen heads result.

It is a matter of building up not only team discipline but individual discipline as well. One must learn self-sacrifice before one can even start to make an intelligent approach to the sport. It is a sacrifice well worth while for, to those of us connected with it, motor-racing is the greatest of all sports. Men on wheels, as the charioteers used to do in the days of ancient Rome, pit their skill against each other in a world of speed and danger—a world where chivalry and sportsmanship are vitally important.

All the great drivers of to-day engage in friendly rivalry, showing their superiority in their skill. There is no " dirty work " so far as the people at the top are concerned and motor-racing in the top flight is probably safer than having to compete as a rally driver in certain minor events that are dangerous out of all proportion to their importance.

On Sunday night after the race we were working on the cars when Abecassis came into our " box "—or garage—in the paddock.

" You have done enough for to-night," he said. " Knock off now, and let's go into Paris. We can discuss our plans for to-morrow over a good dinner and a bottle of wine."

Unfortunately, the party that grew from this well-meaning suggestion gave all three of us monumental hangovers ; Rex Woodgate, who unwisely mixed oysters and whisky, only just managed to reach our hotel before collapsing in agony.

Before the party got out of hand it was decided to test one of the cars at Montlhery the following day, before leaving for Roubaix. We wanted to try four Amals instead of the twin S.U.s and dutifully, though a little late and feeling very brittle, I arrived at the circuit as arranged.

Working on my own it took some considerable time to fit the Amals but eventually the job was done and I took the car round the banked circuit myself. The noise from the four exhaust pipes was thrown back and magnified by the walls of the banking to such an extent that the " locals " were under the impression that a record-breaking run was being made. After one or two hectic moments, I said to myself : " This situation is not for you. With your hangover, you should be anywhere else but in the seat of a fast car." I quickly convinced myself and pulled into the pits.

I was not very pleased with the four Amals. I could not get them to run evenly and consequently this made starting difficult, in view of the fact that it was impossible to use slow running jets. I later made a report to Abecassis in which I pointed out that they were not practical for the H.W.M., and he agreed that we revert to twin S.U.s on both cars. Quite apart from anything else the S.U.s gave much easier handling of the throttle than the Amals.

Barnstorming around Europe with the H.W.M. team in 1950 we had to modify, repair—even rebuild—after a race, using the circuits themselves for testing before moving on to the next meeting. To all intents and purposes it meant working seven days a week, usually against the clock and often with only a few hours' sleep each night.

There was no question of spare cars at Walton being modified in the light of our experience and race reports, then sent out to us whilst the old cars were returned for modification. This is the ideal system—used by the top flight *equipes*—and means that cars are constantly being shuttled to and fro between the various circuits and the factory.

Strictly speaking an *equipe* can only be successful if, as well as having a team of cars on a scheduled programme abroad, it maintains and races another team at home. The technicians at home must be in constant touch with the chief mechanic abroad, so that the cars can be improved and modified in the light of experience on the foreign circuits. Then the cars abroad must be brought home and replaced with the modified ones so that there is, in fact, a constant interchange of cars and a progressive policy of development. And so it goes on ; an endless chain of exchanges, modifications and exchanges.

This is how the Maserati organization works. They have their Design Department and their Constructional Department (which incorporates the work of a Development Department as soon as the cars are completed), with each department under separate management. Then, of course, there is the Competition Department, working very closely with the others.

It is usual for a member of the Development Department to fly to every meeting and, as soon as the race is over, he returns to Modena and incorporates in the car under development in his department any knowledge gained at the race. Such a person not only knows every circuit and its characteristics but also knows the wishes of the team drivers in all matters connected with racing. He is given every opportunity of talking to the drivers during the practice sessions and the race itself. Back in Modena the full facilities of the works are put at his disposal so that if possible any improvement can be incorporated before the *equipe* races again.

It is a system that has never been used by any British team for the simple reason that there has never been a team with sufficient cars, although I suppose we could have worked a modified system with the four H.W.M.s. Instead of taking three cars on the Continent and leaving one at home, we could have taken two abroad and left two at home, under constant development. Naturally, I was not able to suggest such a course to Heath and Abecassis as at that time I did not realize the necessity and importance of such a system.

All I was able to do in those days was establish my own Development Department, as well as look after the preparation of the cars for racing and their transportation from circuit to circuit. I was, in fact, putting the Maserati plan into operation to a certain extent without knowing it.

I tried to carry out any modifications immediately after a race, in the garage where the cars had been prepared prior to the meeting. For instance, if the H pieces broke I would fabricate new ones immediately after the race for there was no time to get replacements from England. I carried the necessary materials with me and one can find welders almost anywhere.

Before moving on to Roubaix, where the Cinquantenaire G.P. for Formula 2 cars was being held to celebrate the fiftieth anniversary of the Northern Automobile Club, I spent the day on the Abecassis car but without success. After Montlhery the car was still misfiring badly at the top and bottom ends, as well as lacking power below 2,500 revs, but at least, by modifying the camshaft chamber, we had cured the oiling up of the plugs.

I know now that the engine was missing because the carburetters were mounted direct on to a solidly based manifold and vibration was causing them to froth. We should have used flexible manifolds but at this time I had no experience of them.

Another problem was the fuel pump. It seemed to me that we either had too much pressure or too little, and what was actually happening, although I did not know it at the time, was that a fluctuation of pressure was causing a loss of power and misfiring as well. This was one of our main, unsolved problems of the 1950 season.

The third team car was sent out from Walton for the Roubaix race and the Moss car returned to England so that Tom O'Hara could fit a new engine. On Friday, at Roubaix, we had confirmation that the car was on its way and I sent Rex to collect it from the Ferry. Meanwhile, Abecassis put up fourth fastest time in the first practice session and was, in fact, going very well. Rosier was the fastest man in his 2-litre Ferrari.

On the second practice day Anthony Baring arrived with his own H.W.M., having purchased it from John Heath with the intention of running as an " independent." This left only the prototype at Walton and, so that the team would have a reserve in the U.K., Heath put another chassis in hand.

When our replacement car arrived, which the Belgian driver Johnny

Claes was to handle as Moss had returned to London, it was in a shocking state. Not only was it dirty, but the windscreen was broken, the engine had not been run in and, as I had expected, the plugs oiled up in practice.

So we went to work. The front end of the cylinder head was drilled and the oil drainage modified. Still the oiling up trouble persisted so I decided to raise the plug level by means of washers and this seemed to cure the trouble. The car went very well but there was no chance of running it in properly and Johnny Claes was told to take it easy during the race. The other H.W.M.s also sounded very healthy at the end of practice and, having cleaned them up, we were ready to do battle.

I have always made a point of ensuring that my cars are properly cleaned before they go on the grid. In 1954, when we were racing the private Maserati with the works team, I prided myself that the car was often cleaner than the works cars. I do not have any time for these slapdash people who will not take the trouble to prepare their cars properly. They usually leave themselves so short of time that it is not possible to find even ten minutes to clean up. I set myself a zero hour for finishing the work on the car and always allocate the last hour for cleaning up.

What a shambles there was on the starting line, with H.W.M. as the star performers. As the flag dropped, Baring ran clean up the tail of the car in front and, having straddled the cockpit with his wheels for a few seconds, slipped down again with the steering arm so badly damaged that he had to retire.

Meanwhile, Abecassis was going very well. From sixth position he pulled up to fourth place at half distance and then to third. Three laps before the end a drive shaft broke and Abecassis pushed his car over the line and was classified as sixth. Johnny Claes obeyed our instructions to take it easy and, in a very sedate manner, came home fourth. The race was won by Sommer (Ferrari).

Afterwards we found that the drive carriers on the rear suspension had fractured and I decided to modify them, using stronger gauge steel, before moving on to Mons. We fabricated and welded new carriers, increasing their thickness from ⅛ in. to 3/16ths in., and by working more or less non-stop for two days and nights in a Roubaix garage, we completed the modification. The weakness had only become apparent since we started racing on the Continent. It was obviously due to faulty design and the use of metal that had not been strong enough in the first place ; metal fatigue, in fact.

The Mons G.P.—a Formula 2 race of 116 miles—was on Sunday, May 14th, and we arrived in the Belgian town on Thursday to find John Heath, Stirling Moss and Tom O'Hara waiting for us. Tom had brought the Moss car over, with its new engine, in the second lorry and our *equipe* was complete, so that we were able to make a maximum effort with three team cars driven by Heath, Moss and Claes—whilst Baring raced as an " independent," prepared by us.

During the first practice session the cars were again oiling up their plugs. It was, in fact, an achievement to get any of them going properly on four cylinders, and revs were sadly lacking at the top end. We modified the oil drainage on Heath's car and this improved matters to the extent that he put up the fastest H.W.M. time of the day ; and he was supposed to be our slowest driver !

I also changed the magnetos on all the cars but this did not make much difference except to improve performance on the Moss car. I then changed to weaker (W.E.) needles on the carburetter of his car and, in a further effort to cure the oiling up, tried an even weaker needle (W.C.) on the front S.U. The car certainly seemed to go better but Moss could not improve on Heath's time of 3 minutes 27 seconds.

On Saturday the situation remained unchanged. The Claes car was missing so much that it was positively embarrassing. It seemed that nothing could cure the trouble and I decided to strip down completely one of the engines to check whether the piston rings had seized or broken and were allowing the oil to pass. I chose the Heath car for the experiment but found nothing wrong with the rings.

The Simca-Gordini team were using the same garage at Mons and in desperation I discussed the problem with Robert, the chief mechanic of the French *equipe*, and asked him whether he considered the use of vegetable instead of mineral oil in the H.W.M.s would improve matters. He assured me that it would do so as they had experienced similar oiling up troubles with the Gordinis, and when I put the question to John Heath he agreed that the mineral oil could be drained from the sump of his own car and replaced with vegetable oil.

It made an astonishing difference and to say that we were pleased when the H.W.M. motored round the circuit without misfiring is an understatement. I felt like dancing a jig or throwing my hat in the air, but simply contented myself with chalking up another triumph over circumstance. If you keep at these problems long enough then you find the answer eventually. The other cars ran just as well on vegetable oil and for the first time since the beginning of the season the entire team was firing on four cylinders !

We were using a very high percentage of alcohol in our fuel, alcohol being a vegetable fuel in its own right, and the mineral oil had not been mixing satisfactorily. We might as well have tried to blend mineral oil with water. When we changed to vegetable oil we immediately improved the burning of the excess of oil that accumulates in the combustion chamber, simply because vegetable oil blends with alcohol fuel and is burned at the same time. The combustion chamber is left in a far cleaner state and the plugs do not oil up.

Morale was high, following the oil change, and we were fully convinced that our troubles had been cured. It was so unusual to be able to wheel the cars on to the " grid," without having had a sleepless night, that I thought to myself : " This is too good to be true. Something is going to go wrong." It did.

I shall never forget the panic at Mons when the Claes car would not start. I was with Heath and Moss whilst Claes, whose practice times had been slow because of misfiring, was on the back row of the grid. As soon as the two-minute signal was shown, the H.W.M.s were started but, looking quickly over my shoulder, I saw that the Claes car had not " fired " and was being frantically pushed backwards and forwards.

As I personally did not wish to remain in the middle of a stream of cars, ran to the back of the grid and reached Claes as the starters' flag fell. We pushed him for almost a quarter of a mile down the straight, encouraged by the Belgian crowd who wanted to see Johnny Claes put up a good show, and I suddenly realized as I straightened up and glanced at the instrument panel that the engine was not switched on !

Tired as I was, and out of breath, I let Claes have the " works " but he was wearing earplugs and did not hear any of my choice phrases. Meanwhile, I leaned over and switched on the ignition. Off he went—with thirty-five seconds to make up—and it seemed that in no time at all he was on the tail of the back-markers. It was incredible. He passed one H.W.M. after another and was leading them all when the race ended.

Claes finished fifth—delighted with the performance of his car—and when the times were worked out we found that if he had not lost those precious thirty-five seconds he could have finished second or third to first place man Ascari (Ferrari). Anyway, the car went like a bomb and the whole H.W.M. team finished in line ahead—fifth, sixth, seventh and eighth, and on the same lap. Admittedly the other cars had not been so fast as Claes but it was nevertheless a great day for us and the first time that a full team had started—and finished !

When I asked Claes about his incident after the race he told me he was sure he had switched on the ignition. However, it was a press-on switch and he must have pulled it out again—perhaps fumbling with his glove—without realizing. How many lessons does one have to learn the hard way ?

We were so pleased with life, and morale was so high, that we decided to strip down completely all the engines, as well as prepare one car for Claes to drive in the G.P. des Frontieres at Chimay whilst we went to Aix les Bains. Actually, Claes won the Chimay race and gave H.W.M. their first continental victory, and we were not there to see it !

It was not our practice to strip down after every race, as you will by now have realized ; there was not sufficient time. Anyway, it was not necessary. What our full programme had told me was that it pays to race as often as possible because one then learns from practical experience how many racing miles a car can complete before certain things have to be checked.

The day after the race I decided to modify one car by fitting a single pipe exhaust. We found all the exhaust pipes cracked after the Mons race and it was necessary to take some action as they had cracked at Montlhery and Roubaix as well. I had Rex to help me.

We were fortunate at Mons in having a very good friend, an executive in the Frigidaire factory. We worked on the cars almost in the factory yard and became very friendly with him. Several times we were invited to his home, where he and his wife entertained us. He had a phenomenally large family of ten or eleven children and the first time I saw them I thought to myself : " Here is someone who has more worries than you have ! "

He organized our garage and accommodation and was always doing something to make our work easier. I used to describe him as " our invisible manager." Certainly, without his help we could not have completed half our work in Mons, either before or after the race. Over the years, in motor-racing, I have made many friends on the Continent.

Wherever we go there is always someone prepared to help, either be ause he (or she) is pro-British or a motor-racing enthusiast.

Our friend from Frigidaire arranged for his engineers to bend the exhaust pipes and then had the necessary welding done. His people cut a new manifold and new brackets for the chassis so efficiently that I asked them to make a second set so that if the prototype was successful we could immediately modify a second car.

On Tuesday I started to strip down Stirling's engine as he had complained about the car going slowly in the race. There was plenty of time to do this as we were not due to leave Mons until the end of the week. On occasions I have taken an engine completely to pieces and rebuilt it between 6 p.m. and 10 a.m. the next morning. It depends, of course, on what one finds when the engine is down but, generally speaking, it should be possible to strip, check and rebuild in sixteen to twenty-four hours.

I was determined to find out why Moss' car had gone so slowly, particularly as the change to vegetable oil had considerably improved the plug readings. I soon found that the ignition timing was not quite right, which was understandable as we had been continually adjusting the carburation and ignition when the mineral oil was causing the plugs to oil up.

With the plugs in their proper clean state, as a result of the vegetable oil, this particular car now required a readjustment of carburetters and ignition. It does show how necessary it is, having cured one cause of trouble, to consider the advisability of readjustments in other directions.

By Saturday the Moss car was assembled and going very well indeed. We planned to leave Belgium the following day and, having loaded the cars in the afternoon, sought out our friend the welder at Frigidaire. He refused to accept any money for his services so we took him out for a meal and a bottle of wine. For hours we talked about nothing but motor-racing and the personalities of the sport. When we eventual y said goodbye he told us that he had never spent a more enjoyable evening.

I have often noticed how the real enthusiast, such as our friend in Mons, can sit in a bar or restaurant and get a great deal of pleasure out of just listening to the reminiscences of people closely connected with the sport. All he asks is the right sort of atmosphere, usually easily provided where the " boys " gather, and he is " there."

The conversation is not always about motor-racing. I have found that in France the main topics of conversation are food, and the laziness of the French people. The French seem to be proud of the slackness of their own nation.

In Germany the main topic is wars, and why they are lost, but I always try to avoid joining in this sort of discussion as it always leads to arguments.

In Italy, as one would expect from a nation so aware of feminine beauty, the subject is invariably women. I have never met an Italian who will not, given the opportunity, express a professional, sincere and heartfelt tribute to an attractive girl. The Italian is a connoisseur and, as such, his forthright remarks are not resented by the fair sex.

I had left the United Kingdom with £100-worth of Travellers' Cheques and every Monday morning there was a business conference with John

Heath, at which I had to account for what had been spent during the preceding week. He then reimbursed me and maintained my float at £100
all the time. I kept a record of expenditure, together with my notes on
practice sessions and races, in a large foolscap diary which I had purchased from Boots in Walton.

With the cars to prepare and the various records to keep I did not have
much time to write home. In fact, my first long letter since leaving
England in April was written on May 24th, the day we arrived at Aix les
Bains. It was my only free day in four hectic weeks.

After writing about the superb scenery in the vicinity I went on to
describe our three races and finished with this sentence : " The course
here is dangerously twisting and one of our drivers, young Stirling Moss,
is exceptionally good, so I have hopes."

Stirling did not disappoint me. On the first day of practice for the
64-mile Formula 2 race, he was no more than two-tenths of a second slower
than Vallone (Ferrari). Everyone was talking about the immaculate way
Stirling was taking his corners. There was no apparent impression of
speed but when he had gone through a corner it left the spectators wondering how it was possible to go so fast with so little visible effort. The
polished performance was there, even in those days.

The pre-race atmosphere in Aix le Bains was terrific. This was the
first time the population had seen a motor race and we could not walk
through the streets or go shopping without someone stopping us and
questioning us about the race and the cars.

Everyone was so kind. We never expected such enthusiasm—in a
health centre—for motor-racing. The Town Council even went so far as
to unveil a head and shoulders statue of Queen Victoria (who used to spend
a lot of time in Aix) in front of the Grand Hotel whilst we were there, and
invited the H.W.M. team to be present at the ceremony as honoured
guests.

There is no doubt that the team—the only British *equipe* of any size
in those days—was very popular on the Continent during that first whirlwind season of 1950. Perhaps it was because, in the usual British fashion,
we were pitting our skill and resources against far stronger and more
experienced *equipes*.

An excess of cream cakes put paid to our chances at Aix le Bains. John
Heath and Stirling went out together the evening before the race and, as
far as I could make out, Stirling not only ate too many cakes but poisoned
himself as well, probably with the synthetic cream in the cakes.

He suffered agonies during the night and was in no fit state to drive.
Nevertheless, as the cars were being pushed on to the grid, Moss appeared
and, white-faced, settled himself in the cockpit of the H.W.M. I admired
his courage for although a reserve driver had been engaged Stirling was
determined to race.

Somehow, he managed to keep going for twenty laps but was then
forced to come into the pits. We sent for the ambulance at once for he
was on the point of collapse.

We were naturally bitterly disappointed. The cream cakes had ruined
our chances for we really felt, on a twisting circuit of this nature and bearing

in mind that Stirling had done so well in practice, that he could have put up a great fight against Vallone and Sommer. The latter had arrived for the last practice session and recorded fastest time, which dropped Moss back to third fastest. Nevertheless, the odds were in favour of a terrific scrap in the final between Moss, Sommer and Vallone.

As it was, there was no H.W.M. in the final. It rained during the heat in which Heath was entered and the car did not put up a fast enough average to qualify for the final. This was just plain bad luck for the other heat had been run in the dry.

I think the incident at Aix les Bains taught Stirling a lesson. In those days he was young but very sure of himself (I am talking about his behaviour off the circuit) and liked to give the impression that he was an expert on how to live well.

He knew all the answers ; where to stay, what to eat, what to do and where to go. Actually, Aix les Bains proved that he was not really grown-up enough to realize what was good for him.

Poor Stirling was very upset about the whole thing. I saw him some days after the race and he was still in bed, feeling very sorry for himself. I think he must have made a mental resolution to be more careful about what he ate in future for, to my knowledge, he has never since been forced to retire for such a reason.

I want to try to explain why we mechanics were so fed up, in spite of the fact that the good people of Aix les Bains were very sympathetic about our bad luck. Their kindness after the race was almost overwhelming.

It is like this. In an *equipe* as large as H.W.M. the mechanics have no idea how the drivers spend their time between the final practice session and the start of the race. But they do know that the cars are " right "—as right as they can make them anyway—and that they should go well if driven properly.

At Aix les Bains we knew that the cars had behaved better than at any time since leaving Walton and we also knew Stirling had recorded some very fast laps. What we did not know was that Stirling had foolishly overeaten and poisoned himself as well. Imagine our feelings when we realized that, due to factors absolutely outside our control, the H.W.M. *equipe* was beaten before it started.

I have seen well-known drivers put up pathetic performances in major events simply because of a " night on the tiles " or an excess of alcohol. Next time a car runs badly in a race don't automatically blame the car. Find out how the driver spent his evening after the final practice.

The public does not make things easy for drivers. They do not always realize that motor-racing is a dangerous sport and that a driver should race only if he is absolutely " on his toes." However, drivers do not like to appear rude by ignoring invitations to parties and often they have to meet a lot of people and drink with them when they would rather be getting a good night's sleep. Although the public have the best intentions they should realize that, in motor-racing, kindness can be dangerous.

The Formula 2 race that preceded the Swiss Grand Prix on the famous Bremgarten Circuit at Berne was our next appearance, and a major event. I wrote a letter home from Aix les Bains and one paragraph in particular shows how difficult it was to make any plans. " Just a few words to say I am not crossing to England mid-June. I am not going to the Isle of Man but to Rome instead ! "

The 4½-mile Bremgarten Circuit demands maximum concentration and is recognized as one of the most difficult in the world. It is in every way a driver's circuit and a man who can do well on the Bremgarten has to be not far short of the top flight. It is situated in the forest of Bremgarten on the western outskirts of Berne, and is a very treacherous circuit. For instance, if it rains some days before a race the surface retains the moisture because of the many overhanging trees ; neither do fallen leaves improve matters. It is impossible to say, on arrival at Berne, that because the sun is shining the circuit is safe ; in any case the sun's rays throw dangerous and misleading shadows in the forest section and have caused more than one accident.

We had three team cars at Berne, but only two drivers, as Moss was not well enough to race. So we tried out Rudi Fischer, a Swiss, who went so well that he was signed on as No. 3. There was some rumour at Berne about Raymond Sommer driving for us, but what actually happened was that Sommer came along to see us at the H.W.M. pit on the first day of practice for a friendly chat. He had become interested in the H.W.M.s at Roubaix and, by the time the races at Mons and Aix les Bains had been run, was a firm friend of the *equipe*.

I remember that his friendship resulted in quite a number of press photographs being taken of him with the H.W.M. drivers. Anglo-French friendship was the theme but some of the other *equipes* were rather jealous of the amount of free publicity the British team received in this way.

Sommer arrived at our pit just as I had finished adjusting the preselector mechanism on Fischer's car.

" Why not take her round," Heath said to Sommer, " I'd like you to have a ' drive ' just to see what you think of the motor-car."

Off went Sommer, and started to lap very fast indeed. He was most impressive and when he eventually pulled into the pit I asked him what he thought of the H.W.M.

" I rather like it," he said, " but I don't like your pedals. They are dangerous."

They were not only too close together for Sommer, but he was used to driving a single-seater Grand Prix car with the pedals on either side of the drive shaft and steering column. If you normally drive a G.P. car, then three pedals all in a line can be disconcerting. This was as near as Sommer came to driving the H.W.M. at Berne.

The Formula 1 cars—with Fangio, Farina, Fagioli, Ascari and Villores —were racing at the same meeting, and I would have liked to watch them in action during practice. As a matter of fact, I felt rather sorry that I was not still in their line of business, as I had been with the G.P. Alta the previous season.

However, I was really far too busy with my own problems to spend any time watching the F.1 cars. In any case, the organizers have such strict regulations at Berne that when the Formula 1 cars practise, the Formula 2 cars have to remain, with the mechanics, outside the circuit. Furthermore, the practice sessions were so well organized (motor-cycles, Formula 1, Formula 2, sports cars, etc.), that we knew to the minute when our particular session would start. We worked on the cars up to the last minute, then drove them over to the circuit gate and consequently never saw any of the other practice sessions.

People have often asked me whether I take an interest in the overall motor-racing scene. I always tell them that the *chef d'equipe* of a team of cars should be so absorbed in those particular cars that his whole world revolves around them. It should not be possible to find the time to take any interest in the sport as a whole.

I, personally, rarely have an opportunity of enjoying myself to the extent that I can watch a race in which my cars are not entered. Once my cars are ready I either try to have a " cat nap " or else worry about the nature of the work I may have to carry out after the race.

A good mechanic cannot also be a motor-racing enthusiast in the true sense of being a spectator. He must be practical and conscientious enough to worry about his own job in the same way that a good flag marshal should worry about his. He should certainly not spectate or take photographs.

I always explain to my apprentices when they join me : " When you go to a race meeting, just imagine you are working in another garage. You must become absorbed in your job."

In the Berne race, against strong opposition in the shape of A.F.M., Gordini, Ferrari and Veritas-Meteor, Abecassis led the H.W.M. team until he was forced to make a pit stop for a punctured carburetter float to be replaced.

The real reason for the float sinking was that the quality of solder used in their manufacture could not stand up to the action of the alcohol fuel. After the Berne race I started re-soldering all the floats myself and they definitely lasted longer.

The race was won by Raymond Sommer in his Ferrari, after he had led for most of the distance. The H.W.M.s did quite well to finish sixth, eighth and ninth—Fischer, Heath and Abecassis in that order, but I shall always remember the race for an incident with the Swiss " polizei." It was rather monotonous, with the cars passing at regular intervals and the pit staff waiting to tick off the next lap, when Tony Hume—who had joined H.W.M. at Berne as Team Manager—dangled his legs over the pit counter.

At the Bremgarten Circuit the Swiss forbid anyone to stand in front of the pits, or even to sit on the counter as Hume was doing, and a Swiss policeman—without saying a word—put his hands behind Hume's knees and tilted him backwards. In an effort to save himself, Hume grabbed at the policeman, pulled off his glasses and broke them. The Swiss hit Hume in the face, and without further ado Hume jumped down in front of the pits and neatly socked him.

The Swiss crowd started shouting and booing and police reinforcements arrived. However, an Inspector, after some persuasion, allowed Hume to remain in control of the pit until after the race.

Next day I was called by Tony Hume as a witness in Court proceedings. I answered the Judge's questions about the incident and then asked if I might make a comment. The Judge agreed and I told him that during the war I had spent some time in a Concentration Camp in Rumania, and that the policeman's high-handed action in dealing with Hume was no better than Gestapo methods. He should have asked Hume politely to move back behind the pit counter and not push him without any warning.

As I am able to speak Swiss-German fluently I warmed to my theme and went on to say : " I helped to fight for liberty and human rights for six years and consider the Swiss police are more like the Gestapo than the police of any other civilized country."

The judge smiled in quite a friendly fashion after this outburst and I was dismissed, instead of being charged with contempt of Court which I had expected. Hume was discharged and the offending policeman ordered to apologize.

CHAPTER 7

BEARDING THE LION IN HIS DEN

*Moss's superb drive in Rome—The missing despatch case—
Living " on tick "—A pat on the back.*

We were due to race three cars in Rome, seven days after the Swiss
Grand Prix, and it was a great personal satisfaction to me that John Heath
had sufficient faith in my abilities to entrust me with the task of getting the
lorries and cars down there safely. We should be taking the H.W.M.
team into the very heart of the continental motor-racing world.

The route I had worked out would take us over the 6,800 feet high
Mt. Cenis Pass, the easiest connecting link between France and Italy for
lorries, and invariably used by the Italian *equipes*. The Customs officials
are so helpful at the frontier that they have been presented with a diploma
of honour, in recognition of their services, by the Automobile Club of France.

At St. Jean de Maurienne, on the French side of the Pass and just before
Modane, there is a famous hotel on Route Nationale 6 where Napoleon
stayed on his way to invade Italy. To-day the manager is a great enthusiast
and the bar walls are covered with motor-racing photographs. It is a well-
known stopping place for drivers.

From Mt. Cenis the route lay through Susa, Turin, Alessandria, Genoa,
and the west coast. I had not been in Italy since the war years and was
looking forward very much to the 700 mile journey. There was a certain
amount of glamour connected with it all. I don't deny that.

I was at this time travelling under an alien's passport and visualized
difficulties obtaining an Italian visa. When we planned our original race
schedule before leaving Walton, it did not include Rome. However, when
I explained to the officials at the Italian Consulate in Berne that I was
visiting Italy in order to go motor-racing, all formalities were swept aside
and the visa was produced in a matter of minutes.

In the afternoon, I went through the accounts with John Heath. The
following items—totalling £26 10s. in English money—give some idea of
our expenses for five nights covering the Berne meeting and do not include
the drivers :—

Hotel for three mechanics	...	...	280 Swiss francs
Tips at hotel	...	...	6 ,, ,,
50 litres petrol for lorries	...	...	30 ,, ,,
			316 ,, ,,

Having made a rendezvous in Rome with John Heath we set off for
Aix les Bains, where I had decided to spend Monday night. We planned a
non-stop run from Aix, as I was due on Thursday morning in Rome and

there would be no time for sight-seeing or sleeping in hotels *en route*. It would be a matter of pressing on regardless.

I decided that it was more necessary to have two people in the large lorry, and it was agreed that Rex and Tom would drive the transporter—taking turns of two or three hours at the wheel—whilst I carried on with the small van.

Every now and then one of them could come into the van for a sound sleep—comparatively sound, anyway—as my cab was more comfortable. I was confident that I could keep going, with only the odd " cat nap " when we pulled up for petrol or food, by using some of the dodges I had learned during the war. I am proud of the fact that I can drive long distances without sleep and several times in recent years have made non-stop runs from Modena to Dunkirk in thirty hours.

I have several means of keeping fresh. First, whilst the cafes are still open, I stop at intervals for a quick cup of coffee and a glass of brandy. This keeps me going for two or three hours. After a few stops of this nature the brandy and coffee no longer has any effect and I then keep a lookout for pumps in villages or small towns. I find that putting my head underneath the tap and really giving myself a good soaking works wonders.

Often at night, when it is cold, I stop the lorry out in the country and make for the nearest ditch. I find that tiredness acts as a laxative in my case, whilst the cold night air, and no trousers, sends me back to the lorry suitably refreshed. Those are my three ways of keeping awake.

Once we had disengaged ourselves from the knot of interested and voluble Italians at the Mt. Cenis frontier, we made for Turin and arrived there safely. Then we got lost—well and truly lost. We had no idea how to get out of Turin and it was almost as though the jaws of the city had snapped shut. We felt trapped in a maze of streets, speeding Topolino Fiats, and signposts that all seemed to point in the same direction.

It was the police force that got us out of Turin eventually, because most of the police seem to speak French and, once I realized this, I was able to ask for directions in a language I could understand. We made good time on the autostrada from Serravalle to Genoa, then lost ourselves again trying to get out of Genoa.

It was most amusing when Rex Woodgate, driving the transporter, stalled the engine in a narrow street and stopped fair and square astride the tramlines. The transporter effectively prevented all movement of traffic and the engine absolutely refused to start. Along came a tram and in no time at all the noisy passengers had disembarked and were pushing the transporter out of the way. They had to push for several hundred yards but as one Italian explained to me : " We like to help you because you have racing cars and anyway we want to get home."

We made quite good time down the west coast via La Spezia, Livorno, Grosseto and Civitavecchia to Rome, and I shall always remember an incident that occurred when we were making our way slowly over the tortuous Bracco Pass, between Sestri Levante and La Spezia, which has a surface in many places no better than a dirt track, with boulders the size of footballs added for good measure.

I was travelling behind Tom and Rex when suddenly I saw an Italian on a motor-scooter approaching very fast. He was riding in the customary Italian manner—almost out of control—and had just rounded a bend in a power slide. Fortunately, as we were climbing the Pass, we were able to slow down but the motor-cyclist could not avoid the transporter and ran full tilt into the front nearside mudguard.

He then bounced along the side of the transporter, keeping his balance in some miraculous fashion, and continued downhill with no reduction in speed. As he passed me he made a brave attempt to smile nonchalantly, and thus not lose too much face, but in doing so hit a small boulder, executed a somersault and came to rest some fifty yards away. Ruefully he picked himself up, collected his motor-cycle and went on his way—a sadder, wiser and very much bruised Italian.

We arrived at Rome on schedule and went straight to the Automobile Club to ask the whereabouts of our garage. Heath went there as well and in this way we made our R.V. In those days I arrived in a strange place, like Rome or Naples, with no idea where to go. I used to stop at the first newspaper kiosk and buy a street map, but this did not prevent us going the wrong way up one-way streets or getting lost at roundabouts.

I learned my lesson the hard way and nowadays I stop at the first taxi rank and ask a driver to guide me to the Automobile Club. It sometimes costs as much as a pound but at least we arrive fresh and without having spent valuable time as impatient, bored spectators of the sort of argument that always arises between the locals when one asks the way on the Continent. The Club officials always provide guides to take us to our garage.

Before the first practice session I went round the Caracalla Circuit in the transporter and decided to use the 4 to 1 axle ratio. It is a road circuit, not far from the Coliseum, where the old Caracalla Baths used to be and I believe the Romans used to race chariots there. It is not " round the houses " like Monaco but more in the nature of a park circuit and, as such, leaves room for error.

It took us some time to change the axle ratios and we did not get to bed until the early hours, but the cars were ready by Friday. However, Rudi Fischer was not satisfied with his ratio so I had to alter it to 4.8 to 1.

For some reason John Heath was not very anxious to drive his own car and handed it over to Tony Hume who promptly hit a kerb and bent one of the front wheels. He also broke one of the rear spring carriers. I realized that it would take all night to repair the car, even if we could find a welder, so we started to strip down immediately after the practice. Fortunately we found a man to weld the new carrier into position and finished assembling the car just in time for an early breakfast. Naturally, we all felt tired out, for we had not had a full night's sleep for days.

On Saturday Fischer complained about his axle ratio again and insisted on having 700 x 16 wheels. I was sure this would mean trouble and told John Heath so. I did not discuss the matter with Fischer ; there are occasions when it is a waste of time to try and reason with a driver. This was just such an occasion.

I knew the drive shafts would not stand up to the additional load, for we had already experienced broken shafts with the standard wheels, and increasing the unsprung weight would not help matters at all. However, John Heath politely but firmly disregarded my warning and the car was fitted with 700 x 16 wheels.

We also had great difficulty obtaining fuel in Rome. We had sufficient of our own for two cars—Moss and Fischer—but John Heath had to use fuel supplied by the Club and I h d reason to describe it in my diary as "very suspicious." Meanwhile, Stirling was in very good form. It was the first time he had driven since his stomach trouble and he was anxious to get back into the fray. In practice he was handling his car in a very polished manner.

Just before the start of the race on Sunday, when I was on the grid and the drivers were in their cars, I stared in amazement as a well-dressed man in a bowler hat approached. "He looks like a Civil Servant," I thought to myself. "He only needs a rolled umbrella." I could not make out how he had managed to gain access to the circuit and evade the ever-watchful Italian carabinieri. There was less than ten minutes before the start of the race.

He came straight over to me, took off his gloves and held out his hand : "I want to wish you the best of luck," he said, "I am the British Consul here in Rome."

I nearly fell over backwards for I never expected to shake hands with a consul on a starting grid. He went on to say : "Will you arrange that after the race you have tea with me in my private house. A team of cars like this does more good in Italy than a dozen consuls like myself."

Needless to say we were honoured to accept his invitation and flattered that he should have taken so much interest in a sport that arouses no enthusiasm, so far as the majority of any political party or government is concerned, in this country.

When the flag dropped I was not at all surprised when Fischer, from his position next to Moss on the second row of the grid, free-wheeled for a few yards and came to rest. A drive shaft had gone !

It was a very exciting race and the first time I had seen Italian spectators in action. I say "in action" because they were like a Wembley Cup Final crowd—surging forwards, backwards and sideways as the mood took them.

Moss chased the Ferraris of Ascari and Villoresi, which subsequently took first and second places, with such determination that he almost sat on their tails and I believe passed them on one or two occasions to hold a brief lead. His driving was absolutely superb and every time the green car passed the pits the spectators rose to their feet as one man and shouted "Stirleeng. Stirleeng."

When the loudspeakers announced that Moss had established a new lap record of 1 minute 58 seconds the crowd went wild with excitement. Hats, programmes, jackets went sailing into the air, and one would have thought Stirling was an Italian protege.

W watched him with increasing admiration as he tore round the circuit. Then came moments of anxiety when he did not appear, whilst we waited impatiently for some news from the loudspeakers. When a driver goes missing, you know fear—real fear. Has he crashed because of some fault in the preparation of the car, in which case you are to blame ? Is he dead, or perhaps injured and crippled for life ? All these thoughts race through your mind. " Damn those loudspeakers. Why the devil cannot someone make an announcement." At last, it comes and your heart beats normally again.

At Rome a stub axle broke and Moss lost a wheel, fortunately without injuring himself. As he tried to make his way to the pits he was suddenly lifted on to the shoulders of enthusiasts who, to show their appreciation of his magnificent effort, carried him back alongside the circuit. Why their presence so near the cars did not cause an accident I do not know.

The pit became very crowded and I could see that Stirling would go to bed with a very " big head " unless I did something about it. I had previously noticed an attractive woman standing behind the wire fence that separated the pits from the enclosure. I pushed my way through the crowd of autograph hunters and enthusiasts.

" Stirling," I said, " there's a lady over there who would like to talk to you."

He quickly walked over to the fence.

" Hello," he said, " you wanted to speak to me ? "

Her reply, in perfect English, was absolutely shattering.

" Really—why should I want to speak to you ? "

Understandably, maybe, Stirling did not say a word to me for the rest of the day.

We had quite a few stub axle failures with the H.W.M.s in that first year and whether it was due to faulty material or faulty design I am unable to say. The cars, after all, had been designed and built by people with limited experience—practical people rather than technicians. Another factor was that lack of finance had forced John Heath to use proprietary parts. The stub axle failures were really a result of a combination of circumstances.

I must admit that, had I been a driver, it would not have given me a great deal of confidence in the car. I was not surprised when Stirling told me later that the incident had upset him.

Moss had a trouble-free run so far as fuel was concerned but John Heath, on the club fuel, had so much trouble that he had to retire. I must not blame the fuel too harshly because, with our limited knowledge of Italian, we asked for alcohol spirit but did not specify its exact composition.

After the race there was the usual weekly conference with John Heath and he told me that as the next race, the Coupe des Petites Cylindres at Rheims, was three weeks ahead one mechanic would have to go back to England. It was an economy measure and I decided to send Tom O'Hara as he was finding the pace of the travelling " circus " rather too hectic for his years.

We left Rome with the two lorries at midday on Tuesday as I was anxious to get away from the high cost of living in the Italian capital, and to reach Rheims without too much delay where we would be better placed for obtaining spares. However, I had not overlooked the possibly of stopping *en route* somewhere for a rest. We should have been " flat broke " in twenty-four hours had we stayed in Rome, and as H.W.M. did not pay us a fixed daily rate a few days in Rome would have cost John Heath a lot of money.

We eventually found ourselves in S. Vinzenzo, an enchanting little village on the Mediterranean coast, south of Livorno, where there is only one hotel and miles of wide golden sands. We stopped there for two nights and I was absolutely astounded when I received the bill. The hotel accommodation for three of us, and including our meals, only came to £4 10s.

We had a real holiday at S. Vinzenzo and it did all of us a lot of good. Whenever I have the opportunity, which is not very often when the " circus " is on the move, I try to relax in this way. When there is time to spare, I would far rather spend it somewhere quiet than in a place like Rome or Naples. And what a relief it is sometimes to get away from the motor-racing crowd, away from everything remotely connected with the sport, and to have sufficient time to send a letter home.

On the beach at S. Vinzenzo I wrote to Sylvia and part of the letter read like a Cooks travel itinerary : " To-morrow I am off to Milan, Turin, and France again. From Rheims I believe we go to Bari in the South of Italy ; then Naples, then Geneva." And then, supreme optimist that I was : " I am sure you are looking forward to your holidays. As far as I know from July 30th until August 20th we have no race unless something suddenly turns up. I hope nothing does ! "

Soon after leaving our delightful seashore village we met an English tourist who offered to take Tom back to England. Off he went, and down went our cash balance by 10,000 French francs and 20 Swiss francs. This left Rex and me with one lorry apiece, and we made for Milan as John Heath had asked me to call at the Borani factory to collect some new wheels he had ordered.

We had a frightening experience in Milan. Having collected twelve wheels from the factory we went into a nearby cafe for a cup of coffee. I took my despatch case with me, as it contained the carnets, passports and various other documents, as well as being 10,000 Italian lire (£6) fatter as a result of meeting John Heath at the factory. I had to smile when he handed me the bundle of lire notes. We had given most of our spare cash to Tom and six pounds would not get two mechanics and two lorries very far.

Carelessly, I left the despatch case in the cafe. Thirty miles along the Turin Autostrada I suddenly had an impulse to feel for the case under the tubular frame of the bucket seat. There was no case ; I was horrified. Frantically I flashed my lights at Rex in front and risking the wrath—not to say fines—of the mobile police we held a council of war on the auto-strada and decided to return to Milan. Maybe I had left it at the Borani works.

We tore back along the autostrada in the small van, having left the large transporter in the village where we turned round, and arrived at the Borani works just as they were closing. We searched the toilets and offices but the case was nowhere to be found.

Miserably we sat in the van.

" How are we going to get out of Italy ? " I said to Rex, " let alone reach Rheims. We have no carnets, no passports and no money."

I could almost hear John Heath letting fly at us and the thought was so depressing that I said to Rex : " Let's go into the cafe and have a drink with our small change."

As we pushed open the door, the proprietor came over to us. " Did you leave a despatch case here this morning ? " he asked.

You could have knocked me down with a feather and once the case had been described to the satisfaction of the Italian we celebrated in no uncertain fashion. When we eventually left the cafe, the proprietor had the symptoms of a hangover, and we ticked off the kilometre posts on the autostrada so quickly that I am sure a record was established for that particular stretch, for a van with a racing car inside.

We picked up the large lorry and then decided to spend the night in Turin, for we were absolutely dog-tired after all the worry of recovering the despatch case. When people ask me what is the shortest and fastest run I have ever made in one day, I answer without hesitation : " Milan-Turin, June 16, 1950." I shall not forget that date in a hurry.

We crossed into France next day, very short of money, having bought 150 litres of petrol in Turin which cost 17,400 lire, and I decided to make for Aix les Bains where I hoped to be able to raise a small loan. I was sure the hotel proprietor, an ex-Pole like myself, would lend me some money or at least keep us in his hotel for a week " on trust."

I said nothing to him the night we arrived and he was delighted to see us again. I just booked two rooms and sent the overalls away to be cleaned, so that everything would be ready for Rheims.

The following day I invited my Polish friend and his wife to dine with me, and I must say we did ourselves very well indeed. I ordered a bottle of champagne and everyone was happy. After the meal I asked my friend whether he could spare a few minutes alone in his office.

I lost no time coming to the point.

" Look," I said, " I'm afraid I have no money. Neither have I any petrol in the lorries, and we must get to Rheims. I just cannot do anything about the bill."

My friend looked hard at me.

" What do you propose that I do ? " he said.

" Well," I replied, " I would like you to lend me twenty thousand French francs, so that I can buy sufficient petrol to get to Rheims, and also keep the bill until we pass through Aix les Bains after the race."

He asked me to follow him to the toilet. There, when he had locked the door, he took out his wallet and gave me thirty thousand French francs.

" Look," he said, " you see my wife and pay the bill in the normal way but under no circumstances tell her that I lent you the money."

He is a good friend and I never pass through Aix les Bains without staying the night at his hotel, even if it means going out of my way. I remember Stirling saying to me once : " What is it that you like about Aix les Bains, Alf ? There must be somebody there. Is it a blonde or a brunette ? "

We arrived in Rheims on June 21st and as the race was not until July 2nd spent ten miserable days, very short of money. In fact, the first thing I did was to borrow five thousand French francs from the hotel manager, which I agreed to pay back when John Heath arrived.

It is obviously much more satisfactory to race every week-end because then, at least, there is starting money to put in the kitty. At Rheims, Rex and I were broke most of the time, sharing a small room and with not a franc in our pockets to spend on ourselves. I wrote in my diary : " How miserable. Have had no money since we left Turin. Living on credit all the time." At Rheims two new recruits joined the H.W.M. *equipe*. There was Lance Macklin, a great friend of Stirling Moss, and a young apprentice mechanic, Frank Nagel, from the garage at Walton.

We had no trouble at the practice sessions for the Formula 2 race and Stirling, in particular, went very well indeed on the fast Rheims circuit. The practices were held at 6 a.m. because part of the circuit is on public roads. It was not a particularly exciting race but the cars behaved themselves perfectly. The engines did not miss a beat and there was not a moment of anxiety in the pits.

The whole team ran like a train, so well in fact that we left the cars alone and did not try to speed them up. They were outclassed because the 3.7 to 1 axle ratio was too low and quite unsuitable for the circuit. The cars should have had 3.5 to 1, which we did not possess at that time. Nevertheless, H.W.M. still managed to come in third, fourth and fifth ; Moss, Heath and Macklin in that order behind Ascari (Ferrari) and Simon (Gordini).

My wife still has a letter written to her by Mr. Alfred Moss : " I am Stirling's father and have just returned from Rheims, where, as no doubt you have heard, the H.W.M.s secured third, fourth and fifth places ; a wonderful performance against such strong opposition. This was mainly achieved by the excellent preparation of the cars carried out by your husband. . . . Although I have not met you, your husband's friendship and help to Stirling prompts me to offer any help I may be able to give you during his absence."

CHAPTER 8

A £1,000 IS A LOT OF MONEY

A fantastic project—Nightmare on the Mt. Cenis Pass—
Lost, one lorry—On fire in the garage—major blunders at Bari.

During the Rheims race Tony Hume took me aside in the pits. " Look, Alf," he said, " you know the Bari race. Well, we have just been offered a fantastic sum—a thousand pounds for the whole team to start. Can you get the cars down there in time for practice next Friday ? "

I knew there was this Bari fixture, but had no idea where the place was and I told Tony Hume I should have to study the map first.

" Well," he said, " everything depends on you. If you can make it, the money is ours. If not, then it's too bad. But you know as well as I do that we don't often get a chance like this to make a thousand pounds."

I don't mind admitting that I brought myself up with a jerk when I saw from my map that Bari was some eleven hundred miles from Rheims. We could just about make it by driving the whole way non-stop, providing there was nothing much to do to the cars once we arrived there, so I gave Tony Hume my answer.

" Everything depends on how the cars behave here. If they finish in good order, then we will get them to the start line in Bari. But I cannot guarantee they will be properly prepared."

This did not worry Hume.

" It does not matter," he said. "A thousand pounds is a lot of money."

This was my biggest problem to date, and whilst the Rheims race ran its course I worked out a rough plan in the pits. To start with there was the old problem of ready cash. We did not have enough to be able to leave immediately after the race on Sunday night, and in any case I had a fairly formidable bill to settle at the hotel, and another one in the local cafe where we had taken our meals.

I knew that I could not possibly move off until all the bills had been met, and I also knew that I should not be able to obtain sufficient French francs until the Automobile Club paid us our starting money on Monday afternoon. However, it seemed crazy to have to waste so much precious time, waiting for the cash, before we could leave Rheims. So I decided to fill up the big lorry on credit at the local garage, and to send it off with two cars first thing on Monday morning, with Rex and Frank. I would leave my own lorry and one car as security in the garage whilst I collected the cash.

I took Rex and Frank aside immediately after the race and told them the plan.

" I want the cars loaded in the lorries. We are not going back to the garage, except to fill your lorry with petrol, and sharp at 7 a.m. to-morrow morning I want you to leave Rheims. All you have to do to-morrow is reach the Hotel Cosmopolitan in Aix les Bains. As soon as you arrive go straight to bed and get some sleep. I shall wait here until Monday evening, pay all the bills, collect some money from John Heath and then drive all Monday night to catch you up. I hope to be with you on Tuesday morning, and Frank Nagel can then take over my van whilst I have a sleep, and we crack on to Italy."

After the race, there were the usual parties in Rheims—particularly at the Hotel Welcome—and at about two o'clock in the morning, when I had finished working on the accounts, I decided that it was time I had a drink myself. I went into the Welcome Bar and there was John Heath with the usual crowd of enthusiasts, hangers-on and well-meaning friends one always finds after a race. I say " well-meaning " because Rex and Frank were there, when they should have been in bed, basking in the limelight of H.W.M.s very creditable performance and collecting drinks left, right and centre. I wonder if those people would have kept them up so late had they realized what a journey lay ahead of us. Anyway, John Heath came over to me.

" Can you remind them that they have a long journey to-morrow ? "

I wanted to tell John Heath that he should have sent Rex and Frank packing hours ago, but I kept my temper and got them out of the bar. I had already arranged with the hotel porter to wake them at 7 a.m. but it was 9 a.m. before they finally moved off. They certainly did not look as though they would reach Aix les Bains, and appeared so ill and tired that I almost felt sorry for them.

In the afternoon I met John Heath after he had collected the starting money. We went through the accounts and he then reimbursed me. At last I was able to pay all the bills and get the small van out of pawn. I then met two Englishmen on holiday with an M.G. and as their knowledge of France was limited they asked if they might follow me as far as Aix. Naturally I agreed, as I was only too glad to have companions for the journey, and we set off in the evening just after 5 o'clock.

With three hundred odd miles to cover there was no time for hanging around; I put my foot hard down and kept it there. I really thrashed the van, and to such purpose that the M.G. driver flashed his lights and signalled me to slow down. They had trouble with their carburetter and, once that had been put right, informed me that I was going too fast for them.

" O.K.," I said, " why don't you go ahead, but try to keep going at a fair speed."

I very soon found they were going too slow for me, and when we arrived in Dijon just after midnight they promptly decided to call off the marathon. In a very friendly manner they pointed out that they were on holiday.

" We want to avoid killing ourselves if we can," said the older of the two, who had been driving.

So I said good-bye to them and continued the journey, refreshing myself during the early hours of the morning with several stops at village pumps and numerous swigs from the brandy flask.

Soon after daybreak, about twenty miles from Aix les Bains, I suddenly stood on the brakes. I could not believe my own eyes. There was the transporter, parked neatly on the grass verge by the side of the road ; I pulled in, expecting to find that it had broken down.

There was no sign of life whatsoever and everything was peaceful and quiet until I neared the cab of the lorry. I have never heard such a cacophony of snoring. Rex and Frank were slumped in the cab, absolutely out to the world ; I felt like committing a double murder and then maybe shooting myself.

These were the two bright boys who were supposed to reach Aix les Bains and have a good night's sleep in a decent bed so that they would be fresh enough to handle the two trucks between them next day whilst I had a sleep. And Bari was still more than eight hundred miles away !

So I banged on the sides of the lorry and woke them up. They had their excuses, of course, and maintained that the carburetters had given trouble. This may well have been the case because on our way to Rheims the previous week the lorry had run out of petrol and we had used racing fuel, which had naturally upset the whole system. However, I was not entirely convinced that part of their trouble was not due to a hangover. I put my cards on the table.

" One thing is sure," I said, " we have to press on and not one of us is even going to see a comfortable bed, let alone sleep in it, until we get to Bari."

We arrived in Aix les Bains soon after 10 a.m. and I suddenly felt the steering behaving in a most erratic manner. The front axle was no longer joined to the chassis ! The whole front end had become a flexible platform and was moving where it wanted, not where I wanted it to move. I was almost too tired to realize what would have happened if the axle had gone during my marathon run the night before—but not quite. I have a vivid imagination.

So I nursed the lorry along to a garage and told Rex and Frank to get some sleep at the Cosmopolitan, in spite of my ultimatum by the roadside, whilst the broken brackets were welded to the chassis. I knew the job would take four or five hours.

We left Aix les Bains in the late afternoon for the Mt. Cenis Pass and what a journey we had over the Pass. I wrote in my diary : " What a life. Why on earth did I ever undertake such a job. It is worse than working in the salt mines of Siberia. We had snow and fog on the Mt. Cenis. It seemed that everything was against us. It must have been the worst night ever on the Pass. I am absolutely worn out."

Mt. Cenis is normally a fairly easy Pass to cross but it seemed on that particular night that the elements decided to play hell. And it was Hell. Somehow we got through to Italy and then it was just a question of pressing on. Rex and Frank drove the large transporter, changing drivers every three or four hours, whilst I continued in the small van non-stop. I had not slept since snatching three hours on Sunday night in Rheims.

It was crazy to carry on like that but we had no alternative. I could not do it these days and when I think of the miles we covered on that trip in little more than four days I realize what a wonderful team spirit there was with H.W.M.

At Piacenza, on the road to Bologna, we stopped for a cup of coffee and were sitting at a table on the sidewalk when we saw John Heath's light Fifteen Citroen. Whoever was driving gave us a toot on the horn, whilst the other occupants waved and gave us a thumbs up signal

Two thoughts crossed my mind when the car had gone. First, I ruminated on the pleasant life that drivers lead compared with mechanics, and then I realized that we must have made faster time from Rheims, in spite of our delays, than they had in the Citroen. Not bad for a couple of clapped out lorries and a bunch of bearded mechanics who were beginning to look like the Long Range Desert Group.

I decided at Piacenza that we would take time off for a bathe, once we reached the Adriatic coast. Quite apart from anything else I was beginning to itch. It would refresh us for the long run down the coast road through Pescara to Bari. So off we went again on the non-stop marathon, through Modena and Bologna to Ancona. Not far from Ancona we left the large transporter by the side of the road and took the small van down a little used track to the sea.

We stripped and plunged into the Adriatic. None of us had a swim suit, but a girls' school outing on that very beach would not have stopped us taking that well-earned dip. We relaxed for an hour or two, stretched out on the warm sand, and the sunshine did us a power of good.

In spite of the rest, we were all very tired and, with another night of driving ahead, I decided that we must change lorries from time to time, so that each one of us would be able to get some sleep and also some variety in driving to ease the monotony. A change of lorries is as good as a rest. I had at last reached the end of my tether. I just could not drive any more and asked Frank to take the small van whilst I climbed into the big transporter with Rex and settled down to have a sleep.

I told Rex to keep an eye on Frank, particularly as it was getting dusk when we moved off. I don't know how long I slept but I remember waking with a start as we rounded a sharp corner and asking Rex if the other van was behind us.

" Looks like it," he replied, and we continued for another mile or two. Suddenly Rex looked in the mirror. " I don't think Frank is there," he said. " Those lights I thought were his must have belonged to someone else."

We stopped and waited. Ten, twenty, thirty minutes. Still no sign of Frank. After two hours we were desperate. I felt as depressed as when I had found the lorry beside the road outside Aix. Where was the gun ? Where was Bari ? I knew the answer to the second question—a hundred and fifty miles away.

There was only one thing to do. Turn the lorry round and search for Frank. We drove back some twenty miles before reaching a fairly large village, and in spite of the fact that it was now well past midnight there were plenty of people still around. Sometimes I wonder just when the Italians do sleep. Yes—they remembered a lorry with *Lucas* on the side but could not say which way it had gone. Why not stop and have a cup of coffee ? There is always to morrow. It was a typical Italian attitude.

However, our luck was in at last. Groping around in the dark we found the tyre marks of the small van leading up a minor road. We knew it was Frank because the tyres were military pattern with a distinctive tread. So off we went again, tearing along the narrow country road in the transporter and keeping our fingers crossed at every blind corner.

At last, after fifteen nerve-shattering miles, we came to another village and, believe it or not, there was a petrol station still open—at 4 a.m. I asked the attendant, in a pantomime of sign language and schoolboy French, whether he remembered a lorry with *Lucas* on the side. Yes, he had seen one, and sure enough when we searched the village there was the van parked in a small square. Frank was sound asleep.

I shook him and his relief at seeing us when he opened his eyes was so great that he burst into tears. You can imagine his feelings. He had only joined us at Rheims and this was his first journey with the *equipe*. He could not speak Italian and was, in any case, so tired when he arrived in the village that he had forgotten where we were going. So he could not even write " Bari " on a piece of paper. His memory just did not work any more. What else could he do but hope and pray that we would find him.

I wonder what would have happened if he had remembered and been directed back along that narrow country road. It could have resulted in a pile up on one of the blind corners, involving the whole H.W.M. team of cars.

Rex and I were so pleased we had found Frank that not a single cross word was spoken. Like the famous Crazy Gang we were together again, and looking back on that hectic journey I reckon we were like the Victoria Palace comics in more ways than one.

We arrived in Bari just before lunch on Friday, one day earlier than we had expected, having completed eleven hundred miles since leaving Rheims on Monday. After the Rheims race I had told John Heath that we would make the trip under one condition. " We shall have to scrap the first day of practice because I am sure we shall not make it by Friday." John Heath agreed and promised that, even if we did arrive on Friday, he would be quite happy to practise only on the Saturday. This was sensible because in any case it was a Formula 1 race of two hundred miles, and our competitors were far more powerful than the H.W.M.s. I knew as well as he did that we were racing at Bari for a £1,000 starting money and for no other reason.

Bari is the sort of city where if you have a racing transporter everyone knows of your arrival as soon as you reach the outskirts. By the time we pulled up at the Automobile Club, Heath and the drivers were waiting for us.

They were all very relieved—particularly Stirling—that we had arrived without mishap. We looked, and felt, like tramps. We had not shaved or washed properly for four days and I for one was not at all surprised that the Italian police gave us some very strange looks as we drove towards the Club.

Then John Heath dropped a bombshell. He insisted that we ought to get one of the cars ready for practice. Quite apart from anything else it meant fitting new tyres, for the H.W.M.s still carried the Rheims treads and they were badly worn.

" We must give the boys a chance," said John Heath.

I looked across at Rex and Frank. They were almost asleep on their feet.

" Frank . . . Rex," I said, in a loud voice. " Go straight to the hotel and get to bed."

At once, Stirling ranged himself alongside me.

" I can take them in the Citroen," he said.

I hoped this would have the effect of reminding John Heath of his promise, but he had made up his mind to practise and, whilst Stirling drove Frank and Rex to the hotel, I got down to it and changed a set of wheels on one of the cars. I can remember very little about the practice. If we had any trouble I certainly cannot recollect putting it right.

I have never been so glad to get to bed as I was after that damned practice session, even though I found myself sharing a small room with Frank and Rex. The Alfa-Romeo mechanics were staying in the same hotel—twenty-eight of them—and they not only occupied most of the rooms but monopolized the restaurant at mealtimes.

According to my diary I woke up on Saturday morning feeling very much better, having had quite a good night's sleep in spite of the combined snoring of the other two. A good breakfast cheered me up a lot and the marathon run was fast becoming a memory. It was not easy to be miserable in such glorious sunshine.

During the Saturday practice session, it was decided to fit 4.0 to 1 axle ratios on all the cars. Bari is a $3\frac{3}{4}$ mile " round the houses " circuit, with race averages around 80 m.p.h., and uses part of the promenade on the sea front. It is a combination of several different types of surface, comprising patches of cobble, granite stone and smooth stretches.

After the practice the cars were prepared finally for the race. I always insisted on the team being absolutely spick and span, and ready to be pushed on to the starting grid, before we went to bed on the night before a race.

My work plan was one I had evolved at Rheims when Frank Nagel joined us. I looked after the three engines, whilst Frank and Rex were responsible for everything else on the chassis. I was whistling to myself and checking the carburetters on Fischer's car in a fairly leisurely fashion, for we were well ahead with our preparation, when suddenly there was an explosion and a sheet of flame. The car was on fire.

Having changed the axle ratio, Rex had started to clean up whilst I worked on the carburetters, and was washing the cockpit with petrol. In those days the cars carried batteries for the self-starter, etc., and whilst he was scrubbing the cockpit with a paint brush dipped in petrol, the metal ring on the handle touched the solenoid switch on the starter. It shorted at once and created a large enough spark to cause a fire, particularly as the cockpit had been soaked in petrol and Rex was also holding a tray of petrol in his hand.

As soon as I heard the explosion, I ran over to the bench for the fire extinguisher, banged it on the floor and waited for a stream of fluid. Nothing happened ? I lifted it and realized at once that it was empty. I picked up another extinguisher and this also was empty !

Meanwhile, the fire had gained a hold and there was so much smoke and flame that I could not see Rex Woodgate, who was gallantly trying to put out the fire with the small and almost useless extinguisher from the car. Both he and Frank were separated from me by a barrier of smoke and flames and any minute now three H.W.M.s, each with some thirty-five gallons of fuel in the tank, were going sky high. I could almost see the headlines in *Equipe* : " H.W.M. team destroyed in garage fire ! Disaster kills three."

I ran into the street to find help and the first person I met was the garage proprietor. He was waving his arms about like a drunken sailor and shouting " Santa Maria. Mia Garagio." In spite of the hysterics he carried a fire extinguisher which he had borrowed from a neighbour. I snatched it from him and he immediately turned tail and disappeared as I advanced on the burning car and directed a stream of fluid over the cockpit.

By the time the local Fred Karno outfit arrived—in the form of the resident fire-fighters—we had the fire under control. Rex Woodgate was badly burned and we lost no time in getting him to hospital. He was not detained but it was obvious that, with his hands bandaged, we could not expect any help from him in the pits during the race.

The fire was the cause of major blunders on the part of Frank and myself. When the explosion occurred, Frank was just about to fill the back axle on Macklins car, having changed the ratio. In the confusion that followed the fire, he forgot all about it and the car went to the grid without any lubricant in the back axle.

For my part, when all the excitement had died down, I forgot to finish checking the carburetters on Fischer's car and consequently the float chamber container was not properly tightened. The fire was, therefore, the real cause of both these cars retiring in the race, and it also kept us working, repairing the damage, until 6 a.m. However, we managed to get two hours' sleep.

In the race Macklin was very lucky. When the axle went solid he was travelling at his maximum speed—about 120 m.p.h.—and spun round and round on the straight like a ballerina. Fortunately, he was able to hold the madly spinning car, and also keep out of the way of other drivers.

Moss drove one of the finest races of his career at Bari. He finished third (and remember it was a Formula 1 race) in front of all the two-stage Maseratis and the Ferraris. The 158 Alfa-Romeos beat him (Farina first, Fangio second) but there was one occasion, in the early stages of the race, when Moss was ahead of Fangio and in second place.

The race times show how well he kept up with the Alfas. Farina 2 hrs. 34 mins. 29.6 secs. ; Fangio 2-35-13.0 ; Moss 2-36-56.8. It was a wonderful performance, more so as Moss was refuelled by a skeleton pit staff. Rex Woodgate was *hors de combat*, and the Italian enthusiasts who joined us to give a helping hand were more of a hindrance than a help.

When Macklin failed to appear after his axle had seized, the news did not reach the pits very quickly and I set off round the circuit to try to find him. At this time Moss was engaged in a monumental dice with the Alfas but, every time he went by, found time to signal that I was going in the wrong direction.

Although he was only a few seconds behind the Alfas, and having to concentrate on what Fangio was doing ahead of him, he still managed to spot me each time round. I just could not understand how, at this speed, anyone could take his eyes off the road long enough to pinpoint the position of someone on the circuit, particularly as their position changed each lap. It seemed incredible to me.

This may not have been the most successful appearance of H.W.M. during the season but it was certainly a magnificent drive on the part of Moss. Both Macklin and Fischer, before being forced to retire, mixed it with the " big boys " but Stirling just walked away from everyone else with the exception of Farina and Fangio.

Admittedly the circuit was suited to the H.W.M. characteristics but, quite apart from this, Sunday, July 9, 1950 was, in my opinion, the day Stirling Moss found himself. I remember so well writing that same evening to Mr. Alfred Moss, quite an achievement for me because I was either too lazy or too tired to write letters under normal conditions. But this was abnormal and I wrote to Stirling's father on these lines : " It is only one son that you have but, believe me, he sure is a champion."

At this time Stirling was still a boy off the circuit, but once in a racing car he was very different. He became part of the team, and his ambition—as it was with all of us—was to prove H.W.M.s were the best cars in their class.

He was in every way a first rate member of the H.W.M. team—an ideal partner—and was not out for personal glory. I liked him, too, because he took a real interest in the work done by the mechanics and tried to help us with our problems by giving suggestions and ideas.

On Monday we had our usual conference to sort out the accounts, and I had a coffee with John Heath and Stirling Moss. This was my first social occasion with Stirling over a cup of coffee, but by no means the last. He described his experiences at the prizegiving, which we had not attended as we were only too glad to get to bed after the race and are not, in any case, usually invited to prizegiving ceremonies.

As Stirling described how he danced with Miss Italy, or maybe it was with Miss Bari, I thought to myself : " This is the other Moss. Still very much a youngster at heart. Very different from the cold, calculating machine in the H.W.M. cockpit yesterday afternoon."

CHAPTER 9

COOKS TOUR

Telepathy and disaster in the Naples G.P.—
Frank Nagel's " suicide " trip—Trouble on the road to Paris—
Introduction to the Nurburgring—Well placed at Silverstone—
Mettet, Perigeux and a " prang " at Garda.

After the Bari race, there was a period of two weeks before our next engagement—the Naples Grand Prix for Formula 2 cars. Moss, Heath and Macklin went off to Capri for a holiday, whilst we stayed on in Bari for a few days. There was very little work to do on the cars and I for one was glad because the heat was almost unbearable. It was so hot that we were only able to work in the morning or late afternoon, and even then did so stripped to the waist.

A check of the compression, valves and oil pressure showed that the Alta engines were in tip-top condition, and when we had fitted a new back axle to Macklin's car and replaced the float-chamber on Fischer's carburetter there was nothing to prevent us moving on to Naples.

We found a first-rate hotel in Posillipo, very close to the sea and not far from the circuit. We did not even bother to unload the lorries, and whilst Moss and Macklin (as we found out later) made a Marathon run to Monte Carlo in John Heath's Citroen, in search of more excitement than Capri could offer, we lazed around Posillipo and joined the tourists. The only difference was that, whereas they had plenty of money to spend, we had very little. Nevertheless, it did not cost me anything to light a cigarette from the hot ashes at the top of Mount Vesuvius.

My diary reads : "This morning : sunbathing in the bay. I cannot believe that two weeks ago I was so utterly weary and at the end of my tether. It is remarkable how quickly one recovers. I am sure that being so busy and having so little time to think is the answer."

I still have happy memories of those few days in Naples. Swimming from the rocks by the hotel, drifting in the bay, sipping Vermouth Bianca in our little cafe in St. Lucia and, of course, the beauty of the bay of Naples at night and the twinkling fairy lights around it. Like most continentals I can find the time to appreciate beauty even though our lives in motor-racing are so much tied up with machines and man-made things.

On the first day of practice at Posillipo, Moss and Macklin were in very good form indeed, partly because they had succeeded in changing the front tyres of John Heath's Citroen for the rear ones without Heath finding out. They had reached Monte Carlo in a day, found that life was almost as dull there as on Capri, and returned in a day ; just a small matter of six hundred miles each way.

On arrival in Naples, having driven the car far harder and faster than

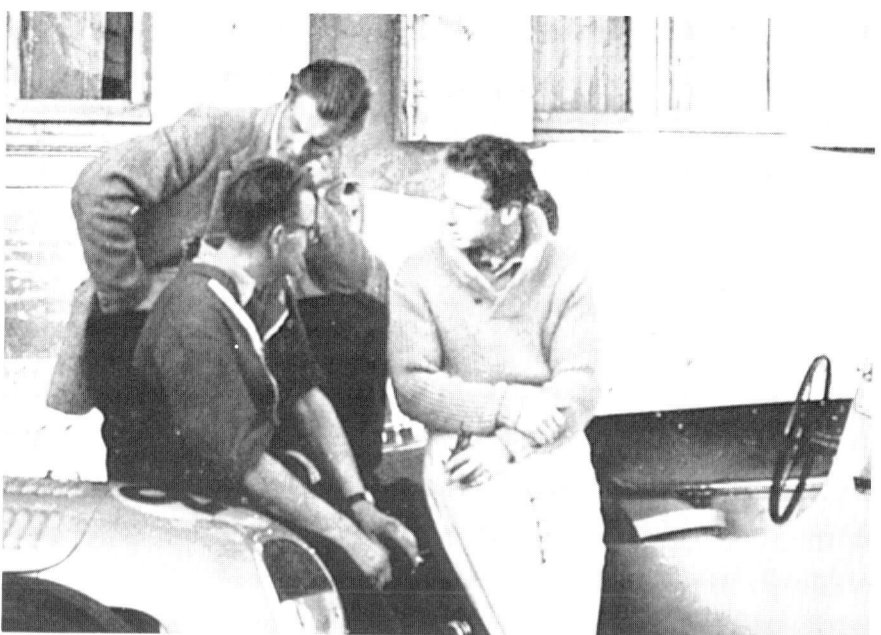

Perigeux, 1950. John Heath, Lance Macklin and Alf Francis with two of the three team cars. Following the long hours and the strain of building the H.W.M.s during the winter of 1949 Alf has already started to wear glasses. Lance Macklin is on the extreme right.

The second of the H.W.M. prototypes, developed from the team cars raced in 1950. Due to stub axle breakages during the season a new front suspension layout was used, incorporating, M.G. standard production coil spring suspension. Stub exhausts, in spite of a slight power loss, have replaced the previous four branch system. Alf Francis is explaining to John Heath the fitting of the Weber carburetters, used for the first time in 1951.

Berne, 1950. This picture of the team cars (A for Abecassis, F for Fischer, H for Heath), was taken just before the start of the F.2 race in which the cars finished 6th, 8th and 9th. Tom O'Hara, who joined H.W.M. at the end of 1949, is standing behind Fischer, and Alf Francis is with Heath. This was the first time since the formation of the H.W.M. team at the end of 1949 that Alf was able to find sufficient time in his hectic programme to have a picture taken of the complete team. Berne was one of the very few races where there was actually time to spare.

John Heath had ever done, they found the front tyres practically bare. Thus, the quick change act ; I am afraid we all worked on the basis of trying to prevent John Heath having anything to get angry about.

On the second day of practice we made second, third and fifth fastest time ; Moss, Macklin and Fischer in that order. The cars were going very well indeed on this fairly twisty " round the houses " circuit. Fischer, as I had expected, made the usual complaints about his seat. I have never known such a fastidious driver. The seat was either too narrow or too wide, too soft or too hard, too short or too deep. It was never right and I often wondered whether there was something radically wrong with his own " seat."

With Fischer the carburetters could have fallen off or the steering wheel come adrift in his hands. But what the hell—provided the seat was comfortable. Maybe he was right—maybe he was just a little prima donna.

The Posillipo race was a memorable one for several reasons. It left me a firm believer in telepathy, and also with a resolve to try to tighten up the control of drivers during a race and of the pit itself in an emergency.

As I have said previously, we did not worry a great deal about race tactics during that first H.W.M. season. The drivers raced very largely for themselves and for their own pleasure, and there was certainly not, to my knowledge, any plan worked out by Moss and Macklin to deal with an incident that brought the crowd to its feet, and left those of us who saw it weak from excitement.

At the start, Cortese (Ferrari) set off at such a pace that he just walked away from the rest of the field but in no time at all Moss was after him. But, try as he might, Moss was unable to pass a slower driver so as to get to grips with Cortese. As Moss moved over to the left, so the other car moved left ; Moss right—the other car right. And so on. The pantomime was carried on for several laps until Macklin closed up. Then, in front of the pits, we were treated to a wonderful display of driving technique.

As if the two cars were linked by a wireless telephone, Moss and Macklin put an audacious plan into operation. Macklin moved up behind Moss, then quickly pulled out as though to overtake the slower driver on the right. The Italian looked in his mirror, saw the H.W.M., assumed it was Moss, and pulled over to the right. Meanwhile, Stirling—with a huge grin— slipped through on the left and took the lead. All over in a few seconds, like the brilliant deceptive footwork of a champion boxer before the knockout. In the pits we laughed, more from relief that the cars had not been involved in a triple crash than from anything else.

However, more drama was to come. On the grid before the start, where two H.W.M.s shared the front row with Cortese, I noticed that the carburetter on Moss's car was leaking. I ran my finger over the leak and sniffed. Water !

Not wishing to upset Stirling, I said nothing to him. After all, it only meant that the car might be difficult to start. Obviously, one of the Wells rings, used in Alta engines as the joint between the water jacket and the cylinder, must have failed.

I did not show concern, hoping that Moss had not seen my finger-sniffing act, and quietly walked over to John Heath.

" We are in trouble," I said.   " We have a leak on Stirling's car.   One of the Wells rings has gone."

Heath looked worried.

" What can you do ? " he asked.

" Not very much," I replied, " unless we push the car backwards in top gear and get the water out of the cylinder on back compression.   But don't worry ; once the car is running in the race it will be O.K."

However, Moss, who has an uncanny knack of sensing trouble, came running over.

" What's wrong now ? " he asked.

There was no sense in trying to fool Stirling so I told him about the water leak ; I could see he was worried.   When he got off the grid, he was not only intent on catching Cortese, but also in building up a large lead so that he would have time to make a pit stop and take on water.   In my opinion it would not have been necessary.   I think he could have run throughout without a stop for water—and won as well.

However, in his usual conscientious way, he did what he thought was right for the team.   He drove flat out, even when he had wrested the lead from Cortese, watching the temperature gauge for that tell-tale increase over ninety that would indicate the leak had worsened and the water had started to boil.

In spite of our signals to slow down, he kept going—driving on the limit—and I could have kicked myself.   I knew why he was doing it.   I did not consider it necessary and yet, through the medium of pit signals, we were unable to stop his suicidal progress.   For we all felt that he was courting disaster.

There is nothing worse than realizing that you have no control over a driver's actions, nothing more demoralizing.   That is why I say that absolute control from the pit is vitally important, and that in nine cases out of ten it is the assessment by the pit manager that matters not the assessment by the driver.

It had to happen.   As Moss was passing a much slower car which he was lapping, I think, for the second time, the other driver spun right in front of him, the hub cap catching the front of Moss' car and splitting a tyre.   Immediately the H.W.M. became unmanageable, with the left front tyre deflated, and Moss careered off the circuit and hit a tree.

Without being aware of it—for he was, in fact, unconscious—he jumped out of the H.W.M. and started running away from the scene of the crash.   As an admirer of Dick Seaman he knew that, after the accident in the 1939 Belgian Grand Prix, Seaman died because no one dragged him out before the car caught fire.   He was badly burned and died later, in hospital.

It is remarkable that the sub-conscious mind has the power to force a driver—who has knocked himself out on the steering wheel, smashed his front teeth and broken a kneecap—to run away from the car.   Moss could not remember anything about it, but from the distance he ran it is quite obvious that he was not thrown out of the H.W.M. as some reports suggested at the time.

As soon as the news came through about Stirling, the pit organization collapsed. The first report said he was dead, the second that he was gravely injured and dying on the side of the road. Rex Woodgate vaulted over the pit counter and started running in the direction of the crash, whilst John Heath went to Race Control.

However, we still had two cars in the race, and it was no use panicking to the extent that the H.W.M. pit just ceased to function. Macklin was in the lead by now, but it did not last long for he saw the wreckage of Stirling's car and this upset him badly. He dropped back to second place. Shortly afterwards Fischer broke a stub axle, our second failure from this cause. Then the race was over, and Macklin came home second to Cortese.

It was at Naples that I realized how necessary it is to have strict pit discipline. Motor-racing personnel have to behave like soldiers under certain conditions, and one thing they must learn is to stay at their posts. Undoubtedly, at that time, strict discipline was lacking in the H.W.M. pit.

No one was more upset about Moss' accident than I, and no one felt sorrier for him, but the important thing to me was that H.W.M. still had two drivers in the race. It was necessary to keep the pit going in order to back up Macklin and Fischer, and in any case we knew nothing definite about Moss ; only rumours.

I want to stress a point. When bad news arrives, make a quiet assessment of the situation before doing anything at all. After all, it is by then too late in any case to prevent the particular occurrence from happening. As it was, Moss escaped with comparatively light injuries, and this is so often the case in motor-racing.

Has there ever been a finer example of iron discipline in pit control than when Levegh's Mercedes crashed at Le Mans in 1955, almost immediately opposite the German pit. The Mercedes personnel saw all the horror of that terrible accident enacted before them, and carried on as though nothing had happened. In times like this, motor-racing is like war. If you expect a driver to remain at his post, then you must remain at yours.

Rodolpho Mailander, the well-known motor-racing photographer, was at the Naples race and took a wonderful series of pictures showing the Moss crash in stages.

We had met Mailander at the Rome G.P. He speaks fluent English and German, and became very friendly with Stirling, so much so that he asked him where was the best vantage point to take photographs. Stirling told him, and Mailander moved into position. It was at this exact spot that Moss lost a wheel and Mailander took one of the best pictures of his career, as Stirling slewed to a stop on the stub axle.

At Posillipo, Mailander again asked Stirling what he considered the best vantage point for photographs. Once more Stirling obliged and once more Mailander got a scoop. Nowadays Stirling refuses to discuss vantage points with anyone. I know photographers who have been most annoyed at what they consider lack of courtesy. Perhaps they will understand now.

After the race it was decided that I should take the Moss car back to England. It was badly damaged, with a twisted chassis, and could not be repaired on the continent. On Tuesday morning we left Naples, feeling reasonably happy about Stirling who was holding court in a hospital bed

rather like a Hollywood film star. The plan was for me to guide Rex and
Frank over the Alps into France, and then for me to make for the U.K.
whilst they carried on to Geneva for our next race on July 30th.

Near Frosinone the transporter stopped. I pulled in behind with the
small van.

" What's the matter, Rex ? " I asked.

" Nothing much," he replied, " just overheating."

We always carried a reserve of water for an emergency such as this and
Rex got a can out of the back of the lorry and started filling the radiator.
Suddenly I noticed water coming out of the exhaust pipe.

" Don't bother," I said to Rex. "We've had it. What a damned fine
start to my journey back to England."

We tried all we knew to start the engine, but it would not give any sign
of life, naturally preferring to run on petrol rather than water. There was
only one thing to do. With the small van I should have to tow the transporter some sixty miles to Rome, where we knew a garage proprietor who
would allow us to repair the damage on his premises.

We arrived in Rome late in the evening and, after a quick examination
at the garage, decided that a cylinder head gasket must have gone ; quite a
normal fault with the Ford V8 engine.

We took off both cylinder heads and, to our surprise, the gaskets seemed
O.K. Then I saw a large crack in No. 7 cylinder, on the right-hand side,
about 25 thou. wide and right through the bore.

" We shall never be able to mend this, or do anything about it," I said
to Rex. "We shall have to take the engine out of the small van and put it
in the transporter so that you can continue to Geneva."

It seemed feasible to me. The Ford Mercury engines in the two
vehicles were identical, and when we had made the change the small van
could be left in Rome with the Moss car until another lorry could be begged
or borrowed. But what a job. I sagged at the knees just thinking about it.
Suddenly I had a brain wave. Why not use Wonderweld (I know, it
sounds like a " commercial," but it's true), and try to repair the crack.

When we found the tin of Wonderweld in our kit, it seemed impossible
that the contents of such a small tin could repair such a large crack. However, drowning people do not refuse to clutch at a straw and we decided to
try. The engine was assembled, minus the radiator, and we poured
Wonderweld into the cylinder jackets and started up. You could have
knocked me down with a feather ; we had cured the leak.

It was well past midnight before we were ready to move off from Rome.
In fact, dawn was just breaking as we drove out of the garage and through
the silent streets. It was now Wednesday and we were due in Geneva for
practice on Friday.

The first part of our journey—to Turin via the coast road—was uneventful, apart from the fact that we drove flat out and only had two hours' sleep
on Wednesday, under the lorries in a market square. It was so hot in
the cabs.

In Turin more trouble was in store. After a refuelling stop I noticed
that the transporter moved away from the garage rather jerkily. I thought
to myself : " Why doesn't Rex take it easy with that clutch," and then

promptly forgot the incident. Some hours later, at the foot of the Mt. Cenis Pass, the transporter slowed down and came to a halt.

I stopped the small van, jammed on the handbrake angrily and jumped out.

" What's the matter now ? " I asked Rex.

" It's no good getting upset," he said. " She just won't move."

It sounded to me like back axle trouble and, sure enough, when all three of us tried to push the transporter, the back axle complained in no uncertain fashion. It was clear that either the crown wheel or pinion had gone.

It was now late on Thursday night. Two cars were entered at Geneva, and there was no object unloading the Moss car from my van and replacing it with one of those from the transporter, for we should still be a car short for the race.

" The only thing to do," I told Frank and Rex, " is to disconnect the drive shafts, tow the transporter up the Pass, and then free-wheel down the other side."

They looked at me in a rather curious fashion. " O.K. I'm mad," I said, " but perhaps one of you can think of something else."

There was, in fact, no other solution, but whilst I was working out how to line up the transporter on a tow rope behind my small Fordson, a Frenchman—driving a large Diesel lorry—pulled to a stop beside us. He was a real friend in need and immediately agreed to take the transporter in tow. Naturally, a fairly considerable sum of French francs changed hands and I had visions of calling at Aix les Bains again if our reserve became further depleted !

It took us six hours to cover the thirty odd miles on the Italian side of the Mt. Cenis and, in the early hours of the morning, we said good-bye to our French friend and set about solving the problem of how to get down the Pass.

Having disconnected the drive shafts, the transporter was left with only the inadequate brakes fitted on the majority of British lorries. They would obviously fade on the way down the Pass, and there would then be no means of stopping the transporter. Not a very happy thought.

It was young Frank Nagel who finally agreed to drive the transporter on what can only be described as a suicide trip, and I told Rex Woodgate to go with him whilst I followed in the small van.

The way they went down the mountain was incredible, and I cannot praise Frank's handling of the lorry highly enough. They went so fast I could hardly keep up with them, and I had a vehicle with both the engine and brakes to stop it, and nothing like so fully laden as theirs. They freewheeled almost as far as St. Jean de Maurienne, a good sixty miles, and just over three hours after starting the downhill " dice " we were in the French town.

We pressed on to Chambery, with me hitching up to the transporter and giving a tow when gradients brought it to a halt, but fortunately our route was downhill most of the way. In Chambery I bought a chain, as the rope was fairly well chafed by now, and started towing the transporter towards the Swiss frontier.

This was not the end of our troubles by any means. When we arrived at the frontier I was told I could not enter Switzerland as my visa had expired. Fortunately I had the address of the hotel in Geneva where Abecassis and Heath were staying. I put a call through immediately, explained my predicament, and then told them that someone would have to come and tow the transporter to Geneva.

Meanwhile, the Customs people were very kind, even going so far as to pay the cost of two more telephone calls in connection with my visa. Whether it was because we were going to the Geneva race I do not know but I succeeded in obtaining a special 48-hour permit to enter Switzerland, and by the time John Heath and Abecassis arrived we were all set to continue the journey.

On arrival at the Geneva Circuit, which is on the outskirts of the city and uses main roads and parkland, we had to change axle ratios. We were, unfortunately, too late to practise but I think you will agree that we had done our best to get there in time. We were all tired out following the journey from Rome, and in the confusion of getting the cars ready in a very short time the wrong ratio was fitted to Macklin's car. It was a case of one damned thing after another because, for the first time that I can remember, John Heath passed the ratios himself on the two cars ; and he did not notice the error.

In the Formula 2 Prix de Geneve, won by Trintignant on a Gordini, Macklin had a miserable drive. He had the Rheims ratio on his car and consequently was slipping the clutch repeatedly, lap after lap, to get round some of the corners. He did very well to finish sixth. Abecassis, in the second car, blew up his engine.

After the race we had to take the engine out of the car that Stirling had crashed in Naples, and put it in Abecassis' car, so that we could run two H.W.M.s in the Freiburg Hill-climb. I began to wonder whether I should, after all, get back to England. It was hard work changing the engines and we had practically no sleep on Monday or Tuesday night. However, the two cars were ready by Wednesday and Rex and Frank left Geneva with them early on Thursday morning. It was agreed that they would take the two cars direct from Freiburg to the Nurburgring for our next race.

With the cars out of the way I decided to have one full night in bed and, having slept like a log, set off for Paris in high spirits, planning to call at the George Bonnet garage to collect some spare parts. However, the Francis gremlin was at large on the Paris road and about a hundred miles from the capital I ran a big-end on the Ford.

Naturally, I could not continue without any oil pressure and, bemoaning my luck, pulled over to the side of the road and proceeded to drop the sump, disconnect the connecting rods and pull out two pistons. I then cut a piece of leather from my trouser belt, so as to cover the oil passages in the crankshaft journal, and held it in position with two jubilee clips. From then onwards, as far as Paris, a Ford V8 ran quite nicely on six cylinders and six sparking plugs.

I did not spend much time in Paris. Having collected the spares from the Deutsch Bonnet works, I then started looking for new big-ends to fit in the Ford lorry, and soon found them. It is quite remarkable how quickly one can pick up Ford spares all over Europe, and so cheaply. I only paid ten shillings for both big-ends.

The lorry was parked outside my hotel in Grand Army Avenue, and I had quite an audience on the Sunday morning when I dropped the sump, took off the cylinder head, then fitted the pistons and connecting rods complete with the new big-ends. At four o'clock in the afternoon I was clear of Paris.

Twenty-four hours later I was in Walton-on-Thames. You will think it strange that I did not call and see my wife at Woolwich, but I knew that a wrecked car and a wrecked engine was in the back of the lorry, and my only thought was to get the car back to Walton so that I could strip down and rebuild. I knew that if I called in at Woolwich it would delay me at least twenty-four hours and prevent any work being done on the chassis by the welder.

I eventually did get home, the following week-end, Sunday, August 13th. It was exactly sixteen weeks since I had left England, and to my astonishment I found that I had covered no less than 5,137 miles, and visited four countries during the course of running the cars in ten races.

Back at Walton, John Heath came to me in the workshop on Wednesday evening.

" Look Alf," he said, " they are having a lot of trouble over at the Nurburgring. Rex says the engines are not behaving at all well. I think we had both better fly over to Frankfurt to-morrow."

So we left next day and on arrival at the famous " Ring " went straight to our Paddock Box where I found the engines of both H.W.M.s stripped down.

I found that we had a new driver for the German G.P., the motor-cyclist Fergus Anderson. He was faster than Macklin in practice, probably due to the fact that he knew the tortuous German circuit better than any of the H.W.M. drivers, but even so had never previously driven a racing car. His performance, first time out, was most creditable and I do not think Moss, had he been there, would have gone round any quicker.

What a circuit. This was the first time I had seen the Nurburgring, described as the most difficult and tiring Grand Prix circuit in the world. Maximum speed is of secondary importance to road-holding and braking, which must cope with something like 175 corners—many of them acute— in a single lap. The Ring is, in fact, nothing more than $14\frac{1}{2}$ miles of twists, turns, ascents and descents relieved only by one short straight.

Quite apart from reassembling the engines at the Nurburgring, we had a lot of trouble with the Hardy Spicer universal drive shafts. They were bottoming every time the car negotiated the famous Karuzel Curve due to the fact that there were no positive full bump stops on the rear suspension units. The Karuzel is steeply banked and cars enter it at very high speed, exerting a tremendous centrifugal force which causes the universals to bottom. In the race, Macklin finished sixth, having stopped one lap too early due to a mistake in lap scoring, and Anderson retired with a broken universal spider.

On Monday we left for England, with very little time to get the cars ready for the Silverstone Meeting on August 26th.   I remember calling in at Woolwich, on the way from Dover to Walton, leaving a parcel of dirty laundry with my wife, and picking up some clean clothing.

A new mechanic joined us at this time and was given the job of changing the clutch on the transporter.   So far as I knew he was fully experienced, and he certainly was of that opinion himself.   However, when we set off for Silverstone late on the Wednesday night I found to my annoyance that the clutch would not disengage.   There was no time to waste, so I started the engine in first gear and went off to Silverstone with an inoperative clutch.

Once the transporter was mobile, and by anticipating the duration of traffic lights, etc., I was able to keep going.   It would have been disastrous had I stopped the lorry on several occasions (when actually I should have done so, although not at traffic lights) for it would have meant using the battery to get going again in gear.   However, it was late at night, there was not much traffic on the road, and we arrived at Silverstone in the early hours of the morning.

On what I suppose we should call our " home " circuit, I had several arguments with John Heath.   It was an extraordinary thing, but the car-buration of the cars used to hold a fatal fascination for him every time we raced in England ;   fatal because his interference usually reduced that particular car from running on a fairly healthy four cylinders to running on a most unhealthy three, or even two.

Heath was, of course, the patron, and fully entitled to do what he liked with his own cars but it was most discouraging.   I was absolutely fed up to the teeth on Friday night, and there is an entry in the diary that more or less expresses my feelings :   " It seems that every time we come to U.K. then J.H. must fiddle with the carburetters.   All our good performances on the continent will be wiped out by a bad show to-morrow.

Perhaps I was a little too pessimistic but I was very tired, mainly due to the fact that on the Thursday night John Heath had insisted on all the drive shafts being changed.   I was, in fact, more fed up at Silverstone— playing at home as it were—than on any occasion on the continent.

In Heat 2 of the International Trophy, Moss showed Chiron's Maserati the way round, and then torrential rain slowed the cars and dropped Fangio's winning race average on the Alfa-Romeo to 76.73 m.p.h. as against Farina's winning time of 90.01 m.p.h. in Heat 1 on a similar car.

In the final Moss was terrific and so was Fergus Anderson, who kept ahead of Moss—and Gerard's E.R.A.—for the first ten laps.   Then Anderson spun, lost third gear on the preselector box and fell right back. Moss then moved up, going like a dingbat, and eventually finished sixth ahead of all the Talbots and Maseratis.   The large crowd of well over 120,000 was delighted with the performance of the 2-litre British car against the Formula 1 machinery.   So were we.

Back to Walton and back to work.   We still had one wrecked car— the Moss car from Naples—and there was still the engine from the Abecassis car to rebuild.   I hardly think it necessary to mention that the character, I forget his name, who bodged up the clutch on my lorry, left at very short notice.

Within a few days Tom O'Hara and I were on the Continent again. Two H.W.M.s (Moss and Macklin) had been entered for the Formula 2 race at Mettet, a Belgian town not far from Namur. It is a fast circuit, out in the country, where average speeds of 90 m.p.h. are possible.

On the first day of practice we had gearbox trouble on Moss' car, and I made an urgent call to Walton for a new gearbox. It arrived by air in Brussels and a friend of Johnny Claes put it on a passenger train addressed : " John Heath. Namur Station. To be called For."

When I went to the station I was told in the parcels office that, as the package was addressed to Mr. Heath, it would have to be collected by him.

" I am Mr. Heath," I replied indignantly. " You can see my passport if you like."

The railway official was suitably impressed by my indignation and waved aside the passport.

" No need for that, Mr. Heath," he said. " Just sign here."

Without thinking, I nearly wrote my own name, but realized just in time and signed J. B. Heath.

It took us most of the night to fit the replacement gearbox, and I cannot recollect any trouble on the second day of practice. The opposition at Mettet was 2-litre Ferraris and Gordinis, but Moss and Macklin nevertheless finished fourth and fifth in the first heat and, on a soaking wet circuit, soundly thrashed the Ferraris in the second heat. Ascari blew up his Ferrari in an effort to hold off the H.W.M.s and two other Ferraris suffered a similar fate. When the heat times were added together, Manzon (Gordini) was classified as first, with Moss and Macklin second and third.

We had a nice welcome on arrival at Perigeux, for the next race, another F.2 event with a field of Ferraris and Gordinis similar to Mettet. It is a fascinating little French town, in the famous Cognac country, and a large sign had been put up on the wall in our garage : " Welcome to our English friends."

It was a most exciting race, with Moss sitting on Manzon's tail for most of the distance ; a continuation of the Mettet duel, in fact. This interesting and exciting circuit takes in the market square, with the cars coming in one side and going out the other. The spectators were running from one corner of the square to the other, bobbing from side to side as though chasing tennis balls backwards and forwards across a net. Moss was third, behind Manzon and Simon both on Gordinis, and Macklin retired with a broken universal spider. Once again, the H.W.M.s trounced the Ferraris.

After the race, Moss spoke to the French public for the first time. I could understand what he was saying into the microphone, but I don't think anyone understood what came out of it.

From Perigeux, we went down to Italy. This time our destination was Lago di Garda, for the circuit of Garda which Ascari was to win for Ferrari. Tom O'Hara and I had a quick journey with no untoward incidents. By now, I was beginning to regard a trip to Italy rather like a Sunday afternoon run from London to Brighton. Down there we met Moss, Macklin and Tony Hume.

Nothing untoward happened on the first day of practice, which was perhaps a good thing because the *equipe* had such a following of pretty girls, all of them fans of either " Stirleeng " or " Mackleen," that I found it rather difficult to concentrate on what was going on.   There was more of a Windmill Theatre atmosphere around the cars in the pits than a motor-racing atmosphere.

On the second day of practice, on this 10-mile lakeside circuit, we had trouble.   Macklin hit a wall near the gasworks and the chassis was badly damaged.   Worse still, it was obvious that Macklin was not going to be able to race.   He was severely bruised and had a black eye that was going to put him out of the running in more ways than one.

Tony Hume asked me to have a look at the car, with a view to working on it during the night and getting it ready for him to drive on the Sunday. I told him it was impossible.

" Look here, Alf," he said, " if you can straighten out the chassis, I will see that you get 10 per cent. of the starting money."

I did a quick calculation.   It worked out to twenty-five pounds.

" O.K." I replied.   " Tom and I will see what we can do, but we will only fix the car up on one condition.   You must come in after you have completed five laps and I will fake engine trouble so that you can retire."

Tom and I got hold of two welding plants and a big blow lamp.   Without taking the engine out of the chassis, and with the assistance of a crow-bar and a nearby tree, we managed to straighten the chassis more by eyesight and judgment than anything else.

In the race, Hume was so pleased with the way the car handled that he tore round and round the Garda Circuit in great glee, turning his head the other way when he passed the pits after the first five laps so that he would not see my frantic signals.

He was really enjoying himself and we had two H.W.M.s going like bombs in that race, for Stirling, absolutely on top of his form, was fighting it out at the front of the field for the lead.

When Hume deigned to call in at the pits he had no intention of retiring. " She handles beautifully," he shouted.   " The car is perfect and I reckon she is better than before Lance crashed."

Fortunately, I kept him to his promise and looking rather crestfallen he clambered out of the cockpit and the car was retired.   The sequel came when we arrived back at Walton some days after the race.   As we were unloading the H.W.M. from the lorry, driving it backwards down the ramp, the front wheel fell off !   It was indeed fortunate that Hume had not continued in the race and possibly lost a wheel at speed on some part of the very tricky circuit.

As it was, Moss was put out of the race by a broken stub axle after a magnificent drive.   He naturally had to retire, and when he arrived back at the pits the first thing he said to me was : " Unless you do something about the stub axles I am not going to drive the car any more."

This was the second time he had lost a stub axle and when he showed me where it had happened—on a twisty part of the circuit that was, in effect, a fast S bend—he had my full sympathy.

The last meeting of the 1950 season was on the bumpy Castle Combe circuit in Wiltshire. Stirling lost considerable oil pressure on his car just prior to the start of the Formula 2 race, and Abecassis, who was still the No. 1 H.W.M. driver in my eyes, was very helpful and offered his own car to Stirling. He is a great sportsman in this way and I don't think anyone knows more than Abecassis how to behave on a motor-racing circuit, whatever the situation. It is a pity more drivers are not like him, and that some people choose to laugh at the "gentlemen" drivers of pre-war days who used to race at Brooklands, Donington and the Crystal Palace.

Moss won the Formula 2 event and then drove the car even better to come home third in the Formula Libre race, astonishing the spectators by the way he "mixed it" with the E.R.A. of Graham Whitehead. I remember, when we got back to Walton, John Heath saying to me : " Now we are going to build single-seaters." He did not satisfy my curiosity but laughingly added : " You have been warned."

CHAPTER 10

FROM SPORTS CARS TO RACING CARS

An assessment of lessons learned—The mixture as before—
Odiham again—A terrifying incident at Goodwood.

That was the end of my first season of racing with a full team of cars. After Castle Combe I relaxed and asked myself what I personally had learned during those hectic weeks on the continent.

People can say what they like about the success of H.W.M. in 1950 but it must be admitted that we ran into a lot of trouble simply because there was no proper organization. Something had got to be done before the 1951 season to strengthen the organization so that it functioned more smoothly.

On the other hand, I had learned the true value of team spirit. There was never any question, whatever the circumstances, of not " having a go." It was an unwritten law that, however much we disliked doing certain jobs, no one ever objected. All of us felt bound to put the maximum effort into the H.W.M. team. We could all have earned the same amount of money that John Heath paid us in a dozen different garages, working normal hours, but the thought never occurred to us.

Whatever has been written about that first H.W.M. season, and of the way we backed up the efforts of John Heath and George Abecassis, no one has really appreciated the tremendous strain under which Rex, Frank and myself worked.

How is it possible to understand the feelings of Frank, lost with the small lorry on the way to Bari, stranded in a country where he could not speak one word of the language and without a lire note in his pocket ? Can you understand how we felt on those occasions when, even though we worked all hours of the day and night, it seemed that nothing would go right, and that there was no way of getting the cars to the grid ; or when we crossed the Alps or the Bracco Pass " against the clock." I want to put on record that, without the loyalty and comradeship of Rex, Frank, and Tom O'Hara we could not have done what we did during the 1950 season.

It was always the same. A query on the lines of " Can you make it, Alf ? " And the answer was invariably : " We will do our best." There was never any question of refusing to try. We were up against it for the whole season, but the morale of the *equipe* was so high that we were able to overcome practically any difficulty. Our morale came from our enthusiasm and it was this enthusiasm as much as anything else that carried us through. What we did then, few people would even attempt these days. And of one thing I am certain ; I would not attempt another season like it myself.

Success also spurred us on. Perhaps it was the challenge of trying to do more than we knew we could do. I felt a deep personal satisfaction at the conclusion of the season, and was proud of the fact that I had been the chief mechanic to the *equipe* at a time when Heath and Abecassis did so much for British prestige abroad. Nevertheless, at the end of the 1950 season I told myself that some radical changes would have to be made because it would not be possible to repeat the formula in 1951. After all, every man—if he wants to be happy—must get some fun out of his work. And there was not much fun in motor-racing for me during that whirlwind season.

There was a certain matter that I was determined to put right—the comfort of the mechanics. We are the chaps, after all, who have to spend days and nights either working in a garage or sitting in a lorry. I challenge anybody who has not experienced anything other than the comfort of a saloon car to try just twenty-four hours non-stop in the driving seat of the sort of lorry one sees around the British circuits. Not the latest type, but those that people have to use because their finances will not run to anything better.

When a team is planned, considerable thought should be given to the comfort of the mechanics. Whilst a team manager cannot afford to spend too much money on this aspect of the *equipe*, he can at least ensure that the transporters are built in such a way that maximum comfort, taking various factors into consideration, is provided for the men who will have to drive and work in them. After all, they often have to start work as soon as they arrive at a circuit, after hours of non-stop driving over many hundreds of miles.

There is always something to do, even if it is only change the tyres, and it is not very easy to do the job quickly and efficiently if one arrives tired out. I don't expect mechanics to travel around in Rolls-Royce luxury, with a mobile bar in a trailer as well as all mod. con., but I would like to think that the people who run an *equipe* appreciate that this very important point has a great deal of bearing on team morale. So far as H.W.M. were concerned, I am quite sure that when John Heath bought the two Fords in the first place, he had no idea that we would have to make those fantastic journeys in the 1950 season.

My main concern, from the point of view of the cars at the end of 1950, was to make them safer and something had got to be done about the stub axles and drive shafts. I was also determined to get rid of the preselector gearboxes. They were unnecessarily heavy and by no means the type of gearbox easily adapted to conditions of circuit racing. Preselector boxes are designed for women drivers, not racing cars, and anyone who considers himself a racing driver and cannot change gear with a crash box should keep away from the circuits.

A crash box is simple in its design, easy to maintain and very reliable ; so why employ complicated, fragile gadgets on a racing car—expensive gadgets that require skilled men to look after them. I can strip and reassemble an engine in less time than I can a preselector box.

Admittedly the preselector ratios were nice ones but the box was never made for this type of work. I have yet to hear of an Indianapolis racing car with fluid flywheel or a torque converter. Things of that sort are made for people who are lazy.

I was also anxious to put over a point concerning the number of cars in the team. I felt that we should run three cars on the Continent with the third in reserve all the time, and concentrate more on the preparation of the cars—as we should be able to do with only two in action—and their development from race to race.

In 1950 there had been no time to develop and extract more power from the engines in the light of that development. The main concern was to get the cars from circuit to circuit as quickly as possible ; get the full team on the grid and collect starting money. We were very lucky on occasions to finish well up, but that was never our intention in the first place. Admittedly, the season was economically successful, but the H.W.M.s were definitely outclassed and it was thanks to our drivers that the cars put up such a good performance.

Another thing that upset me during the 1950 season was lack of funds. It puzzled me why we had such an inadequate allowance, because there was never any question of spending money on ourselves. I did not go motor-racing in order to throw parties all over Europe. No, we raced on a shoe-string in 1950, and it caused me, personally, great embarrassment on several occasions and no end of frustration and worry.

People used to look at me in a rather curious fashion when I asked for a loan. They must have thought to themselves : " Why is he broke ? " With three racing cars, two lorries and two other mechanics, he surely does not travel around Europe with only five pounds in his pocket ! "

There was no time wasted in the construction of brand new cars for the 1951 season. The success of the H.W.M. two-seater sports cars in single-seater events had convinced John Heath that we should build a team of pukka racing cars. The question of purchase tax entered into it as well, and in this connection readers may wonder why the cars never raced at Le Mans in 1950 as was originally intended.

It was simply that if the H.W.M.s had been fully assembled as sports cars, and taxed in accordance with the Le Mans regulations, heavy purchase tax would have been payable. That was why the idea was abandoned. It was not worth the money or trouble, although I remember John Heath tried to get some relief from the Government. The politicians, however, could not care less about motor-racing prestige abroad—any more than they do nowadays—and that was that.

The team cars of 1950 were pushed aside. One had been sold early in the season to Baring, and a second was sold at the end of the season to Tom Meyer, who purchased the car on condition that one of our mechanics accompanied it. That was how we lost Tom O'Hara.

A third car, fitted out in full sports trim, went to a Swiss enthusiast, and I think he took delivery of Stirling Moss' car, which he sold at a later date to Twentieth Century Fox. They used it in the film " Such Men are Dangerous," and it was involved in that monumental prang caused by the poodle in the early part of the film. The H.W.M. was destroyed ; a sad end to such a famous motor-car. Oscar Moore purchased the fourth of the 1950 team cars.

We planned a stronger permanent staff for 1951. Jack Tolly, the welder from Coopers at Surbiton who had been so helpful in 1950, joined us, and also Frank Webb. Frank had been an apprentice with Aston-Martin at the same time as John Heath, and was engaged as our head mechanic at base, responsible for handling major repairs in England whilst at the same time supervising the building of more cars.

Rex and Frank stayed with us and they were joined by a youngster, Richard Curtis, who had just left Eton and wanted something to do between leaving school and starting his National Service. He was, I think, more interested in travelling around Europe than in working on the cars. Nevertheless, he was to prove very useful. Then we had Frank Green, the tool-maker from John Heath's factory just outside Walton who had given us such a lot of help during the manufacture of the 1950 cars. He was attached to us again.

It was not quite the same as it had been the year before. Then there was only Tom O'Hara, Rex and myself. Now we had at least twice as many people working on three cars, but no increase in floor space. It was crowded to say the least and not such a cosy atmosphere. Even though I was chief mechanic, I did not feel so closely connected with the new cars as I had been with the old ones.

My main task was to develop the power units and I took an engine to Geoffrey Taylor's workshops. I was with him for six weeks, trying to improve performance on the test bed, and succeeded in getting something like a 12 per cent. increase in power.

It was a matter of tuning, by valve and ignition timing, and trying various combinations of carburetters in an attempt to improve the carburation. We also used different type camshafts, designed and fitted by Geoffrey Taylor.

Generally speaking, we were only playing about and I am afraid I regarded it in this light. It was really a waste of time, because the engine lacked so much power in 1950 compared with our continental rivals that it required specialized tuning attention.

With my limited experience and background, I could not hope to compete in the development field with the big boys. Our 12 per cent. increase still left the Alta with less b.h.p. than the continentals had produced in 1950, and I knew very well that they would be getting even more power in 1951.

We should definitely—during this slack period—have found someone more specialized in tuning to develop the engines ; Geoffrey Taylor was, I feel, rather leisurely in the way he tackled the problem. I felt that if we were to get the best out of the Alta engines in 1951, they would have to be developed and tuned to their maximum efficiency by someone who knew how to do the job in the least possible time, someone who already knew the answers that we were having to find the hard way.

There was one particular component part of the engine that I disliked intensely. It was the fuel pump, a gear type fitting with a shabby arrange-ment of a release valve, and I am sure that at least half our troubles in 1950 could have been traced to this component. Flooding the carburetters could easily have been caused by the pump, which was quite incapable of controlling the fuel pressure. There was either too much, too little or none at all.

It was finally decided that we would build five cars for the 1951 season, so that four could be raced and the other sold. The plan was to take three cars on the continent and keep the other in reserve at Walton, so that in case of emergency it could be sent over to us at short notice.

The new cars were very different from the 1950 ones. The front suspension, for instance, was entirely changed, and incorporated coil springs of M.G. type, with the exception of the uprights which were taken from a Standard Vanguard. The stub axles were also of Vanguard design.

The idea was to use production parts wherever possible, reducing their weight whenever practical. We also lifted the roll centre of the car slightly by modifying the pivoting of the bottom wishbones and by using the Standard Vanguard uprights. At the rear end we dispensed with the independent type of suspension and changed over to a De Dion type axle with quarter elliptic springs and torque arms.

The diameter of the brake drums was increased and also the width of the linings, but much to my disappointment the preselector-type gearbox was retained. The chassis was built on similar lines to the 1950 cars and consisted of two longitudinal tubes with four cross members. It was different in that we incorporated an S bend in front of the engine in an effort to drop the chassis at the rear end by three inches.

Making the De Dion tubes with Jack Tolly was most interesting. I had not previously been responsible for a job of this magnitude and, with Jack welding, we succeeded in making the tubes without using expensive jigs and achieved quite a remarkable degree of accuracy. There was so little distortion, after welding was finished, that it was hardly worth worrying about. Tolly was one of the most skilled welders I have ever met and knew exactly where to start and where to leave off.

Morris Minor rack and pinion steering was used on the H.W.M.s, not because of Stirling's marked preference for going round a corner by this method but because it suited the new type of front suspension. Briefly, the use of transverse leaf front springs in 1950 had called for track rods of slightly longer dimensions, and British rack and pinion steering was unsuitable. However, with the M.G. type coil spring suspension we could use the Morris Minor steering with only a slight modification to allow for the rack and pinion being a little shorter than in our previous steering geometry.

We were just as busy building the 1951 cars as we had been the previous year; still working late hours and with the same arrangement of half-a-crown a night for a cup of tea and some cakes in the local cafe, because we were too hard pressed to get back to our digs for an evening meal.

Rex, who had a very good technical background, worked on the prototype with John Heath, as he had done the previous year, and many of his ideas and suggestions were employed. I was responsible for the actual team cars.

It was the mixture as before; building a prototype and a team of cars against the clock, so that we could have them ready for testing well before the start of the season. Abecassis fulfilled his usual function of acting as

The prototype of the 1951 single-seater racing cars at Odiham. This was the first appearance of Alf Francis after his motor-cycle crash and, wearing his Polish Army beret, he is standing next to Frank Nagel. Next to Nagel is Rex Woodgate and then Frank Webb. After six weeks at home Alf felt in his own words, "like a fish out of water."

It was no less hectic than it looks. The pit stop at Zandvoort in 1951 when Moss, in second place with his H.W.M., came in when the race was within a few laps of the finish. Alf Francis recalls that although he is taking out No. 3 plug, whilst Alfred Moss stands by expectantly with a replacement, he is in fact looking at the magneto, the real cause of the trouble. It was always good Public Relations with Stirling to change No. 3 plug ! Note that the ram pipe (seen on the prototype above) has been removed, following the recommendation of the Weber experts at Monza.

The phenomenally light 2-litre Formula 2 Alta, the only one ever made in this class by Geoffrey Taylor, and no more fortunate than the ill-fated Formula 1 G.P. car. It has Bugatti-type wheels specially cast from Elektron and incorporating brake drums, and the stub exhausts follow H.W.M. practice. Stan Ellsworth is changing the plugs prior to the La Baule Grand Prix.

On the road to Syracuse in March, 1952, with Peter Whitehead's well-equipped transporter. In southern Italy, where this picture was taken, the heat was intense at sea level but in the mountains it was freezing cold. Alf Francis and Stan Ellsworth are suitably attired.

referee when the inevitable and sometimes very stormy technical arguments with John Heath assumed an almost violent aspect.

I threw a fairly large spanner in the works by falling off my Velocette motor-cycle one Sunday evening when returning to Walton after a week-end at Woolwich. I hit a private car at New Cross Gate and broke a bone in my foot, which kept me at home for six weeks.

My absence slowed down the programme and I felt very miserable having to take a back seat whilst the cars were being built. My wife was, of course, delighted with this turn of events. She had hardly seen me at all in 1950 and my presence at home, even though I was very short-tempered trying to get around on crutches, was very much appreciated.

She had told me after the Castle Combe meeting that she hoped I was not going to spend another full season away from home, but I could not very well pack up with H.W.M. at this stage, partly because I wanted to see it through with the new cars and partly because I wanted to complete my third full season as a racing mechanic with a British *equipe*.

I promised her that although I would be going abroad again this would be the third and final season. She agreed and few people can have had such an understanding wife. In her shoes, I would not have put up with it. There is no fun in being married to a racing mechanic even when the season does not include races abroad.

When I eventually returned to work, one of the cars was almost ready for test. I felt an absolute stranger, almost an outcast. It was all very strange and it took me some days to regain my confidence. I had not had very much to do with the new cars, yet I was still the *chef d'equipe*.

I noticed at once that Rex seemed to be disagreeing with me even more so than in the past. There had never been very much love lost between us in connection with motor-racing matters, although as a man I liked him, and the climax was reached when he bluntly refused to work with me any longer. After a discussion between John Heath, Rex and myself, Heath decided that if Rex felt all that strongly about me, then the best thing would be to let him go. And so Rex left us.

I was upset, for after all he had built the prototype of the new car, and it seemed a shame that he should leave us just at the commencement of the season. Technically speaking, he was very clever but would sometimes make a clever suggestion that was not practical. He would get offended and argue the case, when there just was not the time to argue. My main concern on these occasions was to get on with the job and not waste time discussing something which I knew from previous experience would not work.

Early in March we took one of the new cars to Odiham and once again I had the privilege of being the first person to drive the latest design from H.W.M. Once I had warmed up the car, Abecassis and Heath took her round the airfield circuit. They were delighted with the performance and we all returned to Walton in high spirits. This was a strictly private test, before inviting the official team drivers, and consequently Stirling was not there.

On March 9th, the second team car was tested at Goodwood and Moss and Lance Macklin were invited. When we tried to push-start the H.W.M.

it just spluttered and refused to fire.   Investigation showed that the valves were bent and there was nothing we could do except remove the cylinder head and take it back to Walton, whilst the car remained locked up in a shed at Goodwood.

It turned out that the engine had been assembled incorrectly, in that the timing chain was too long.   Two of the links were doubled up on the chain in such a way that the folds escaped our notice.   When the pistons moved, the camshaft remained stationary and consequently the valves were bent.

We had to work all night fitting replacement valves and, in the early hours of Saturday morning, set off for Goodwood again with the new head. Moss and Macklin arrived, and according to both of them the car was more powerful and definitely superior to those we had used the previous year. Moss proved this to himself by spinning the wheels on acceleration, which he had never been able to do with his 1950 car.

He also went so fast round Woodcote that he spun.   On returning to the pits he was fully convinced that, whilst the car was undoubtedly more powerful, it also oversteered badly.   We went back to Walton and set about solving the problem.   John Heath wanted to modify the whole of the rear suspension, but I argued that we had no definite proof that the rear end was causing the oversteer.   It seemed to me that Heath's solution was too drastic, and I suggested that we tried to find a more logical reason before committing ourselves to a major task.

Heath even went so far as to contact W. O. Bentley, as well as many other technical experts, and it is of interest that "W.O." considered the fault lay with the steering geometry at the front end.   By carefully checking the geometry we confirmed his views.   In the static position of the chassis, the geometry was perfect, but when the car rolled on corners it was inducing the front wheels to point more into the corner, thus causing oversteer.

Our solution was to modify the steering arm, to create understeer on rolling, and this proved successful.   By trial and error we had altered the characteristics of the car from excessive oversteer to slight understeer.

Now Abecassis, who was a first-rate test driver, came into the picture. It was decided to make one more visit to Goodwood so that the carburation, as well as the new steering geometry, could be checked on the circuit before the Easter Monday meeting.

We took the third car—which in any case needed running in—and I covered sixty or so laps.   When Abecassis arrived, he completed another twenty-five laps and then brought in the H.W.M. so that the plugs could be checked.   He was quite happy about the car which, according to him, now handled very well indeed.

The carburation was, however, much too rich and, having weakened down, he did a lap in 1 minute 47 seconds, which was very quick indeed in those days.   The H.W.M. came in again and, whilst Abecassis was chatting to Duncan Hamilton, I checked a plug and found that we could weaken a little more.   Meanwhile, it had started to drizzle, and I could see that the circuit was becoming dangerous with a thin film of moisture. Just before he set off, I warned him to be careful.

I watched him into Madgwick and Fordwater, and then the car disappeared from view for a few seconds as it went through St. Mary's. From the sound of the engine Abecassis seemed to be going very well and very fast. Hamilton and I saw him come out of Lavant Corner and make for Woodcote. " Take it easy," I muttered to myself, as the H.W.M. streaked down Lavant Straight.

Suddenly, the car was spinning and careering off the track. Then there was silence. I was not too worried because Abecassis was a fully experienced driver. I expected to see him, after a minute or two had elapsed, walking towards the pits. But there was no sign of him, and with a St. John's Ambulance man I started running towards Woodcote Corner.

What we did not know was that following his spin he had run backwards into the barrier and that one of the lateral concrete sections of the barrier was missing and had allowed the tail of the car to run underneath.

It was Abecassis himself—or rather his neck—that eventually stopped the car. The top section of the barrier hit the filler cap and wrenched it off, then hit Abecassis, broke his collar bone and knocked him out. It also forced him forward on to the steering wheel and broke some ribs.

When we arrived, Abecassis was unconscious in the cockpit, jammed between the concrete barrier and the wheel. He was still wearing his crash helmet and there was no sign of cuts on the face but, to my horror, I saw a thin trickle of blood from each ear and from his nose. I could only imagine that he had internal injuries and was gravely hurt. I honestly thought it was the last I should ever see of George Abecassis.

I felt sick as we lifted him out of the cockpit and on to a stretcher. The one thought in my mind was " Who is going to tell Mrs. Abecassis ? " Then the ambulance took him away.

I drove straight to the hospital as soon as I had loaded the car into the transporter. To my surprise, I found that he was still alive. He had not only broken his collar bone and ribs, but there was a suspected fracture of the skull as well.

' He is on the danger list," the Sister-in-Charge told me, " and we shall not know anything definite until the morning when we can take some more X-rays of the skull."

Still, he was alive and that was all that mattered then.

The car was not badly damaged, although during the spin it must have hit something in the grass beside the track with the front wheels because on one side the steering arm and track rod was bent. With the exception of the petrol tank filler, the tail was undamaged.

It was an unpleasant incident and brought home to all of us at Good wood on that occasion—Moss and Macklin were there with Duncan Hamilton—the unpredictable dangers of motor-racing. A spin—yes ; even an encounter with the safety fence ; but who could have foreseen the exact circumstances, resulting in multiple injuries for Abeccasis, that were to keep him out of a racing-car for two months.

However, he turned up at the Goodwood Meeting on Easter Monday, only a few days after his accident. I have never met a man with such remarkable stamina. Admittedly, X-rays showed that his skull was not fractured, but even so it took guts to get out of a sick bed and make the journey to Goodwood.

Parnell, in his 4 CLT Maserati, made fastest times of the day during practice and set up a new unofficial lap record of 90 m.p.h. Moss, in the new H.W.M., was second fastest at 87.3 m.p.h. but was not very happy with the handling. He was driving the No. 2 team car and was convinced there was something wrong with the back-end.

" I just can't hold the car on the road," he said, " and I don't like the position of the pedals."

We set about modifying them (so far as I could see there was nothing whatever the matter with the back-end) whilst Moss took over the No. 1 car from Macklin and put up the very fast time of 1 minute 39 seconds.

Macklin recorded a much slower time in the No. 2 car, but we just could not make out why the two H.W.M.s should be so different. After the practice session we checked the rear end of the No. 2 car and there was no reason at all why it should have given Moss, or Macklin for that matter, a different ride to No. 1.

One cannot get away from the fact that from time to time a driver will take a dislike to a car for no particular reason other than that he does not feel it is right. He will naturally complain about the handling of the car— usually steering or suspension—but even he will not know the real reason and this, of course, makes it very difficult for us to do anything about it.

It was an exciting Meeting, partly because at Goodwood they have bookies on the circuit and for some reason or other Eric Brandon was favourite in the 5-lap Lavant Cup, even though Moss had recorded fastest time in the 2-litre class. We could not understand the reason for this apparent lapse on the part of the bookies, and the cognoscenti grabbed the opportunity of putting a few " bobs " on Stirling. I never bet on cars, or horses for that matter, otherwise I might have done quite well that day.

When the flag fell, Brandon was first off the grid in the Cooper J.A.P. 1100 and increased his lead considerably on the first lap, whilst Moss lagged behind. Then suddenly the H.W.M. started to go like a bomb and Moss passed Aston (Cooper) who was lying second and tore after Brandon. These two had a terrific dice and Moss just managed to win by no more than four-fifths of a second. Macklin was fourth.

The H.W.M.s were unplaced in the Formula 1 Richmond Trophy, and in a five-lap handicap race, but we were quite pleased with their performance. It had not been spectacular, but then neither had there been any serious trouble, and it was undoubtedly a more successful first meeting of the season than the previous year.

After Goodwood I organized a small dinner party (on H.W.M.) at the " Swan " in Petworth, for myself and the boys. I try to have these parties after every race, because I am a firm believer in building up team spirit and tradition in this way. I shall always remember walking into a hotel in Brackley after the Silverstone meeting in August, 1950, and finding the entire Ferrari *equipe*—manager, drivers and mechanics—dining there. This, I discovered, was normal practice and it impressed me very much.

The Italians, and the French as well, know how to cultivate the family atmosphere that is so much a part of team spirit. The drivers are part of that family, no more or less than the apprentices, and it is a tradition that the whole *equipe* gets together after a race. I am sorry to say that this is not generally the case with British *equipes,* and consequently the drivers and mechanics tend to drift apart instead of getting to know each other through acquaintance away from the circuit.

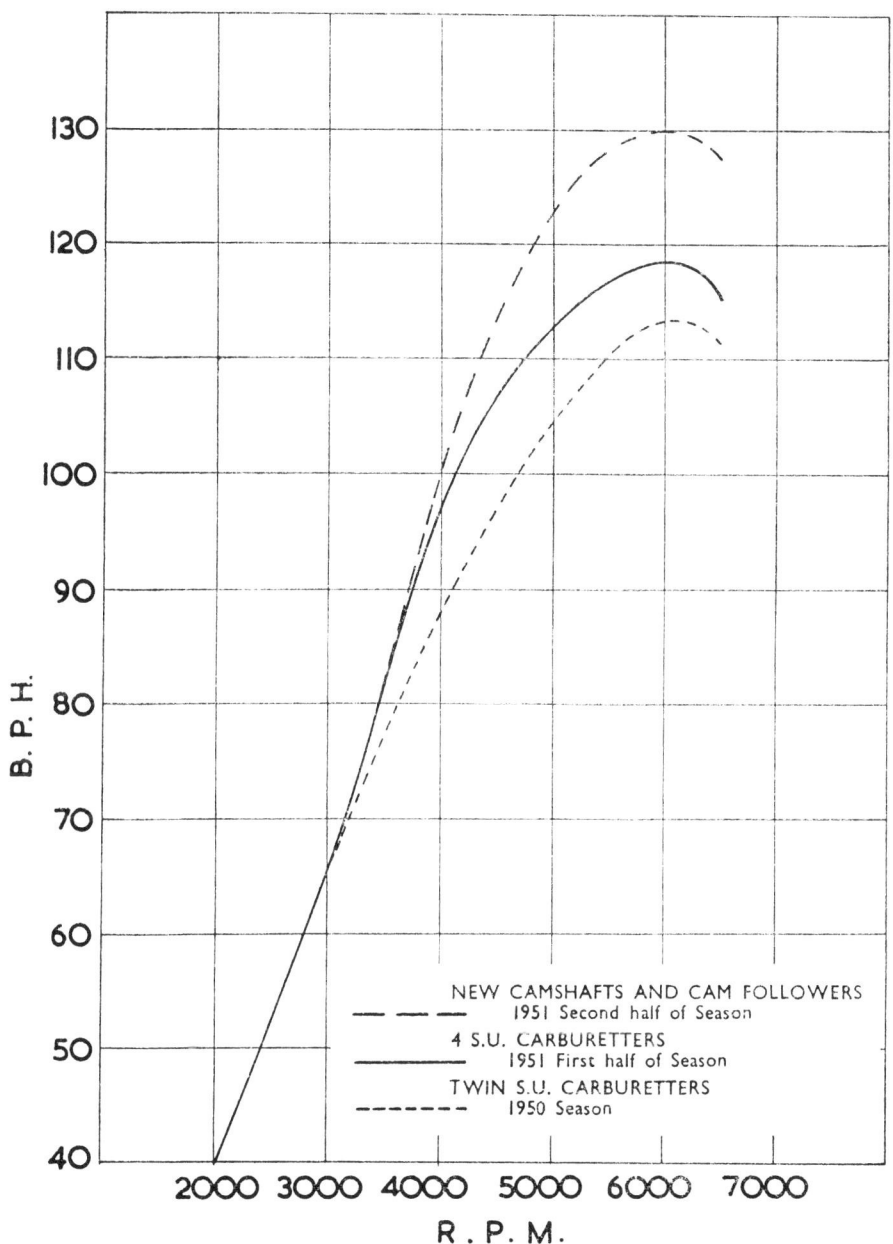

B.H.P./R.P.M. Graph of the Alta 1960 c.c. engine showing various stages of tuning. The four S.U.s were rarely used in 1951. Once the new camshafts had been fitted, twin Webers were used.

CHAPTER 11

SECONDS OUT OF THE RING

Moss third at Marseilles—We meet the Foreign Legion—
Our routine with the H.W.M.s—Louis Chiron drives for us—
A miserable race in Bordeaux—I go on strike.

We had only a few days to get the cars ready, as H.W.M. had been invited to race at Marseilles in the Formula 2 event two weeks after Goodwood. I could not help wondering, as we loaded the lorries, whether the 1951 season would be a mad, crazy whirl of events similar to the previous year. I hoped not.

We had a new system of accounts for 1951. Keeping the books during 1950 had taken up far too much of my time—time that I could ill afford to spare—and it surprised nobody that the accounts were a shambles by the end of the season. I suggested to John Heath that everyone should be paid travelling expenses at the rate of 22s. 6d. a day for the mechanics and 25s. a day for myself.

I was able to convince him that, from the psychological point of view, it would be a much more satisfactory system and not only give us a certain amount of independence but simplify the accounts as well. It would only be necessary to keep them from week to week on the basis of the daily flat rate.

It was also agreed that all members of the *equipe* could draw £1 a week of their wages in local currency, with £2 for myself, and John Heath then told me that he was thinking of employing someone to give me a hand with administration.

This was good news, for I would have more time to concentrate on the cars, and Steve Watson—who had been engaged by John Heath to make a film of the H.W.M.s racing during the 1951 season—was told to help me by taking on the job of paymaster and cashier.

We took three cars to Marseilles in the faithful Fords that had been used the previous season. Actually H.W.M. had been given an old Oxford City double-decker bus, but the coachbuilders were unable to convert it to a racing-car transporter in time for the Marseilles event.

It was typical of the H.W.M. organization that we did not leave Walton until 7.30 p.m., although we were due on the quayside at Dover by 9.30, so you can appreciate that all records were broken on the way to Dover, particularly as I had to call at Woolwich and pick up a suitcase of clean clothes. My wife had already resigned herself to not seeing me for several months. We arrived at Dover at 11.15 on Monday, April 2nd, and were very lucky to get on the boat.

I suppose it was too much to expect that we should reach Marseilles without trouble. In the first place there was a lengthy hold-up at Dunkerque with the Customs. We disembarked at 3.30 a.m. and eventually got away from the port at 11 a.m., feeling very miserable and cold.

This was a serious setback and we only managed to get as far as Rheims for our night stop. I made a note in my diary before turning in. " Engine on F.O.P. (the large transporter) is running at 180° F. Seems rather hot."

Sure enough, when we pushed on next morning, F.O.P. was still running hot. I could not understand what was wrong, for both water and oil were O.K. and then—at St. Seine l'Abbaye, some sixteen miles from Dijon—the cylinder head gasket " blew " on the nearside bank.

We replaced the gasket and continued our journey but after only a few miles the engine started running hot again, and we found water pouring from the opposite side of the V-bank of cylinders. Due to overheating, the cylinder head had cracked ! It was now midnight, so we decided to go to sleep. Next morning I drove into Dijon in the small van, bought another cylinder head (those wonderful Ford spares) and returned to the transporter.

We worked until mid-day Thursday fitting the new head and then set off on a non-stop run to Marseilles, as we were a day behind schedule. I telephoned John Heath from a cafe some twenty-five miles from the port on the Friday morning at about half-past eight to explain why we were late. After the initial explosion that one always expected from John Heath, he told us to get to Marseilles as quickly as possible and to take the lorries straight on to the circuit.

Bira drove for us at Marseilles, where the opposition was mainly Ferraris and Gordinis, and made up the team of three H.W.M.s with Moss and Macklin. One important outcome of the 1950 season was that drivers of his calibre were pleased to consider an offer from us, and we no longer had to scrape around if we found ourselves in need of a replacement at short notice.

Bira, of course, was a first-rate driver. In my opinion, all he needed after his performance at Goodwood in the 12-cylinder OSCA, was the right car. The OSCA did not seem to handle at all well, but Bira nevertheless won the Richmond Trophy and I remember saying at the time that I would like to see him in an H.W.M. An intelligent and very polished driver is my summing up of Bira.

We had a lot of trouble at the Friday practice session. Each car was spilling oil from the back axle and also suffering from flat spots. Moss was going round the very bumpy, twisting 1¾-mile circuit in the Borely Park in 1 minute 24 seconds and Macklin in 1 minute 25 seconds, but Bira did not practise until the following day. If I remember rightly, we had to alter the seat position to accommodate his short legs.

John Heath cured the back axle leaks on the Friday night, but the carburation troubles still remained and neither Moss nor Macklin were able to better their times on Saturday. It was Heath who succeeded in improving the carburation and flat spots. We were using twin double choke Webers in 1951 and I had no idea how to adjust them. They were to give us a lot of trouble in consecutive races, entirely due to the fact that none of us really knew how to handle them. Don't laugh, but we did not even have an instruction manual !

Bira, to our disappointment, was rather slow in practice and I made an entry in my diary : " We hope that once he gets used to the handling of the car his times will improve." It was, of course, the first occasion he had driven an H.W.M., not having had an opportunity to do so after Goodwood.

The race times were much faster than the practice sessions. The best lap put up by Moss was 1 minute 19.8 seconds, as against his 1 minute 24 seconds during the Friday practice period ; he went very well indeed, to the delight of the French crowd, and finished third when Ascari went off the road. Stirling's time was only a fraction of a second slower than the lap record set by Ascari, before his accident, of 1-19.2.

The race was won by Villoresi (Ferrari). Trintignant (Gordini) came home second and Macklin was fifth. Bira retired with fuel trouble but out on the circuit after the race we found plenty of fuel in his tank. We thought that lack of air supply to the tank had caused fuel starvation, and that could have been the reason, but I have a strong suspicion that the fuel pump was to blame all the time.

We had Jack Tolly with us at Marseilles, as I had promised at the end of the 1950 season to take him on the Continent. He had never been out of England and enjoyed himself immensely. His classic remark when he returned home was : " You cannot beat good old England. There is no fish and chips over the other side."

The night after the Marseilles race we found ourselves in a night club on the waterfront, where a bottle of wine for six of us only cost a few shillings. Most of the customers were Foreign Legion soldiers and the tariff was obviously based on their low rate of pay. We were there all night, drinking on bare wooden tables with the Legion and applauding with them the toughest and most fearsome collection of dancing girls I have seen anywhere in the world.

As soon as the Legion boys found out we were connected with motor-racing, they insisted on treating us and the sum total of our expenditure during the night was 10s. The way the Legion treated the dancing girls was the licentious soldiery at its worst !

Unfortunately, our night on the tiles had serious consequences. We were taken to the Club by a Polish friend of mine who had settled down in Marseilles and bought a restaurant, and was only too pleased to help us celebrate the good performance of the cars.

When we took him home next morning, his suitcases, containing his worldly goods, had been left outside the main entrance of the restaurant. The last time I saw him was when we left Marseilles on the Tuesday and he had still not been able to see his wife. Trying to entertain us he had not only lost his wife but his restaurant as well.

Our next race, in two weeks, was at St. Remo in Italy, so we had plenty of time to get there and prepare the cars. The Marseilles papers on the Monday were most complimentary about the performance of the H.W.M.s and our morale was high, in spite of the fact that we were all suffering hangovers as a result of our night out.

The manager of the garage where we had kept the cars, a large Renault agency, was so impressed with the performance of Moss and the green

H.W.M.s that he refused to present us with an account. So we all went out together for a few drinks which probably cost us more in the long run.

The transmission on all cars was O.K. and we had obviously cured the oil breathing trouble experienced at the first practice session. Apart from this, there was very little else to do, although on checking Macklin's engine I found that the camshaft was lacking oil and liable to seize up. The trouble was traced to a blocked reduction valve in the lubricating system. Having put this right, I tightened the magneto on its mounting (it had worked loose in the race), changed the coil springs on the front end and the car was ready for the routine post-race checking procedure.

This is how we worked. Every member of the *equipe* was entirely responsible for a particular job on each car. For instance, I checked the engine, ignition, carburation and transmission, also the " band " adjustment of the preselector gearbox.

Richard Curtis, who did not know much about the mechanical side, was responsible for the wheels, tyres and spokes, and also for the organization of spares and the positioning of the cars inside the lorries. Everything had to be kept in the right place, otherwise chaos resulted when we suddenly had to do something in a hurry.

Frank Nagel looked after the steering geometry, including the wheel and column, and also gearbox, back axle and the mountings and fittings. He not only had to watch oil levels, but to look for cracks in the casings and also make sure the universal joints had not come adrift and that the various bolts on the transmission were tight.

Jack Tolly was responsible for checking the chassis for cracks or other damage and in this way he was very helpful indeed. That was the system I put into operation after every race, a rather more precise way of doing things than in 1950.

Preparing the cars for the actual race was another matter, but here again we worked to a definite system. I made myself responsible for the fuel, and for consumption tests, whilst Richard Curtis looked after tyre pressures. During practice we found, by trial and error, what were the most suitable pressures, and it was then up to Richard to ensure that the cars went to the grid with them right to the nearest half-pound. A race can be lost by incorrect tyre pressures for a particular circuit.

As I have explained, the maintenance work was carried out after the previous race and there was not a great deal for us to do before the first practice session. The most important job was to change axle ratios and as soon as this had been done the cars were filled with fuel and oil under my supervision.

Finally, we all worked on cleaning and polishing the H.W.M.s prior to covering them up for the night and getting ourselves a few hours' sleep before the actual race. We never packed up until the cars were absolutely ready to go on the grid. It is one of my strictest rules.

We were looking forward to our visit to San Remo because John Heath had given us a few days' holiday. Lance Macklin, who knows that part of the world very well, had promised to find us somewhere reasonably cheap to stay.

It has also been arranged that a new mechanic would join us, a Frenchman who was at that time chauffeur to Madame Macklin and apparently interested in gaining some experience of motor-racing. I was rather anxious to meet this man because I had only apprentices with me. Admittedly they were first rate, and I could not have asked for better, but I was sorely in need of an experienced man.

We left Marseilles on the Thursday morning, having spent Wednesday on the cars. My diary indicates that I adjusted the gear selectors on each car and checked transmission, valve clearance, ignition timing, points, etc. Valve clearances are an important guide to engine reliability. If the clearance increases, it indicates that the engine has been over-revved and the valves distorted. This means an immediate check of the pistons.

If the clearance decreases, it indicates that the valve stem has stretched and is liable to break, or that the valve seats have come adrift. Whether clearances increase or decrease, the cylinder head still has to come off.

We arrived at Rocquebrun, Cap Martin, on Friday morning where Lance Macklin had booked accommodation for us at the Hotel Les Diodato. It is one of my favourite hotels on the continent and even on that first visit the proprietor and his wife treated us like friends.

The Diodato was originally an old castle, dating from the time of the Napoleonic wars, and has been converted to a hotel. Madame Macklin has her house almost next door and Sir Winston Churchill paints in the vicinity.

We spent nearly a week at Rocquebrun, lazing in the Mediterranean sunshine, and it was here that the new mechanic, Richard Millani, joined us. He was a Monegasque of Italian origin, and could speak no English, but I took a liking to him at once. My judgment was not at fault, for he turned out to be the hardest working mechanic the H.W.M. *equipe* has ever had.

On the Wednesday before the race we left Rocquebrun, crossed the border and drove along the Italian Riviera to San Remo. At practice on Thursday each of the three H.W.M.s had carburation trouble, especially the Moss car which was oiling plugs badly. Each time a plug test was taken, the mixture was still too rich and we were weakening down so much that it was becoming dangerous to continue. Maybe the mixture was too rich, maybe it was the fitting of the carburetters, or perhaps the fuel pump was not functioning properly.

When softer plugs were used, there was pre-ignition at the top end ; it seemed that we were going around in a vicious circle and we just could not cure the persistent misfiring.

The only thing to do was strip the engine right down, for it could be that a piston ring had collapsed, so we worked until 3.30 a.m. stripping the bottom and top end, whilst the engine remained in the frame. Having checked all the pistons and found nothing wrong, I had no alternative but to reassemble. However, I did fit a new magneto.

On Friday we were still having a lot of carburation trouble, although Stirling was inclined to think his car was in better form. Louis Chiron, who had been invited to drive for us at San Remo, suggested that we use a smaller choke. Although this was not the first time I had met Chiron, it was the first occasion I had worked with him in the same team. I found him a most likeable person, with a wonderful personality and sense of humour.

Nothing is too much trouble for Louis Chiron and he will go out of his way to help people. He is inclined to be theatrical at times but his displays of temperament have endeared him to motor-racing enthusiasts all over the world.

In Monte Carlo, where he lives, the townspeople idolize him. He is a personal friend of Prince Rainier and runs the Prince's motor-racing stable.

I remember saying to Chiron once : " You must be the oldest racing driver in the game ; why don't you retire ? "

His reply was typical. " I could never retire. And if I begin to feel too old to drive, then my coffin will be a racing car."

He is probably the most charming person in the game, and a first-rate sportsman and driver. What more could one ask.

But back to our carburation problem. At that time my French was about equal to Louis Chiron's English so we conversed in a peculiar jargon that no one else could possibly understand.

"Alphons," he said to me, " there is one thing you must remember. Motor-cars are like women. You must regard your H.W.M.s as three sisters. But do not regard them as all being the same. They are not.

" You must have one car different from the other two ; maybe two are the same, but never three. It is the same with cylinders. They can be compared with sisters but, like sisters, they are not absolutely the same. You must adjust the carburation for each cylinder."

I worked most of Saturday, keeping Chiron's excellent advice in mind, and by trial and error managed to get the three cars running reasonably well. On Macklin's car I had an air bleed jet of 180, a main jet of 210 and the choke at 32 mm. ; fuel level 6½ mm. Moss had the air bleed at 220, the main jet at 230 and the choke at 32 mm. ; fuel level at 7 mm. Chiron had the same settings as Moss.

Chiron's theory had, in fact, worked out. One car was different from the other two and yet, in general, there was an all-round improvement in carburation. We did not, however, finally get the Webers right until we went to Monza at a later date. At this time we did not really know whether we were coming or going with the blessed Webers !

We were not sure what axle ratio to use at San Remo. Chiron insisted on a low one (4.56 to 1) because he knew the circuit well enough to use more revs and gain a lot of time on the uphill sections, whilst Macklin and Moss were satisfied with the higher 4.1 to 1 ratio.

During the race, which was a Formula 1 event, Moss went very well, but Macklin came in repeatedly with carburation trouble. Chiron was fairly streaking round the circuit, driving like a man possessed, whilst Moss gave the 4½-litre Ferraris (Ascari and Villoresi) and the Talbots, not to mention the supercharged Maseratis, a run for their money.

When Chiron suddenly disappeared from our lap chart I was not surprised. He was bound to break something. We soon knew the worst, for he arrived at the pits on foot.

"Alphons," he said, " I have broken a universal drive shaft. You know

I always like to finish every race in which I start. What can you do ? "

"O.K." I said, "we will take a drive shaft out to the car."

And off we went. I have never considered myself a mountaineer but I did very well that day. It took us fifteen minutes to make our way round the hilly circuit, clambering from level to level and cutting off the corners to save time. I don't think a Commando could have done better.

We were almost exhausted when we reached the car, but the drive shaft was replaced in under five minutes. Chiron climbed into the cockpit and proudly continued in the race, just as fast as before, and came home eleventh.

Moss finished in fifth place, ahead of several Formula 1 cars, and Macklin came in seventh. "Bearding the lion in his den," was how a Frenchman described the H.W.M. challenge.

We left San Remo on Tuesday *en route* for Bordeaux and travelled as far as Aix en Provence in convoy, where Frank left for England. He took the Moss car (Silverstone followed Bordeaux) in the small van whilst we continued to Montpelier and stopped for the night.

We set off early next morning and had difficulty crossing the Massif Central. The roads were very slippery and there were some nasty moments with the transporter. More trouble was to come. Soon after midday the cylinder head gasket blew on the offside bank of cylinders, and up there on top of the Pass, with Frank miles away by now, I realized how fortunate it was that we carried spare gaskets.

We changed the faulty gasket and it was 2 a.m. on Thursday before we arrived in Bordeaux. In the morning I changed the magneto on Macklin's car, as I was suspicious that something had come adrift in the San Remo race, which was why the H.W.M. had performed so badly. The mag. was indeed very loosely fixed in position and needed shims.

We also took the carburetters off both cars, as I felt that the manifold pipes were not in correct alignment, and the carburetters themselves were out of line with the ports. By the evening we had completed one car and started work on the second.

It had occurred to me that perhaps the reason for our carburation troubles was the intake tube, a tube joining both the carburetters and designed to pressurize the intake at high speeds. I suspected this tube because, according to the plug reading, No. 1 cylinder was always O.K., whilst No. 4 was always rich, which indicated that it was running partly choked.

We had a miserable race in Bordeaux. Macklin retired whilst Chiron somehow managed to finish seventh. Carburation was the trouble and it was becoming increasingly obvious that we should have to do something about the Webers. Maybe change back to S.U.s.

As soon as the race finished, we loaded up and set off for England and the *Daily Express* B.R.D.C. Silverstone Meeting, stopping on the way in Paris to collect some spares for John Heath. Twenty miles outside the French Capital, on the way to the coast, I pulled into a garage and bought some petrol, and a cup of coffee. As I was driving away, I noticed one of those pernicious French gullies, that so successfully slow down traffic in villages, and eased back on the throttle. However, I was not quick enough and the whole front end of the transporter collapsed.

We jumped out of the cab and found that both half-elliptic springs had broken. What on earth could we do ? There was not much object in going back to Paris, where there was a public holiday, on the offchance of finding some garage open where we could buy replacement springs.

The only thing to do was tackle the job on the spot and with the help of the petrol pump attendant we managed to get the transporter to the side of the road so that it was no longer holding up traffic. Then I had a bright idea. Why not use the M.G. coil springs that we carried as spares for the team cars. However, when the front end of the transporter was jacked up, it was obvious that the springs were much too long. They would, in fact, be ideal at half the length. So I sawed one of the springs in half.

With half coil springs on either side of the broken elliptic springs and with towing ropes locating the axle in position, we set off with our "Heath Robinson" front end and reached the Channel without incident. In fact, we went all the way to Silverstone like it and then back to Walton.

It was at Silverstone that I went on strike and refused to work any longer. John Heath, in the way he always did when we came to England, was fiddling about with the carburetters and exasperated me to such an extent that I just packed up and left him to it.

I went over to the transporter, climbed into the cab and took no further interest in the proceedings. I thought to myself : " What is the use of continuing in this crazy game ? When we are on the Continent, whatever our difficulties, we do at least keep running. Here, in our own country, we are worse than anywhere else."

The Moss car, in particular, was missing very badly and the best time that Stirling could put up in practice was 2 minutes 15 seconds, compared with Farina (159 Alfa-Romeo) at 2 minutes 6 seconds. Stirling actually went round quicker in a " works " XK120 Jaguar.

When I had calmed down, I spent the whole of Friday night with the boys, fitting new drive shafts in the de Dion axles and, as usual, the H.W.M. team was ready for the race.

This was the Silverstone Meeting that should have been a " benefit " for the 159 Alfa-Romeos but was ruined by torrential rain. The final was stopped after only six laps, with Stirling in eighth position, because of the appalling weather conditions. In the paddock, the other two H.W.M.s stood forlorn and silent. In their respective heats Abecassis had blown up his engine and Macklin had experienced gearbox trouble. That is one Silverstone Meeting I shall never forget, summed up in my diary by two words : " Terrible race."

CHAPTER 12

ITALIAN INTERLUDE

Drama on Mt. Genevre—Our biggest success to date—
The pros and cons of axle ratios—Ferrari-baiting at Genoa.

There was very little time after the disastrous Silverstone Meeting to prepare for the F.2 G.P. of Monza eight days later. We had to collect spares from Walton and the double-decker bus from Reading. The A.E.C. was quite a handful to drive and I could not make a quiet gearchange, however hard I tried. I thought to myself: "This is going to be fun. Driving round Europe and crashing the gears all the time."

I drove the bus to Monza with Frank Nagel and Richard Millani and could not help feeling that George Abecassis and John Heath saw us off from Walton partly because they wanted to express their disapproval of my gearchanging. I did not disappoint them.

I started in first gear and moved away from the garage into the roadway, where I attempted to engage second. You have never heard such a crunching of gears! Abecassis and Heath were roaring with laughter, thumbs jammed in their ears.

I braked to a standstill and tried again, with the same result. My face was as red as a beetroot and as I became more and more flustered, the H.W.M. partners became more amused. Finally, I put the bus into second gear and succeeded in moving away from the garage in a fairly sedate manner.

When I reached Streatham Hill I changed down to third, then down to second. Half way to the top, I took my courage in both hands and slammed the lever towards first gear. I say "towards" because I was not very optimistic about it reaching " home base."

Luckily, I found first gear before the bus started to run backwards. "What a heap," I told myself. "Just wait until this old crate comes up against the Alps and the Mt. Cenis Pass."

There were two cars in the back of the bus and a complete set of axle ratios for the full team; a third car was supposed to join us at Genoa. The A.E.C. was fitted with a special tank so that up to a hundred gallons of alcohol fuel could be carried, as well as a full complement of spares for the whole team, including twenty sets of wheels and tyres. We were well stocked because the odds were against us returning to England until the end of the season.

Naturally, we had left Walton late, following the usual panic and, having called at Woolwich to say "Hello and Goodbye" to my wife as I had not been able to get home since arriving for the Silverstone Meeting, we were late at Dover on the Monday night.

On the quayside I was told that even if we had been early, there was no firm booking for the bus, so I sought out the bearded Loading Master, who had been helpful on previous occasions, and put the problem to him. He dealt with it in a most effective manner by "organizing" some space for the bus and then, somehow or other, contriving to shunt the railway coaches backwards and forwards on to the Night Ferry, thus delaying loading operations whilst I went through Customs.

Last on the Ferry meant that we were first off in the early hours of Tuesday and we were soon bowling along the roads of Northern France, with the most peculiar clanking noises coming from the Diesel engine, apparently without any ill effect.

We tried all we knew to coax more than 32 m.p.h. out of the bus, but that was her maximum and she would not go a mile an hour faster. As Richard Millani said to me—

" Even if we dance on the steering wheel, Alf, I don't think this bus can go any quicker."

When we eventually arrived at St. Jean de Maurienne, early on Thursday evening, having "clanked" our way non-stop from Dunkirk, we were informed that a heavy snowstorm was raging in the Mt. Cenis Pass and that it was closed.

I certainly had no intention of ignoring the warning, but the only alternative was a long detour. Nevertheless, we had to push on, as Moss and Macklin expected us in Monza on Friday. I turned the bus round and drove back almost to Chambery, then took a minor road which by-passed Grenoble and led to the Lauteret Pass. Once across the Pass, we continued to Briancon, Mt. Genevre and Susa.

If we had been able to cross the Mt. Cenis, we should not have had to tackle Mt. Genevre in the early hours of Friday morning, and would probably have spent most of the night in a comfortable bed in Susa. The detour took us 130 miles out of our way and lost eighteen hours of running time.

I shall never forget taking the bus over Mt. Genevre, and there is an entry in my diary: "What a ride . . . . . clouds, mountain mist and darkness. The Pass was only wide enough for one vehicle at a time to squeeze through the narrow gap left by the snow-plough. The snow was as high as the bus on either side."

It was a devilish climb, in first gear most of the way. I was not driving in the real sense of the word. With the wheels at the back spinning most of the time, it was more a matter of climbing by slewing from side to side and clouting the snow every now and then. I dared not stop when the radiator boiled because I knew it would not be possible to get the bus moving again. So the A.E.C. boiled like a kettle on the hearth most of the way up the mountain, and there was so much steam inside the coach that it was like a Turkish Baths.

It was impossible to see through the windows, and in any case there was not much to see because the snow clouds were very low and as dense as fog. I dread to think what would have happened if anyone had been coming down the Pass. Fortunately, no one else was as mad as we were that night and the Customs people told us so when we reached the top.

They were astounded to see the bus loom out of the mist in the early hours of the morning. They congratulated us, stamped our carnets and mentioned casually that they thought we were either mad or doing it for a bet. Then the Chief Customs Officer said:

" You will, of course, not carry on down the mountain to-night."

Frank Nagel was inclined to agree but I knew that within a few hours it would be light and that it was essential to reach Monza without further delay. So off we went and, as neither Frank nor Richard could handle the bus with its A.E.C. Diesel engine, I settled down in the driving seat once more and set off down the mountain.

It took me three-and-a-half hours to cover forty miles to Susa. The bus almost slid clean off the road on several occasions and we frightened ourselves on countless occasions; it was a nightmare. Frank and Richard tired themselves out peering through the windows beside me, trying to foresee the prang that we all felt was bound to come, and after the first hour just curled up on the floor––exhausted––and went to sleep.

It was an incredible journey. I literally felt my way down the mountain. In front all the time was just blackness, and I had no idea whether I was heading for the ravine or keeping more or less to the road. To make matters worse, the wind blew the protective snow barrier down on the outer edge of the road and piled the snow high on the inside.

There was nothing to guide me on the corners. All I could see was the blackness, the snow clouds and––when it was almost too late––the mountain, as an indication of the way the road went. On several occasions I turned the steering wheel at the very last moment before plunging into the ravine.

I felt sick from fear. When eventually I reached Susa, I was so exhausted that I had not even the strength to shift the gear lever into neutral when the bus stopped. The engine stalled in top gear, and there we stayed––in the street. I just collapsed over the wheel and for two wonderful hours slept like a man poleaxed.

At 6 a.m., suitably refreshed, I decided to push on to Milan. Compared with our effort the previous night it was an uneventful journey but, as we were crossing the piazza by the Palace Hotel on our way to the Monza Autodrome, I heard someone whistling and shouting at us to stop. It was Stirling.

He came running over and pulled open the door of the bus.

" Where the hell have you been ? " he said.

I took my blistered hands off the steering wheel and held them so that he could see the palms.

" Look, Stirling," I said, " we did our best. We had to come over Mt. Genevre last night. I am sorry to be late."

Stirling took one look at the blisters.

" No need for you to be sorry, Alf," he said. " It is I who should be sorry."

The first practice session for the Monza race took place during the late afternoon of Friday and we were not very happy about the performance of the H.W.M.s. The engines would not go beyond 5,400 revs. and it was almost as though regulators had been fitted.

After practice, I listened politely to at least ten different reasons for the lack of power, and then took myself off to a quiet corner where I could think about the problem without outside pressure.

There are more people who "know the answers" in motor racing, I should imagine, than in any other sport. If only they realized how ridiculous their "know how" sounds, they would adopt an attitude similar to my own —" See all. Hear all. Say nothing."

I was convinced that pre-ignition was the trouble but no one would agree with me, except Louis Chiron. He and I had a meal together in Milan and it was agreed that next morning, before the official practice, we would test out my theory.

" I will take one of the cars round for you," said Chiron, " and switch off when the revs reach 5,400. We shall then see whether the engine continues to fire."

Sure enough, pre-ignition was the trouble. After a few laps on the Saturday, Chiron came into the pits beaming all over his face.

" She just went on pulling," he said, " after I had switched off."

I immediately fitted harder plugs (R.L.51), although I realized John Heath would strongly disapprove if he found out I had replaced the .49 type plugs that he favoured. Anyway, he was not at Monza and I took a chance. The result was very good indeed, with Chiron reaching 5,700 revs. quite easily.

However, I was still not too happy about the Weber carburetters and spoke to Mr. Galletti, the Chief Technical Service Representative of the Weber competition organization.

He came straight to the point.

" The best thing to do if you want to cure all these troubles is to remove the ram pipe from each Weber. Your idea of using the speed of the car to feed air under pressure to the carburetter by means of the pipe will not work. You will only upset completely the carburation."

There was nothing to lose by following his advice and I removed the pipes. Moss and Macklin were quite impressed with the improvement in performance, so there must have been something in what he said. At last we were running on four cylinders again and sounding quite healthy as well. It had been a good day's work. What a pity we had not known about the ram pipes at Silverstone.

Moss put up a fantastic performance against "works" Ferraris and Simcas in the Monza race. He was fourth in the first heat, third in the second and, when the heat times were added, third in the final. It was in the second heat that he "slipstreamed" Villoresi's Ferrari so successfully and for lap after lap, almost a hundred miles, tore round the Monza circuit never more than a few feet behind the Italian. Afterwards, Stirling told me it was the most tremendous dice he had ever had.

It was one of his finest, and most exhausting drives, exhausting because very little daylight separated the two cars and Moss was not able to relax for twenty-five breathless laps. His *average* was 100 m.p.h. for 58 minutes 16.8 seconds and, after this terrific performance, Villoresi congratulated him. The speed of the H.W.M., tucked in behind the Ferrari, had us all chewing our nails in the pits. What a race!

I wrote home: "In Monza I think we had our biggest success yet—being third on the fastest course in the world."

I cannot remember exactly what it was that caused Macklin's car to put up such a mediocre performance at Monza. The ram pipes had been removed from both H.W.M.s, so there was no reason why Macklin should have suffered from carburation trouble any more than Moss.

I don't think the Webers were to blame on this occasion, although some of the reports said so, and we entered the mediocre performance under the heading of "possible fuel pump failure."

Nevertheless, after the race I removed the carburetter from Macklin's car and took it back to the hotel, where I stripped it down piece by piece in order to study the principles on which it worked. We still had no instruction manual for the simple reason that the Webers on the H.W.M. were special competition carburetters and the only ones of their type.

John Heath had bought them and even if the Weber people had given him a set of instructions they would have been in Italian and incomprehensible to us.

I sat up until well after midnight and eventually took the Weber, still in pieces, to bed with me. I must have fallen asleep, for when I woke next morning there was the chambermaid regarding me as though I were crazy. She was rather a pretty girl.

" Do the English always sleep with bits and pieces from their racing cars ? " she asked coyly.

I had the answer, but put the carburetter together instead!

Our next race was at Genoa and, on the day we arrived, I took the bus round the circuit and decided to fit all the cars with 4.1 axle ratios, which I considered would be ideal. The circuit is very fast, as well as dangerously bumpy, and comprises a dual carriageway, running beside the sea, with 340° corners at either end, joining two straights of approximately a mile in length. The kerbs are quite a hazard.

Abecassis was now fit again, almost exactly nine weeks after his accident at Goodwood, and brought a third car out from England in the small van, sharing the driving with that wonderful character, Charlie Brackenbury.

However, when Abecassis arrived, we found that the car had no carburetters. According to him, the Weber people were supposed to deliver them to us at Genoa so that they could be fitted at the circuit. I took a rather dim view of this because it meant that someone would have to go down to Bologna if the carburetters had not already been despatched. It was already Thursday, and with the race on Sunday I could not afford to go short-handed.

I had a talk with Abecassis about the Webers and he told me that John Heath wanted one of the H.W.M.s sent to Bologna after the race so that the Weber people could get the adjustment right. Charles Brackenbury would go with the car as test driver. It was never difficult to find Charles. Usually he was within one or two cafes of where we were working on the cars. The diary tells the story of one evening out with him: "Charles Brackenbury sure can drink! "

On the first day of practice only Moss and Macklin went out, as the carburetters had not arrived for the Abecassis car. Macklin made fastest time of the day, but Stirling did not do too well and asked for a different axle ratio. He reckoned that 4.1 was too high and wanted 4.46. This I could not understand, because Macklin's time was faster than Ascari, so surely there could not be much wrong with the ratio I had chosen.

I was not able to do anything on the Friday because the Webers arrived, and I worked all night on the Abecassis car, but on Saturday I changed the ratio on Moss' car to 4.46, and Abecassis decided on this ratio as well. Unfortunately he was not able to practise, because I did not finish fitting the manifold in time. It was a skilled job and there was so much else to do in preparation for the practice session, that I had to leave the carburetters. Luckily, the organizers said Abecassis could start from the back row of the grid.

We had quite an argument on Saturday night about the axle ratios. Neither Moss nor Macklin could make up their minds whether they wanted 4.1 or 4.46, whilst Abecassis favoured 4.3. It was a ridiculous state of affairs, to have the three drivers all asking for different ratios, so I sent a telegram to John Heath at Walton and asked him what I should do. Back came the reply : " Use your own initiative. Fit the ratios you think right."

Moss had not taken a very active part in the argument prior to my cable to John Heath and, having made my decision to put 4.1 on the Moss and Macklin cars and 4.46 on the Abecassis car, I asked Stirling why all three of them had favoured different ratios. "It just does not make sense to me," I said.

With a shrug of his shoulders, Stirling replied:

" There is a lot to learn about this axle ratio business before one can talk with authority."

From the very first day he started racing, Stirling knew more than the average driver about ratios. Today, he knows instinctively what is right for a particular circuit and few drivers can equal his knowledge.

I consider that his experience with 500 cc. cars—where the choice of axle ratios, because of the small power unit, is much more important than with G.P. cars—taught him most of what he needed to know. Owners of 500 cc. cars can afford to have a selection of different sized sprockets, and only have to change one sprocket as against a crown wheel and pinion on a G.P. car.

It is no trouble at all to the 500 cc. driver and he becomes so adept at choosing the right sprockets for a circuit that, when he eventually graduates to a different class of car, he is able to tell at once whether the axle ratio fitted is the right one.

It is impossible to work out axle ratios without the full co-operation of the team drivers and a driver has to be "honest" with his rev. counter before he can express an opinion. Normally, I gear up to the maximum speed. If a car is peaking at 7,000 revs. down the straight, but reaches its peak well before the end of the straight, then the driver should note this and report to the pits. The ratio is obviously too low.

On the other hand, if a car reaches only 6,500 or 6,600 before the braking point, the ratio is too high and the driver should report on these lines when he gets back to the pits.

On short straights, between corners, a driver cannot always tell whether second gear is too low or third gear too high.   In these circumstances he must report in such a way that we can decide what ratio will save the most time on such sections.   The result may mean that the driver has to lift his foot on the long straights, but this is preferable on a circuit where there are several low gear and what I call acceleration sections.

Choosing the right axle ratio is really basically a matter of co-operation and agreement between the drivers and team control.   From the point of view of morale, a driver likes to feel that he has the best available ratio for the circuit and thus a fair chance of doing well.   A driver who can really "feel" a circuit, like Moss, is absolutely invaluable.

We almost missed the start of the Genoa race.   It was supposed to be at two o'clock, but no one expected the Italians to be punctual, and we arrived just before two p.m. to find all the cars lined up on the grid.

We had four minutes in which to get the H.W.M.s ready and there was not a plug spanner between us!   With two minutes to go, Frank arrived— strolling nonchalantly along in front of the pits with the spanners—and we pounced on him.   Poor Frank hardly knew what hit him.   By a supreme effort we just managed to change the plugs and start the engines.   As we evacuated the grid, the flag dropped and the field was away.

It was a couple of laps before I had recovered my breath sufficiently to unload the spares from the lorry and organize the pit.   When I did get time to check up on the race positions, there was Moss in the lead with Macklin second, Villoresi third and Ascari fourth.   I could hardly believe my eyes.

The two Italian aces, in "works" 2-litre Ferraris, tried unsuccessfully to pass the H.W.M.s.   Moss and Macklin really had the bit between their teeth.   Unhappily, it did not last.   First of all Macklin came into the pit and switched off.

" I can't see a damned thing," he shouted.

I could only advise him to keep going as fast as possible in an effort to finish.   As he accelerated away from the pit, I thought to myself: "Now what; do I have to be an optician as well as a mechanic ? "

I was perhaps a little harsh but it was a disappointing development, because Macklin had, by the time of his pit stop, established himself comfortably in second place.

Less than a minute later, Abecassis came in with a sticking throttle. I lifted the bonnet and found a return spring broken.   A few seconds was enough to fit a replacement and Abecassis was off again.   Two laps later there was no sign of Stirling.   We waited for a loudspeaker announcement, hoping against hope that he had only spun and was by now back in the race, but it was worse than that.

" The Englishman Moss has retired.   He has walked away from the car."

It transpired that the differential had seized solid but we never found out why.

There was more excitement to come.   Suddenly we noticed fuel leaking from the tank of Ascari's Ferrari.   It was being sprayed all over the circuit and we tried to draw the attention of the Ferrari pit to the danger.   It seemed to us that the fuel would very soon catch fire on the exhaust pipes and, sure enough, as the Italian approached the pits down the straight there was a spurt of flame and the car went on fire.   It was burned out completely but fortunately Ascari got out unhurt. And so the race ran its course. Macklin, although he could not see very well, finished a very creditable third whilst Abecassis came home in fifth place.

Abecassis congratulated me after the race on my speed in dealing with his pit stop.

" It was so quick," he said, " that I still do not know what you did."

The H.W.M.s had put up a wonderful show and many people came along to the pit and congratulated us. I felt really sorry for Stirling, as he had been forced to retire his 500 cc Kieft in an earlier race, when the swing axle suspension cable broke, but even in those days Stirling was philosophical about misfortune. He is a good sportsman and never broods on his bad luck or becomes moody. It has always been the same and few people can hide their real feelings in the way he can.

His self-discipline is tremendous and it is impossible for an outsider to realize that he has had a stroke of bad luck. At Genoa we knew what wretched luck he had experienced and felt very sorry for him. He had led two races for a considerable distance, only to have victory snatched from his grasp in each case. My diary summed up our feelings: "It has been a bad day for Stirling Moss."

It seems that sleeping with the carburetter had done some good, for I had never seen the H.W.M.s go so quickly or show such a clean pair of heels to the Ferraris as at Genoa. However, credit was not entirely due to an improvement in carburation, because when I watched part of the race from a corner it was obvious that the 4.1 axle ratios were giving the H.W.M.s more torque lower down than the Ferraris. Undoubtedly Moss and Macklin were going round the bends quicker than the Italians and gaining about twenty yards on each of the two corners. By the time they reached the next corner the Ferraris were almost up with them, but always the H.W.M.s increased the gap until the presence of the Ferraris was no longer an immediate menace.

CHAPTER 13

KEEPING UP WITH THE " CIRCUS "

Signal honour at Berne—Weber carburetters—
Taking a chance at Aix les Bains—The ingenuity of Louis Chiron—
Round the houses at Angouleme—Arrested by the French police—
Birthday party at Rocquebrun.

We all realized that H.W.M. did not stand much chance in the Formula 1 Swiss Grand Prix, a full length World Championship event where the opposition consisted of 4½ litre Ferraris, 159 Alfa-Romeos, supercharged Maseratis and 4½ litre G.P. Talbots. I wrote in my diary: "This is not a race for us." However, the organizers had invited the H.W.M. team as representatives of Great Britain, and it was a signal honour. We were determined to do our best in spite of the fact that the Swiss race was only seven days after our appearance at Genoa.

I reached Berne with the bus on Wednesday, having sent Richard Millani to Webers with Charles Brackenbury and Macklin's car, and found John Heath and George Abecassis waiting for me. On Friday evening Duncan Hamilton arrived at our hotel, the Volkshaus in Berne, having come to Switzerland in rather an unorthodox but typically Hamilton fashion. Unable at short-notice to obtain a permit to land his light aircraft, he faked engine trouble and made a forced landing, whereupon the Swiss officials told him he had forty-eight hours to clear out of the country. This was exactly what he had planned. It would take in the Swiss G.P. nicely.

During the Saturday practice session we carried out consumption tests and found that a stop for fuel would be necessary during the race. Stirling, however, was anxious to attempt a non-stop run. As he explained:

" It will be difficult to keep up with the big cars, but they will have to come in for fuel, and if we can keep going then I think there is a good chance for H.W.M."

There was logic in what he said, particularly as our consumption tests indicated that a non-stop run would only drop the fuel level to around two gallons. It was worth trying and John Heath agreed with Stirling.

The tests are very necessary on circuits where the race distance is of full G.P. length. In case the surface is not quite level, I usually mark the position of the car wheels in front of the pits and then take a reading with a dipstick of the fuel in the tank. The driver goes off, covers either five or ten laps at race speeds, and the tank is then refilled to exactly the same level on the dipstick, using half gallon measures. We thus know exactly how much fuel the car will use under race conditions.

Nowadays I make a practice of taking a dipstick reading at the pits before the first practice run. This means that, if I am unable to carry out consumption tests because of pressure of work in other directions, I only have to take another dipstick reading at the end of the day to have some idea of fuel consumption.

Moss put up a magnificent performance on this dangerous Bremgarten circuit, in streaming rain and against the finest drivers in the world. He held on grimly to seventh place, ahead of all the 4½-litre Talbots, until the last lap, and then spun just before reaching the grandstand straight. He ran out of fuel at the same time and was just able to coast over the line. As he did so, Louis Chiron came up behind him in a supercharged Maserati to snatch seventh place.

People in the grandstands had been making bets throughout the race as to whether Moss would finish ahead of or behind the Frenchman, and there was tremendous excitement as Chiron caught and passed the H.W.M. However, quite apart from the spin, Moss had been driving for well over half the race at a great disadvantage.

A stone hit his windscreen, shattering it, and as he wore a visor the wind was getting underneath and practically lifting him out of the cockpit on occasions. He was driving past the pits, a flat-out section, with only one hand, whilst he held on his helmet and visor with the other. We thought he must be trying to make some new sort of signal and just could not make it out.

Abecassis retired with magneto trouble, one of several misfortunes during the season from this cause, and our continental tour was almost at an end before we got to the root of the trouble. We found that misalignment of the magneto drive with the camshaft was forcing the magneto to turn in the direction of its rotation and this had the effect of retarding the engine, which naturally became "woolly" and started missing.

Before the real trouble became apparent, we used to blame the actual magnetos, changing them on several occasions. We assumed that engine vibration had loosened the clip holding the magneto in position, and just tightened the clip, with the result that the same trouble occurred all over again.

I felt sorry for Abecassis. He seemed fated with H.W.M. Something of the nature of this magneto trouble put him out of the running in almost every race—although he did finish the course at Genoa—and I began to wonder whether he was perhaps harder on the cars than the other drivers. Engine vibration seemed to be the cause of most of his trouble, such as when a carburetter float chamber fell off or an exhaust pipe broke. It seemed feasible to assume that he drove harder than the others, perhaps using more revs. on occasions, and that the engine was more frequently at its peak of vibration. It was significant that other drivers did not have troubles that could be directly attributed to vibration.

After the Berne race there was the usual Monday conference to settle the accounts and make plans for our next engagement, at Aix les Bains. John Heath and I pooled our information at these sessions so that the cars could be improved in line with the drivers' comments to Heath and in line with my observations during the race.

After discussing technical matters, I pointed out to Heath that the daily allowance was not sufficient, and after a fairly lengthy argument it was agreed that the allowance for the mechanics would be increased by five shillings to twenty-seven shillings and sixpence and that my daily allowance would be raised by the same amount to thirty shillings.

I used to dread these interminable arguments about money and felt like a housewife who knows her husband is running the home on a shoestring but who, nevertheless, has to ask for a bigger allowance in order to exist.

At Aix les Bains I booked in at the Cosmopolitan and lost no time reassuring my Polish friend that there was plenty of cash to meet the bill! Richard Millani arrived from Bologna with the other car; the carburetters had been tuned and naturally Webers had made a very good job of it. They sent a detailed report with Millani, which enabled us to tune the other cars, and from then onwards our carburation troubles were negligible, although from time to time John Heath insisted on fiddling, not always with the best results.

Generally speaking, we had been basically wrong in our tuning of the Webers. With this type of carburetter it is a matter of mixing air with fuel in the orifice of the main jet before it finally reaches the choke and the induction manifold; this air/fuel ratio requires very careful adjustment. If it is not right, then naturally the whole performance of the car is upset. The slow running jets are not very important, but the pump jets, which are partly working with the main jets, have to be very accurately synchronized otherwise performance is hopeless.

When I think of the number of races where carburation on the H.W.M.s affected the result, it amazes me that we were able to achieve any measure of success at all. Just imagine Ferrari or Maserati going motor-racing with a thimbleful of knowledge about the carburetters!

In the first practice session at Aix les Bains, on the Friday following the Swiss G.P., Stirling put up second fastest time in his H.W.M. and then took John Heath's car out and recorded fastest time of the day. He seemed to think Heath's car was better than his own but so far as we were concerned there was no difference between them, apart from the fact that Stirling's own car had, even at this early stage of the season, been fairly well thrashed and had covered more racing miles than the others. It was perhaps more flexible in the transmission than Heath's car.

The fast time put up by Moss had the effect of getting Heath a better grid position and we could not resist pulling his leg and asking whether this elevation to the front row of the grid meant that he was going after the 1951 World Championship.

On Saturday, Rudi Fischer (the Swiss driver with ants in his pants) arrived and put up fastest lap of the day in his 2-litre Ferrari. The car went faster than any 2-litre I have ever seen, and in my opinion was remarkably quick and very similar in performance to the $2\frac{1}{2}$-litre car he had used the previous week-end.

It was interesting to compare Fischer's time with those of Raymond Sommer when he had driven a 2-litre Ferrari at Aix in 1950. I considered Sommer a faster and more capable driver than Fischer, and for the Swiss (even in the 1951 car) to put up times faster than Sommer was a remarkable performance.

On the small, twisty Aix circuit, driving skill is more important than engine capacity, unless of course one car is far more powerful than the others, and I could not see how it was possible for Fischer to go round so fast in a 2-litre car.

It was a good race, run in two heats and a final, and if Stirling had not hit a kerb in his heat I think he would have beaten Fischer in the final. As it was, he trounced Cortese on a Ferrari and Manzon and Trintignant on Gordinis to such good effect that he won the heat, but when the car came into the pits after the race I could see that the H.W.M. had a bent track rod and steering arm. There was only thirty minutes before the final, and no time to repair the damage, so John Heath suggested that Stirling drive his car.

" We can adjust the seat," said Heath, " and so far as I am concerned I will not race in the final."

We tore out the seat, made various adjustments to suit Stirling, and put it back in the car again. We could have saved ourselves the trouble because when we came to start Heath's H.W.M. we found that two of the gears had jammed during his heat. In the excitement Heath had forgotten to mention this.

With only five minutes to go things were desperate and it was Stirling who made up our minds.

" I'll use my own car," he shouted.

So he went on to the grid in a car that had a two-and-a-half inch toe out of the front wheels!

The flag dropped and Moss went away, hard on the heels of Fischer. And he stayed right behind the Swiss for the whole of the sixty odd mile race. Strangely enough the toe-out did not seem to affect the handling of the car at all, or the exuberance of Moss who gave Fischer no respite, but it was obvious that he would have gone just that little bit faster had the wheels been correctly aligned. As it was, he beat Simon (Gordini) and Cortese (Ferrari) and was only twelve seconds behind Fischer at the finish.

In the first heat Macklin's gearbox seized up in the same way as the gearbox on Heath's car. The preselectors used to arrive at two gears at the same time, due to some failure in the automatic adjusters, but I do not think this was the main cause of our troubles. Personally, I think the failure on most occasions could have been traced to insufficient lubrication.

Later in the year, when I was having to strip down two damaged gearboxes in order to make up one good one, I found that it was usually the planet gears and bushes that had seized on the shafts. It seemed to me that centrifugal force kept the gears running dry but it was not possible to do anything about it.

On the Monday after the Aix les Bains race it was decided that Frank Nagel would take the Moss car to Rome in the small Ford van, whilst the rest of the *equipe* went to Angouleme. Heath had agreed to race one car in Rome because the starting money was so good.

Angouleme is a true "round the houses" circuit, right in the middle of the town, and the enthusiasm of the townspeople is tremendous. The pits are actually opposite the Cathedral. Can you imagine a race round the streets of Chester or Bournemouth ?

At Angouleme the irrepressible Louis Chiron drove for us again, teaming up with Lance Macklin. Chiron is very much a business man and I could not help but admire his method of obtaining more starting money. He did not take out a car on the first day of practice (Macklin was the only H.W.M. driver and put up second fastest time to Fischer) and then informed the organizers that he would probably not go out on the second day either unless they arranged for him to have an increase in starting money.

" I am, after all, the fastest man on this circuit," he told them, " and I do not consider that you are paying me enough."

His ingenuity was matched by an official who told him that if he succeeded in making fastest time of the day, then extra starting money would be forthcoming. It was boiling hot and the sun's rays were blinding, but without more ado Chiron climbed into the cockpit of his H.W.M. and sallied forth on to the circuit. His problem was not other drivers and their practice times; it was the sun shining directly in his eyes on certain parts of the circuit.

One lap; two laps. I was astounded at his times. How was it possible to go so fast! The sun was so bright that I could not even see as far as the corner, let alone make out which way it turned. Nevertheless, he put up fastest time of the day and when the H.W.M. rolled to a stop I asked him how on earth he managed to go so fast, particularly in front of the pits.

" It is quite simple," he replied. " I watch the chimney pots at the end of the straight. They tell me when to turn. I have landmarks all round the circuit."

I was rather surprised by Chiron's insistence at Angouleme that I seal the car at night, and in fact on any occasion when I was going to be away from the H.W.M. for any length of time. He was not concerned about Macklin's car, only about his own, and provided seals, clips, and plenty of wire to seal the filler caps, bonnet, wheels, steering wheel—anything, in fact, that could be sabotaged.

Chiron said to me:

" It is no good, Alphons; I cannot sleep unless I know the car is protected. After all, they dope horses you know. Is there any reason why a car should not be, as you say in English, ' nobbled ' ? "

He checked the seals before going to bed and I realized that his views must be based on some experience or other during his long motor-racing career. He never told me about it and, in fact, used to say that motor-racing is one of the cleanest sports in the world but always added: " It is better to be safe than sorry."

I trusted people in those days and I still do. I have never sealed cars except with Louis Chiron. Even with the Moss Maserati in 1954, I only went to the extent of trying to get a garage on my own—unless I was with the "works" team—or else loading the car into the transporter, locking it securely and taking it back to the hotel car park.

After Chiron had delighted us all by recording fastest lap of the day and confounding the organizers, and Fischer as well, he insisted on richening up the mixture all through the range. He recalled that the carburation had been troublesome at Monza and, choosing to ignore my assurance that the Webers were now very much better, insisted on running the richer mixture. He maintained that it would be better on a short circuit like Angouleme and enable him to put up even faster times in the race than his practice ones.

He was wrong, and it was quite obvious as the car stood on the grid before the start that the engine was not behaving itself properly. He was on the front row with Macklin and, after he had run the engine and switched off, Chiron shook a fist at me in his typically theatrical manner.

I did not take much notice at first, until the public started booing me. This was too much; after all, he had told me to alter the carburetters. I shook my fist under his nose and the booing became louder and louder. Not to be outdone, Chiron pointed at me and shouted:

" Pas bon mechanicien. Pas bon mechanicien."

I managed to register my reply a few seconds before the first engine broke into life:

" Pas bon pilote. Pas bon pilote," I shouted.

With a huge grin on his face, Chiron settled down in the cockpit of the H.W.M. and all was forgiven.

When the flag dropped, the engine seemed to regain its form and he went away like an express train, hard on the heels of Macklin. On the first lap he was involved in an accident with a spinning car on a bend. The H.W.M. was not badly damaged but Chiron had to reverse before he could get going again and consequently lost several places. When the race finished, the first thing he said to me (one of the few English—or American —phrases he had learned) when he arrived at the pits was:

" That son of a bitch."—And then in French: " I am going to finish his motor-racing."

And he did just that. I understand that, through the F.I.A., Chiron succeeded in having the offending driver's competition licence taken away.

It was not too bad a Meeting for H.W.M. Macklin won his heat and came second to Fischer in the final, whilst Chiron made fastest lap in the final and came home sixth. Fischer had the experimental 2-litre car, under development for the new Formula, but if Moss had been at Angouleme I am sure he would have won.

The new lap record established by Chiron was significant, for he is a good driver though getting on in years, and I think it definitely proved the stability and safety of the H.W.M.s. It was, in fact, a very pleasant Meeting. There had been very little to do after the practice sessions and for the first time in weeks we had gone to bed at a normal hour.

We had also been able to check both cars thoroughly, without missing out any part of the procedure, and our preparation had not been hampered by having to rush some job through at the last moment.

Moss and John Heath had a rough time in Rome and Frank Nagel was certainly kept busy. During practice, the timing chain broke, bending the valves and damaging the camshaft bearings. How on earth Moss managed to finish fourth I just do not know, for he had magneto and gearbox trouble as well. After the race, Frank Nagel remained in Rome, having been told by John Heath that we would collect him on the way through the Italian capital to Naples—the venue for our next race.

We decided to break the journey to the south at Rocquebrun and to stay at the Diodato for a few days. It was, however, a tiring cross-country journey from Angouleme to Monte Carlo, and there is an entry in the diary : " Our A.E.C. bus did not like this journey very much. The roads were very narrow and we had an accident with a horse and cart near Barberieux. I was arrested and taken in a Black Maria to the police station."

This is how it happened: suddenly, on rounding a bend, we were confronted by two horse-drawn carts, one trying to overtake the other. In the split second before the crash I saw the horses rearing, and remember thinking that the shafts might come through the screen and hit Richard Curtis, who was sitting beside me. I pulled over to the right, hit the leading cart on the side, and the horses broke loose as one of the shafts snapped.

Millani jumped out of the bus and found one man in the ditch with the cart but there was no sign of his companion. I sat in the cab nursing a strained wrist as the force of the impact had wrenched the steering wheel out of my hands. As Millani was speaking to the Frenchman we suddenly heard moans from the other side of the bus, where the second Frenchman had landed, having been thrown clean over the top of our vehicle. He had broken his collar bone.

This was not all. A small 750 cc Renault had run into the back of the bus and more or less concertina-d itself. The driver had been relaxing and following us at a steady forty miles an hour, and our violent braking came as a rude awakening. We did not feel the impact because of what was going on at the front end.

Richard Millani walked to the nearest farmhouse and telephoned for the ambulance and police, and as soon as the gendarmes arrived I was politely but firmly placed under arrest in spite of my protests. I told them that we could not delay too long but it was explained that I should have to remain at the scene of the accident until details and measurements had been taken.

Eventually they allowed us to move the lorry but this was no easy task as the brakes were locked solid, and we could not budge it an inch until the clevis pins had been removed from the brake rods. We were then taken to the local police station and a solicitor called, who eventually established that the accident had not been our fault.

We were released after an hour and taken back to the lorry in the Black Maria. Our next move was to get it repaired and we drove the A.E.C. slowly to a garage. The front axle had been bent and the locating U-bolts broken, but after four hours of hard work the lorry was ready for the road again; having spent the night in the village of Barberieux we set off for Monte Carlo next morning.

It was my birthday the day after we arrived at the Diadato and Louis Chiron and his wife invited Richard Millani and me to join them at the famous La Turbie restaurant.

I sent a postcard to Sylvia: "Having a little party to-night. To-morrow we move on to Naples, then back to Berlin; then Rouen in France. I may be able to arrange a few days' holiday . . . . . so get your passport ready just in case!"

What a hope—as you will shortly see.

I don't think I am speaking out of turn when I describe Chiron and his wife as the happiest couple in the motor-racing game. They are very fond of each other and it is reassuring to spend an evening with them, reassuring because the sport has ruined so many marriages.

We noticed, when cleaning down Chiron's H.W.M. after his first drive for us at San Remo, that two very small hearts pierced by an arrow had been drawn on the side of the car. We had no idea who had put them there, and during my birthday dinner I asked Madame Chiron if she knew anything about them.

" It was I who put them on the car," she replied. " I do so every time I am at a Meeting where Louis is racing."

We had a wonderful meal, impeccably ordered by Chiron and impeccably served by the maitre d'hotel. The champagne corks popped frequently and as the other diners drifted away we stayed on, whilst Chiron reminisced about more than twenty-five years in the motor-racing game.

The Chef, a good friend of Chiron, joined us and was so flattered by our praise of his excellent cooking that he asked a favour in return.

" I would like to see one of these English racing cars that you call H.W.M. Is that possible ? "

Chiron looked at me.

" How about it, Alphons. Can we go back to Rocquebrun and get the bus ? "

I was feeling on top of the world and immediately agreed. He drove me down the coast road and in the early hours of the morning a party of late night revellers outside the Casino stared in amazement as the bus passed them on the way to La Turbie.

The Chef was, of course, delighted when I backed one of the cars down the ramp and invited him to sit in the cockpit. As he tried the seating position and controls, I warmed to my task and explained various technical details. He warmed to *his* task and the champagne corks popped more frequently, until eventually Chiron and I were trying to open a bottle of champagne with a plug spanner, whilst the Chef struggled valiantly with a corkscrew to make some impression on a sparking plug. I still have some flashlight photographs of that very enjoyable party, which eventually finished at daybreak.

CHAPTER 14

NO PEACE FOR THE WICKED

Naples and the antics of Schell—1300 miles in 3 days—
Airlift to Berlin—I frighten myself at Avus—
The H.W.M.s are outclassed—" Red tape " at Rouen—
Mediocre performance at Mettet—I cross swords with John Heath—
Assorted troubles at Zandvoort.

When we arrived at the garage on the outskirts of Rome, where Moss, H.W.M. had been prepared, there was a familiar figure at the petrol pumps' serving an Italian in a Lancia. It was Frank, more or less in pawn at the garage until we arrived, and he was naturally delighted to see us.

" I am absolutely flat broke," were his first words when we pulled up.

It transpired that Heath had left him very little money, being under the impression that we were on the way, and not knowing that we planned to stop at Rocquebrun.

After a day or so of waiting, Frank realized there must have been a hold up and had to admit to the garage proprietor that he had no money to pay the accounts. The Italian was very reasonable and told Frank the settlement could wait until we arrived, and that if he would like to work on the pumps and do some servicing there would be a small wage. It was the same old story. We bought Frank out of pawn, which was quite an expensive business, as he had been sleeping, eating and living at the cafe attached to the garage—all on credit.

The Naples race was a Formula 2 event and, as Moss and Macklin were driving at Le Mans, John Heath engaged two drivers new to the H.W.M. *equipe* ; the Franco-American, Harry Schell, and a Neapolitan sports car driver, Rocco.

We had a lot of fun with the Italian during practice for he could not speak English, neither could we speak Italian. We tried to understand what he was saying about the car, listened attentively when he complained, and regarded his gesticulations with solemn respect—but we had no idea what he was trying to tell us. So we just continued looking after the car in our own way.

There is an entry in my diary : " Rocco is complaining about something but who can understand what he says. Anyhow why worry. He is not fast enough to worry."

Harry Schell is a wonderful character. This was the first time he had driven in the H.W.M. team, although I had met and helped him at Angouleme, where he and his mechanic stripped down a J.A.P. engine and then could not retime it properly.

It is great fun to go out with him on a party. He impresses everyone, from the cloakroom attendant to the maitre d'hotel, for when Schell arrives anywhere it is as though a Crown Prince at least has deigned to grace the establishment with his presence. To the local people he appears as a man of considerable wealth.

He is a great practical joker and will walk into a restaurant and demand to see the Chef. The proprietor, convinced that Schell is either Royalty, a Hollywood film star travelling incognito, or some important person connected with the Shell Oil Company, produces the Chef as quickly as a conjuror produces a rabbit out of a hat. Schell then says:

" I would like to see your kitchen and satisfy myself that it is clean."

In the kitchen he will taste the soup and, having spoken in glowing terms of the Chef's abilities, then retires to the dining room where he invariably gets extremely good service.

He accepts things as they come and is just as much at home in a smoke-filled night club as at a cocktail party in the George Cinq in Paris. Good humoured and with a pleasant personality, he is very similar in many ways to Louis Chiron and likes to put on the odd act from time to time for the benefit of the public.

He goes down very well indeed with the fair sex and the odds are that Harry Schell will have the prettiest girl at any party. Without mentioning names, I know of several famous drivers who reckon they only have a fifty-fifty chance of coming away from a party with their companion, if she happens to be particularly attractive and Harry Schell is there on his own.

It was great fun having him with us at Naples. He drove during the race in a most spectacular manner, almost bouncing out of the cockpit as he changed gear. Every time he made a change, not being used to the pre-selector lever on the steering column, he lifted himself off the seat as though forcing the lever into place and then slid back again with a mighty bounce as he released the foot pedal.

This went on for the whole race and the antics of Schell with the gear lever resulted in his shirt rising higher and higher until it was screwed up round his neck like a handkerchief. He came roaring over the line, second to Ascari, naked from the waist upwards, having driven a very sound race and beaten Cortese (Ferrari) for second place.

The H.W.M.s were really doing very well at this time. There was never any question of the cars trailing round at the back end of the field. Either we retired, or finished well up; there were no half measures. We either covered ourselves in glory or went despondently back to the garage with cars that had been put out by silly, petty breakages. No one could describe us as a team that ran reliably throughout the season, and the H.W.M. motto in 1951 could easily have been " Flat out or bust."

Both Heath and Rocco retired at Naples. The Italian had gearbox trouble and we put this down to the fact that he had not previously driven a car with a preselector box. He came into the pits during the race, gesticulating wildly in the general direction of the wheels.

We jacked up the car and made a quick check of the tyres but that was not what he wanted. However, as none of us could understand exactly what he did want, I eventually let the car down off the jacks, slapped him on the back and shouted in his ear one of the few Italian words I knew at the time—"Avanti."

Off went Rocco like a scalded cat and tore round for another ten or fifteen laps, obviously enjoying himself when he did not have to cope with the intricacies of the preselector box, and then retired. I cannot remember anything being the matter with the car, so we just put it down as "Dislike of gearbox," although naturally this was not given as the reason to the Press.

After Heath had retired, we discussed with him the best way of getting to Avus, in the Western Sector of Berlin, for the Avus G.P., and it was decided that we would load up two of the cars in the bus immediately after the race and set off as soon as possible for Rome, where it would be necessary for me to call at the German Consulate for visas.

I was delighted to learn that we were to fly into Berlin via the famous airlift. The last thing I wanted to do, as an ex-Polish Army man and only a naturalized Englishman, was fall foul of the Russians. We were assured by the race organizers that all we had to do was get the cars to Brunswick and the British Army would do the rest.

John Heath told Richard Millani and Richard Curtis to take one of the cars back to England in the small Ford van whilst Frank, Steve and myself took the bus to Berlin. As there was a fairly considerable mileage to cover in a short time—thirteen hundred miles in three days—we decided to have a really good meal after the race, with some nostalgic Neapolitan music thrown in for good measure.

Steve Watson had already found a charming and romantic restaurant in Naples and the three of us went along there. I shall always remember the musical trio that moved in a slow and melancholy fashion around the tables. It might almost have been romantic had not Steve been on one side of me and Frank on the other.

There were two singers supported by a violinist who accompanied the romantic songs of Naples in a bored, leisurely fashion. In fact, I was sure he was asleep on his feet and wondered idly to myself whether a pin would perhaps help him to take more apparent interest in the proceedings.

The violinist woke up when the singing stopped for the simple reason that his hat was the one handed round for the grubby lire notes. Then he went to sleep again and it seemed as though he was musing to himself: "Hurry up and finish the song so that I can pass the hat round again."

It was well after midnight when we left Naples and eight hours later we were in Rome. As soon as the city stirred, I hailed a taxi and told the driver to take me to the German Consulate. It was early but I have never seen such a queue, not even in Oxford Street during the rush hour.

A quick calculation showed that the queue, several hundred people long, was moving at the rate of one visa application every five minutes or so, and I could see that unless I did something desperate we should be in Rome for hours, perhaps days.

Naturally, I speak German and, making my way round to the rear of the Consulate, was able to persuade a porter to take me inside and introduce me to the Consul's secretary. There was much clicking of heels (I was in the Polish White Lancers for my National Service) and stiff, jerky bows from the waist in typical German fashion. After a formal handshake I was taken to the office and within half-an-hour there was a set of visas for all of us.

I am convinced that my heel clicking act did the trick, particularly as I introduced myself as the Renabteilung Fuehrer (which translated means Racing Leader) and this obviously impressed the Consul's secretary. I think, too, that the Germans welcomed the opportunity of dealing with someone who could click and bow in the best German fashion, in preference to the long queue of Italians outside, none of whom I am sure could either click or bow. Such is life. I never thought I would be favourably treated by the Germans.

We left Rome after lunch, having planned a fast run to Brunswick, and there was no question of stopping for food or sleep. We bought bread, cold meats and Coca Cola and made our own sandwiches to eat en route. As the bus could only manage a top speed of thirty-two miles an hour, I decided that all three of us would take turns, and that we would drive flat out and change every three hours. It was organized in such a way that we all had equal spells of driving, map reading and sleeping. There were two hammocks suspended inside the bus and it was no easy matter to get to sleep whilst the bus was rolling about all over the place. We reckoned to cover, on the flat sections, something like one hundred and ten kilometres in three hours, and the old crate was driven to the limit all the time.

Our route took us through Grosetto, Livorno and over the Apennines, which Stirling crossed in the incredibly short time of just over an hour in the 1955 Mille Miglia, the race he won for Mercedes. It took us about four hours but nevertheless we were pressing on at a fair rate.

We did not bother to stop for a change of drivers. On a straight stretch of road the relief just climbed from the passenger seat into the driving seat whilst the driver slid out of the seat and went straight into one of the hammocks. The man who had been sleeping was woken up so that he could navigate.

From Bologna, we cut back along the Via Emilia to Modena and then headed northwards again for Verona, Trento, Bolzano and the Brenner Pass. Just before reaching the Brenner I heard strange noises (perhaps I should say stranger than usual) coming from the back axle, but there was not much we could do about it except nurse the bus over the Pass and make for the Munich Autobahn. Once on the comparatively flat, dual carriageway road we could proceed at a leisurely pace, without straining the axle too much, in the hope of reaching Brunswick before having to do anything about it.

However, the bus only managed to get as far as Nurnberg. On the outskirts of the German city the back axle became so noisy, and the speed of the bus was slowed down so much, that we had no alternative but to stop and change the axle. Fortunately, we had a spare worm and drive, which I had been meaning to fit for some weeks as its ratio would give us a higher cruising speed—in the region of 40 m.p.h.

We pulled up at a large commercial lorry workshops and I jumped out and asked the German foreman if he would help change the axle. He was most co-operative and, with the assistance of some of his mechanics, the job was finished in a little over four hours. This was no mean achievement as none of us had ever stripped down an A.E.C. bus back axle and none of the Germans could speak English.

Undoubtedly the Germans excel when really up against it. They like taking on tough jobs at short notice and then delighting themselves and surprising everyone else by finishing the work in half the normal time.

From Nurnberg, we continued our journey on Wednesday to Brunswick, all of us tired out by now, having driven night and day since leaving Rome on Monday. It meant driving really hard for unless we reached Brunswick in time to catch the special train laid on for our cars and those of other competitors there would be no H.W.M.s at Avus. So we pushed on, the old bus fairly bowling along the boring, featureless Autobahn at its new maximum of 40 m.p.h.

We arrived at Brunswick Railway Station at about 8 a.m., with very little time in hand, having completed the journey from Rome in 65 hours The cars and spares were unloaded from the bus and manhandled on to one of the platforms. The organization for getting these trains through to Berlin was most efficient, and the German railway employees dealt with the H.W.M.s and the marked spares as though they had been handling racing cars all their lives.

The Germans told us to leave everything on the platform and get to Hanover as quickly as possible where an Air Lift plane would take us to Berlin. I must admit to a pang or two of conscience as I drove the empty bus away from Brunswick Station. After all, what I had left on the platform represented a considerable amount of starting money at Avus and I shuddered when I thought of what John Heath would say if the cars failed to arrive.

The bus remained in a Brunswick Garage so that it could be thoroughly checked, for the A.E.C. had covered some 3,500 miles since I had driven it away from the H.W.M. works at Walton eight weeks previously. We took a taxi to Hanover and in no time at all were flying down the Air Lift Corridor in a dilapidated and disturbingly noisy Dakota, which nevertheless got us safely to Berlin.

Officials and guides of the organizing club met us at the airport. Accommodation had been arranged at the hotel Savigny where I found that a suite of rooms had been reserved for me, including a bathroom and even an office. I suppose the Germans were under the impression that the H.W.M.s were the British equivalent of Mercedes-Benz and indeed, as Chief Mechanic, I was treated very civilly.

The rather superior receptionist looked at me oddly when I told him I had no luggage with the exception of my small suitcase. I felt rather like a visitor from the provinces arriving at the Dorchester with pyjamas, a toothbrush and nothing else.

I ate very little breakfast next morning and don't mind admitting I was in a very worried state of mind. What if the cars had not arrived? What if the Russians had off-loaded them at the frontier ?

Soon after 10 a.m., fearing the worst, I set off for the circuit and the adjoining Exhibition Halls where competing cars are garaged in special cubicles. To my relief, in one of them we found the two H.W.M.s complete with all spares.

Nothing had been mislaid, nothing damaged. Someone had worked very hard for in less than twenty-four hours the H.W.M.s had crossed the frontier by train, been unloaded at Berlin Station, and taken out to the

Exhibition Halls.   There they were in the cubicle, in perfect order, and everything as we had left it on the station platform.

The practice session was in the afternoon so that we had the morning to prepare the cars.   There was no need to motor round the Avus circuit to find the most suitable axle ratio for it is not, strictly speaking, a road circuit but more in the nature of a track, the fastest in the world.

Avus is a dual carriageway, used by main road traffic in the ordinary course of events.   At one end is an acute hairpin and at the other the cars soar up on to a forty-foot high banking which is, of course, not part of the ordinary road system.   The only thing we could do was fit 3.7 axle ratios, the highest we carried, but I knew they would not be high enough and that we were going to be well and truly out-classed from the start.

After his first practice run, Stirling complained about a flat spot.

" There is just no power over 5,200," he told me.

That started an argument.

" Look," I said to him, " a few days ago Harry Schell drove this car like a bomb in Naples and wasn't much slower than Ascari.   What do you want me to do ?   Take a car to pieces that is O.K. ? "

One thing led to another and eventually Stirling got really annoyed.

" If only you could drive yourself," he said.   " The trouble is you are afraid."

That was too much.   I snatched the crash helmet out of his hand and climbed angrily into the cockpit of the H.W.M.

Off I went.   It was not too bad starting away from the pits and accelerating along the straight towards the hairpin; in fact, I was beginning to enjoy myself.

On the back leg of the course, after leaving the hairpin, I put my foot down.   The needle of the rev. counter crept round tantalizingly slowly—4,800 .... 5,000 .... 5,100.   The wind took my beath away and, gritting my teeth, I pushed the needle round to 5,200.

From then onwards I stopped looking at the rev. counter, for it was as much as I could do to keep the car on a strip of concrete that, all at once, had suddenly become much too narrow for my liking.   There was also a banking not very far ahead.   I forget all about the flat spot and whether or not it was possible to exceed 5,200.

And then the car was on the banking and I was terrified.   Upwards and outwards; it was as though the H.W.M. was on the end of a long chain and someone was swinging it with every intention of letting go.   I felt as helpless as an unwilling passenger on a scenic railway approaching a banked curve.

Suddenly it was over and I found myself coming off the banking and running down to the straight and pits.   I smartly put on the anchors, pulled up and got out of the car.   White as a sheet I leaned against a rear tyre.

" I quite agree with you," I said to Stirling, who was standing there smiling, " the bloody car is no good at all."

Not wishing to discuss the matter further, I whipped up the bonnet and with rather unsteady hands started to strip down the Webers.   I had to do something whilst I was recovering from my sortie round the Avus. I certainly scared myself that day and made a mental resolution that next time Stirling complained about a flat spot, I would not question it—not by trying the car, at any rate.

In the Saturday practice session Macklin succeeded in putting up a faster time than Moss, by using the slip-stream technique and tacking himself on to one of the German cars which were cracking along down the straight at nearly 160 m.p.h. Moss did not seem quite himself for, if anyone can slip-stream, he can. In addition there was magneto trouble with his car.

It was a disastrous race. As soon as the flag dropped it seemed to me that the engine on Moss' car was over-revved, and I told myself that probably the valves had already been bent. I was right. On the third lap the engine just disintegrated when the crankshaft broke and split the crankcase in half. There was very little for us to collect after the race.

Stirling told me frankly that he had scared himself stiff (that made two of us on the same car, but for different reasons, in two days) when the engine blew up for the H.W.M. was travelling at maximum speed.

" It felt to me as though the whole car was exploding," said Stirling.

He was certainly shaken.

Macklin only lasted fifteen laps and then his engine blew up as well, and that was the end of the H.W.M. challenge. It must have been a great disappointment to all the British servicemen who had come out to Avus to see us.

After the race, when we went to collect what was left of the cars, I heard some of the German spectators talking about us.

" Look at them," said one youngster, " they are still smiling and yet their cars put up a disgraceful performance. Cannot understand these British."

It was not unexpected, for a German is never prepared to believe that the British accept disaster so complacently. I clapped Frank Nagel on the back.

" Laugh, you ' so and so,' " I said. " That will annoy them even more."

In my opinion we should never have entered the H.W.M.s at Avus and risked blowing them up. It is a track only suitable for streamliners and it was just downright silly to race the H.W.M.s there, cars that had been designed and built for a different type of circuit. I was furious for we had driven the bus non-stop from Rome, with very little sleep or food, and now we had a couple of wrecked engines on our hands. We had worn ourselves out for nothing.

Is it any wonder that I wrote to my wife after the race: "We have blown two of our cars to pieces so a lot of hard work is in store because we are racing in Rouen a week from to-day. I am sincerely sick of motor racing and I shall be glad to retire from it so am only looking forward to the time when my season will finish. Forgive this scrawl but I can hardly see. It is now 1 a.m. and we have just finished putting the cars and stores away in the cubicle in the Exhibition Hall. The Germans will collect the cars from there and put them on a sealed train which will cross the border to-morrow."

On Tuesday morning we left Berlin for Hanover and Brunswick. I had, of course, been in touch with John Heath at Walton, who was busy rebuilding the car which Richard Millani had taken back from Naples, and also preparing the fourth H.W.M.—our reserve car.

The idea was for the three of us in the bus to get to Rouen as quickly as possible and to strip down one of the Avus cars so it could take a spare engine that Richard Millani was bringing from Walton, together with the Naples car.

Our system of keeping a car in reserve, planned at the beginning of the season, was paying dividends and it was a wise decision John Heath made in sending a car back from Naples for a complete overhaul. Undoubtedly, had the Avus misfortune occurred during the previous season, there would have been no H.W.M. entry at a race only a few days afterwards. As it was, we had to work very hard indeed between the time of our arrival in Rouen, on Thursday morning, and the first practice session on Friday.

Soon after we reached Rouen, Richard Millani and Richard Curtis arrived with the Naples car and spare engine. Millani left for Dunkirk again almost immediately with one of the two wrecked Avus cars, whilst the fourth team car was sent off from Walton. It was arranged that Millani would cross on the Night Ferry, hand over the Avus car and collect the other H.W.M. He arrived back in Rouen soon after lunch on Friday and I then found that the car he had collected still had to be run-in.

I managed to put in about thirty laps on the fast Essarts circuit with the brand new H.W.M., running it in on roads occupied by ordinary traffic, and it was decided that Giraud Cabantous would drive the car in the race. He was warned to take it very easy, as the H.W.M. was by no means fully run-in.

Stirling had the car that had been sent back to Walton from Naples and hurriedly checked over. It was mobile but ropey, for John Heath had not had very much time to do anything with it.

Nevertheless, even in a ropey car, Moss was more than a match for strong Ferrari and Gordini opposition, and held the lead for quite a while. He might well have won this race on the Essarts—very much a drivers' circuit—if he had not been disqualified.

On the morning of the race we were told by the organizers that, following a pit stop for any reason, the car would have to be started on a mechanical starter and not pushed. We at once asked for permission to keep the engine running during a refuelling stop, as it was obvious we would have to make one, but the organizers would not agree. They were adamant. The engine would have to be switched off, in spite of the fact that we had stub exhausts and there was no danger of fire.

The race was as good as lost before it started and Moss was in a very angry mood on the grid. I have rarely seen him so angry—or angry at all for that matter on the starting line—but how would you feel, as a driver, to be told that irrespective of how hard you drive you cannot win because, when you make a pit stop for refuelling, the engine will have to be switched off and there is no means of starting it again.

Nevertheless, Moss was far from beaten and during the early stages of the race sailed easily away from the opposition. Eventually, the H.W.M. came into the pits. The engine was switched off and the car refuelled in accordance with the regulations.

Then, with the mechanics standing there helpless, Moss pushed the car himself to get it started. It was a stout effort for it meant pushing the H.W.M. slightly uphill and also overcoming the resistance from the pre-selector box. When people say that physical fitness does not matter, I tell them this story.

I felt like punching someone on the nose. How ridiculous to insist on the cars being mechanically started in the pit area. It is a highly dangerous method. Quite frankly, in the heat of the race and whether it is Stirling Moss or anyone else, I have not enough confidence to stand in front of a car and start it mechanically. There is no danger in pushing from the rear. After all, if the car starts suddenly, all that happens is that you fall flat on your nose.

With a few well chosen words directed at marshals in the pit area, who were shouting, " It is forbidden," Moss rejoined the race, but not for long. After twenty-seven laps he was forced to retire with the old bugbear of gearbox trouble. Cabantous was unfortunate and broke the back axle on the brand new H.W.M. He was driving very nicely, not taking any chances and nursing the engine, but I don't think he was happy with the preselector box.

Marzotto, in a Ferrari, was the winner and at the prizegiving the organizers gave a bigger prize to the second place man, the Frenchman, Trintignant. To add insult to injury it was announced after the race by the disgruntled organizers that they were going to strip down the Ferrari and check its capacity. Incidentally it was 2 litres.

Is it any wonder that, as soon as the prizegiving speeches started, the Italians, together with the entire H.W.M. *equipe*, stalked out of the room in protest.

We had to do some more chopping and changing to get a team of four cars ready for the Mettet race, a week after Rouen, to be driven by Moss, Macklin, Heath and the Belgian racing motor-cyclist, Roger Laurent.

I sent Richard Millani to Dunkirk with one of the cars in the small van whilst, at Walton, John Heath finished the preparation of two cars, so that our Base Mechanic, Frank Webb, could bring them out to Mettet and then stay with the *equipe* to give me some assistance.

By the time I arrived in Mettet, Webb was there and Richard Millani as well, having handed his H.W.M. over to the Walton transporter at Dover and returned on the boat with Webb.

On the second day of practice, we had some gearbox trouble on Stirling's car. The other three H.W.M.s behaved themselves quite well and, after giving all four cars the pre-race check-over, I told the rest of the boys to get some sleep. I intended to take the Moss gearbox to pieces and it was more or less a one-man job. However, young Frank Nagel insisted on staying up with me and we set to work.

I had no alternative but to try to assemble one serviceable gearbox out of the Moss gearbox and bits and pieces from other preselector boxes. At this stage of the season I did not have one complete spare gearbox. We had experienced so much trouble that all I had was odds and ends.

It is a complicated business, assembling a preselector, and we worked all night, making up one gearbox from two cannibalized ones. We were absolutely dog tired and I remember sending Frank Nagel for some spring washers and wondering vaguely to myself why he did not return after more than an hour.

Next morning there was still no sign of Frank. I wandered round the garage calling out for him and even looked in the toilet and offices. It seemed that he had disappeared into thin air and then, as I was clearing up, I found him in the back of the lorry, fast asleep on the floor, using the box of spring washers as a pillow. He was absolutely dead to the world.

I shall remember Mettet for another reason. Lance Macklin had with him a strikingly beautiful model from Paris, a blonde. She was very keen on motor racing and asked me, during practice:

" Why is Moss faster than Macklin ? Is it because Lance is a bad driver ? "

It was rather difficult for me to explain that Moss was the better of the two, because I did not want to upset her, so I said that John Heath always gave Moss a better car.

I did not see her again after the Mettet race, which was a pity because she was not like some of the empty-headed nuisances who straggle from circuit to circuit, knowing nothing and caring less. So many of these motor racing popsies attend Meetings under false pretences, basking in the reflected glory of a driver but frequently quite unconcerned about the possibility of him being injured.

Still on the same subject, it is my opinion that a driver should not have his wife or fiancée watching him at a Meeting. Chiron's wife disappeared when Louis was engaged in the serious business of driving and would not dream of remaining in the pit area. This is as it should be.

It was not a very interesting or successful race for H.W.M. Admittedly we had all four cars on the starting line but none of them was running really well. After several pit stops, Stirling finished fourth. Try as he might, he could not improve his position during the race, although he was running second for a few laps in the early stages. Moss' car had put in some really hard racing miles since the beginning of the season and sounded very woolly indeed towards the end of the race. The other H.W.M.'s finished well down the field.

The next race, a major Formula 1 Grand Prix, was at Zandvoort and John Heath invited a Dutch driver to make up the team. We did not want to give the Dutchman our best car, so after the Mettet race the engine was taken out of Heath's H.W.M. and put in the Moss car. The engine that Stirling had been using went into Heath's car for the Dutchman. We also split the team, Frank Webb and Steve Watson taking one car to Sables d'Olonne with Giraud Cabantous.

Apart from changing over the engines, there was a lot of work to do on Macklin's car. I found that the magneto drives were not properly aligned, which could have accounted for ignition trouble in the race. I was sure this misalignment was to blame because the locking pins used to break so frequently. I decided to use $\frac{3}{16}''$ pins of silver steel on the magneto as an added safeguard.

It meant working all Monday night and I was worn out by Tuesday morning. I had forgotten just how long since I had spent a full night in bed. Over and above my keenness for motor racing, I was beginning to wonder why on earth I had ever joined H.W.M. in the first place.

I had been given too much responsibility. It was a lot of work to look after four racing cars and make sure they were not only as fast as they could be when they went to the starting line, but one hundred per cent. safe as well.

On Thursday we left Mettet for Zandvoort. Richard Millani and Frank Nagel took the bus with two of the cars whilst I drove John Heath's H.W.M. There was no room for it in the bus, and Webb had taken the trailer with him to Sables d'Olonne.

I had a frightening experience that could have had serious consequences. Soon after leaving the hotel and before I was clear of the town, somebody pulled in front of the H.W.M. and waved me down. A letter had just arrived from my wife and the Hotel Manager thought I would like to have it before leaving Mettet. Naturally I was very pleased, and switched off the engine whilst I read the letter.

When the time came to move off, I suddenly realized there was no one to give me a start. With the picture still in my mind of Moss pushing the H.W.M. at Rouen, I decided to attempt a similar feat. The gradient was a downhill one and I was sure that if Stirling could push an H.W.M. uphill and start it, then I could do the same downhill.

All I succeeded in doing was to run myself over! After a few yards the engine fired but I did not get into the cockpit quickly enough, and the rear wheel somehow or other ran over my right leg and pulled me backwards into the road.

I could easily have broken my leg, but I had very little time in which to sympathize with myself, for there was the H.W.M. freewheeling down the hill. I covered ten yards remarkably quickly, scrambled into the cockpit, started the engine again and away we went.

It was great fun driving a racing car, with no number plates and a very throaty exhaust note, on the public roads. The officials at the frontier were most enthusiastic about the H.W.M. and insisted on giving me a push-start after my passport had been stamped.

In Holland I amused myself at crossroads, seeing how close I could get to the Dutch policemen on traffic duty, most of whom took it in very good part. Maybe I'll try it in England one day, on the way to Silverstone or Goodwood.

There was one exception, a rather rotund policeman, who abandoned ship, as it were; he vacated his little platform in the middle of the road and made for some shrubbery.

We had more trouble in Zandvoort. Stirling was not at all happy with his car, which was oiling up, and told me bluntly that it was not quick enough. On referring back to my race records for Genoa and Monza I came to the conclusion that the only way to stop the plugs oiling up was to run the engine hot, by using harder plugs and weaker jets. After all, with eighty per cent. alcohol, there should not be much danger of the engine over-heating to the extent of burning the pistons. I had a word with the famous Italian ex-racing mechanic and driver, Giulio Ramponi, about this and he agreed with me.

It was necessary to use subterfuge for John Heath would never agree to a change of plugs, so I had a word with Moss and Macklin on the quiet and we decided to experiment without saying anything to Heath. I weakened the jets, put in 51 plugs, took several "cuts" and showed the results to Ramponi who agreed that it should be perfectly safe.

These mixture cuts have to be taken in close co-operation with the driver, who allows the engine to labour up to its peak. If the peak is 6000 revs. the driver takes her right up there and then switches off and disengages the clutch. Then he freewheels to the pits and we have a look at the plug readings; they tell us whether the mixture is right or wrong. Ramponi is, of course, an expert on such readings and confirmed that we had not only succeeded in keeping the plugs clean but had gained some speed as well. Naturally, Stirling and Lance were delighted.

On the second day of practice, it just so happened that John Heath spent most of the time in the pits and very near the cars. So I carried the 51 plugs in my pocket whilst I warmed the engines on the soft ones. Suddenly Heath came up behind me.

" Which plugs are you putting in ? " he asked.

I decided to try to bluff it out with a white lie.

" 49's," I replied.

John Heath looked at me.

" They are the plugs you were using yesterday ? " he questioned.

I nodded.

" Let me have a look," he said, and at once spotted that they were 51.

" You are a liar," Heath said.

" Well," I replied, " that may be so, but it seems to me I can only get the best results for H.W.M. on occasions such as this by not consulting you. You have never been right about the plugs and we have ' lost ' them on many occasions, whereas I have found that harder plugs are best; and now an expert—Ramponi—confirms it! I am only trying to do what is best for H.W.M."

" You are not going to tell me what to do with my own cars," replied John Heath. " I want 49's and the same jet settings we had previously."

I was furious.

" As long as I am your Chief Mechanic and responsible for these cars —and until you dismiss me, which you can do here and now if you want— I shall look after the plugs and jets the way I want."

We were soon engaged in a slanging match, and it was John Heath, admittedly calmer than I was, who asked me quietly to continue the discussion behind the pits. I was very angry, fed up to the teeth with the damned cars and tired out as well!

However, I saw his point of view when we were on our own. He pointed out that, whatever my personal views, he was the patron.

" There must be discipline," said Heath.

I knew he was absolutely right and immediately set about altering the carburetter settings on the four cars. It was a pity because, although John Heath would not admit it, the cars definitely went better on the harder plugs and both Stirling and Lance reckoned they were getting an extra 100 revs. with the 51's.

Then we had trouble with the Dutchman. He bluntly refused to drive his H.W.M., maintaining that we had given him the worst car. After all the trouble we had taken, painting the car in the Dutch colours of orange, we were all well and truly fed up with this latest development. The Dutchman was quite right. We had given him the worst car but to prove it was not as bad as he made out we asked Stirling to do a few laps.

Moss fairly streaked round the circuit, only half-a-second slower than the best time in his own car, and ten seconds faster than the Dutchman. It did not make any difference. The Dutchman bluntly refused to drive, so John Heath had to take his place.

This left three H.W.M.s in the race—Moss, Macklin and Heath. As it was the full Grand Prix distance we had to arrange fuelling stops, but it was vitally important that we cut their duration to the absolute minimum. This was one way we could perhaps gain a few seconds against the $4\frac{1}{2}$-litre unsupercharged Talbots.

During the race, even though I say so myself, our pit stops were very good. I used the system I had seen the Alfa-Romeo *equipe* use at Berne in 1948, and called in the slowest car first so that we could more or less practise on it and iron out any errors in pit control by the time the fastest car came in for fuel.

We brought John Heath in first and managed to put in fifteen gallons of fuel and check tyres and oil in twenty-six seconds. Then we refuelled Lance Macklin and knocked two seconds off our time. Finally, two laps later, we brought in Moss and handled his pit stop in twenty-two seconds.

I do not consider these times at all bad, times incidentally taken by the official timekeepers and not by us, and I cannot understand why the pitwork of the H.W.M.s at Zandvoort was criticized so harshly in one of the motoring journals after the race. Apparently the pit was disorganized and we were at sizes and sevens. It was a harsh criticism because we did not use pressure fuelling, just churns and a funnel, and I was controlling the signals to the other cars as well as supervising the actual refuelling in the pits.

I wonder whether the criticism was levelled at us more for an incident later in the race. Moss overtook the Talbot of Etancelin and almost immediately afterwards started misfiring. It seemed to me that the magneto had come adrift again because I could see no reason why he should have suddenly oiled up.

On the next lap the car came into the pit and, as I knew Stirling would want reassuring as usual about No. 3 cylinder (he always attributed misfiring to this cause but I was never able to confirm it), I whipped off the bonnet and started unscrewing No. 3 plug whilst at the same time looking at the magneto.

Sure enough the magneto had moved, but there was no sense in rushing the job as I could see the bracket had broken. I just changed the plug— which had the effect of reassuring Stirling—and he naturally wanted to get away again, not knowing anything about the magneto.

" Let's go," he shouted.

At the same time I called to Frank Nagel—" Put the bonnet on." I was afraid we might be disqualified if the H.W.M. went away from the pits without it.

However, when Frank took off the bonnet he had put it down on the track side of the white line marking the pit area, and a friendly official (who could have disqualified us for this breach of the rules) lifted it and put it on the correct side of the line. Stirling could not wait whilst the bonnet was located and went off again without it. He managed to finish third, in spite of the fact that the car was not running on more than three-and-a-half cylinders.

Heath came home sixth but Macklin had to retire when the fuel pump on his H.W.M. threw a fit of temperament and refused to pick up the last few gallons in the tank. Those fuel pumps caused a lot of trouble. They were not self-priming and if there was a surge in the tank—even with as much as four gallons of fuel—the pump would not pick up.

For some reason or other Stirling never had fuel pump trouble but it certainly chased everyone else. Stirling's gremlin—or so he thought—was the piston ring on No. 3 cylinder. Every time he came into the pits I started unscrewing No. 3 plug, even if I knew the trouble was something entirely different. I found that it was good for the driver's morale to change No. 3 plug as a matter of course, although it probably made no difference to the performance at all.

This matter of pit stops is not an easy one. What time is there to decide exactly what is wrong with a car and then put it right ? Maybe you are in the lead, only ten seconds ahead of the next man. A pit stop drops sixty seconds immediately—or half-a-minute at least—without anything having been changed. Just looking takes that time. It is not possible to take things calmly, decide what is wrong and then put it right. It can mean losing a race.

In the official works teams, when there is trouble in the nature of mis-firing, they do not bother to touch the car. It is retired, unless the driver himself knows exactly what is wrong and it can be put right at once. On the other hand, if the No. 1 has trouble and it cannot be quickly traced, another car is called in and the drivers swopped. Naturally, we could not work to such a system with H.W.M. If we had called in Macklin at Zandvoort I doubt very much whether we would have finished third. It was only five laps from the end of the race, and I personally think Stirling should have carried on, with the engine missing ; with any luck we might have finished second.

CHAPTER 15

THE LAST LAP WITH H.W.M.

A race against time—Complications at Albi, and at Erlen too—
Back home again—Rebuilding the team cars—
Moss beats the handicap at Dundrod, the first outright victory for H.W.M.—
My first visit to Modena—New plans for H.W.M.—I resign.

The question of finance reared its ugly head again after the Zandvoort race. It was decided, when we had our usual Monday conference, that H.W.M.'s would compete at Freiburg and Albi. As the Albi race was not until August 5th, John Heath asked whether I would prefer to take the whole *equipe* back to England or stay on the Continent. A quick calculation showed that the fares for all the mechanics would cost more than staying on the Continent, so I promised John Heath that we would find somewhere cheap and at the same time give ourselves a few days' much needed rest.

We eventually found a little village in the Black Forest, about fifty miles from Freiburg, and a delightfully situated, cheap and charming little country pub. Full board at fifteen shillings a day per head was not too bad. So we settled down there; Richard Millani, Richard Curtis and myself. Young Frank had gone off to visit a friend in Lille and we did not expect to see him again until the Hill Climb.

What a pleasant change it was to sit in the local beer cellar and talk to people who were remarkably, but refreshingly, disinterested in motor-racing. We were in bed by nine o'clock and that was how it was for the next four days. They say a change is as good as a holiday and this was no exception to the rule. The diary tells the story:

" Last night I slept properly after a nice bath. How nice it feels to be back on earth again. I almost feel human. We have been in the swimming pool all day. The Jerrys still do not speak to us very much. I suppose it is the war ."

All good things come to an end and eventually we had to leave our little village and move into Freiburg, where we had a rendezvous with John Heath and Stirling Moss.

We practised on Thursday and followed John Heath's instructions to detune the cars completely, running on very low tyre pressures and very soft plugs. It was all beyond me as I had not had any previous experience of hill-climbs, but it seemed there was more preparation required than for a straightforward circuit race.

However, I did not have to worry about the Hill Climb for as soon as Steve Watson arrived at Freiburg with the car Giraud Cabantous had driven at Sables d'Olonne, Richard Millani and I set off for Albi with Macklin's car.

We were not clear of Freiburg until the early hours of Friday morning, having been considerably delayed by the late arrival of Steve Watson, and we had a journey of five hundred miles ahead of us which had to be completed in just over twenty-four hours if we were to run the car at Albi in the last practice session.

It was a terrifying journey and meant driving the small van non-stop all night through Switzerland, and then over the Central Passes with the attendant menace of fog. We drove flat out, taking turns of three hours each at the wheel, and undoubtedly our time schedule forced us to drive quicker than was safe.

I dislike driving against the clock, particularly at night on tortuous mountain passes. With the mist swirling around the van I found it quite impossible to relax when Richard was at the wheel. Neither could he relax when I drove, and his foot repeatedly stamped an imaginary brake pedal on the floorboards.

We could hardly keep our eyes open and several times I found myself dropping off to sleep at the wheel. On one occasion the van almost went off the road into a ditch, and its crazy progress as we bumped along a grass verge for twenty yards or so woke me up as effectively as if Richard had wrung out a sponge over my head.

Our route took us through Basle, Belfort, Chalons, Lyon, St. Etienne, Mt. Dubrac and Rodez. We were pretty well worn out when, just after 6 a.m. on Saturday, we arrived in Albi. I stopped the van outside the Automobile Club and promptly fell asleep over the wheel. A policeman who tried to wake us, convinced that we were drugged as we slept so soundly, gave it up as a bad job and came back about an hour later with a colleague, by which time an interested crowd had gathered to watch the two of us having a quiet, uninterrupted shave.

We found ourselves a hotel and garage for the car, where the axle ratio was changed, and then made our way out to the circuit for practice in the afternoon. There was no sign of Lance Macklin but Duncan Hamilton was there and told me he was supposed to drive the second team car instead of Abecassis. This was news to me, and anyway we did not have a second H.W.M. I told him that the car had arrived at Freiburg too late for it to be prepared for Albi.

Naturally, Hamilton took a dim view of the situation and was very annoyed about the expense of getting to Albi.

"Look," I said to him, "Macklin is supposed to drive this car but, as he has not arrived for practice, I suggest you do a few laps. At least you can qualify the car."

So off he went and, as soon as he was circulating in his usual carefree way, a dishevelled, unshaven Macklin arrived. He looked like a tramp and it turned out that his Simca had blown two tyres and that he had walked for miles. By this time the practice had almost finished and I brought in Hamilton and sent Macklin off to do a few qualifying laps.

That night Duncan Hamilton saw to it that the telephone wires fairly hummed to Abecassis in Walton and John Heath in Freiburg. He wanted to drive instead of Macklin but I am glad John Heath would not agree, for Macklin drove a very good race on the fast Albi circuit and came in seventh.

He had no trouble with the car and in fact the Meeting was an uneventful one for us.

The next appearance of the H.W.M.'s was at Erlen in Switzerland, a week after the Albi race, where three cars were entered.

We had to wait until Monday afternoon so that I could collect the starting money, and did not leave Albi until Tuesday morning. We had 150 gallons of Esso fuel, which we had collected after the race, and this presented no small problem at the Swiss Customs. They are very strict about these things and we very nearly became involved in serious trouble at the frontier through acting as Good Samaritans.

Just previously we had picked up two English hitch-hikers, both men.

" For goodness' sake don't say anything about the fuel in the back of this lorry," I warned them, " otherwise we shall all end up in clink."

When the Swiss Customs officer asked what was in the drums I told him it was a special oil, with which we were experimenting with a view to running the car on it. That was a good enough explanation for the official and, having asked me whether the drums were full or half full, he was about to wave us on when one of the hitch-hikers said in a loud voice:

" But you said this was fuel, not oil."

It would have given me the greatest pleasure at that precise moment to hit the fellow with a monkey wrench but it was not necessary. The Customs official did not speak English sufficiently well to understand what had been said and waved us on.

At Erlen, Moss had gearbox trouble after only two laps in the first practice session, and de Graffenried, the Swiss driver who had been engaged to handle an H.W.M., suggested that Moss might like to try his car. The Swiss had gone very well indeed, and not only put up a faster time than Macklin on the third H.W.M. but was second fastest of the day. However, de Graffenried complained about the brakes on the H.W.M.—which were normally absolutely first-class—and after Moss had taken out the car, and knocked 4/10 of a second off the time recorded by the Swiss, he confirmed that the brakes were almost non-existent.

Meanwhile, on Macklin's car there was trouble with the valve seats and he was unable to practise on the first day. I think someone must have over-revved the engine, perhaps at Albi, and bent the valves. One thing followed another and the valve-seating went to pieces. I worked all night on the two cars and managed to get all three H.W.M.'s ready for the second day of practice, when Moss put up fastest time at 1-24.9.

In the race, as soon as the flag fell, Stirling went into the lead and quickly built up a nine-second margin over the next man. He drove very well indeed, absolutely on top form, and to our delight stayed out in front for half the race distance. Then, to our disappointment, the top of one of the suspension wishbones broke, and the car pulled into the pits to retire. It was the one and only occasion during the season we experienced wishbone trouble and undoubtedly the failure lost us the race. Macklin finished fifth, whilst de Graffenried's gearbox seized solid.

At the Monday conference, John Heath told me that Steve Watson would be leaving and that I would have to take over the administration of the *equipe* again and look after the financial side. Steve went off to Monte Carlo.

That afternoon we loaded the cars into the transporters and Richard Millani was told to go straight back to England with one car whilst I picked up some spares in Paris. On Wednesday, Frank Nagel and I were in Paris and, on Saturday, at Dover. It was such a long time since I had seen England that the green of the countryside was a tonic. It looked so different from anything I had seen in Europe, and luxuriant in its greenery. We stopped on the road to Maidstone and took a deep breath of good English fresh air. It was grand to be alive. On Sunday I went home for a few hours—the first time since the beginning of the season—but it was only a brief respite.

The H.W.M.'s were on their last legs. There was a great deal of work to do and each engine was completely stripped down whilst at the same time a thorough check was made of the chassis and steering geometry, and damage to the bodywork repaired. The cars were, to all intents and purposes, taken to pieces and rebuilt again.

I made myself responsible for the engines and took one over to the Alta works where, with Geoffrey Taylor, I checked output and endeavoured to find some more power. That was our trouble in 1951, lack of power when compared with our continental rivals. However, time was short, for Frank Nagel and I planned to leave with two cars for Ireland on September 5th, and I achieved very little with the engine on the Alta test-bench.

I under-estimated the Welsh roads and we just managed to catch the boat at Fishguard. It was the first time I had travelled through Wales, and I classify the roads as more difficult in parts than those in the Central Massif. When we arrived during the late evening at the docks in Fishguard, I asked an official whether it was possible to take the lorry across to Ireland. The Fordson is quite a tall van and I was concerned from the point of view of bridge clearance.

" Of course," he said, " there will be no difficulty." I asked him if he was sure, and he replied: " Look, I know what I am talking about. Don't worry."

I wish I *had* worried for when we arrived in Ireland it was not even possible to get the Fordson out of the docks! There was a bridge in the way and although we tried all the dodges known to transport people for getting lorries under low bridges, it was hopeless. British Railways even unloaded the Fordson, removed the wheels and hoisted the chassis on to a railway truck. That was no good; still not enough clearance.

After Frank and I had spent almost a day, fuming at the delay and cursing the smug, complacent official in Fishguard, we decided to abandon the transporter and get two lorries from Dublin. That was how we arrived at the circuit, in a couple of hired lorries.

The Commanding Officer of the Barracks at Curragh, where we were billeted, was quite a character. He could not have been more charming. As soon as we met, he looked hard at me.

" You are not English ? "

" No," I replied, " Naturalized English."

He must have thought I looked sympathetic, for he lost no time putting me in the picture about the Irish troubles. As we crawled from bar to bar, and consumed Guinness after Guinness, he became more eloquent until I found myself almost feeling sorry for him. I did not bother to argue. I always find that the easiest course in a foreign country is to agree with whatever the locals say. You have to fit into the company otherwise you can run into a lot of difficulties.

I was given the best bed in the barracks which adjoined the circuit and the H.W.M.'s put in the best garage by the man who now described himself as "a friend for life." His rapid rate of Guinness consumption also gave me my biggest hangover of 1951.

We consumed vast quantities of Guinness in the Sergeants Mess at Curragh. It seemed to me that every sergeant was six feet tall and almost as round as tall, with great beefy hands and a cheerful, red face. They were a grand crowd. I don't reckon anyone can live in Dublin long without getting a fairly considerable " corporation."

After the first practice session it was necessary to change axle ratios as they were too low. Frank looked after this whilst I dealt with the engine checks. In the second practice session Stirling had only completed two laps when the back axle seized solid. There was not a drop of oil in it! Naturally, I was given a sound ticking off by John Heath for lack of supervision.

In spite of our "black" with the axle, the H.W.M.'s did very well indeed, for Moss not only won the race outright but established a new lap record, and won the handicap class. Duncan Hamilton came in second.

The opposition was not considerable and included Ken Wharton with an E.R.A., the late Bobbie Baird with a Maserati and some local " boys." The main problem H.W.M. had to overcome was the handicap. It was such a heavy one that Moss drove remarkably well to beat it.

During the race we had to call Moss in for fuel, as we had calculated that if he took things quietly it might just be possible to complete the distance without a stop. However, Stirling drove "flat out" to beat the handicap and we had to make a snap decision to call him in three laps before the finish.

The refuelling was carried out very quickly. In no time at all he took on five gallons, and the engine was not even switched off. As Stirling tried to ease himself out of the cockpit, he was roughly pushed back again and tapped on the shoulder as a signal to get going. Even with this pit stop we still beat the handicapper.

This was the first outright victory for H.W.M. and Frank and I decided to celebrate. We knew no one in Dublin, apart from our Guinness-drinking friends in the Curragh Barracks, and decided to take in a film first before getting mixed up with them in what would probably end up as an all-night party.

We were sitting on the end of a row in a Dublin cinema when one of the attendants came down the aisle and told me that somebody was waiting downstairs who would like to have our autographs. This was the first time I had ever been asked for an autograph.

" We are not the drivers, you know," I said.

" I understand that," replied the attendant, "but these people would still like to have your autograph."

" Well," I replied, in the best prima donna manner, " you will have to wait until the film finishes."

That seemed to settle the matter but a few minutes later the attendant returned and asked us to call at the Cash Desk on our way out of the cinema. We did so, and introduced ourselves to the cashier, a very pretty girl, who told us she was not so much interested in our autographs as having us at a party she was giving in Dublin that night.

When we arrived at her house, an embarrassing situation arose connected with Frank's trousers. In all the excitement of the pit stop for fuel, they had split in half down the seam. This did not worry Frank at the cinema, as he was wearing a raincoat, but a problem arose when our hostess told Frank to take off his coat. He could not very well refuse, so took it off and then worked himself into a strategic position in a corner of the room where the large expanse of white pants was hidden from view.

As the party grew larger Frank became even more insistent on staying in the corner. He refused to dance and the girls eventually became suspicious. He blushingly fought back when they questioned him but eventually had to admit that he had a large tear in his pants. There was an immediate call for volunteers, and Frank was ushered into th bathroom and told to take off his trousers and to hand them round the door. This he did, and in no time at all the trousers were repaired whilst Frank remained locked up in the bathroom.

We left next day for England, rather crestfallen and not a little upset by a decision made concerning the prize money. We had a system which Stirling had insisted on John Heath introducing, that ten per cent. of the winnings in any race should go to the mechanics. Stirling maintained that we needed some sort of compensation for the long hours of hard work, and had fixed the arrangement earlier in the season.

The prize money in the Dublin race was quite high but, because of our error in not filling the back axle on Moss' car, John Heath told us quite frankly that we would have to pay for the damaged axle with our commission.

Fate plays funny tricks. It was Stirling who made it possible for us to share in the winnings, and his car that made it impossible for us to do so on an occasion when H.W.M. won quite a considerable sum.

Frank felt pretty rotten about it but I told him not to worry.

" We are a team—you and I—we have to stand or fall together."

We only had a few days at Walton, as on Sunday, September 23rd, we were due to race in Modena. Frank, Richard Millani and myself went in the A.E.C. bus and left Walton on the Monday with two cars, arriving in Modena on Thursday evening after an uneventful journey.

This was the first time I had visited a town that was to become very much a part of my life. I did not realize, being so much immersed in my own problems with the H.W.M.'s, that I had arrived in the very heart of motor-racing, the home of Ferrari and Maserati.

I made a mistake by not booking at the famous Hotel Reali, where sooner or later most people in the motor-racing game stay for a few days.

From the prestige point of view it would have been a good thing to have the bus standing outside.

The practice session was an unusual one, for Macklin was a second faster than Moss, recording 1 minute 58 seconds as against the fastest time of the day, put up by Ascari, at 1-54. Stirling was not very happy about the engine of his H.W.M. so I made a thorough check of the valves and ignition.

On the Saturday, Macklin was again faster, and I think Moss was of the opinion that the engine in Macklin's car was a better one. Personally, it seemed to me that Macklin was absolutely at home on the Modena circuit and driving extraordinarily well.

On race day, as soon as the flag dropped, Moss fairly streaked away from the third row of the starting grid and in doing so ran over the toes of the Chief Mechanic of the Ferrari *equipe*. Fortunately, the man was unhurt and Moss settled down in fifth position and behind Froilan Gonzalez, who was lying fourth. Moss actually passed Gonzalez, who was driving a Formula 2, 12-cylinder Ferrari.

Soon afterwards the engine started missing and Moss came into the pits. Without stopping to reason why, I changed No. 3 plug, as I knew he would want me to do this anyway, and the car was soon away. However, the H.W.M. continued to misfire, and John Heath agreed that there must be something wrong with the magneto.

" It's no use letting him struggle round on three-and-a-half cylinders," I said to John Heath. " We may as well call him in."

It was certainly nothing to do with the plugs, for the missing was inconsistent.

I prepared a spare magneto and all the necessary tools, then put out a signal. In his usual sensible and obedient fashion Moss came in on the next lap and, without saying a word to him, we tore off the bonnet. It took 4 minutes 38 seconds to change the complete magneto and re-time the engine.

We push-started the H.W.M. and it sounded very well indeed. Although we had lost so much time there was the satisfaction that Moss was driving a healthy car and it was just sheer bad luck when, in the latter part of the race, one of the sparking plugs blew out of the cylinder head.

I think the plug must have been cross-threaded when it was screwed into the head, perhaps in the excitement of changing the plug on the first pit stop, or even earlier when all four were changed from soft to hard just before the race started.

Macklin finished third. He was passed by Gonzalez but stayed in front of Cortese, Rosier and Marimon. There was constant passing and repassing and Macklin was really mixing it with the experts as well as with the local Modena talent. I have never seen him drive better than on that occasion.

That night, in Modena, John Heath gave a dinner for the *equipe*. He wanted, amongst other things, to talk about the coming season, as the Modena race was the last major event of 1951. We had a first-rate meal at a famous Modena restaurant and, after the coffee had been served, John Heath made a speech outlining his plans.

He lost no time telling us that he had every intention of building a lighter car with a lighter chassis which, in his words "Will give us better roadholding." This announcement came as a shock to me. I could see myself spending several months at Walton again, as I had done at the end of the 1949 and 1950 seasons, cutting and welding and going through the entire wearisome business of making a new chassis all over again.

When Heath had finished, I stood up.

" Could I have your permission to ask the drivers their views about the handling of the 1951 H.W.M ? " I said. " In my opinion the roadholding is good and I cannot see why we need a new chassis."

Heath granted my request and I asked Moss for his views.

" I cannot see much wrong with the handling of the cars as they are at present," he said. " All we need is more power."

Macklin agreed and added that if we could find another 20 brake horse power we might be a match for the Ferraris. " All we need," said Macklin, " is an engine that will pull the lower axle ratios so we can use more revs."

With such powerful support I did not hesitate, and put it to John Heath that, instead of spending all the winter building new cars of unknown quality (against the clock and calendar, as usual), we concentrated on our present ones which had already had their chassis developed and proved.

" After all," I pointed out, " in the entire season the only trouble we have had is a broken wishbone at Erlen and a bent steering arm, due to an accident, at Aix les Bains. Let's concentrate this winter on developing the engine," I argued. " Let's find that other 20 b.h.p."

I was told in so many words not to be silly, and sat down a sadder but wiser man. However, it had upset me and after the dinner I asked John Heath if I could have a word privately with him. I had made up my mind to give notice!

I felt bad about it, particularly as Macklin had done so well in the Modena race and Moss and Hamilton so well in Dublin, but what could I do ? How could I put a maximum, conscientious effort into such a project ? My conscience told me that I would not be able to do a satisfactory job of work, and in motor-racing if one does not believe wholeheartedly in matters of major policy it is best to get out and not to be a fake.

I could see that we should be working flat out again during the winter months, building and developing yet another new car—the third H.W.M.— in a devil of a hurry, whilst we should have been remedying the persistent troubles connected with the magneto, fuel pump, gearbox and carburation. If we could have put those things right and then gone motor-racing again in 1952 with the same cars, I think H.W.M. would have finished well up in the honours list. It would have been early enough to think of a third H.W.M. in time for 1953.

We were on the verge of success at the end of 1951—at the crossroads— and John Heath took the wrong turning. If he had taken the right one, we could have been the Prancing Horse of Britain. The Modena race proved that although the H.W.M.s had less power than the 12-cylinder Ferraris our cars had certain qualities, such as cornering and braking, which were superior to the Italian cars.

We knew that at the end of the 1951 season Enzo Ferrari intended to smooth out any troubles with his chassis and engines and had no intention of building a new car. We should have followed his example.

We argued and argued, but I was determined that, if John Heath went ahead with his plans, it would be with a new chief mechanic.

I was quite frank.

" I have had enough," I told him. "After all, I have done forty meetings with H.W.M. and I, personally, do not want to get mixed up in something brand new when we are so near success with the present cars."

The argument continued until 4 a.m., John Heath trying to persuade me that I was looking at the whole thing from the wrong angle.

" If we have a lighter car," he said, " we won't need the extra revs. The power to weight ratio will be the answer to more power."

I stuck to my guns. I just was not interested in power to weight ratios. All I wanted was an extra 20 b.h.p. out of that Alta engine, and I knew I could get it.

" Give me the time," I told John Heath, " and we will find it."

The discussion ended when I told him that, if he was agreeable, I would leave as soon as the British Racing Mechanics dinner had taken place at the Park Lane Hotel on November 21st. Naturally, I wanted to stay on and finish the season; there were still a few races to run at home.

I sometimes wonder whether my decision was the right one. I think it was. After all, from the point of view of chassis design, the H.W.M.s were the most reliable cars on the circuits. Look back through the records and you will see what I mean. In twenty race meetings in 1951 the cars had no chassis troubles and there were no stub axle breakages or incidents with wheels coming off. So far as brakes were concerned the Girling two leading shoe brakes with Alfin drums were terrific, beyond praise. We could beat any Ferrari, or any other car for that matter, on brakes alone.

Our problem was lack of acceleration and power throughout the whole range. Taking all these factors into consideration, I felt it only logical to make the car more reliable from the point of view of the engine and gearbox for the 1952 season. Let me say here and now that there was nothing basically wrong with the engine. It was, in fact, a very good power unit and from the point of view of reliability we only had two timing chains break in forty meetings over two years.

To be honest, I must admit there were other reasons for my decision to leave H.W.M. In the first place I knew that, whether or not the proposed new chassis was successful, I would still be the person responsible for keeping the cars running week after week. I had no intention of shouldering that sort of responsibility for the third successive season without a large enough expert staff to ensure that the organization would function as efficiently as possible.

The chaps who worked with me, particularly Richard Millani, had enthusiasm and a great team spirit, but I realized during 1951 that this was not good enough. I was held responsible if anything went wrong with the cars, and yet certain incidents occurred during the season that were a direct result of carelessness or slackness on the part of someone else. Those particular incidents would never have taken place had I been able to double-check everything myself, which unfortunately I never had sufficient time to do.

The drivers naturally held me responsible for the cars. If they behaved well, then they were for me; if they behaved badly, then I got the blame in no uncertain fashion, as Chief Mechanic, irrespective of the cause of failures.

It was not a very happy situation, at only £10 a week, and I had frequently been the subject of constant criticism. At the same time, the team spirit of the drivers in the H.W.M. *equipe* was tremendous and I knew I should miss working with Moss and Macklin in particular. I had grown to like and respect them both very much.

Another factor had become very obvious during the 1951 season. I did not enjoy sufficient authority or freedom of action. In the few races, such as the one at Monza where I ran the *equipe* on my own, we were comparatively successful. When everyone else was there, I was still Chief Mechanic but without the authority to do things my way, and we were not so successful.

I gave a great deal of thought to this matter and came to the conclusion that I had worked twice as hard at meetings where John Heath had been present and usually ended up in bed during the early hours of the morning, if at all. At meetings where I had looked after the cars in my own way I had frequently been in bed before midnight.

Reluctantly, for I had grown up in motor-racing with H.W.M., I came to the conclusion that I had been given a raw deal. For two seasons I had worked like blazes, saddled with a very heavy responsibility, but without sufficient authority, freedom of action or strong backing in the form of more personnel.

CHAPTER 16

I PROVE MY POINT

I may have sounded over optimistic at the Modena dinner with my plans for more b.h.p. but I was confident that the extra power could be found. Admittedly, I had not got very far the previous year with Geoffrey Taylor at the Alta works for we had been fighting a losing battle.

My idea, as it had been previously, was to get the right man to tune the engines and extract every available ounce of power from them. I had no illusions about doing the job myself but I am confident that, given a free hand and the right man, we could have worked wonders with the Alta power unit.

In actual fact, my knowledge of the Webers enabled me to prove my point to a marked degree. There were a few meetings still to be run in England when we arrived back from Modena and, with the permission of George Abecassis and John Heath, I took an engine over to Geoffrey Taylor. By careful tuning from the carburation point of view, we were able to recover some 15 b.h.p., and increase from 110 to 125 b.h.p.

We decided to instal the more powerful engine in Abecassis' H.W.M. as it was almost in the nature of an experimental engine, and the car went like a bomb at Winfield. It was certainly much quicker than the other H.W.M.s. and Abecassis led the race for a long time. He had no difficulty whatsoever in passing Moss and the reason why he did not win the Winfield race was because he wanted Moss to chalk up a victory. He felt that Moss deserved it after all the good work he had done for H.W.M. I shall always remember Abecassis as a true gentleman and sportsman on occasions such as this, and he is one of the people I am very proud to have known in motor racing.

After the race, Abecassis asked me to take the engine back to Geoffrey Taylor's and to continue with its tuning and development. I had proved my point and it was my last race with H.W.M.

When the time came for me to leave H.W.M. I found that no one in the office knew about my departure. I don't think John Heath had taken me seriously at Modena and no one was more surprised than he when, on the morning of the Mechanics Dinner, I asked for my cards.

I had no intention of going back on my word, for my views remained unchanged. Someone had to make a move. John Heath was equally unrelenting and that was that.

He asked me to take the mechanics to the Dinner, which I was glad to do, and that was my last official undertaking as Chief Mechanic of H.W.M.

Moss was there and told me that he had not signed a contract with H.W.M. for 1952. If I remember rightly these were his exact words.

" When the Chief Mechanic goes, I may as well go too."

Like myself he was depressed about the way things had turned out. Like me, he wanted H.W.M. to be great and was sure the *equipe* could have been if John Heath had not insisted on sweating out another entirely new design.

There is one point I want to make absolutely clear; John Heath and I parted the best of friends. This may sound strange but, although we fought tooth and nail on occasions, I had great admiration for John Heath and for his courage and "drive" in racing the green H.W.M.s all over Europe. Undoubtedly he and his partner, George Abecassis, brought much needed prestige to this country.

Having left H.W.M., I decided to take a job as workshop manager in a small garage on the outskirts of Berwick. It was a new life. All I wanted to do was settle down quietly to a nice, steady job with regular hours and forget about circuits, axle ratios, temperamental drivers and patrons; to forget everything to do with motor-racing.

I started off in good form, with every intention of finding somewhere in Berwick where I could live with my wife, but soon realized that life away from the circuits is very, very empty. I found I could not cut myself off so easily from the only life I had known for three years, a way of living which more often than not consists of tearing about all over Europe, always fighting against time.

Are you surprised that I could not settle down in Berwick ? After only four weeks, and every day seemed like an age, I did what many people do these days, and tried to drown my sorrows by drinking heavily. I soon realized that if I continued in this manner I would finish up as an alcoholic, every bit as bad as some of the human wrecks I had met around the European circuits.

I wrote to my wife.

" Definitely, so far as I am concerned, I cannot stay in a job like this. Even though I told you I would only complete three seasons, I realize now that motor-racing is my life. I cannot give it up, and that is all there is to it. I think you will understand."

Was it fate, I wonder, that only a few days later I received a letter from Geoffrey Taylor asking me if I would like to join Peter Whitehead and look after one of the new 2-litre Altas that he had ordered from Taylor.

To the utter amazement of my landlady, I threw the letter over my shoulder at the breakfast table, pushed back my chair, dragged her out of hers and danced her round the room.

" You must be mad, Mr. Francis," she said.

" Not mad," I replied, " just happy, that's all. I am back once again in motor-racing."

CHAPTER 17

FOR LOVE OF THE SPORT

Equipe Whitehead—The 12-cylinder Ferrari—Off to the Syracuse G.P.—Trouble at the frontier—A " nice, comfortable race."

I knew that working for Peter Whitehead was going to be very different from working with the H.W.M. *equipe*. Instead of having to look after a team of three or four cars, and the varied requirements of several drivers, I should be working with one man, a sportsman who goes motor-racing purely and simply for love of the sport. Whitehead is in no way a professional and I knew from the start that our motor-racing would be on a strictly amateur basis.

He interviewed me in the bar of the White Hart, near his garage in Chalfont St. Peter, and I accepted the job over a pint of bitter. It was all settled very quickly. We had met previously on many occasions and there was no need for him to tell me his requirements, for he knew I understood his views.

I like Peter Whitehead very much as a person and consider him one of the gentlemen in motor-racing as well as a first-rate driver. His approach to the sport is rather an unusual one. He leaves himself a greater margin of safety than a professional, or perhaps a more ambitious amateur. It means that in action he is slower than his capabilities but there are occasions when he puts his foot down a little more firmly and then he is as good as some of Britain's top drivers.

He is undoubtedly very skilled but as his racing is a private venture he has to bear in mind that every blow-up costs money. So he endeavours to preserve the car as well as leaving himself a safety margin. He certainly does not take unnecessary risks and is a downright sensible driver with a downright sensible approach to a sport that some drivers make far more " dicey " for themselves than is necessary.

He is knowledgeable about the mechanical side but rarely discusses the subject. So far as his racing cars are concerned he leaves the whole shooting match to his mechanics, and this is a most refreshing outlook.

I realized, when I joined him in January 1952, that at last I was going to be able to do things my way and that I was going to have responsibility and authority without the heavy hand of officialdom as with John Heath. However, I wondered whether I would be able to cope, particularly with the Ferrari owned by Whitehead as I had very limited experience of foreign marques.

When I first started at Chalfont I lived in digs and it was the intention that the garage would loan me sufficient money to buy a motor bike so that I could get home to Woolwich every day. They eventually bought me a pre-war Rudge Ulster, a terrific—repeat terrific—piece of machinery which gave me one or two very nasty moments. I fell off more times than I care to admit and there was one particular roundabout that caught me out on several occasions and caused me to abandon the Rudge—as it were—in mid-stream.

However, it carried me from Woolwich to Chalfont and back, and I was covering seventy miles daily, leaving Woolwich at 7 a.m. every morning and getting back some twelve hours later.

At Chalfont, when I joined the Whitehead *equipe*, the Alta had not been completed and consequently I was able to help the other mechanic, Stan Ellsworth, strip down the 12-cylinder Ferrari in readiness for the 1952 season and give the car its normal winter overhaul. The Ferrari was equipped with two engines, one of 2-litre capacity and the other a 1½-litre supercharged unit. They were interchangeable and it was thus possible to enter the car in different classes according to the event.

The *equipe* consisted of Peter Whitehead as the driver, Stan Ellsworth and myself. Stan was responsible for the Ferrari whilst my job was to look after the Alta, but although the work was divided in this way it was agreed that if only one car was being raced then both Stan and I would work on it. I was appointed *Chef d'Equipe*, with similar administrative duties to those I had been given by John Heath.

We had a brand new Ford Thames van, with a Perkins Diesel engine. However, the Diesel restricted our speed to forty m p.h., which was to prove rather boring on our first trip of the season to Syracuse in Sicily. I was surprised at the quality and quantity of the spares carried by Peter Whitehead. He had an incredible collection for just one car and more I think than the whole of the H.W.M. team with its four cars. I was very impressed with the way in which the *equipe* had been organized from this point of view and it was obvious that money had been no object.

I got on very well indeed with Stan Ellsworth. Before I took the job we had a discussion over a pint in the White Hart, when I pointed out that if he did not want me in the *equipe* he had better say so before it was too late.

" It is better to tell me now," I said, " if you do not like my face because it will save us a lot of trouble later on."

Stan was very decent about it.

" Alf, there is no doubt you have had the most experience and I shall be only too glad to work with you."

From that day onwards we never had any unpleasantness for we had got off on the right foot.

I found the Ferrari a delightful car on which to work, although much more complicated than the H.W.M., and it soon became obvious to me that a tremendous amount of thought had gone into its design and construction. It was a sound engineering proposition, having been built 100% for the job in hand—motor-racing—and was exactly as I had always imagined the perfect G.P. car. It had been designed carefully, logically and with plenty of time to spare during the development stage. No panic building here.

The designer had certainly not gone out of his way to make the car easy to maintain between races and it took us a long time to do certain jobs. For instance, it was a major operation to change the axle ratio and I could see the designer had not cluttered up his mind trying to save people like ourselves time and trouble. I can understand the point of view. Why compromise on a racing car when all the energies of designers and constructors should be directed towards maximum efficiency in action.

I am sure that in this country we concentrate too much on ease of maintenance to the extent that in some ways a car is improvised; this is a bad thing to my mind. Admittedly, there are British cars where it is a simple matter to change ratios, gearboxes—even engines for that matter—but is this necessarily a good thing when, in the first place, the designer has set off with so many problems to solve in connection with ease of maintenance and operation that he has not concentrated sufficiently on the basic requirements of the car for circuit racing.

At Chalfont, before we left for Syracuse, I did not have to work anything like so hard as I had during the two previous winters with H.W.M. My average day was an eight-hour one, whereas with H.W.M. it had been anything up to twelve or fourteen hours, and I could not help wondering how the boys were getting on at Walton with the prototype of the new car.

I had far more time to talk about motor-racing at Chalfont than ever before and used to have the most interesting and lengthy discussions in the White Hart with Mr. Charles White, Managing Director of the garage. I had been so engrossed in a job with H.W.M.—a job that was almost too much for one man and a seven-day week—that I never had any time to stop and think or talk about it. As a matter of fact, we did more talking at Chalfont than good honest hard work, and I spent a great deal of time talking "shop" in the White Hart with a pint of bitter in my hand.

Both engines were taken to Syracuse with the Ferrari, as we planned to run the car in the Formula 1 race at Turin after the Sicily venture, and this would mean replacing the 2-litre engine with the $1\frac{1}{2}$ litre supercharged unit.

Even with H.W.M. I had never undertaken such a long trip and Stan and I decided to give ourselves plenty of time, as during March most of the Passes are closed and there are few alternative routes.

We decided to go via Monte Carlo and Ventimiglia and, having consulted our maps, reached the conclusion that it should be possible to drive ten hours a day and complete the journey in eight to ten days.

We left Chalfont on Monday, March 3rd, and it was a pleasant change to proceed in a leisurely fashion to Dover and then board the Ferry without any difficulty. From Dunkirk we pushed on to Paris, via Abbeville, and stopped for the night in the French capital. Sufficient to say that we spent a very enjoyable evening there, so much so that we realized the sooner we pressed on the better it would be for our finances. Stan was not only a good partner in the workshop but equally good on a night out.

I could see, at this early stage of my association with the Whitehead *equipe*, that we were not going to have a series of embarrassing situations on the Continent regarding our expenses. I was never short of ready cash with Peter Whitehead and he made a point of checking that I always had sufficient reserve to meet sudden emergencies, such as a lorry breakdown which could mean a rush job in a local garage.

On Wednesday, a little the worse for wear, we left Paris and reached Chalon Sur Saone for our night halt. The following day, driving non-stop for almost twelve hours and covering 405 miles, we reached Rocquebrun—

and the Diodato. The Fordson Diesel went very well, bearing in mind that our maximum speed was restricted to 40 m.p.h.

We planned to cross into Italy on the Friday but ran into trouble on arrival at the frontier. The French authorities asked for our Permit of Circulation and were amazed when I pointed out that we had not been asked for one at Dunkirk and had, in fact, travelled from north to south without one.

A new law had been introduced for commercial lorries, about which I knew nothing and neither did Peter Whitehead. Apparently, lorries entering France and carrying goods required a special road permit. As the Customs Officer explained;

" We wish to prevent foreign lorries transporting French goods."

I must admit to a feeling of disquiet on our journey to the south for everything had gone so smoothly. There had been no driving by day and night, non-stop and against the clock, neither had there been any breakdowns. It had all seemed too good to be true.

I was not at all surprised when, although the French allowed us to leave France, we ran into real trouble at the Italian Customs Post at Ventimiglia. They would not let us through, insisting that I ought to have a special licence authorizing the Whitehead *equipe* to carry Italian goods in the shape of the Ferrari and its spares, as well as the large quantity of English tyres and spares.

The officials were adamant. It was no use arguing for the Customs Officer was the worst type of Italian in uniform, a proper little Fascist in fact, and there was nothing for it but to stay on the frontier for the night. It was a waste of time to explain that we were motor-racing and to request special facilities.

I caught the early morning train to Milan and left the lorry with Stan at the frontier. My intention was to enquire about the necessary permit at the Automobile Club, although the Customs people had, in a most objectionable manner, refused to tell me where to go. The Club was unable to do anything. As one of the officials pointed out ;

" This is the law and we have to observe it. We are, in this case, Italian citizens before we are motor-racing enthusiasts."

I was naturally disappointed and set off back to Ventimiglia, calling at San Remo on the way as I knew personally the President of the Automobile Club. He is a lawyer and gave me a letter stating for what purpose I carried the tyres and spare engine, afterwards telephoning the Frontier Post and explaining matters to the officials.

By the time I arrived back at Ventimiglia the Customs Officer was prepared to let us proceed, but only if I left 1 million lire as a guarantee that I would not sell the tyres or the engine!

" Don't be such a clot," I told the Italian. " Where in hell am I going to find a million lire ? "

He shrugged his shoulders.

" So—the engine and the tyres—they will have to stay here at the Frontier."

I eventually persuaded him to settle for the engine and only thirty of our tyre stock, and leaving them there we set off for the south, three days behind schedule and with a thousand miles still to cover. To this day I do not know what sort of permit we should have carried. I think my face must have upset the Customs Officer, and indeed it was a case of mutual dislike at first sight. Moral: Always be courteous with the Customs when you have a lorry full of spares.

Once clear of Ventimiglia we pressed on down the Mediterranean coast and, by driving more or less non-stop for 400 miles, reached Civitavecchia in one day, negotiating the formidable Bracco Pass in the process. We had not done too badly with the Diesel Fordson since leaving Paris, having reached Chalons in one day, Rocqueburn in two and Civitavecchia — 80 kilometres from the Italian capital—in three days of driving. I wonder how many people with private cars would attempt to reach Rome in three days from Paris.

The road from Rome to Naples is not too bad but conditions are shocking beyond the seaport. We had a hair-raising journey southwards from Naples to Lago Negro, travelling down the Via Calabria which is famous for its serpentine corners. Time and time again we had to reverse—and then reverse again—to negotiate a corner and it was late at night when we eventually arrived in Lago Negro. I have never since experienced such a journey. There seemed no end to the interminable corners and winding roads.

We stayed the night at a most impressive, Roman built hotel and having signed the Visitors Book, a small boy appeared and asked whether I would like him to look after the lorry. I immediately agreed because I knew that if I refused, he and his friends would be the first to break open the Fordson and steal the spares. I offered 500 lire and promised him twenty cigarettes if the lorry was intact in the morning.

In the hotel there were washbasins in every room but no running water. When I complained to the proprietor he was not surprised.

" They cut off the water," he said, " because I cannot pay the bills."

So we had to carry our own water from the market square in buckets and all the manager did was supply the buckets.

I asked him why such an impressive building was in such a neglected state.

" Well," he replied, " in years past this hotel was quite a famous one in the health resort of Lago Negro but the town has fallen on bad times and most of the people are on the verge of starvation. We have no visitors except once in a blue moon when people like yourselves stop here. There is no trade."

His reply did not surprise me for there is no doubt that the standard of living south of Naples is very much lower than in the north. It was obvious from the dilapidated state of the buildings and the tattered clothes worn by the lower classes.

Next morning, we found a different boy guarding the lorry.

" What are you doing ? " I asked.

" Watching the lorry all night for you," he quickly answered.

" Well," I said, " I paid someone else to do that."

" I know," he replied, " I don't want any money. I punched him on the nose and took the five hundred lire. I thought you would rather have a stronger boy to guard the lorry than that weakling."

I laughed. I would have done the same thing myself in similar circumstances, so I not only gave him the twenty cigarettes but another 100 lire as well.

From Lago Negro we pushed on next day to Palmi and after a night in a flea-ridden hotel, with what appeared to be a wrought-iron mattress on the bed, we continued our journey and arrived at the toe of Italy, Reggio Calabria. We crossed to Sicily on the ferry in company with Peter Whitehead in his XK 120 Coupe Jaguar, who had allowed himself five days for the journey as against our eight.

We pushed on southwards down the coast and it seemed to me that the Sicilian roads were in a better state of repair than those in southern Italy. Our route to Syracuse took us through Catania and then over the famous Primo Sole Bridge where a brigade of the Durham Light Infantry fought a long and bitter battle with the Hermann Goering Parachute Division in July 1943; a white stone memorial stands just north of the bridge in memory of the officers and men of the D.L.I. who lost their lives in the battle.

It had taken us six days of driving to get from Paris to Sicily ; three days to Rome and then one day to Lago Negro, one to Palmi and one to Syracuse. And we had driven by day and slept by night. However, to make the journey in comfort requires eight days.

When I spoke to members of other *equipes* in Syracuse I found that I should have taken the Adriatic coast route through Bari and Taranto, which is longer in terms of miles but not so difficult and can be covered more quickly.

As Peter Whitehead had not raced at Syracuse previously he was not sure about the characteristics of the circuit and uncertain about which axle ratio to use. I consider Syracuse a miniature Rheims, for it is triangular in shape and has two long straights and a shorter one joining them together. The race average is in the region of 100 m.p.h. and the top speed on the fastest section approaches 150 m.p.h.

At the first practice session on the Friday, Whitehead soon discovered that the axle ratio was unsuitable. He came into the pits, stopped the engine and in a most polite fashion said to me:

" Please yourself but I think the ratio is wrong."

Please myself! This was a new one on me. I had never known a driver express his views on an axle ratio in such a courteous manner. It is, however, typical of Peter Whitehead. He seemed almost embarrassed, realizing fully that it would take us all night to do the job.

We finished at 3 a.m.—for it takes two people six hours to change the axle ratio on the Ferrari—and then found that our beds had been given to someone else. We slept on hall chairs in the foyer of the hotel. It was just like the old days with H.W.M.

The car went quite well in practice on the Saturday and next day Peter Whitehead drove what I would describe as a nice, comfortable race. There was no excitement in the pit as both Stan and I realized that Whitehead was not exactly fighting for the lead or intent on challenging Ascari and Villoresi on their "works" Ferraris. As I have explained, he enjoys motor-racing as a sport and at Syracuse I found that the pit "drill" is to pass information about lap times rather than attempt to speed him up in the normal way by indicating how far he is behind the man in front. He is an easy driver to control from the pits.

The car ran perfectly. There was no trouble with engine or chassis and Whitehead finished fifth. He might well have been fourth had he lapped just under one second faster each lap, but he knew exactly how quickly he wanted to go and was delighted with his placing.

After the race, he thanked both Stan and myself for the way we had prepared the car and invited us to join him for a drink. I had enjoyed my first outing with the Chalfont *equipe* although it was a very different atmosphere from that of H.W.M. There we had worked against the clock and our main object had been to win races.

With Whitehead the whole approach was a much more sober and sedate one. I never looked for or expected thanks from John Heath or anyone else in the H.W.M. *equipe* because it was a strictly business proposition. With Whitehead it was different; I felt that every effort was appreciated to the full and that the driver really did acknowledge what was done for him and the car. It was not an impersonal business proposition for either the driver or the mechanics.

I really enjoyed working on the Ferrari. Admittedly it took us a long time to change the axle ratio but, apart from this, there was no other work required on the car. Whereas in 1950 and 1951 we had experienced our teething troubles with H.W.M. in practice sessions and the races themselves, most of the teething troubles on the Italian car had been located and remedied before that particular model left the Maranello factory.

With its 2-litre engine the car was not tremendously powerful, developing something like 140 b.h.p. or 150 at the most, and weighed a good sixteen to seventeen hundredweight. It was not as light as the H.W.M.s and there was not a great deal of power low down or for acceleration through the gears, but the Ferrari handled beautifully and was a stable, sturdy motor car.

Incidentally, I did not share any of the spoils with Peter Whitehead. He paid all my expenses—very handsome ones—as well as a salary and consequently, as no bonus was involved and from a strictly business point of view, his final placing in a race was not very important to me.

CHAPTER 18

A TALE OF TWO FRONTIERS

We were anxious to get away from Syracuse in view of the fact that the 1½-litre engine would be needed for the Turin G.P. and it was still under lock and key at Ventimiglia.

The journey back via the Adriatic route was uneventful, and all we had to do was press on at the rate of four hundred miles a day and a maximum of 40 m.p.h. The Fordson went remarkably well, bowling along for hour after hour, and on Thursday afternoon we arrived in Modena, having left Syracuse on Monday morning and driven for twelve or more hours each day.

We spent the night in Modena at the Albergo Europa—a comfortable, modern and reasonably priced hotel that I can thoroughly recommend—and left for Milan next morning, having collected some spares for the Ferrari from the Trade Counter in Modena. I was disappointed that we were unable to visit the famous workshops at Maranello.

The Customs people were waiting for us when we arrived at Ventimiglia two days later. The Chief Customs officer listened impatiently to my plea and then point blank refused to grant my request.

"Turin or no Turin," he said, "we will not let you take the engine and tyres into Italy unless you produce an Import Permit. If you would care to leave 2 million lire deposit that is a different matter. Otherwise you are wasting your time hanging around here."

I felt like punching him on the nose but, with visions of twenty-four hours or so in the guard hut if I did so, Stan and I withdrew in best military fashion to the village of Ventimiglia and held a council of war. I knew it was useless trying to obtain assistance from the Club in Milan and even if we did succeed I had an idea at the back of my mind that the character at the frontier post would find something else that was not in order.

Stan and I talked the matter over and suddenly I had a bright idea.

"Why don't we turn the lorry round and go back into France? Then maybe we can cross into Italy by some other route."

We both agreed that even the unpleasant Customs official could not prevent us collecting the engine and tyres and then leaving for France, so we drove back to the frontier and pulled up outside the customs shed.

"What are you proposing to do now," demanded the Chief Customs Officer.

"Well," I said, "in the first place I am going to load up the engine and tyres and return to England, and in the second place I am going to thank you for all the help you have given and for your sporting co-operation. If all Customs Officers were like you, our job would be much easier. I have been so impressed with your kindness that I shall report your behaviour to the Royal Automobile Club in London. Thank you once again for all your help."

The Italian was flabbergasted, not knowing whether I was pulling his leg or not. However, he could no longer hold our engine and tyres under lock and key, and with a bad grace he released them. He watched suspiciously as we loaded the lorry, obviously unhappy about having to release such a valuable prize. Then, with arms akimbo and his cap pushed on to the back of his head, he stared hard at us as we drove away and pulled up at the French frontier post.

Naturally, the French Customs Officers had a few questions to ask. They had cleared the lorry when we originally passed through on our way to Italy and had watched with great interest when the tyres and engine had been unloaded by the Italians. They noted the fact that the Italians held us up for three days on that occasion, and then held us up again on our return journey. Then they had watched the pantomime of Stan, myself and a hired help staggering to the lorry with thirty tyres and an engine.

However, when I explained about the unpleasant and stupid attitude of the Italian official, the senior French official smiled and said:

" Well, at least we will not add to your difficulties. Why worry about the Italians. Why don't you try another Pass ? "

" That had occurred to me," I replied, " but the next Pass is Mt. Genevre and that's a long way to go."

The Frenchman rubbed his chin, pondering for a few seconds.

" Why not try the La Tenda Pass ? It is a much more difficult road but you may be able to get through if you enquire whether the tunnel is high enough for your lorry."

We thanked our friend profusely and set off for Rocquebrun in high spirits where, in the garage of the Diodato, we set about replacing the 2-litre engine in the Ferrari with the $1\frac{1}{2}$-litre one. I was not taking any chances. At least, if we had to leave an engine at La Tenda I should have the right one in the chassis for Turin.

We changed the engine in record time. It took from Monday morning until lunch time on Tuesday and, having checked the chassis, we loaded the Ferrari and spare engine and set off for the La Tenda Pass. It was a difficult route that involved crossing two other Passes before reaching La Tenda, and whilst Stan drove the Fordson as fast as he dared on the winding road I sat and worried about our chances. Just before reaching the frontier I stopped the lorry at a kiosk, as I wanted to send a postcard to my wife. Whilst I was looking through the cards a furtive little Frenchman tugged at my sleeve.

" How about some dirty postcards, Monsieur ? "

This gave me an idea. If I bought half-a-dozen pictures of nudes and mixed them up with the lorry papers and carnet, I knew the Italians on the frontier would be more interested in the postcards than in the carnet and spares. Pornographic pictures are forbidden in Italy.

The gamble worked. On arrival at the frontier I got out of the lorry and walked into the Customs shed where I put the carnets on the table. The Italian in charge soon found the postcards and became so engrossed in them that he even forgot to stamp the carnet and I had to remind him.

" I wonder," he said, " if you would mind leaving one or two of these with me."

I naturally agreed at once.

" So far as I am concerned," I replied, " you can keep them all."

With a cheery wave he sent us on our way. We felt on top of the world for not only had we succeeded in getting into Italy with the right engine in the chassis but we had the spare engine and all our tyres. I knew that Peter Whitehead would be delighted.

We left the lorry in Turin as Whitehead wanted us to have a few days off in England and had booked sleepers on the train. Both Stan and I appreciated his thoughtfulness, and it was a most comfortable journey.

Having bought some bottles of Chianti on Milan station we invited the train attendant to join us. It was well worth while because we crossed three frontiers without being awakened by the Customs. The attendant explained, before he started drinking with us, that if we left our passports on the table just inside the door the officials would open the door and stamp them without waking us. I must say the attendant gave us very good service before he passed out!

Those few days at home in Woolwich were very welcome. Sylvia summed up my feelings.

" It seems that at last you have a civilized job."

But it was only a short respite for we left London on April 2nd for Turin and the Formula 1 race in Valentino Park. The location of the circuit, in an artificial park rather than a natural one, is most attractive and it is a real drivers' circuit. There is a variety of different surfaces, the circuit is reasonably fast and cars are subjected to considerable stresses.

At one particular intersection drivers go from a minor to a major road, cross a dual tramway line and cope with a change of camber all at the same time. During the first practice session on the Friday I watched Taruffi in his $4\frac{1}{2}$-litre Ferrari hit the alteration in camber and become airborne until the car landed on the far side of the intersection. Naturally, the cars took a hammering from this treatment and after the race we found that the chassis of our Ferrari had cracked, even though it was not driven as hard as the "works" cars of Taruffi and Villoresi.

Peter Whitehead had raced at Valentino Park before and knew the back axle requirements. We used the 14-50 Syracuse ratio, 14 teeth on the pinion and 50 on the crown wheel, with a reduction gear mounted in the axle. On the second day of practice, he was in very good form and recorded fourth or fifth fastest time. I found that invariably his times were in the first five on most circuits and Stan and I almost took it for granted that they would be.

On Saturday we fitted a Lucas magneto in place of the Marelli and found it very satisfactory. The car went even better, particularly when we fitted 700 x 16 tyres which had the effect of slightly altering the axle ratio and saving revs. We had been using 6-50 x 16 on the Friday.

A petrol leak during the race probably lost us a place. When the chassis crack developed it must have split the fuel tank at the same time but so far as I can remember the car did not come into the pits. Whitehead must have noticed that the Ferrari was not handling properly and, by slowing down, automatically conserved enough fuel to complete the race. In spite of the chassis trouble he still managed to finish fourth and was very pleased.

He had driven against powerful "works" opposition and to come home fourth was no mean achievement for a private owner.

In two races and with the same car we had finished in the first five and also had a good night's rest with remarkable frequency. It was quite a change to lead an almost normal life.

We arrived at Chalfont on Thursday—having left Turin on the Monday —and set about welding the cracked chassis and repairing the petrol tank so that the car could race at Goodwood on the following Monday. The Ferrari was also overheating, due to a kink in the water hose, and I think the radiator and hose must have been assembled out of alignment when the engines were changed before crossing into Italy at La Tenda.

I was not sure whether the 4.9 to 1 axle ratio with the 700 x 16 tyres we had used at Syracuse and Turin would be suitable for the Sussex circuit but I need not have worried. At Goodwood on the Saturday we found that the ratio was just right and I made a note in my record book that the characteristics of the two Italian circuits and the British one are very similar.

However, we had trouble with the Ferrari. The gearbox broke down and we went straight back to Chalfont to investigate. At least the Ferrari box was a normal crash one with a "dog" engagement, and there was time to locate and possibly remedy the trouble, but having worked all night and Sunday morning as well, we found that third gear had been stripped. Unfortunately we did not carry that particular type of spare so the Ferrari had to be withdrawn.

Nevertheless, Graham Whitehead (Peter Whitehead's step-brother) took the B. type E.R.A. to Goodwood so we had a race after all. We had bad luck with the E.R.A. In the Chichester Cup, Graham spun after leaving the chicane, whilst in the big race of the day, the Richmond Trophy, he " lost a plug " on the starting line.

He is a very highly strung person, whom I was never able to keep calm, and a driver who tends to rev. the engine unnecessarily before the flag drops, so that by the time the flag falls at least one, and sometimes two, plugs are gone. It is fatal to risk oiling up these $1\frac{1}{2}$-litre supercharged engines.

My normal procedure in the paddock is to warm the engine on soft plugs and thus keep the combustion chamber as clean as possible. I do not like to start up too long before the flag drops because an engine on hard plugs is better if it labours. If it is kept running freely it oils up very easily and fills the combustion chambers with oil.

On this occasion Graham was not quite sure of himself and insisted on starting the engine three minutes before the flag fell with the result that the plugs oiled up. Nevertheless, he really made the E.R.A. motor in this race and came home fifth. I wrote in my diary: " Very good going for Mr. Graham but what a pity he oiled a plug. We might have finished fourth."

CHAPTER 19

AN ANGLO-ITALIAN EFFORT

The Formula 2 Alta—Disappointment at Marseilles—
The Ferrari at Silverstone—Alta gearbox trouble again—
Albi, the B.R.M.s and faulty race tactics—The Ferrari excels at Monza.

Our first race with the Alta was a Formula 2 event at Marseilles on April 27th, and precisely one week beforehand I went over to Tolworth to collect the brand new racing car. Geoffrey Taylor had been working against the clock but even so the Alta was not ready, which meant staying at Tolworth on the Sunday night.

The new F.2 Alta was a nice looking car. The wheels were of Bugatti style, cast from light alloy and widely spoked. In fact, the car looked rather like a Bugatti. It had a similar but much lighter version of the suspension system on the Grand Prix Alta—double wishbones front and rear. However, the rubber blocks on compression were directly connected to the wishbones, not connected through a radial cantilever action as on the G.P. car. The back axle was identical on both cars and so was the gearbox. The F.2 engine was supposed to give over 150 b.h.p. but we never succeeded in extracting this much power.

We eventually left the Alta works in the transporter at seven o'clock on the Monday evening and just managed to catch the Night Ferry to Dunkirk. With the transporter stowed on the car deck, Stan and I relaxed in the bar.

" This has been some rush," I said. " I hope it is not an ill omen."

We left Dunkirk in the early hours of Tuesday morning, stopped the night some sixty kilometres from Dijon and arrived in Marseilles just after lunch on Thursday. I drove straight to the Renault Garage, where we had been given so much help the previous year, and found the H.W.M. team already there. This was the first time I had encountered the Walton *equipe* in the 1952 season and I am glad to say there was no ill feeling. It was rather the reverse.

Having been given permission by the proprietor to use his garage I then asked John Heath whether he would mind me sharing the facilities with H.W.M.

" Of course you can, Alf," he said. " After all, you are the man who found this garage for us in the first place."

He told me that their lorry had crashed en route to Marseilles, and that it could not be used, so I offered him the use of the Chalfont transporter to ferry the H.W.M.'s to and from the circuit.

On the first day of practice we changed the Alta axle ratio to 4.3 to 1 but it was obviously not entirely satisfactory. The carburation was also very troublesome and it seemed to me that the mixture was far too rich. We were " losing " plugs regularly.

At the second practice session, at 4.30 on Saturday afternoon, we had trouble with crankcase breathing. Having more or less sorted out the carburation on the previous day the car was going quite well, except that every two or three laps the engine suddenly sneezed and covered the engine and driver with oil. Geoffrey Taylor was there, having decided to accompany the car to its first race, and whilst he is a first-rate designer he is not exactly the right man for curing troubles on the circuit in the shortest possible time.

After the first sneezing fit we examined the engine but could find nothing wrong with the oil system. We started the car, off went the Alta and sure enough—after a few laps—Whitehead came in again, having been smothered in oil for the second time. We had not experienced trouble on Friday and it occurred to me that perhaps a piston ring had collapsed. There was only one way to find out; strip down the engine.

It meant working all night, otherwise we should never have the car on the grid for the race next day and, as soon as we could do so, Geoffrey Taylor, Stan and I left the circuit, made our way back to the garage and got down to it. We reckoned to have the pistons out by midnight but, as we were stripping down the engine, Geoffrey Taylor pulled one of them through the crankcase instead of taking it out of the top end. In his anxiety to see the piston rings he had overlooked the consequences of such action.

As soon as he extracted the piston in this fashion, and the ring had come away from the bore, it still had another half-an-inch to travel in the aluminium crankcase and became jammed. I struggled with the piston but could get it neither in nor out. It was well and truly jammed and I was furious.

It was going to take something like ten hours to take the engine out of the chassis, strip and reassemble. There was plenty of work for Stan and myself without added complications and I am afraid I lost my temper, although Geoffrey Taylor had only been trying to help. I straightened up and faced him.

" You designed this engine," I shouted, " and you don't even know which way to pull out the pistons. You ought to know better. I wish you would leave us alone."

Geoffrey Taylor could see that I was in a belligerent mood.

" I feel rather tired," he said in a most polite manner. " I think I will go to bed now."

We eventually succeeded in getting the pistons out, only to find that the rings had not collapsed. At six o'clock in the morning we had completed reassembly of the engine, but were both so tired that I insisted on double checking everything for tightness when the body was replaced on the chassis. It is a lot of work to remove the body and engine from the chassis, strip the engine and remove the head, take out the crankshaft and pistons, and finally reassemble the whole issue and put it back in the chassis.

There is no margin for error and it is the mechanic who takes the blame if anything goes wrong with the car in the race that can be traced to faulty assembly. I wonder how many people realize just what sort of responsibilities we have to accept, and the very tight schedules—with little or no sleep— that are involved.

That night at Marseilles was one of the most tiring I have ever spent and, having replaced the body on the chassis, I told Stan to pack up.

" It is no good going on like this," I said. " We are both finished. Someone has to be awake to look after the car during the race and the best idea is for you to get some sleep whilst I finish the preparation. I will wake you for the race."

I wish I could say that the Alta, on its first appearance, did well but unfortunately this was not the case. Peter Whitehead completed forty laps, at a rather slow pace compared with the rest of the field which included Ferraris and Gordinis, eventually retiring with oil breather trouble. In addition, he was not very happy about the steering.

We were all disappointed with this performance but in all fairness I think the 4.3 to 1 axle ratio was wrong. I consider we should have used 4.8 to 1 or even 4.9 to 1, for the circuit is a very slow and bumpy one and it is necessary to increase the power out of corners and the acceleration low down.

We left Marseilles on Tuesday, having caught up on our sleep, called at the Simca works in Paris for some spares on Wednesday evening and crossed from Dunkirk to Dover on Thursday night. Next day we drove to the Alta works; Geoffrey Taylor intended to strip down the engine and find the cause of the oil trouble as well as check the steering geometry.

We had other problems. The Ferrari had been entered for the Formula 2 International Trophy at Silverstone the following weekend, and there was still no sign of the new gearbox parts from Modena. Fortunately, they arrived on Wednesday and by the evening a new third gear had been fitted and the assembly of the gearbox completed. Next day, at Silverstone, I made a rather feeble attempt to modify the air intake scoop on the Ferrari but only succeeded in upsetting the entire carburation system. So I quickly abandoned my theory, gave best to Mr. Enzo Ferrari and fitted the original intake.

On race day the car went very well indeed, and finished seventh in the first of the trophy heats after an exciting dice with Schell on his Maserati. Whitehead drove impeccably and his handling of the Ferrari was a pleasure to watch. The heat was won by Hawthorn in the astonishing Cooper-Bristol.

I certainly got excited in the final. The H.W.M.s (Macklin, Rolt, Collins and Hamilton) were out in force, to say nothing of the Gordinis and Hawthorn. Peter Whitehead was not exactly going slowly at Silverstone, sharing fastest lap with Hawthorn at 88.35 m.p.h., but neither was he trying to beat the " works " teams.

I knew the potentialities of both car and driver and wanted Whitehead to "have a go" on our home circuit particularly as the H.W.M.s were there. I suggested the "faster" signal to David Yorke (later team manager of Vanwall) who was running our pit at Silverstone, convinced that both the car and driver could be pushed a little in perfect safety.

" Give him a signal. Do something! " I pleaded. " He is going so well."

However, Yorke would not agree. I suppose he was right. He knew very well that Whitehead would take no notice and probably be annoyed as well. I was disappointed for it was hard to get used to this new approach of driving within certain limits as against the H.W.M. attitude of "flat out or bust." Nevertheless, although perhaps a little wistful I was glad that Lance

Macklin won the race for H.W.M., his first major victory. Rolt's H.W.M. was second whilst Peter Whitehead was a very creditable fifth.

At Chalfont, after Silverstone, we had to change the engine on the Ferrari and fit the 1½-litre supercharged unit for the Formula 1 Albi G.P. It was also necessary to alter the back axle ratio, which we were able to do at Chalfont, as I had a complete list—provided by the Ferrari works—of ratios for the various circuits. This was easier than trundling around in the lorry and finding out the hard way.

Peter Whitehead was anxious to get the car over to the continent because its Italian carnet was due to expire and this meant that we should have to convert the transporter to carry two cars, for both were entered at Monza after the Albi race.

I knew a garage in Calais where I should be able to carry out the work and took the Ferrari over there in the transporter. In three days, I modified the lift and completed the job and, having loaded the Ferrari on the top runners, I left the whole outfit in the garage, returned to London by train and went straight over to Tolworth to help with the Alta.

Within a few days I was back in the Renault garage at Calais again, having towed the Alta from the ferry, and once the car had been loaded in the van we set off for Montlhery where the Alta had been entered in a Formula 2 event. It was an uninteresting race with Ferraris first, second and third— and the Alta retired with gear selector trouble after only a few laps. I was very fed up about it for I knew so much about the Alta gearbox, having experienced its frailty on the G.P. car, and it looked as though we were going to be plagued with similar trouble on this latest car as well. It still had the same synchromeshes, which were preventing successful gear changes and causing the selector to break when the driver used force to engage the gear lever.

We took the Alta to Cataneos in Paris, a garage belonging to a friend of Peter Whitehead, and stripped the gearbox to try to find out why the selector had broken down. However, there was not much time to spare, as the following week-end the Ferrari was due at Albi, so we just checked the box and modified the gear selector. It was rather a "bodging up" process for there was only time to strengthen the selector when the real necessity was for the gearbox itself—the synchromeshes—to be modified.

We were practising in Albi on Friday and, with 700 x 16 tyres, the Ferrari went very well. What a difference! There was no trouble at all and in the evening there was so little to do that we were able to relax at the corner cafe and have a quiet chat. We even went to bed early.

The B.R.M.s were at Albi. They were most impressive in practice and shook all of us. We had heard so much about them and their disappointing performance but when, during the practice sessions, Fangio and Gonzalez took them round, it was fantastic—almost beyond imagination. Fangio not only went faster than the previous lap record but knocked off something like eleven seconds as he lapped at over 114 m.p.h.

The performance of the B.R.M.s put the rest of us in the shade and all we could hope for was another B.R.M. breakdown which, on past performance, was fairly certain. The rest of the field could then sort itself out in a comparatively leisurely fashion. Certainly, had the B.R.M.s kept going for the whole race at similar speeds to their practice times the other competitors would have come home as stragglers.

Having made a consumption test I found that we should need to take on five gallons of fuel in order to complete the 190-mile race, but according to our calculations it would be run at such a high speed, even if the B.R.M.s did pack up, that we should in any case be several laps in arrears at the finish and would not need to take on the extra fuel. We, therefore, decided to run throughout non-stop.

However, the B.R.M.s were out of action before twenty laps had been completed and we suddenly found, to our consternation, that several other very rapid cars—including Schells 1½-litre supercharged Gordini—had also retired and that Peter Whitehead was lying fourth, *on the same lap as the leader*. It became apparent at once that we should have to cover the full race distance and I asked David Yorke what action he proposed to take.

" Do we or do we not call in the car for fuel ? "

Yorke was uncertain because, as I have explained, we did not tell Peter Whitehead what to do in a race. He made up his own mind, based on the information we passed him, and Yorke decided to leave the decision to Whitehead who knew as well as we did that he was on the same lap as the leader. Meanwhile, we would prepare for a quick refuelling stop.

I went to the back of the pits to get the churns and mechanical starter, then worked out a quick plan with Stan.

"As soon as the car stops," I told him, " I will put in the funnel and you can pour in five gallons of fuel whilst I get the starter to the front of the car."

Having worked everything out carefully we sat back and waited for Peter Whitehead. However, during the course of the race he must have forgotten about the fuel situation for it was obvious that he had no intention of calling at the pits. Maybe it was because, very near to the end, he started to close on Giraud Cabantous (4½-litre Talbot) who was lying third. I could not help feeling that we should have given some sort of signal, warning him of the position, but instead we just stood there like clots and waited for the inevitable.

I hoped against hope that the Ferrari would come in for some other reason but it was not to be. The car ran out of fuel but, by an incredible stroke of luck, Whitehead was able to freewheel to the pits. Nevertheless he not only lost fourth place but a great deal of time as well for the Ferrari ran itself absolutely dry and the fuel pump, being a mechanical vane type, is not easily primed. Although our refuelling drill worked perfectly, the pump refused to co-operate.

The car rolled to a stop and within seconds Stan had snapped back the filler cap and was pouring in the fuel. He slammed the filler shut again.

" Funnel out," he shouted. " Let's go."

I pressed the button of the starter and the engine turned over but that was all. There was absolutely no sign of life and I kept the starter going so long that it began to smoke. It was almost red hot.

There was still no sign of life and, in desperation, I shouted at Stan to blow down the tank, meanwhile making a mental note that Fischer's starter was at the next pit and very conveniently placed if our own gave up the ghost. Stan must have blown down the tank with gale force for suddenly the engine fired and Whitehead went away. I relaxed and watched the car until it was out of sight then turned round to congratulate Stan.

There he was, flat on his back in front of the pit and unconscious. The fuel had obviously blown back into his mouth and a combination of heat, exertion and fumes had put him out for the count. I had to find some water or something without delay. There was a bottle of Coca Cola standing on Fischer's pit counter and I quickly grabbed it, knocked off the top and poured most of the contents into Stan's mouth. This brought him round, but he was still very shaky and pale.

I forgot all about the Coca Cola until Fischer arrived at his pit, absolutely dying for a drink. He had probably had visions of ice cold Coke all through the race and, when the bottle could not be found, rounded on everyone including his wife.

" I put it there myself," he shouted. " Where is it ? Who has taken it ? Does no one have any consideration for the drivers ? "

I did not say a word, for I knew very well that if I told what had happened whilst he was in his present excited state he would probably knock me down. A minute or so afterwards Gonzalez came along the front of the pits. He must have seen the whole incident with the Coca Cola bottle, and Stan passing out. He slapped me on the back and said in perfect English: " Bad mechanic," then continued his journey. Just those two words, probably one of the few English phrases he knows besides " Good mechanic."

The next engagement of the Whitehead *equipe* was a Formula 2 race at Monza on June 8th and Peter Whitehead decided to race both the Alta and Ferrari, handling the British car himself whilst Peter Walker drove the Italian car. This meant changing the Ferrari engine and I have never had a season of motor-racing where I have changed engines on so many occasions.

There was very little else in the nature of hard work to do on the Ferrari. In view of Peter Whitehead's outlook we did not have to tune the car to the highest degree as with the H.W.M.s. Once the carburation had been set in England, then it was hardly altered from race to race. There was no question of fighting for extra horses.

On arrival at the Monza autodrome we unloaded the lorry and booked our lock-up garage in the paddock. Almost before we had got the cars on to the circuit for the first practice session there was gearbox trouble with the Alta. As with the G.P. car, centrifugal force was driving out the lubricant with disastrous effects. The first gear bush had broken, also the distance pieces.

It was not an easy task finding phosphor bronze on Friday evening in the town of Monza but we eventually succeeded and returned to the autodrome. We worked all night, fabricating new bushes, but the Alta was not practised on Saturday, although Peter Whitehead took out the Ferrari and was very pleased with it.

On race day both our cars were on the grid in Heat 1, cars and drivers rather overshadowed by the opposition which included Ascari, Farina, Gonzalez, Fangio, Villoresi, Simon, Bonetto and Fischer. Ascari won the heat, Fangio crashed and was seriously injured, whilst our Ferrari and Alta ran in more or less team formation and finished sixth and seventh respectively.

In the second heat a carburetter float chamber fell off the Alta but the Ferrari fairly whistled round the circuit, with Walker at the wheel, and when the heat times were added he was classified as fourth, only 7½ seconds a lap slower than the winner, Farina (Ferrari).

I asked Walker just before the start of the second heat what sort of pit signals he required.

" Look, Alf," he replied, " I am going flat from the word ' go. ' I am not interested in plus or minus. I am going as fast as I can and I only want you to signal how many laps remain."

I consider this Monza Grand Prix one of the finest races Peter Walker has driven and he told us an amusing story when, on the Sunday evening, we dined with Peter Whitehead in Milan. Walker explained how he saw Ascari in his mirror as the Italian moved up to lap him in the new type 4-cylinder Ferrari. Walker, of course, was on a much older, slower and heavier car. Lesmo Corner was approaching and Walker resolved to hold off Ascari through the corner.

" I never lifted my foot," he said. " I just kept her going flat, and halfway through the corner Ascari goes by on the outside. I almost passed out in the cockpit."

Peter Walker is apt to press on regardless but is a first-rate driver and a first-rate sportsman as well. He is rather different from Peter Whitehead in that he is ambitious to "have a go" whereas Whitehead is just as much of a sportsman but will never "have a go" to the extent of attacking the works cars unnecessarily, thus running the risk of an expensive blow-up.

CHAPTER 20

MAINLY ABOUT THE ALTA

Wizardry with Webers—The F.2 Alta impresses at Silverstone and Comminges—A broken crankshaft at La Baule—Loss of face at Monza

After the Monza race it was decided to fit Weber carburetters to the Alta. Mr. Galletti of Webers, who had been so helpful the previous year in connection with the H.W.M.s, was confident that they could find at least another 6 or 7 b.h.p. by fitting twin Webers. Peter Whitehead was most enthusiastic, and I told Galletti that we would let them experiment with the Alta engine provided there was no charge if they were unable to justify their claims.

At Webers in Bologna we lifted the engine out of the chassis, fitted it on the brake and made a run on S.U. carburetters. At 6,000 revs. it was developing 117 b.h.p., not a great deal when compared with the 170 b.h.p. of the new Ferrari. The Alta engine was running exactly as fitted in the chassis, with the normal foot-long stub exhaust pipes.

Next day we fitted Weber carburetters and a new manifold, and although we were in a hurry and only guessed the jet sizes, the power increased to 124 b.h.p. Without any special tuning, we had already found 7 b.h.p. I was beginning to see daylight and wrote in my diary: "I am sure we are going places with this Alta. The car is beautifully light and if we can get even more power out of the engine then we shall really be able to scrap with the opposition."

The Weber people did not work on the Saturday afternoon so Stan and I took this opportunity of stripping down the Alta gearbox and found that the synchromesh locating pins had broken. I had new pins fabricated in Bologna by a private individual and he made a remarkably good job of them. They were certainly as good as, if not better than, the original ones; for three pins he charged only 4,500 lire, approximately £2.10s.

We carried on with our carburetter development on Monday. The Weber experts suggested a further modification to the manifold, as they did not like the angle of induction from the carburetter and, sure enough, when the new manifold was fitted the power increased to 129.8 b.h.p. We had found no less than 12.8 b.h.p. since our arrival and were all striving for a final figure in the region of 150 b.h.p.

On Tuesday we ran the engine on the bench all day, experimenting with different lengths of exhaust pipe, but nothing would induce it to produce more than 130 b.h.p. However, by altering the ignition timing we found another 4 b.h.p. Total to date 133.8 b.h.p.

Next day the Weber people—who had been most enthusiastic since the start of our experiments—fitted an entirely different type of carburetter with much larger chokes, 38 mm instead of 36 mm. The result was terrific, the engine producing no less than 136.8 b.h.p.

In five working days we had increased output by 19.8 b.h.p. but no one believes me when I tell this story. People think I am shooting a line, or that I must have taken inaccurate readings, and it is very difficult to convince them that such gains in b.h.p. are possible mainly with carburation adjustment. However, the figures are at Weber for anyone to see, and the explanation for the large increase that followed the change from S.U. to Weber is quite logical.

There is no doubt that S.U. carburetters are ideal for normal production motor cars that are driven largely on part throttle. This type of carburetter requires very careful setting of the needle jet, but once it has been adjusted properly a much better m.p.g. figure can be obtained than with other carburetters because the mixture adjusts itself to perfection for all engine speeds. This is not so with a fixed choke carburetter such as a Weber, which is set to run rather rich in places so that the performance is as near perfect as possible at the top end and in the middle range.

However, from the competition point of view a car is not driven on part throttle. The object is to obtain the maximum b.h.p. throughout the whole range of engine speeds and for this purpose I consider the Weber is more satisfactory.

From the point of view of thermo-dynamics the better streamlined Weber carburetter is bound to give a more satisfactory performance. With a fixed choke it is possible for a different size of choke to be used, which increases or decreases the air speed through the carburetter. Thus one can, to a certain degree, lower or raise the torque of the engine at different revs., and the performance of the engine at high speeds can be increased. The S.U., with its dashpot and adjustable choke, is not streamlined in the same sense, and an air speed blockage occurs as with a car that is not streamlined.

We wanted to celebrate but I could not induce Mr. Galletti and Mr. Gallini—the two Weber chiefs—to join me for a meal. They are very strict about this sort of thing and absolutely refuse to accept favours from their customers. As one of them explained to me:

" We do our job and are only too pleased to help but after all it is a strictly business proposition."

It suddenly occurred to me that June 18th was my birthday and when I pointed this out they could not very well refuse to join us for a celebration dinner. Mr. Weber congratulated us on achieving so much with the Alta engine, wished me good luck for the rest of the season and said he would send his interpreter to the dinner party as neither Galletti nor Gallini could speak English. The interpreter was an attractive brunette and, having wined and dined extremely well, we eventually ended up in a dance-hall with Stan monopolizing the interpreter and Gallini, Galletti and I struggling along without one.

The day after my birthday party, on the recommendation of our friends at Webers, we fitted different type diffusers—with long, tapered extension tubes of Ferrari-style—and this increased the brake horse power yet again, to a figure of 143.

At this stage it was decided to abandon further experiments and the engine was taken off the bench and stripped down completely. It had been well and truly thrashed, yet the bearings were in perfect condition and we only changed them because, with the engine down, it was convenient to do so. I wrote in the diary: "I wonder how much all this is going to cost."

The account was a pleasant surprise. The Weber people were very fair and only charged 146,000 lire, approximately £80. This covered five days' bench testing of the engine as well as the manufacture of new manifolds and supplying the carburetters and all necessary parts.

In high spirits we left Bologna, met Peter Whitehead in Milan and went out to Monza to test the car. To our great disappointment we had fuel pressure trouble and it is a good example of successful development in one direction resulting in a fault elsewhere.

On the bench we had used a gravity supply, with fuel fed from a tank some six metres above the engine. With the engine in the chassis once again we had to use the normal type of pressure pump and it could not cope. This was not our only problem. We broke every single one of the synchro-mesh pins during testing!

"I wish it was logical to take all the synchromesh out of this gearbox," I said to Stan. "It will make a mental case of me otherwise."

What this Alta required, as did the Formula 1 G.P. car, was an entirely different design of gears and engagement "dogs."

Our next race was at Rouen on July 6th and I took the opportunity of going via Paris so that I could "thrash" the gearbox at Montlhery. I drove the Alta round and round the banked inner circuit for two hours until I felt thoroughly sick from being bumped about so much. I tried all I knew to break the gearbox. Again and again I went up through the gears and down again, changing with and without the clutch. I really gave the Alta the treatment.

Then we took the car to Cataneo's garage and stripped down the gearbox. There was not a thing wrong with it.

"I reckon it is O.K. now," I said to Stan and, having assembled it, we set off for Rouen and the Formula 2 French Grand Prix. The Alta faced stiff opposition, including the "works" Ferraris, six-cylinder Gordinis, and a number of V.12 Ferraris as well as Maseratis, H.W.M.s, and Hawthorn in a Cooper-Bristol.

The Ferraris, absolutely superior on the twisting Essarts circuits, fairly romped away with the race and finished first, second and third; Ascari, Farina, Taruffi. The Alta, having completed twenty-five laps of the 3.17-mile circuit, was retired when in eleventh place with a broken gear selector lever. It was some consolation that at least nothing had gone wrong *inside* the box.

Two weeks later, both cars were entered at Silverstone in the Formula 2 British G.P. Graham Whitehead drove the Alta whilst Peter Whitehead handled the Ferrari. On the first day of practice we had trouble with the cylinder head gasket of the the Italian car and, leaving the Alta in the Shell tent, we took the Ferrari back to Chalfont where the head was removed. It took the two of us all Thursday night, because taking the cylinder head off a Ferrari is no easy matter, and we found a leak in the copper jointing.

Having dealt with this problem we returned to Silverstone and practised the Alta, only to have trouble with one of the rear hubs which came loose and damaged a half shaft. One of Geoffrey Taylor's mechanics drove to Tolworth, collected a new shaft and, for the second night in succession, we went without sleep. After this series of misfortunes it was more than gratifying to see both cars on the grid for the 250-mile British G.P.

Neither car put up a brilliant performance against the strong opposition, which included Ferrari, Maserati, Gordini, Cooper-Bristol, H.W.M. and Connaught, but at least they both finished, the Ferrari tenth and the Alta twelfth. I got quite a kick out of Chalfont vanquishing Walton for only one of four H.W.M.s finished and that was in thirteenth place. Ferraris—Ascari and Taruffi—were first and second.

Having loaded the cars we were in jubilant mood for this was the first occasion the Formula 2 Alta had completed a full race distance without breaking down. I had taken my courage in both hands at Chalfont before the race and removed synchromesh on first and second gear, and Graham Whitehead was full of praise for the performance of the gearbox.

Morale was high and it seemed that at last the Alta teething troubles had been cured. In an effort to consolidate our triumph over circumstance we took the car back to the works at Tolworth and fitted new type gears in the box, on needle rollers. I was as happy as a sand-boy that, after nearly four years, something was being done about the gearbox. We also stripped down the engine for a complete overhaul and spent ten days at Tolworth before leaving for the Comminges F.2 race in the South of France.

The brakes were re-lined the day before the first practice session and, with a 4 to 1 axle ratio and 600 x 16 tyres, Peter Whitehead managed to record 2 minutes 2 seconds on the 2.738-mile road circuit. We were delighted, for the car gave no trouble at all, and Whitehead did not bother to practise on Saturday as it was raining and we knew it would not be possible to better the Friday times. I made an entry in my diary: "Alta is going well. This is one occasion we have not had to work on the car all night before a Meeting."

Peter Whitehead drove a very steady race, in spite of the fact that an engine bearer broke, and after a non-stop run finished fourth behind the Ferraris of Ascari and Farina, and the Gordini of Behra, beating de Graffenried (Maserati-Plate) and Giraud Cabantous (H.W.M.) in the process. Afterwards Whitehead told me that the steering had suddenly become stiff and I found, on driving the car away from the circuit, that the weight of the engine was resting on the steering column.

It was in 1952 that I started a system of driving a car to and from the circuit so that I could compare its handling—at slow speeds at any rate—before and after a race. Getting into the cockpit and driving a car immediately after a race told me a great deal about brakes, suspension and general handling qualities.

This was the second long distance race the Alta had completed and we decided to make a thorough inspection of the car and find out exactly how everything had stood up to several hundred hard motor-racing miles. First of all the gearbox was stripped down and checked. Fourth gear had worn slightly but, apart from this, the box was sound as a bell. However, I found the clutch housing cracked and this had to be reinforced and welded, and on inspecting the chassis we found the front cross member broken on the weld joints.

We had to remove the engine, fuel tanks and body so that the chassis could be reset to its normal position and the engine supports modified. We then removed the drive case of the engine and sump, afterwards checking connecting rods and bearings and finding them absolutely O.K. Then we had a look at the brakes and found the linings worn quite considerably, particularly at the front end, but there were no cracks in the drums. Finally, the back axle was checked and found O.K.

We took the car to the local Citroen agent so that he could carry out some of the work under our supervision for we could never have done it all ourselves. Even so, we only finished working on the car a few hours before we were due to leave Comminges for La Baule. That night I wrote in the diary: " We are tired out. The car has been practically rebuilt."

The 2½-mile circuit at the Atlantic Coast resort of La Baule is partly on public roads, partly on airfield service roads. The car did not sound too good at the first practice session and next day I had a look at the camshafts and magnetos but could not find anything wrong, so we reassembled, then cleaned the car for practice. We were still too slow and the range of revs too short and it seemed to me that the 4 to 1 ratio with 600 x 16 tyres was not quite right, but at least the gearbox gave no trouble. The diary tells the story of the race: "Broke crankshaft after only two laps. What rotten luck. We are all fed up." Ascari won and H.W.M.s were fourth and fifth.

It was at La Baule that I had a crew cut. My long hair had been annoying me for years and I told the barber to give me the full treatment, as with the Americans. I had the "modification" carried out one evening whilst Stan was on the beach, and arrived back at the hotel looking like an Indian brave.

The receptionist did not recognize me, neither did Stan when he returned. I was on the bed, with my feet up and facing away from the door, and when Stan came into the room he went out again at once, thinking the rooms had been changed and apologizing profusely for intruding.

We sent the Alta back to England from La Baule and concentrated on getting the Ferrari ready for the Italian Grand Prix. The axle ratio was changed and the car thoroughly checked before we left for Italy but I am afraid the Chalfont *equipe* lost considerable "face" at Monza, together with the H.W.M. team (Gaze, Collins and Macklin) and Bill Aston in his Aston-Butterworth.

On Friday the Ferrari did not go at all well on the very fast circuit. Whitehead was lapping in 2 minutes 20 seconds, which was some fourteen seconds slower than Ascari and five seconds behind the slowest Connaught (McAlpine). It seemed the car was lacking some 200 revs. and I suspected the magneto.

" Whatever happens, we must qualify," I said to Stan.

However, having checked the points, magneto timing and carburetters, the car was still very slow at 2-18.8 when we practised on the Saturday. We even cut back the exhaust pipes at the suggestion of Tony Vandervell but still could not make up those elusive 200 revs. "Seems we are going to see the race as spectators," I wrote in the diary on Saturday night. And on

Sunday : " Seen race from Terrace Box. What a disgrace, but H.W.M. are in the same boat."

The Formula 2 Alta ended its first season of racing in a most violent manner. In October we entered the car at Castle Combe and Peter Whitehead was involved in a bad crash. That was its final appearance in 1952 as, although Whitehead was not hurt, there was considerable damage to the car, which included a twisted chassis, and damage to the steering and front wishbones.

CHAPTER 21

THE RAY MARTIN COOPER-ALTA

*An interesting project—I leave Peter Whitehead—
Trials and tribulations—An almost impossible task—
Somehow we get to Goodwood—I leave Ray Martin.*

A chance meeting with Stirling Moss in the drivers' changing room at Goodwood towards the end of the season left me in a curious state of mind. Stirling asked how I had enjoyed racing with Peter Whitehead.

" To tell you the truth," I replied, " it has been interesting but not much fun. Admittedly, I have lived a more or less civilized life, but it has been a continuous holiday rather than hard work. As you know, Peter Whitehead is not such an ambitious driver as the average amateur, and I have missed the incentive of working for success that we had with H.W.M."

Stirling's reply was intriguing but non-committal.

"Well, frankly speaking, I have not had much of a year either. I am pretty well fed up about everything and would like to have a talk with you some time. I may have a proposition to put to you and I suggest you speak to John Cooper of the *Autocar.*"

He did not satisfy my curiosity and I heard nothing more about the proposition until one evening at the Steering Wheel Club in London when I met the late John Cooper. I knew him quite well. We had often met around the circuits and I regarded him as one of the nicest people in motor-racing.

He lost no time coming to the point, sitting me down in a corner of the bar and outlining plans which he and Moss were making to build a racing car of their own shape and design.

" The idea," explained John Cooper, " is that Stirling and I will decide on the rough characteristics of the car but the detail design will be carried out by Ray Martin of Ray Martin Motors."

This was the first occasion I had spoken to John Cooper for any length of time, and as he warmed to his theme I could see that people had not exaggerated by describing him as a gifted engineer and clever designer. He emphasized time and again during our discussion that this country ought to manufacture and race a Grand Prix car.

"I am convinced," said Cooper, "that the right people are available in England to do it. That is why I approached Stirling and Ray Martin. I know Stirling's capabilities and his insistence on racing a British car. I also know he has been disappointed with the E.R.A. and that there is no other British car available at the present time to exploit his talent. I want to help build one for him."

John Cooper continued : " We need you to help build the car. How about joining us ?   Both Stirling and I reckon you are the best man to supervise its construction under the guidance of Ray Martin."

My reaction wa immediate.   In the first place I knew I would like nothing better than to work with Moss and Cooper.   On the other hand I did not see how I could possibly let down Peter Whitehead.   I was still working for him and he naturally assumed I would be staying on for the 1953 season.

" I appreciate your kind thought," I said to Cooper, " but how can I leave Peter Whitehead at such short notice ? "

That was how our first discussion about he proposed car ended ; but John Cooper was not prepared to let the matter rest there and put on the pressure by coming over to see me at Woolwich on successive Saturday evenings.   We used to spend hours talking about the car even though I still had not made up my mind to leave Peter Whitehead.

Eventually, his insistence convinced me that I should join the team and I must admit that he wore down my resistance by firing my imagination. He was a man with national prestige very much at heart and put over his arguments in such a way that in the end I did not like to refuse.

I felt, as Cooper did, genuinely enthusiastic about a British G.P. car in the hands of Stirling Moss and it was after all an honour to be invited to join such a team and to plan and work on such a project.   I was still a comparative newcomer to motor-racing and the offer from Cooper and Moss flattered me.   There was one other very good reason why I wanted to join them.   I should be able to have a crack at the " works " teams.

My wife saw the whole problem in a much more logical light.

" You have not been able to find anywhere at Chalfont where I can join you," she said, " and you cannot go on for ever, travelling over a hundred miles each day in all weathers."

And so I made the decision to leave Peter Whitehead.   He was naturally disappointed and rightly so.   However, in a most courteous manner he dismissed the matter with a few words.

" I cannot understand why you must leave, Alf, but if that is what you want, then you had better go."

It was embarrassing and I felt an absolute heel.   I could not justify my action for I was leaving a secure job, with the best working conditions I had ever had, to chase what might well turn out to be a will-o'-the-wisp.

I joined Ray Martin Motors at Mitcham just before Christmas and was employed as Works Manager.   We had to have more personnel, yet the finances of the firm were limited and we could not afford skilled fitters, so I advertised for motor-racing enthusiasts willing to help in the construction of a British G.P. car.

I succeeded in finding four enthusiasts who were prepared to earn a living in this manner and employed them on a full time basis.   They were so keen to learn about the practical side of building a racing car that I think they would have worked on the project for nothing if I had suggested it. They were a grand bunch and used to work twelve or fourteen hours a day for a very small wage ; I believe it was in the region of £5 a week.

It was decided that our target date would be Easter Monday and the Goodwood Meeting, which gave us no more than twelve weeks in which to build the car. Whilst this would have been sufficient time under normal circumstances, the construction of this particular car was such a complicated business that it inevitably became a rush job.

I am not going to describe in detail how we set about building the chassis but, by explaining some of our difficulties, the reader will appreciate what we were up against during those twelve weeks. In the first place Stirling wanted to use a modified version of a Cooper chassis and to improve the road-holding by altering the suspension. Having discussed the matter we considered the best solution would be to use a de Dion at the rear and double wishbones at the front.

The other John Cooper (of the Cooper Car Co. Ltd., Surbiton) agreed to supply a standard chassis and body but no sooner had they arrived than Ray Martin reached the conclusion that to modify the chassis would take longer than for us to build a special one, incorporating our ideas on suspension. Coopers finally agreed to supply the material only so that we could fabricate a chassis according to our own design.

We did not really get going until January and soon found that making the actual chassis was not as complicated as we had thought. However, as the car took shape around it, various complications arose. Normally, when one builds a car of one's own design, the procedure is to contract out to various firms for the necessary component parts which are naturally specified in such a way that they fit the general scheme of things. However, as the car was going to be called a Cooper, the Surbiton firm insisted on most of the parts—such as wheels and chassis tubes—being used as originally specified for the 2-litre Cooper-Bristols that were being built at the time. It meant that not only did we have to use our ingenuity in adapting certain parts but we were having to do twice as much work.

For instance, in line with the policy of the late John Cooper, of the *Autocar*, and Ray Martin, a de Dion tube was used at the rear end, and as the weight of the tube is heavier than the normal Cooper transverse leaf and bottom wishbone suspension we were forced to move the rear brakes inboard. This in itself involved considerable complications. Then when Stirling agreed with Girlings that they could experiment with disc brakes at the front end we were faced with the problem of using Cooper electron wheels with stub axles of our own manufacture to incorporate disc brakes. More complications arose when it was agreed that the wheels would be of the knock-on type.

On the front suspension I suggested that we use shock-absorbers mounted on the chassis instead of the Cooper telescopic type. We had a lot of discussion about this particular point because I insisted that by mounting the " shockers " in this way they would be less subject to vibrations than if mounted on the unsprung part of the car. My idea was adopted and we eventually used double wishbones with the top ones incorporating the shock-absorbers.

One way and another the car from beginning to end was the most complicated project on which I have ever worked. During the building there was very little that could be described as practical from the fitting point of view. Even accommodating the seat was difficult and, looking back, it seems to me that we never had the chassis the right width in the first place.

Trying to save weight, it is probable that Ray Martin cramped the whole design of the car.

Stirling Moss wanted to use a Maserati 2-litre 6-cylinder engine, which he was confident of being able to import from Italy, but I was against this course of action.

" If we are going to build a British car," I said, " let's use a British engine. After all, I know quite a lot about Alta engines so why not buy one from Geoffrey Taylor."

John Cooper of *The Autocar* was in full agreement, and Stirling was quick to see my point about national prestige, so we placed an order with Alta Engineering. Whilst work continued on the chassis, a dummy engine was used—supplied by Geoffrey Taylor—which was supposed to be precisely the same dimensions as the one he was building for the car.

The Cooper Car Co. Ltd. did not mind what sort of engine was used. They were so pleased that Stirling would be driving a car with a Cooper chassis and body, which might become a prototype for future production models, that they were not particular whether it was powered by a British or foreign engine.

An Alta engine meant an Alta gearbox of the same design as that used on the Formula 2 Alta and the Grand Prix Alta driven by Abecassis. I was anxious to avoid the sort of troubles we had experienced in the past, and suggested mounting the gear change mechanism on the chassis where it would be less subject to vibration from the engine. I could not redesign the gearbox but could at least attempt to improve matters.

My main concern was to avoid breakages of the gearchange lever itself. This raised the problem of joining, by means of flexible linkage, the gear change mechanism to the selectors. However, I must point out that modifications had resulted in the use of needle roller-bearings in the Alta " box," instead of bronze bushes, and double helical cut gears which did not produce any side thrust at all.

After eight weeks with Ray Martin, working seven days a week and twelve hours a day on this complicated project, I am afraid our relationship became very strained and I complained to the late John Cooper, who sympathized with me. Nevertheless, I continued with the project although it was not a very happy association, for I was determined that no personal feelings would prevent me from finishing the car in time for Goodwood. Eventually the chassis was more or less completed and I took it to Cooper Cars at Surbiton so that the body could be made. I had decided to keep one of the four fitters with me for the season of racing, and made a wise choice in selecting Tony Robinson of Neasden.

The Alta engine arrived eleven days before the car was due to race at Goodwood and to our consternation we found that it would not fit the chassis. The engine was of a later type and longer than the dummy originally supplied, and we found that the rack and pinion layout, designed and made by Ray Martin, would have to be altered so that the engine could be accommodated. This, of course, meant redesigning the entire steering geometry.

During those last days prior to Easter Monday we worked from 8 o'clock in the morning until the early hours of the following morning and rarely had more than four or five hours' sleep. We worked on Good

Friday, Easter Saturday and Sunday, right up to the time we left Surbiton for the Sussex circuit.

Stirling came over to see us in the middle of that hectic week.

" Do you honestly believe it is possible to have the car ready for Goodwood ? " he asked.

" Well, Stirling," I replied, " we promised you the car for Goodwood and you are going to get it. We are not going to give in. This car will be finished and once it is completed—even though it may not be initially successful—we shall at least have something to develop and modify."

Charles and John Cooper of Cooper Cars were convinced we should not finish the car in time; Keith Challen of the *News of the World*, who came over to Surbiton on Good Friday, was just as pessimistic !

"Alf," he said, " you have set yourself an impossible task."

" Don't talk nonsense," I replied. " Just leave us alone and don't come snooping around because it is all getting on my nerves. I've got too much work to be able to discuss or argue about the project with anyone."

Poor Challen, who is one of the best informed of the newspaper motor-racing correspondents and a very likeable character, wondered what had hit him verbally ; but we dealt with everyone in the same manner, just told them to get out and pressed on.

The springs for the front suspension did not arrive until Good Friday. Here we were building a British Grand Prix challenger and all along the line there had been frustrating delays of this nature. Perhaps one day someone will be able to convince the motor industry that the supply of component parts for Grand Prix cars should be given priority.

The Cooper-Alta was finally completed in the early hours of Monday morning. We had put the finishing touches to the car with it raised on stands several feet above floor level, but when we removed them and let the springs take the full weight, the whole perishing oufit collapsed on the floor.

I was too tired to lose my temper ; I just stood there with Tony and we looked at the car as though it were something from another world. " You devil," I muttered between my teeth, " you rotten devil."

It was no use despairing. We had promised Stirling the car would be ready for Goodwood and something had got to be done in double quick time about the springs. Finally I decided to improvise by using twin coil springs, one mounted inside the other. The job took three hours or so to complete and it was 7 a.m. on Monday before the Cooper-Alta was finally ready to leave the works. Whether or not the rate was right for the coil springs, I did not know.

There was more trouble when we tried to load the car into the brand new Commer lorry delivered only a week previously by the Rootes Group Service Engineer and Public Relations Officer. We had supplied data on the car to the bodybuilders before the measurements of the Cooper-Alta were finally settled and having got the car up the ramp we then found it was too long for the lorry ! This was almost the last straw.

" Is nothing going to go right with this ruddy car ? " I said to Tony.

Perspiring freely we manoeuvred the car around inside the lorry until it was fixed securely in position, but on the slant, with the front part hoisted up on the top runners and the back end on the lower ones. I slammed the doors at the rear and climbed in o the driving cab with Tony, convinced in my own mind that something would happen to prevent that damnable car ever reaching the circuit.

We were both ravenously hungry, having lived for a week on nothing else but fish and chips in the cafe next to the Cooper works. We looked dirty and unshaven and felt even worse than we looked. I was tired, miserable and in a filthy temper.

In Ripley I saw a transport cafe with an inviting notice : " Ham and Eggs."

" Damn it," I said to Tony. " I promised to have the car at Goodwood by 10 o'clock but I am going to have a really good breakfast, even if it makes us late."

We parked the lorry, went into the cafe, and wolfed a plate apiece of eggs, bacon, sausages and fried bread. If more people would stop at transport cafes on their way to various circuits they would discover what comprises a really well-cooked and plentiful English breakfast.

It was half-past ten before we reached Goodwood. There was Stirling, standing just inside the entrance gates, waving us to slow down and stop.

" Where the devil have you been, Alf ? " he said. " You are half-an-hour late."

I said nothing—just ignored him—and drove into the paddock where the Cooper-Alta was unloaded. After all, Stirling did not realize that we had only slept a total of little more than thirty hours in a whole week or that the car had collapsed on its springs the previous night.

Stirling settled himself in the cockpit, started up and set off to do a few laps. The engine had been run-in on the bench but never in the chassis, whilst neither the clutch nor gears had ever been tested. This was, in fact, the first time the Cooper-Alta had ever been tried on a circuit.

After a few laps Stirling came in and complained that the engine was misfiring. Almost immediately the car was surrounded by people, many of them only " rubber-necking." The Cooper-Alta had been given considerable publicity in the motoring press and everyone was anxious to see it.

Twenty-five or thirty people crowded around the car, jostling me in the process and doing everything but climb into the cockpit. If only people would realize how irritating and annoying it is to have a bunch of enthusiasts, even though they are customers, gawking over you when you are trying to work on a car before a race. I could feel the tension rising inside me ; I felt that something was going to burst. What with Stirling's admonition, the crowds around the car, and the S.U. technical representative getting in my way and vice versa I suddenly lost control.

" Have it. Have it," I shouted. " Take it all, the ruddy lot of you. I am clearing out."

I went stalking off to the lorry, climbed inside, settled down in the corner of the cab and shut my eyes. I could not care less what happened to the car. There were so many technical " advisers " around that they could do without me.

It transpired that the reason for the misfiring was a slightly damaged dashpot on the S.U. carburetter, and once Tony got the car firing on four cylinders. Stirling went round reasonably fast. His times were good considering that the Cooper-Alta had no proper springing. The suspension at both front and rear was resting on the full bump stops and there was hardly any movement.

However, Stirling seemed quite pleased with the performance. He came over to the lorry.

" Don't look so damned miserable, Alf," he said. " I think this is going to be a real good motor-car."

This cheered me up a lot and I returned to a normal state of mind, regaining my interest in the car and Meeting, but unfortunately the Cooper-Alta did not run very well. Frankly, I cannot remember the trouble but I have a note that it only ran in its first race and was " scratched " from the other two in which it had been entered.

The day after the Goodwood Meeting I returned to Ray Martin's works at Mitcham. With the Cooper-Alta completed I was curious to learn what plans he had for the remainder of the season. As soon as I arrived Ray Martin asked me to step into his office. Having shut the door he turned to me.

" It seems we just cannot get on well together," he said. And then— waving aside my protest : " I am afraid I cannot see things the way you do and I think it is better if we terminate our agreement."

This rather bald statement of fact took me completely by surprise. I did not know what to say. In three months, for £11 a week, I had worked very hard indeed on a project that might have led to a great deal of business for Ray Martin Motors Limited. Now all this was apparently forgotten and my services were no longer required. Nevertheless, I knew that he and I would never be able to work together amicably and did not bother to argue. Within a few days our agreement was terminated.

CHAPTER 22

I JOIN STIRLING MOSS

Long hours at Surbiton—Mr. and Mrs. Alfred Moss—
Stirling crashes in the C-Type Jaguar—Equipe Moss is formed—
I scare myself at the Crystal Palace—The Commer transporter—
Nonsense at the Nurburgring—Stirling shows his mettle—
Disaster at Rheims

I was not unemployed for long because Stirling knew of Ray Martin's decision and telephoned me almost at once. Could I call and see him at his private address in Challoner Mansions ? I went over there at once on my Rudge Ulster and was delighted when Stirling asked me to join him on a permanent basis.

" I should like you to look after the Cooper-Alta, Alf," he said, " and to work for me personally."

I pointed out that Tony Robinson would want to stay on and Stirling had no objections. Within twenty-four hours we were both on the pay roll of Stirling Moss and it was now up to us to modify the Cooper-Alta wherever necessary and improve its performance. I knew that I should have full co-operation from John Cooper of *The Autocar* and from Cooper Cars.

There was a great deal to do before the Silverstone Meeting in May and we based ourselves on the works at Surbiton. One of our biggest problems was the spring rate ; I was determined to make the suspension work properly which had certainly not been the case at Goodwood. Until we had done this, it was impossible to judge the handling characteristics of the car. However, we were held up for our second set of springs, as we had been with the first set, and were not able to test the car with its proper springs before Silverstone.

The braking system was another problem. We not only had oil leaking from the back axle to the inboard brakes but our ratings were incorrect, and we could not get the right balance between the disc brakes at the front and the normal drum brakes at the rear. The combination was not at all satisfactory although I must admit we had no fault to find with the disc brakes themselves. The Cooper was one of the first cars to use them and they were excellent.

However, there was something peculiar about the overall braking system because the car became difficult to handle as soon as the driver applied the brakes. It may have been due to the flexibility of the chassis which was not a very rigid one.

We worked late at Coopers on the Thursday before Silverstone, fitting the springs which had only arrived that afternoon, and Stirling came over to see how we were getting on.

" The job should be throu h in the early hours of to-morrow morning,"
I told him, and then added, " if we are lucky."

He suggested that the best course of action would be for us to drive
out to his father's farm at Tring as soon as the car was finished, so that
we could have an hour or two in a comfortable bed before going on to
Silverstone Friday morning. This we did and found Alfred Moss waiting
for us at 4 a.m. with a steaming hot jug of coffee. He had waited anxiously
since 11 p.m.

His gesture was very much appreciated but not a surprise for one
almost expects a kind thought of this nature from Alfred Moss. He is
that sort of man and I have always got on very well with him. We have
always been the best of friends and I can see eye to eye with him on most
things.

Alfred Moss is very practical and not the sort of person one meets so
often in motor-racing who knows all the answers but never gets around to
doing anything about a particular problem. He is more than ready to
take off his jacket and help strip down a car if necessary and did so often
in the early days when Stirling had the Cooper before joining H.W.M.

I am convinced that Stirling would not be where he is to-day if it were
not for the help and support given by his father and mother. They have
been the backbone of his support during the whole of his professional
career. His mother is a wonderful woman, if only because she is able to
repress her fears. After all, Stirling is her only son and she must have
suffered agonies of apprehension in more races than she can remember.
Mrs. Moss has learned to conquer fear and that is her way of supporting
Stirling in his hazardous profession.

For all their good points, the Moss parents are an absolute menace in
any pit. They get so excited, following their son's progress, that it is as
much as the pit staff can do to calm them down, let alone pass signals to
the driver and look after all the other problems connected with pitwork.
The atmosphere in a pit should be cool, calm and collected and soon after
I joined Stirling I asked him if he would kindly tell his mother and father
to keep out of the pit.

" I fully agree," replied Stirling, " but why not tell them yourself ? "

" Wait a minute, Stirling," I said. " I cannot tell your father that.
After all, he is your father. I think you should speak to him yourself."

We eventually reached a compromise and agreed that just before a race
Stirling would call his father and, in my presence, ask him not to watch
the race from the pit. It worked on occasions but not very often for Alfred
Moss is not easily pushed around, and neither is Mrs. Moss.

I can remember some terrific rows before, during and after a race over
this vexed question of the pit being banned to the Moss parents. Nevertheless, I have never had a violent argument with either of them and in
fact Alfred Moss has supported me on many occasions when I have had
policy arguments with Stirling. I have the greatest admiration for him
and would like to work with him again one day.

It was on the Friday at Silverstone that Stir ing had his crash with the
C-type Jaguar. A change of surface caus d the accident. The Jaguar
was drifting and suddenly went from the concrete to the normal road

surface at the edge of the track. The drift immediately developed into a dangerous slide and the car turned over. Stirling had been driving at his maximum on the concrete and the more slippery surface would not take the car. So far as I know, this part of the circuit is still the same but most of the drivers are aware of the danger.

I was working on his Cooper 500 at the time. As soon as the crash occurred everyone disappeared from the paddock but I did not know it was Stirling who had overturned until Alfred Moss brought me the crash helmet he had been wearing. It was split in half and had undoubtedly saved Stirling's life when the car turned turtle. The medical people made a thorough check to see whether he had any internal injuries and then pronounced him fit to drive. I don't think we practised any more that day.

I suggested to Stirling that he did not race the Cooper 500 as the vibration in these small cars is terrific.

" You have been badly bruised," I said, "for goodness' sake don't give yourself a shaking by driving the Cooper."

Stirling agreed and confined his activities on race day to the Cooper-Alta.

The 500-c.c. car had been in the stable since the beginning of the season but we were only responsible for looking after the chassis. Francis Beart tuned the engine whilst from the maintenance point of view the car was the responsibility of Tony and myself. I did not have very much to do with Francis Beart. We spoke on several occasions but I would describe him as a man with a genius for tuning who likes to be left to himself.

The International Trophy was run in two heats and a final. In the first heat the Cooper went like a bomb, Stirling driving remarkably well considering he had crashed at over a hundred miles an hour the previous day. I don't mind admitting I was worried. I had a nasty feeling that perhaps the doctors should not have passed him as fit and that he would have a black-out.

I was beginning to feel an almost fatherly affection for him and ticked off the laps nervously as he hung grimly on to the tail of de Graffenried's Maserati and came home only six seconds behind the Swiss, having tied with him for the fastest lap. I was more than pleased for he had beaten Bira (Maserati), Rolt (Connaught), Rosier (Ferrari), and Hamilton (H.W.M.) amongst others.

In the final of the International Trophy, Moss shared the front row of the grid with Hawthorn's Ferrari, de Graffenried's Maserati and the Cooper-Bristol of Ken Wharton. He finished ninth, largely due to the fact that the car had to make a twelve-second pit stop for five gallons of fuel as the tank was not large enough to carry sufficient for the race duration of just over one hour. Moss was lying sixth at the time and his pit stop enabled Peter Whitehead to move up a place.

It irritates me the way some designers tackle the tankage problem. They design the body, then the chassis, then try to fit the tank in what remains. No one seems to consider, when the original design is worked out, how much tankage the car is going to carry and where.

Most of the British designers I have known treat the problem in this way, and the result is that cars appear on a circuit with anything up to half-a-dozen tanks. Under the seat, behind the driver, in front of the driver—everywhere but on top of the driver. Such car have a multiplicity of fuel pipes running all over the place, as difficult to follow as the Paris Metro. It is a plumber's nightmare, with pipes going left, right and centre. It is ridiculous so far as reliability is concerned because it stands to reason that every additional fuel pipe union is a potential cause of failure in a race.

A car should be designed to take a tank large enough to carry sufficient fuel for a full length championship event. The extra weight of a larger tank is only a few pounds and it is not only silly but dangerous as well to have to add fuel tanks for long distance events.

Immediately after the Silverstone Meeting there was a full-scale conference at which Stirling, Ken Gregory, Alfred Moss and myself were present. This resulted in the formation of *Equipe* Moss, with Ken Gregory as Business Manager and responsible for the entire administration of entering the car and getting it to circuits at home and broad. It was also agreed that he would pay our wages here in England, and it came as a great relief to me when he took over the accounts as well and left me free to concentrate on the car.

I had met Ken Gregory for the first time when working on the Cooper-Alta at Surbiton. On that occasion he did not strike me as being a particularly astute business man. I regarded him more as a friend of Stirling, who helped to sort out some of the business affairs connected with his professional career.

I soon discovered that he was hard headed, ambitious and shrewd. It became obvious to me that he was determined to " go places," and indeed he has done so in no uncertain fashion since those early days. He is now not only a Director of Stirling Moss Limited but the energetic secretary of the British Racing and Sports Car Club, and the man who handles the fortunes of several well-known drivers as well as Moss, including Peter Collins.

Nowadays he is as much a professional as Stirling and, as such, cannot accurately be described as a motor-racing enthusiast. He makes his living at the sport in the same way as a motor-racing journalist, and I imagine it has ceased to be a sport with him. He is a clever businessman and everything is filed neatly away in his brain for future reference. Gregory listens to what people have to say but does not fall into the common error of saying too much when his turn comes.

There was a marked dividing line between Ken and myself. It was his responsibility to pay my wages, and my job to look after the cars. When the *equipe* was first formed, he took an interest in my work but when he discovered—as so many other people have done—that I like to be left to my own devices he accepted the situation. As a team we worked very well together but, nevertheless, apart.

The dividing line was there and whilst we were always ready to help each other if asked, we normally kept on our own side of the line. That, I think, was one of the reasons why the Moss *equipe* functioned so successfully. We did not interfere in each other's activities and in this respect no one is more sensible than Stirling about leaving people alone to get on with their work, unmolested and in their own way.

The next race for the Cooper-Alta was at the opening of the new Crystal Palace Circuit on Whit Monday, two weeks after Silverstone. As well as working on the F2 car, we had to take the engine out of the 500 so that Francis Beart could make some modifications, and what with one thing and another we were kept very busy.

It was becoming evident that, in spite of the performance of the Cooper-Alta at Silverstone, it was not exactly a winner. Stirling was beginning to realize that the car was not as bright in colours as he had thought. It definitely lacked good handling qualities and we could not make out what was wrong, particularly the reason for its marked oversteer.

We carried out all manner of experiments with the torque arms, regulating them and trying to induce artificial understeer, but without success. In my opinion the gearing of the steering box was too high. We had only three-quarters of a turn from lock to lock and with such high geared steering there was always the danger that the slightest error of judgment by the driver would be over-corrected. I think that was the main reason why the car was difficult to handle. It was too sensitive for any driver and also lacked the normal understeer characteristics.

Frankly, the Cooper-Alta was quite a handful and it took a driver of the calibre of Stirling Moss to handle it. I don't mind admitting that it frightened me on the few occasions I drove it, and I recollect the remarks of other drivers who tried the car, usually on the lines of " How on earth does Stirling manage ? "

I was annoyed with Stirling at the Crystal Palace because he would keep grumbling about the car. After a practice run, when the criticism had been particularly strong, I said to him in disgust : " Give me the crash helmet. I want to have a go. At least I will see for myself what is the matter with the blessed car."

I had forgotten all about my sortie at Avus with Moss' H.W.M. and away I went in the Cooper-Alta. I looked in the mirror soon after leaving the paddock and there was Ken Wharton on my tail in his Cooper-Bristol.

I kept it up for three laps and really scared myself. I did not notice whether the car was handling well or whether it was not. All I knew was that I went three times round the circuit, far faster than I had wanted to do, and that Wharton was breathing down my neck all the time. I came in eventually and said to Stirling, having cooled down considerably : " I quite agree with you ; I think there is something radically wrong with this motor-car."

On race day, the car did not go at all well. Rolt in his Connaught, and Wharton in the Cooper-Bristol, were more than a match for the Cooper-Alta and Stirling could only manage fourth place in Heat 1 of the Coronation Trophy and fifth in the final. However, he won the 500-c.c. race so that it was not entirely a black Whit Monday.

After the Crystal Palace Meeting, we went to the Nurburgring in Germany for the Eifelrennen on May 31st. It was our first trip to the continent in the new transporter and we added another vehicle to the *equipe* —a Vespa for Stirling's personal transport.

The left-hand drive Commer was the most modern of the racing-car transporters and a pleasure to handle. It had been designed specifically for the job in hand, with the object of providing fast, reliable transport between Meetings. How much easier our job as mechanics would have been had we been able to use the Commer with the H.W.M.s.

The chassis of the van was a standard Commer forward-control 5¼-tonner with a 13 ft. 6 in. wheelbase. The 4,750-c.c. 6-cylinder overhead valve engine was placed on its side under the floor of the cab, thereby allowing maximum chassis space for the body. The Commer had a four-speed gearbox and a two-speed rear axle and Tony and I soon found that the powerful engine, developing 109 b.h.p., enabled us to cruise the lorry for mile after mile at speeds in excess of 60 m.p.h.

The body was built by Associated Delivery Limited of Reading and incorporated tinted perspex skylights running the full length of the vehicle on either side to provide interior illumination. A hand-operated winch, which was used for pulling the Cooper-Alta into the lorry and for raising the 500 on a lift so that the larger car could be run underneath, was mounted on the forward bulkhead. The loading and unloading of the cars was simplicity itself and Tony and I were able to put on our travelling clothes for a journey and keep them on, whereas with previous lorries a pair of overalls was necesssary before we dared venture into the greasy interior.

The right-hand side wall was specially strengthened to take ten spare wheels and the lorry carried three fuel tanks of fifty-gallons capaci₁y and two of twenty-five gallons. Home comforts at that time included a wash basin supplied from a water tank, a built-in Calor gas cooker and a separate adjustable bucket seat for the driver. We made many improvements at a later date as you will see.

As this was our first trip abroad with the new lorry, Charles Cooper of Cooper Cars decided to travel with us. However, when we disembarked at Dunkirk I found that he did not have the special permit required to enter Germany.

"We had better make for Lille," I told him, "in the hope that the German Consul there will issue one."

However, there was no Consulate in Lille and we pushed on to Brussels. When we eventually got away from the Belgian capital with the necessary permit we were well behind schedule and had to drive the lorry flat out. We really thrashed the Commer, keeping the speedometer needle above the 60 mark wherever possible whilst Charles Cooper, perspiring freely, sat hunched in the corner of the cab, asking in a plaintive voice from time to time if I would "Please take it easy and slow down." That was the only journey Charles ever made with me.

Charles "suffered" again when Stirling took us all round the Nurburgring in his Jaguar saloon when the circuit was opened to traffic after the practice session. Tony and I sat in the front with Stirling whilst Charles Cooper sat in the back with Sally Weston. The Jaguar lapped the "Ring" in just over twelve minutes with five people up, which I considered very good indeed. Poor Charles Cooper, visibly perturbed, did not like it at all.

The rest of us felt quite happy for Stirling inspires tremendous confidence in his passengers under such conditions. He is a convincing driver and does not take excessive risks. One realizes instinctively that the car is being driven in an absolutely safe manner, though very fast indeed.

Tony and I did not worry. We chatted and joked whilst Stirling described the line he took through different corners in the Cooper-Alta : " Here the car does this ; here it does that."

He explained all the corners and I marvelled how he had learned so much about the circuit in such a short time. It takes a very active and receptive brain to memorize even part of the Nurburgring but Stirling seemed to be doing exactly the right thing at every corner.

Poor Charles Cooper was finished. When he got out of the car he disappeared and although he was with us in the pits during the race I never saw him again after the Meeting ; I think he must have hitch-hiked back to England with someone else.

I had a row with Stirling at the Nurburgring and it does show how, when tension mounts before a race, it is silly to play the fool as I did. The night previously we had a meal together and as Stirling had no small change to pay the bill he asked me to lend him two Deutschmarks.

Next morning he repaid me but, on arrival in the Paddock some time later, asked : " Oh, by the way, did I pay you back those Deutschmarks ? "

Jokingly I replied : " No, you have not paid me back yet."

" Don't tell lies, Alf," said Stirling, " I paid you back this morning."

" Well, what did you want to ask me for ? " I said—and added : " Please don't call me a liar."

When we pushed the Formula 3 car on to the starting line for the first race the driver and mechanics of the Moss *equipe* were not on speaking terms. He was on the front row, having put up fastest time in practice, and went away like a bomb. There was little signalling from the pits and we did not take much notice of his meteoric progress round the $14\frac{1}{2}$-mile circuit. We were not on speaking or signalling terms all over two Deutschmarks and a joke.

Stirling drove the 500 so quickly that he beat the second place man by minutes, not seconds. Maybe he went so fast because he was angry ; I don't know because we never discussed the matter again.

Stirling finished sixth in the Formula 2 race, run over seven laps of the Nurburgring. He did not attempt to go fast on this tricky circuit, particularly as there was steady rain during most of the race and he knew the handling of the car was not right. In fact, the Cooper-Alta was a very " dicey " car on a circuit like the " Ring." The race was won by de Graffenried on a Maserati, with H.W.M.s second and third after the drivers, Collins and Frere, had fought a tremendous duel for second place.

We returned to England with the Cooper-Alta, whilst Stirling went on to Zandvoort for the Dutch Grand Prix. There he drove one of the Connaught team cars and was ninth—the only one of four Connaughts to finish the race distance.

Stirling was not at all happy about the Cooper-Alta but two weeks after the race in Holland the Moss *equipe* was on the continent again, *en route* for the Grand Prix of Rouen, a Formula 1 race over sixty laps of the tricky Essarts Circuit. Farina and Hawthorn on Ferraris were the main opposition.

No sooner had Stirling completed a few laps on the first day of practice than there was gearbox trouble. The synchromesh clutches seized solid on the slide and would not disengage, which meant that I had to work all night trying to free them so that the car would be ready for the second practice session. So far as I can remember the car was not finished in time and the roads had been opened to the public again before I was able to tell Stirling I had completed the job.

It seemed that all my work had been in vain, for in the first few laps of the 60-lap race the Cooper-Alta lost first gear. On a circuit containing two sharp hairpins, Stirling was at a great disadvantage without his lowest gear and virtually out of the running. I had the greatest admiration for his dogged determination and the way he plodded on, lap after lap, with an outclassed motor-car.

Other drivers would have given up, but not Stirling, who managed to keep going and finish last, seven laps behind Farina, the winner. Often I have noticed that he displays his best driving form when the dice are loaded heavily against him.

From Rouen we moved on to Rheims for the French Grand Prix, on Sunday, July 5th, that fantastic " race of the century " that centred around Fangio on a Maserati and Hawthorn on a Ferrari, which the British driver eventually won. It was one of the most exciting races I have ever seen and, like most people in the pit area, I was caught up in the wild enthusiasm of the French crowd as time and again the two duelling red cars tore up from Thillois and screamed through the pit area with hardly the width of a tyre separating them. It was a terrific " dice " which I will never forget.

During practice the Cooper-Alta did not behave at all well. As at Rouen we again had gearbox trouble but this was not our main problem. It was the first time it had been raced on an ultra-fast circuit such as Rheims, and Stirling found that coming down the straight towards Thillois hairpin at over a hundred miles an hour the car would not keep straight. It weaved from side to side in a most alarming manner, alarming for Stirling and equally so for any other driver in the vicinity.

In the limited time at our disposal we tried to modify the steering geometry but could not succeed in making any improvement. I wrote in the diary, twenty-four hours before the race : " S.M. does not like the car. He thinks it is dangerous. I quite agree."

Of all the circuits to have to race a " dicey " car Rheims is one of the worst because it is so fast but it was trouble of an entirely different nature that put the Cooper-Alta out of the French Grand Prix whilst the Maserati and Ferrari were engaged in that tremendous duel. The clutch housing split open within a fraction of an inch of Stirling's foot and the clutch disintegrated. His legs were scratched by flying metal but that was all. If the housing had split slightly lower it could well have cut off his legs.

It happened when the engine was at its peak, almost 6,000 revs, and whilst the car was streaking down the far leg of the course towards Thillois at over 140 m.p.h. The clutch, its housing and the gearbox became a solid mass, and at once the Cooper-Alta went into a spin which Stirling managed to control. We later found that the force of disintegration had bent the chassis !

Stirling walked back to the pits, very shaken.

" It's no good, Alf," he said, " I am not going to drive this car any more."

I was angry for only the previous season, when the clutch housing had broken on Peter Whitehead's Alta, I had modified the housing and notified the clutch manufacturer of what I had done. If Moss had lost a leg and been invalided for life, I would have blamed the manufacturer for not modifying their most recent clutch in line with our racing experience. We all know motor-racing is dangerous but for goodness' sake let's keep it as safe as we can.

After the race we sat down quietly to discuss our plans for the future, and it was decided there and then that the car would never be raced again. We were fed up, disappointed and miserable. On that day, when Stirling's fortunes were at their lowest ebb, the fortunes of Mike Hawthorn, the winner of that fantastic race, were at their highest.

CHAPTER 23

THE SECOND COOPER-ALTA

We start all over again—Building a car in eleven days—
A brilliant "drive" in the German G.P.—Subterfuge at Sables d'Olonne.

The Cooper-Alta had been a disappointment but there was absolutely no question of throwing in the towel. Stirling decided that we would return to England, purchase a standard Cooper chassis and start all over again.

"We can use a preselector gearbox," he pointed out, "and fit it behind the driver, thus avoiding the use of a clutch."

With these thoughts to cheer us up we left Rheims and returned to our home base at Tring. The 500-c.c. Cooper was unloaded at Surbiton for an overhaul and then, having removed the engine from the chassis of the 2-litre car, I took it over to Barwell Engineering in an effort to find more power. At last I could put into practice my theory of letting an expert tune the Alta engine.

Their first reaction was that the camshaft would have to be redesigned.

"Look," I said, "I am terribly sorry. Whatever work is required on the engine must be finished inside four days, and in that time you cannot redesign the cylinder head and camshaft. Let's get cracking and do what we can with the breathing of the engine in the time available."

I must say they backed me up when I explained the problem.

"We are due to race in the German G.P. on August 2nd, less than four weeks from now, and we have not even started to build the car. This engine is all we have at present."

We worked hard, long hours in the small tuning shop at Chessington and, having slightly modified the ports and altered the valve timing, gained something like 19 b.h.p. With the improvement in valve timing alone we gained 10 b.h.p.

As soon as the engine was ready we went straight to Coopers. In sixteen days' time we were due to leave Surbiton for the Nurburgring, and our plan was to put the tuned Alta engine into a standard Cooper chassis with an Armstrong Siddeley "box" behind the driver so that the gearbox and back axle would be joined in one.

Whilst Tony went with Stirling and the 500 Cooper to the Silverstone British G.P. Meeting, I stayed at Surbiton and worked out a plan for building the new car. As soon as I had done so I contacted Ken Gregory and asked him to order all the necessary component parts such as stub axles, drive flanges, rear shaft drives, fuel and oil tanks, the flywheel and radiator.

I soon found that our original idea would have to be scrapped. A standard Cooper chassis could not be used for the simple reason that we were fitting the gearbox in a different position, as well as using different

Easter Sunday, 1953. Alf Francis and Tony Robinson knock off for fish and chips and a bottle of Pepsi-Cola. This was one of the few breaks in over a hundred hours of almost continuous work during that fantastic week when they were putting the finishing touches to the Ray Martin Alta.

The controversial Formula 2 Cooper-Alta, the first British racing car to use disc brakes, built by Ray Martin and with a body designed by Alf Francis. Great attention was paid to undercar streamlining and the car was very well proportioned. In this picture the Alta is being push-started by Tony Robinson following a routine stop for fuel at Silverstone.

The Cooper-Alta that was built in eleven days for Stirling Moss to drive in the 1953 German Grand Prix. The engine, which was taken from the Ray Martin Alta, developed amazing power on nitromethane. Here, Moss is driving the car to victory during the September Crystal Palace Meeting.

In the French Alps, en route to Modena and the Maserati works which he had never previously visited, Alf Francis takes time off to photograph the Commer van loaned to Stirling Moss by the Rootes Group. Alf made this journey single handed and could not complete it quickly enough for the Maserati works were ready to start building Stirling's own 250 F brakes, larger capacity fuel and oil tanks and a different type of radiator. We wanted to build a car that could run in all the important long distance events without being handicapped through lack of fuel capacity.

Having talked over the problem with John Cooper he found the obvious solution.

" You will have to make your own chassis," said Cooper. " There's the jig, there are the tubes, and you can borrow my welder so what are you waiting for, boy ? "

It was a typical sporting gesture by John Cooper.

I recollect the Secretary of the German Automobile Club visiting the works at Surbiton and asking him : " By the way, where is this car of your make that Stirling Moss is going to drive at the Nurburgring ? "

Cooper turned and pointed to a bunch of tubes on the floor.

" That's it," he said.

" I cannot see any car," replied the German.

" Well, that's it," insisted Cooper.

" How can you possibly build a car in such a short time ? " questioned the German. " You have only ten days before the practice begins."

" Don't you worry," said John Cooper. " We shall do it."

With the fullest co-operation from all the boys at Surbiton we got on top of the job remarkably quickly. The whole of John Cooper's staff was put more or less at our disposal and within seven days the car began to take shape. A standard Cooper-Bristol chassis was made up on the Cooper jigs, and modified whilst it was actually being built, so that it would take the Alta power unit (heavier than the Bristol engine), the gearbox, transmission and back axle.

The chassis also had to be altered so that Girling drum brakes could be used on all four wheels instead of the Lockheeds favoured by Coopers. We also replaced the Armstrong Siddeley shock-absorbers with Girling's.

Strangely enough we did not work such long hours as with the original Cooper-Alta because, in spite of our modifications, this was much closer to a standard Cooper chassis and body and we had at our disposal eight or nine people very skilled in their work and with years of experience. We worked until 10 or 11 o'clock every night but never until the early hours of the morning

I complicated matters to a certain exten by trying to fit S.U. fuel injection on the car, rather a novelty at the time, and this undoubtedly resulted in a considerable increase in power. Unfortunately, there was not sufficient time to test the engine on the bench. Furthermore, we had to work rather in the dark to the extent that Geoffrey Taylor supplied us with data and the S.U. people then made the necessary modifications to their fuel injection outfit so that it would work with the Alta engine. We were not very fortunate with our experiments and could not get the injection system to function properly, eventually reverting to the old faithful four S.U.s

The Cooper-Alta was finally finished the day before we were due to leave for Dover and only eleven days after we had started to build it. This must be a record for a Formula 2 car.

However, when we installed the engine in the chassis and started up, I found to my dismay that the drive case was cracked.

" This is going to be another unlucky Cooper-Alta," I said to Tony. " Even if we finish the car there will be a hoodoo on it."

With only twenty-four hours before our sailing time we took the engine out of the chassis and worked all through the night improvising a drive case. There were none in stock at Geoffrey Taylor's so we borrowed one of an earlier design from John Heath and re-machined it to our requirements. Dawn was breaking as we put the finishing touches to the job.

The only sleep we had after leaving Surbiton was on the boat crossing the channel, and from Dunkirk we pressed on with the Commer, driving night and day and finally arriving at the Nurburgring on Friday morning in time for the first practice session.

During practice this new Cooper-Alta behaved very well, and there was not a great deal of work for us to do, bearing in mind that the car had never been track-tested any more than had the original Cooper-Alta. This new one sounded very healthy and I think Stirling was pleased with it. We were certainly hopeful about Cooper-Alta No. 2 on our side of the pit counter.

Twenty minutes or so before the start of the race, with the car fully prepared and standing in the paddock which is on a lower level than and partly underneath the circuit itself, Stirling decided to make a short run around the pits.

He started up and drove off whilst Tony and I carried all the necessary spares and fuel over to the pit. We had no sooner reached there than Stirling pulled up on the other side of the counter.

" I have no gears," he shouted. " There is only second and I cannot get out of it."

In fifteen minutes the race was due to start. I looked at him blankly. " What can we do ? " he said.

" There's nothing to do," I replied. " You will have to start the race on second gear, retire as soon as you can and collect the starting money."

I suddenly realized that with the gear jammed in second there was every likelihood of the engine stalling on the start line. The ratios are very close, and first gear unusually high, so that second gear is not suitable for a racing start. In the few minutes still available we took off the cover of the gearbox and by using a crowbar disengaged second gear and forced home first.

" You can start the car a few seconds before the flag drops," I said to Stirling, " and slip the bands so as to keep the engine at peak revs."

Miserably we pushed the Cooper-Alta on to the fourth row of the grid behind Marimon's Maserati. The car had gone very well in practice and Stirling had put up fastest time of the British entries, lapping the lengthy circuit in 10 minutes 48.3 seconds as against the fastest practice lap, set by Ascari on a Ferrari, at 9 minutes 59.8 seconds.

We pushed the car backwards, then forwards. The engine fired and Stirling kept revving hard. Down slashed the flag and away went the field. To my surprise Stirling seemed to be well up with the leaders.

"At least," I said to Tony, " the car has left the grid and we shall get our starting money."

Slowly we strolled back to the pits, knowing quite well that for the rest of the race we should be spectators. It would be ten minutes before we could expect the first cars and Stirling would certainly not be with them.

Sally Weston was on the pit counter with the lap-scoring chart, and had just watched the tail end of the field disappear beyond the North Turn. At the Ring the cars double back on their tracks after going through the South Curve, passing the pits on the opposite side to the start and finish straight within a minute of leaving the grid.

Sally was quite excited. " I think he was fourth or fifth into the North Turn," she said.

" That's impossible," I said irritably, thinking she had made a mistake in identification. " You must have been seeing things. Anyway he has retired by now. He cannot go round the Nurburgring with only one gear."

But Sally was right. Just over ten minutes after the start the field roared by the pits. The first car—Ascari's Ferrari—tore past the grand-stands followed at intervals by Fangio, Hawthorn, Farina, Villoresi, Bonetto, de Graffenried and—sure enough—towards the back end of the field, Stirling Moss in the Cooper-Alta.

I could hardly believe my eyes. Tony and I sat on the pit counter and tried to work out what could have happened in the gearbox, for it was obvious that Stirling had already changed gear quite a few times by now, with something like 173 corners per lap. Even so it took us almost three laps, just over half-an-hour, before we accepted the fact that our car was in the race and likely to stay in it. We began to organize the pit for the fuel stop.

Everything went smoothly when he came in. We dared not tempt fate by asking why the gearbox was in working order, and I kept my fingers crossed as the car accelerated away from the pits. There was no trouble at all. Up through the gears went Stirling. Everything was under control and when he came by the pits as he approached the North Turn he gave the " thumbs up " sign.

He drove brilliantly in that German G.P., in a brand new car which had been built in eleven days, and out of a field of thirty cars came home sixth. The opposition from the " works " Maseratis and Ferraris was about as tough as it could be, and it was most exciting to watch the car— on its first outing—put up such a good performance on a circuit as difficult as the Nurburgring. It handled much better than the original Cooper-Alta and was, from the point of view of the chassis, in every way as good as one would expect a Cooper-Bristol to be.

It was a very fine drive and when Stirling brought the car into the pits we were all anxious to find out why the gearbox had righted itself.

" How did it happen ? " I asked. " How were you able to continue ? "

" Well," replied Stirling, " it was like this. In the heat of the moment I just changed gear automatically, without thinking, and the blessed gear went in. When the flag dropped I went up to six thousand in first and selected second as I would normally do. To my surprise the selector worked, so I tried third and that was O.K. So I just kept going all the time and used the gearbox in the normal way."

Stirling went on to explain that there were certain bumpy parts of the circuit where he had not been able to select a gear successfully and, as the race progressed, he stayed in top for these sections.

After the race I stripped down the gearbox in an effort to find the reason for the original failure and discovered a loose nut. It was floating on the inside of the selector mechanism, where there is a bus bar that engages the toggles, and must have been in the gearbox when it was originally supplied. On some corners the nut had obviously slid backwards under the bus bar and prevented the bar from disengaging the previously selected toggle or engaging the already selected one. Stirling found that when he applied the brakes all the gears were usable again, and it must have been that, as the nut slid forward under braking pressure, the bus bar was freed.

In the practice session the nut must have jammed in a certain position where it could do no harm or interfere with the selectors and then, fifteen minutes before the race, dislodged itself and jammed the bus bar. The nut had obviously jammed occasionally during the race but at no time as firmly as during that short run before the start.

Our next race was a Formula 2 event at Sables d'Olonne, a week after the German G.P., and in practice Stirling had difficulty in selecting gears. It was nothing to do with the trouble at the Nurburgring and this time I was inclined to blame it on the actual selector mechanism on the outside of the gearbox, which had a tendency to overadjust itself. Even so Moss put up some very fast times on the short, twisting circuit and the Cooper-Alta started from the front row of the grid.

During the race there was a terrific " dice " between Moss and Jean Behra. Although handicapped by the troublesome gear selector mechanism Stirling really fought it out with the Frenchman, but Behra in his Gordini inevitably pulled away and eventually established such a large lead that he lapped Stirling.

This irked Moss, who proceeded to " hold " the Gordini although there was a six-second gap between the two cars. As we did not stand much chance of winning the race in any case I decided to have some fun and games, and said to John Eason-Gibson who was managing our pit : " Let's give him a signal—minus 6."

" Don't be silly," replied Eason-Gibson, " he is one complete lap and six seconds behind."

" It doesn't matter," I said, " let's annoy Mr. Gordini."

Eason-Gibson agreed. No one likes a spot of fun and games in this fashion more than he does. He is a man I admire, most of all for his wonderful sense of humour and dry wit. I have never seen him angry and the popular Secretary of the British Racing Drivers' Club is one of those fortunate people who are able to take most things in their stride.

The Gordini pit was only a few yards away from us and when I held out the minus 6 signal I could see from the expression on the face of Amedee Gordini that he was puzzled. Stirling saw the signal and, whether or not he knew that he was a lap behind, the fact remains that he speeded up. Next time round when we timed him he was minus 5 ; next time minus 4.

To the bewilderment of the Gordini pit we passed information to our driver to the effect that he was on the same lap as Behra and gaining a second a lap.

I could see Gordini checking up on his lap charts, probably wondering whether his lap scorer had miscalculated to the extent of a lap. He must have decided as a safety measure to speed up Behra just in case we were on the same lap. Anyway, there was a certain amount of alarm and despondency in the enemy camp and out went the faster signal.

Next time round there was no sign of Behra and we began to feel a little guilty. Sure enough he had gone too fast and run out of road. Fortunately he was not hurt and we were able to congratulate ourselves on our tactics, although they had not been put into operation with the object of knocking Behra out of the race in this manner. It had all been a joke and Stirling finished third, having gained a place, one minute behind Louis Chiron in his Osca who was second to Rosier's Ferrari. The H.W.M. team finished fourth, sixth and seventh.

It was as a result of this little piece of subterfuge that I decided to have my own signal board, not using any of the existing code systems. I could see that if we could pass signals to our driver which other *equipes* could not interpret, there were interesting possibilities.

CHAPTER 24

FUEL INJECTION

Trouble at Charterhall—Nitromethane at Monza—
Moss versus Rolt at Crystal Palace—Stirling crashes at Castle Combe.

After the Sables d'Olonne race we returned to London at once, and at one of our periodic conferences of *Equipe* Moss it was decided to use fuel injection. We had only been getting something like 160 b.h.p. from the Alta, and I knew that if we could get a fuel injection system to work properly on the car it would considerably increase the b.h.p.

Geoffrey Taylor was already developing his engines to run on fuel injection so by arrangement with the S.U. factory a kit was supplied for the use of *Equipe* Moss. When bench tests had been carried out, the results were so promising that the system was fitted on the car. The improvement in power was incredible, the injection system giving us at least 20 b.h.p. extra.

However, as there was only a week between the Sables d'Olonne race and the appearance of the Cooper-Alta at Charterhall, our experiments were made in far too short a time and I for one did not expect a startling performance north of the border.

As I had expected we experienced a lot of trouble during practice and changed from injection back to carburetters. Although there was less power with the S.U.s the engine kept running consistently, whereas with injection Stirling could not rely on the car behaving itself on acceleration coming out of the corners. It was impossible to predict whether, after leaving a particular corner, it would fire on three cylinders or four. When it fired on all four it sure went like a bomb.

Stirling nevertheless decided to use injection in the Formula 2 race, probably because he had put a faster time with it in practice than any of the other F.2 cars. He was ill advised for the car retired early in the 50-lap race with over-lubrication in the fuel injection equipment.

There and then Stirling decided to run the car in the Formula Libre race with the four S.U.s, and whilst he took himself off to the Formula 3 race we started to dismantle the injection system. I was not in a very good mood and thought to myself : " Stirling wanted this fuel injection, which we never had an opportunity to test on a circuit, and thanks to him all I am doing is working hard on a new project without being able to spend sufficient time to make the car reliable."

I spoke my thoughts aloud to Tony and added : " It is time Stirling realized that if we are going to play with fuel injection we must do it at home, not during an actual Meeting."

One cannot get away from the fact that a car in its standard form, even if it is " the devil you know," is always a better proposition than one with a new gimmick that has not been properly tested and developed.

The car went very well in the Formula Libre race, like the wind in fact, and Moss had an exciting " dice " with Rolt's Connaught but unfortunately the Alta engine started to flutter. He came in for a change of plugs and shortly afterwards the car stopped again, with the carburation all over the place, and we retired.

It was probably due to the fact that we had been forced to fit and adjust the four S.U.s in drizzling rain, in little over half-an-hour. If we had not fooled with fuel injection for this Charterhall Meeting I am sure we would have put up quite a good show.

We were, nevertheless, determined to use the injection system and took the Cooper-Alta to Barwell Engineering, where I had the engine out on the bench and invited the Chief Chemist from Shell down to Chessington so that we could try out different fuels. One of them happened to be nitromethane—a fuel that had already been used by Bob Gerard successfully in his Cooper-Bristol—which was becoming quite popular.

Several drivers in the 500 class had used it with startling results and we thought it might be a good idea to chalk up a victory, or at least some fastest laps, by using a fuel that can only be described as liquidised dynamite. We experimented with the nitromethane and, to my amazement, the power output of the engine went up from 178 b.h.p. and exceeded the 200 mark. We were getting 100 b.h.p. per litre. It was terrific.

Briefly, S.U. fuel injection is a system where fuel is supplied by primary pump at a pressure of over ten pounds per square inch to a secondary pump, which is a metering device as well as a pump. The fuel is then delivered through a distributor to the injectors. It is, in fact, injection of fuel under pressure into the manifold.

We were pleased with the results but soon found that the distributor plate was being attacked by the nitromethane, becoming full of pores within a matter of minutes. However, that was not a particularly tough problem and in any case I had resigned myself to the fact that the use of nitromethane would probably result in sundry mechanical disorders. We had to ask ourselves the question : " Do we go quickly for part of the race or do we go slowly with the idea of finishing. The answer, it was agreed, would be to go quickly.

Our next race was the Italian Grand Prix at Monza, that fantastic Grand Premio when Fangio won for Maserati after a race-long battle with the Ferraris, in which Fangio, Farina and Ascari raced in each other's pockets for most of the time.

Our plan was to show the Italians that a British car could go quickly and that a British driver could keep up with the big boys even if the car did not finish. We ought to be able to do this with the nitromethane but it meant taking it all the way to Monza, two hundred gallons of liquidised dynamite.

We could not get the fuel in Italy and would have to carry sufficient for practice and the race itself, bearing in mind that the Cooper-Alta was only doing four miles to the gallon on nitromethane and would have to make at least three pit stops for fuel during the race.

For'unately the Commer was fitted with sufficient tankage to carry that quanti y of fuel but it was such a dangerous cargo that we took it to Italy in secret ; no one knew anything about it. I felt like the lorry drivers in the French film " Wages of Fear," where a convoy carrying nitroglycerine at empted a hazardous journey over unmade roads and all but one lorry was blown up.

I did not relax for a minute, particularly on the mountain passes. I never felt comfor able and dared not even light a cigarette. Tony was just as scared and we both collected a crop of grey hairs on that trip. We viewed oncoming vehicles with suspicion and distrust and gave them a very wide berth.

At Monza the car went like a bomb in practice and Stirling put up tenth fastest time, ahead of all the other British entries. His speed of 2 minutes 6.6 seconds compared very favourably with Ascari's time of 2 min. 2.7, which gave the Italians' Ferrari " pole " position on the grid.

The Cooper-Alta was not only very fast but very smelly and I think every driver and mechanic complained about nitromethane fumes. Admittedly it was a shocking smell and I was not at all surprised when officials told me I could not warm up the car in the paddock or in front of the pits. They would not even allow us to warm the engine on the grid before the race and we had to use hard plugs, with the engine absolutely stone cold.

On the day of the race we wheeled the Cooper-Alta on to the grid, hoping that after we had started up on hard plugs a few seconds before the flag fell, the car would go well. We need not have worried for the Cooper-Alta fairly streaked round on that first lap. When the field came past the pits I could hardly believe my own eyes. There was a bunch of four red cars and, right on their tail, the green Cooper-Alta. Next lap round there was no change. At least we were showing the massed Italian crowds that a British car and driver could keep up with the Italian aces.

However, Stirling was soon in the pits. A front tyre had thrown its tread and, after we had changed the wheel and refuelled the car, he was away again and storming round the circuit. The Cooper-Alta sounded very healthy and Stirling was enjoying himself immensely.

Four laps later he came in again, with another tread gone. In fact, treads went at the rate of one every four laps, mostly on the rear wheels, and we only had to change one wheel at the front end. It was rather a depressing sight to see the car in the pits every four or five laps, in spite of the fact that—between stops—it was going like the wind.

Then the Cooper came in for a different reason ; a side fuel tank was leaking. Fully resolved to continue the race, although by now we had dropped well back because of the pit stops, I shouted to Tony : " Change the tyres whilst I mend the tank."

He lost no time and, with a bunch of Dunlop people in the pit examining the tyres and trying to find the reason for the tread trouble, he changed two wheels and refuelled whilst I set to work on the leaking side tank. My intention was to cut the supply to the tank, drain it off, plug it and continue racing on the rear tank and the other side tank.

Working under the car I had to drain off nearly four gallons of nitro-methane, and a pool of the dangerous liquid rapidly formed underneath the Cooper-Alta, whilst the top of my overalls was soon saturated with the foul smelling stuff.

Suddenly there was a loud explosion and my first reaction was to evacuate the pit area as quickly as possible. I did not stop to find out what was happening but got away to a flying start and must have covered fifty yards in well under ten seconds.

When I paused to look back the car was still there, standing absolutely on its own, with our pit empty and also the ones on either side. To my surprise there was no sign of a fire so I decided to return. Everyone else, including Stirling, came back as well and rather shamefaced we continued as though nothing had happened. Actually a tyre had blown in the pit and, whilst the Dunlop boys knew this, they were not sure why I suddenly got out from under the car and ran like a hare down the track. They thought, as of course I did, that the car was about to catch fire and explode.

I completed the job and Stirling went off again. He eventually finished thirteenth, after eight or nine pit stops, and we changed at least six sets of rear wheels as well as refuelling on four occasions. Stirling must have been lapping very nearly as fast as the Ferraris and Maseratis when the Cooper-Alta was in full song.

He gave the Italians plenty to think about. For some considerable part of the race he was either passing or being repass d by Bonetto, who in those days was considered quite a driver. Whenever Moss felt like " taking " Bonetto he would wait until the cars were about to pass the grandstand and then, out of sheer devilment, scream past the Maserati.

He did the same with Mike Hawthorn on one occasion, when the Cooper-Alta was running in close company with the " works " Ferrari. Stirling hung back until the cars were almost level with the Press Tribune and then " took " Mike, giving him the Churchill sign to the delight of the spectators. So far as sheer speed was concerned the fuel injection Cooper-Alta was more than a match for most of the field.

On Monday, with the famous autodrome strangely quiet and almost deserted, we set off for England in the Commer as the 2-litre car was entered at the Crystal Palace the following week-end. We were confident that the car, with 200 b.h.p. available, would take the Palace trophies easily so long as the fuel injection behaved as well as it had at Monza.

I was not surprised when Stirling put up fastest time of the day on the London track, an unofficial lap record at 1 minute 6.2 seconds. During the Meeting the reigning king of the Crystal Place circuit—Tony Rolt in Rob Walker's Connaught—had to give best to Stirling. Nevertheless the first heat of the Formula 2 race was a very close thing because there was oil on the pedals of the Cooper and Moss' feet kept slipping ; only two-fifths of a second separated the two cars when Moss and Rolt crossed the line. In the second heat Stirling beat the Connaught by two seconds.

Undoubtedly that Cooper-Alta with fuel injection could really motor and was first rate on a circuit like the Crystal Palace. It had terrific acceleration—with this combination of fuel injection and liquid dynamite—acceleration that was superior to any of the continental cars. However, Monza and the Palace told us a home-truth. The road-holding of the car was not equal to its performance and the braking by no means adequate. How many people, I wonder, have found that an increase in power can only be made in line with development in other directions. It is plain common-sense but a fact that is often ignored.

The Castle Combe Meeting, where Stirling tried to beat Rolt's Connaught in the F.2 race by using the 1,100 Cooper-J.A.P. instead of the Cooper-Alta, was the last appearance of the Moss *equipe* in the 1953 season. I was not very keen on the idea of Stirling driving the Cooper-J.A.P. and said to him :

" The car will be dangerous used in this way. It is so light that anybody following you closely will find it most uncomfortable from the point of view of braking. Your retardation will be much greater than the car following which will probably be more than twice the weight. I think you ought to use the Cooper-Alta."

However, Stirling had made up his mind. He was sure the Cooper-J.A.P. was the answer for the Castle Combe Circuit and, by working long hours, Coopers got the car ready at Surbiton. As I had feared, Stirling was involved in an accident. Although he took the lead in the Formula 2 race, first Salvadori then Gerard passed him and on the second lap Rolt sat on his tail as the cars approached Quarry Corner. Stirling braked sharply and Rolt was unable to prevent his front wheels touching the rear wheels of the Cooper, which turned over. Stirling was thrown out but fortunately not badly injured.

When we went to collect him with the ambulance men he was unconscious and looked so pale that I thought he had been injured more seriously but in fact it was only a broken shoulder, the penalty of an unwise decision.

CHAPTER 25

MARKING TIME

" Hotting up " the Standard 8—Modifying the transporter—
The decision to " go foreign "—My theories on preparation.

Sitting in the flat at Challoner Mansions, discussing plans for the 1954 season, Stirling suddenly said : " Whatever happens, Alf, I would like you to stay with me. Something is bound to turn up. I may join Ferrari, Maserati or Mercedes-Benz, and if it is Mercs. then I shall want you to come along as personal mechanic and interpreter."

I considered this a great compliment, from a person I had grown to admire and respect, and it pleased me that Stirling had been so well satisfied with me during 1953. Whether there was work or not, he still wanted me to stay on. Quite frankly I could see no reason for him keeping me because there was nothing for me to do.

We all knew the Cooper-Alta would not be raced in 1954 having come to the conclusion that the chassis, as originally designed by the Cooper Car Co. Ltd., for use with a Bristol engine (a power-unit never used by us) developing 120 b.h.p. or even as much as 140 b.h.p., was an excellent motor-car for sprint races on short, twisty circuits like Goodwood or the Crystal Palace but not suitable for full length races on the Continent. The Monza race had shown that we had found much more power with fuel injection and nitromethane, but the braking and road-holding did not match the increased performance. This was understandable.

It looked very much as though Stirling would have to " go foreign " because there was no sign of a British car for him to drive that would match his abilities. Whilst the Moss family and Ken Gregory thought around the problem, Stirling bought a Standard 8, very largely I believe to keep me employed.

" There you are, Alf," he said, when I was shown the car for the first time, " that will keep you busy for the next two or three months. I think you ought to be able to make this a very nice little town carriage."

A few days later I took the Standard down to Barwell Engineering as I wanted to deal with the engine before tackling springing and suspension. I knew that once I had "hotted-up" the power unit it would then be necessary to improve the road-holding. I was on my own as Tony had returned to Ray Martin, having promised to do so at the end of the 1953 season.

We did not do a great deal to the engine. John Lucas checked the cylinder head for gasflow and cleaned out the ports ; then we increased the compression ratio slightly and fitted twin Solex carburetters. These modifications gave us another 14 b.h.p., quite a considerable gain.

The biggest improvement was made in the roadholding dep rtment and to such effect hat the little Standard became almost a saloon version of a Grand Prix car.   Its roadholding was so impressive that it would have given drivers of the calibre of Ascari and Fangio the greatest pleasure to handle it.

The secret lay in lowering the centre of grav ty.   The rear springs were modified in that the camber was re-set an inch lower and I then cut a coil out of each front spring.   I also fitted harder shock-absorbers and the whole front end became a much more rigid unit.

By the time I had finished with the Standard, at the end of January, Stirling had a car that held the road remarkably well and accelerated in a most impressive fashion.   He was delighted with it and undoubtedly the Standard was a terrific little motor-car, comparable to the Fiat 1100 T.V.

People can say what they like about big cars but I think it is much more fun to drive a small car like the Standard and Stirling shares my point of view.   A production car of this size, fitted with a slightly larger engine and with various modifications such as better brakes to match the extra power, would give a lot of fun to a lot of people.

You could " hit " a roundabout " flat " in the Standard, go on drifting all the way round and come out quite safely on the other side.   Stirling gave me a lift to Coventry on one occasion and we came to a roundabout which was rather narrow at its entry and exit.

" Shall I cut straight through ? " he asked.

"For goodness' sake," I replied.   "This is a roundabout. You cannot go over the top in this country."

" What I mean," said Stirling, " is 'flat' all the way round.   Let's see anyway."

We managed to negotiate it safely, without hitting the kerbs, and this proved to me that the Standard really handled well enough for its extra performance, a factor that many people overlook when they "hot-up" their cars.   How many enthusiasts, for instance, give any thought to the friction area of brake linings when they increase power and top speed, often by as much as 20%.

I collected the Commer transporter from the Rootes Group on February 1st, having left it at Ladbroke Grove immediately after Christmas so that they could give it a thorough check-over, decarbonize the engine and repaint the body.

I was determined to make the Commer the most efficient and comfortable racing car transporter around the circuits.   Not enough thought is given to the comfort factor when lorries are designed.   We are always talking about making cars more comfortable so that the averag private owner can spend perhaps a dozen hours each week in the driving seat in comfort, but not very much thought is given to the seating position for a professional lorry driver who spends practically all of his working day at the wheel.

I had every intention of travelling round Europe with the minimum of effort during the 1954 season.   I had given some thought to the transporter before Christmas and come to the conclusion that if I planned everything sensibly inside the Commer, I should probably be able to cut down by half the energy and effort required. I wanted to avoid all this scrambling over oil drums, tearing overalls on awkwardly positioned spares and barking my shins on similar obstacles. With this in mind, I set about tidying up the layout inside the Commer so that everything had its proper place, was fixed securely in position and could be easily reached on arrival at a circuit.

One of my main concerns was to ensure that I could travel a thousand miles at short notice and flat out, secure in the knowledge that the car would be safely housed and that nothing would fall on top of it. I did not want a repetition of the incident in 1948 when the streamlined Alta had come adrift and bent its nose. I am a great believer in eliminating unnecessary work.

There seemed little doubt that we should cover a considerable mileage during the 1954 season, more than I had ever done previously, and I knew there would be numerous occasions when we should have to repair the ravages of one race and transport a racing car hundreds of miles across Europe and prepare it for the next event, often in less than a week.

As well as being a transporter the Commer would have to be a work-shop and office for myself and my assistant. Every inch of space would have to be used and, as a start, I found room above the driving cab for twenty-two spare tyres and a fireproof cash box.

On many occasions, both with H.W.M. and Peter Whitehead, I had lost sums of money whilst looking after the finances of the *equipe*. This time I was taking no chances and welded the cash box to the body so that the Commer would have to be destroyed or driven away before anyone could remove the box or its contents.

Inside the body I had a work bench, with a vice and grinding wheel fitted and, on the wall above the bench, clips for all my tools, bins for the nuts and bolts and shelving for spares. Under the bench was a tank which carried twenty gallons of oil, and there was space next to the bench for a wash basin. On the nearside wall I fitted clips to carry two collapsible chairs although there was precious little time ever to use them.

Having tidied up the interior of the Commer I then made better arrange-ments for our suitcases. After all, they carry our personal clothing and we like to be able to get out of our overalls and into a decent suit once in a while.

If suitcases are left lying around in the back of a lorry they are easily damaged and, apart from the expense of frequently replacing them, the contents get spoiled ; so I solved that problem by fitting luggage racks well above floor level.

I then modified the work bench so that it could be used as a bed. Nothing is more uncomfortable than trying to sleep in a cramped position in the cab of a lorry. I wanted to be able to pull off the road, put a sleeping bag on the bench and have an hour or two of deep sleep with my legs stretched out. It could also be used as a bed on a non-stop run when the spare driver wanted to relax properly.

The amenities were further improved by fitting a kitchen cabinet so that sufficient cutlery and crockery for six people could be carried. Sylvia gave me a very efficient coffee percolator—I am not a great tea drinker—so that a cup of coffee could be brewed when I felt like it.

A small bar was incorporated in the cabinet which always contained at least one bottle of brandy, that wonderful morale booster, and the cabinet also included a chest of drawers where I planned to keep the necessary data on the car, lap charts and stopwatches. On top I fitted a small portable gas cooker.

Like some kitchen cabinets this one had a " pull-out " table top and I covered it with aluminium sheeting so that it was easy to keep clean, and a simple matter to prepare and serve a meal or just cut sandwiches. Mrs. Moss kindly supplied a set of mugs and cutlery sufficient for six persons.

Inside the cab there was a navigating table with a shaded light, so that the reserve driver could check up on the route.

When Dunlops had fitted a brand new set of tyres the Commer was as good as new. Both engine and chassis had been completely overhauled and the interior was second to none, both from the point of view of practicability and comfort. I even had an ashtray fitted in the driving cab.

Whilst I was working on the Commer, Ken Gregory went on a continental trip to try to sign up Stirling for 1954. He went first of all to Mercedes-Benz and, from what I gathered afterwards in a conversation with Ken and Alfred Moss, the Germans were not at all pleased to see him and not particularly interested in the possibility of Stirling driving for them. Ken was bluntly told that Stirling did not have enough experience and that it would be a good idea if he purchased and raced a potent piece of Italian machinery, such as a Maserati or Ferrari, and proved his worth before applying to Mercedes again.

This led to a family conference. How could Stirling purchase £5,500 worth of Italian motor-car ? It is typical of the Moss family, and the way they stand by each other, that there was never any doubt that Stirling would eventually get a Maserati or Ferrari. It was simply a matter of how quickly the money could be raised. Alfred Moss told me that, if necessary, he would put all his savings into buying a car and it was the same with Mrs. Moss and Pat ; the whole family was prepared to make whatever sacrifices were necessary.

One evening towards the end of February I was invited to join Alfred Moss and Ken Gregory for a meal at the Steering Wheel Club. It was Alfred Moss who opened the conversation.

" Ken has just been to Italy and placed an order for a 250 F. Maserati."

This was indeed good news.

" That's wonderful," I replied. " I only hope I shall be able to look after it properly."

I must admit that I had qualms about whether I could prepare the most recent design of Colombo for World Championship events and keep it going in first-class trim. I was not altogether sure that I could support Moss' driving ability with my limited technical knowledge, particularly with a car such as the 250 F. Maserati. I was perhaps a little more dubious than pleased, for I knew very little about either the latest Maseratis or Ferraris.

However, Alfred Moss reassured me and then went on to explain that the family had helped finance the project and that Stirling—in Sebring—knew very little about it.

Alfred Moss continued : "As soon as Maserati are ready to start build-ing the chassis they are going to let us know. They have promised not to start assembling until you arrive in Modena."

This was very good news indeed for I feel very strongly about being with a car right from the beginning if I am going to look after it. If there is one thing I dislike it is being given a car to maintain and race which I have not built myself. I was, therefore, delighted when Alfred Moss told me that I should be able to keep closely in touch with the assembly.

I realized, as did Alfred Moss, that it would mean living in Modena for weeks—perhaps months—but the advantages far outweighed the dis-advantages for I should get to know the car. This, to me, is a vitally important factor.

I believe it was Alfred Neubauer who once said : " Ninety per cent. of success, or lack of it, with a racing car is in its preparation." In putting forward this point of view, Neubauer knows that the preparation of a car goes right back to the day the first chassis tube is welded, and that the preparation continues throughout the programme of construction until the first appearance of the car on a circuit. Only after the initial tests are successful can one say that the first ninety per cent. of the requirements of success have been achieved.

The next five per cent. of the maximum requirement of one hundred per cent. lies with the driver. He has to get the feel of the car before he can extract the maximum performance from it and soon he should—if he knows his job—be aware of its capabilities.

He will judge how fast he can go without over-straining either the car or himself. We all know that a car and its driver are subjected to severe strain, on some circuits more so than others, but only a top flight driver knows at what stage it becomes excessive and how long it can be tolerated without collapse.

The car has been prepared properly ; the driver knows how to treat the car. What is the final five per cent. that can bring success ? It lies with the *ecurie*, particularly the pit personnel. They are the eyes and ears on the circuit of a calculating machine and technical brain, which should be able to tell exactly how much wear is taking place in the brake system, tyres and transmission, as well as be aware of how much punishment the engine can take.

Unless one has this combination of meticulous preparation, a driver who can " feel " the car, and pit personnel who are in sympathy with the mechanical stresses imposed then one cannot say " well prepared motor-car."

Next comes a second stage in preparation, when the car is prepared for different circuits, which I describe as the development stage. Every circuit has its own peculiarities and, if this development is to be successful, an *equipe* must not miss any major event. It is these events which build up the progress graph of a particular car and show how it compares with others. It is a graph which indicates where you are, how you are progressing and how good you are. Thus the organization for success is very slow and requires infinite pains and patience.

Motor-racing is an endless battle of skill, technical knowledge and common-sense—with the emphasis rather on common-sense. There is no indication that the constant struggle for success and prestige is diminishing ; a struggle between drivers, technicians, mechanics—and the oil companies, who can do so much to ensure success with their development of new fuels.

It is a long road and a difficult one, with many obstacles and chicanes, but the struggle gives much pleasure to people like myself and holds out a continuous challenge. In meeting and often overcoming that challenge— by doing more than one thinks is humanly possible—I find the greatest satisfaction of all.

I often wonder why, in this country, a mechanic charged with the responsibility of looking after a particular car often has difficulty in convincing the team manager or proprietor of an *equipe* what is best for the car. It seems strange to me. Why, in the first place, appoint a man and give him the responsibility of dealing with the car from the technical point of view and then override his decisions. After all, he gets to know the car inside out and is quite capable of taking the logical view in most matters.

I cannot help feeling that too many decisions are made in British *equipes* against the advice of the head mechanic, and often without consulting him at all. I know from experience how many races have been lost because the owner of a car has persisted in approaching a problem from the wrong angle simply because, in the Steering Wheel Club or some similar venue, he has been convinced about a course of action entirely by hearsay.

The racing mechanic has to do what he is told, often against his better judgment, and in my own case it has on occasions resulted in an inferior performance by the car. A mechanic who knows his job should be as good in his own sphere as a top flight driver. No one attempts to alter a driver's technique of control so why interfere with the mechanic's techique in the vitally important sphere of preparation.

The Rootes Group Service people at Ladbroke Grove in London were ever ready to help and to place their facilities at the disposal of *Equipe* Moss. Whilst Rootes Group mechanics are working on the Commer, Alf Francis and Tony Robinson are changing the axle ratio of the 250 F.

The " boxes " at Monza. Warming up the 250 F. Maserati prior to the 1954 Italian G.P. which was so nearly won by Stirling Moss. Bertocchi, chief mechanic and tester for Maserati (wearing his Pirelli cap) is checking fuel and oil levels whilst Alf Francis is operating the throttle. Following a violent argument with Maserati the previous night there was nevertheless maximum co-operation from Bertocchi on the day of the race. Alf recalls that this was a fine example of the *esprit de corps* that is characteristic of racing mechanics.

Pit scene at Pescara in 1954. Moss has just put up a very fast practice time of 10 minutes 23 seconds around the sixteen mile circuit. Alf Francis, sporting his famous woollen hat, originally supplied by Stirling Moss who bought his mechanics one each in Germany, has just removed the bonnet. He is about to replace the hard plugs with soft ones whilst Harry Schell seems more interested in the revolution counter.

CHAPTER 26

MODENA, HERE I COME

On Monday, March 15th, I made an entry in the diary : " To-day I am starting my season." We were all anxiously awaiting a letter from Maserati, notifying us that they were ready to start work on the car. I was on tenterhooks for I knew that as soon as the letter arrived I should be on my way to Modena within twenty-four hours.

Meanwhile the original Cooper-Alta, built by Ray Martin, was collected from Tring by the Ferodo people as they wanted to continue with their experiments in connection with brake linings. The car was under contract to Ferodo, as it had been partly financed by them, and Stirling had agreed that after the 1953 season they would be free to use it as a guinea pig for development purposes. The other Cooper chassis had been returned to Cooper Cars at Surbiton after the engine, gearbox and rear axle had been removed so that the original Cooper-Alta could be made a " runner " again.

When Maserati informed us what sort of fuel would be required for the 250 F. I collected from B.P. 200 gallons and 60 gallons of oil, ranging from 30 to 60 S.A.E. for the sump, back axle and gearbox. I did not know how long we should be on the continent and was taking no chances. I have never had a great deal of confidence in oils I buy over there, even those in sealed cans.

A contract with Shell and B.P. had been signed soon after the Maserati was ordered. Actually, I had been with them since leaving H.W.M. for Peter Whitehead raced on Shell and both Cooper-Altas had been with Shell.

With the transporter and fuel organized I turned my attention to tyres and, as we were signed up with Dunlop, took delivery of a batch sufficient to cover half-a-dozen races. Then, in the sacred cause of publicity, four cases of Lucozade had to be collected for Stirling so that we had a permanent supply in the lorry.

One way and another I had a very busy time. There were travellers' cheques to sign, documents and authorizations to obtain and a spares list to be worked out. I also had to pick up two gallons of paint from the offices of Stirling Moss Limited, in William IV Street, as Stirling is very particular about his colours and was anxious that the Maserati should be painted in true British racing green. At the same time I collected a set of off-white seat covers for the cockpit and a set of metric tools. Back at Tring the last item of equipment to be loaded in the Commer was a hundred-weight of rags, which Alfred Moss had obtained as he knew we had always been short during the previous season.

At last the long awaited letter arrived from Maserati and I set off for the continent on March 20th. The diary entry is as follows : " Collected a brand new Vespa to-day for transport at the circuits. Everything has been settled and Alfred Moss worked overtime last night on my dentures so that I could have them for the trip."

The Vespa had been loaned to Stirling for the 1954 season, and I made a proper fixing for it as our previous Vespa had not been held securely and had been badly damaged.

It seems that someone had plans for Scandinavia during the tour for a further diary entry indicates that I carried £153 Travellers' Cheques for Europe and £50 for Scandinavia. We never went there. I am still waiting!

I drove to Modena on my own, the first time I had ever travelled solo with the Commer. Tony was still with Ray Martin, but we had already spoken to him and it was agreed that as soon as he could leave Ray Martin he would join us.

How different from those early days with H.W.M. I arrived at Dover in a leisurely fashion soon after 7 o'clock on the Saturday evening. I almost felt like singing as, with the wireless playing, I cruised slowly along the promenade, parked the lorry and went into the Shakespeare Bar where I had a Guinness before embarking.

Perhaps it was as well that, at this stage of the journey, I did not know I should cover over fifteen thousand miles in the Commer during that memorable 1954 season, cross the Channel nine times, negotiate the mountain passes of the Alps fifteen times, and cross more than thirty international frontiers in order to deliver the Maserati safely to fifteen major meetings in seven European countries.

I was clear of Dunkirk by twenty minutes to five, having been awake most of the night, and as excited as a schoolboy at the prospect of my visit to Modena and the Maserati works. I pressed on from Dunkirk to Chalons, a distance of four hundred miles, at a fair old chat! I cruised the Commer whenever possible at sixty miles an hour and in the process collected a fine of 1,8 o francs for speeding, administered by a couple of incredulous motor-cycle cops.

When I passed the two policemen the Commer was travelling at 110 kilometres an hour (68 m.p.h.). After catching me the police complained that it was dangerous to drive the transporter at such a speed, and that they had nearly been blown off their motor-cycles by the slipstream. I claimed that the speed was safe for the road and, to avoid getting further involved, eventually settled for a fine on the spot.

However, even a fine for speeding could not upset my morale, which was higher than it had ever been since I started motor-racing. I thought to myself before I turned in that night : " This is it. I shall never have a chance like this again." I was determined to put everything I knew and all my effort into the Maserati project.

Next day I stopped in Lyons for lunch and inquired about the state of the passes from the offices of the Automobile Club de France. I discovered that Mt. Cenis was closed and that the only Pass open, apart from the Ventimiglia route which I had no intention of using, was Mt. Genevre and Lauteret.

That night I stayed in a pleasant little country pub twenty miles from Briancon and next morning set off on my journey through the Passes. The scenery at this time of the year is breathtaking in its beauty, and with the sunshine glistening on the snow it was one of the most picturesque, yet dangerous, journeys I have ever made over the Alps.

It was rather slippery and as the Commer was not fully laden it did not exactly sit down on the road as it should have done. I had a feeling that something was going to happen and suddenly, on entering a tunnel on the winding road, I felt the back end sliding sideways on a surface as slippery as an ice rink. The sun could not penetrate the entrance to the tunnel and the treacherous black ice had not melted.

There was a dull thud. The Commer was well and truly jammed against the roof of the tunnel and I dared not try to move either forwards or backwards for fear of holing the roof. I had to leave it there whilst I walked half-a-mile to the nearest emergency telephone and contacted Pass Control. They told me a snowstorm was raging at the top of the Mt. Genevre Pass and that they would send a snow plough to get me out of the tunnel and then clear a path to the top of the Pass. The French officials were most kind and helpful.

The snow plough straightened the Commer in the tunnel by dragging it sideways, and then followed a tedious two-hour journey behind the plough, which could not travel faster than five miles an hour. After a few miles of this, on a comparatively clear section of the road, I decided to pass.

As I drew level the driver shouted at me : " Get behind us. It is all right here but you will never keep on the road higher up."

How right he was. Suitably chastised I fell in at the rear again and was pleased not to have ignored his advice for as we climbed higher I could not see the road at all. To me it was just a plateau of snow and even though the plough had only come down the Pass a short while previously the wind had blown the snow over the road again and completely hidden it from view.

It was late on Tuesday evening when I arrived in Susa and, having had a good night's rest, I pushed on to Modena and reached the Europa soon after 7 o'clock. My old friend Bruni, the receptionist, was delighted to see me and obviously very proud that Stirling Moss' racing transporter was parked outside his hotel.

CHAPTER 27

ENTER THE GREEN MASERATI

The Red Carpet—Guerino Bertocchi—
Some embarrassing situations—The 250 F. engine.

I still have a photograph, taken as I drove through the gates of the Maserati factory the morning after my arrival in Modena. I needed no introduction, as the name Stirling Moss was prominently displayed on both sides of the Commer, and there had been a brief item in the early morning news bulletin on the wireless to the effect that the mechanic to Stirling Moss, the British racing driver, had arrived in Modena to collect his Maserati.

Forewarned, the " works " gave me a terrific welcome. It seems that everyone was there, including Mr. Orsi, Jnr., Mr. Montcaliery—the Secretary—and a man with whom I was to become very friendly, Guerino Bertocchi, the Head Mechanic.

As a mechanic myself I had never expected such a welcome and after I had been introduced to a dozen or so people I invited them all to inspect the interior of the Commer.

" Once we have the car," I said to Mr. Orsi, " we intend to look after it properly."

The Italians were most impressed by the way the Commer had been fitted out and particularly with the cooking facilities and miniature bar. The latter interested them more than the various ingenious devices connected with the transportation of the actual car.

By the end of the day I was tired out, having been shown over the large Maserati works and introduced to all those people who would be involved in the building of our 250 F. I met everyone, from the Chief Body Designer and other departmental chiefs, to the foremen, mechanics and fitters.

They all had a surprising knowledge of Stirling and his activities whilst some of them had watched him in action on several occasions. All had a great regard for him and several people told me during the course of the day : " We are proud and honoured that he has decided to buy and race a Maserati."

There was no resentment in the works that I should have been sent to Modena to watch the car being built. The Italians were delighted to see me and put me at my ease from the very first. They even went so far as to invite me to park the Commer in the factory yard. This was a great privilege, as customers' lorries normally have to remain outside the works.

My interpreter, who had been instructed to stay with me all the time, explained that Modena is a pro-Communist town. " We do not want any incidents involving your British lorry."

He then explained that although Maserati wanted my advice and views whilst the car was being built, they did not expect me personally to do any work.

"I think you will soon get bored," said my friend, "for there will be very little for you to do."

I met Roy Salvadori during my tour of the works. He had been at the Autodrome testing Syd Green's new 250 F. and was most impressed by its performance. Stirling telephoned me at the Europa that night and I told him that Salvadori was delighted with the handling of the car.

"From what I can make out," I said to Stirling, "this Maserati really goes."

Next day I was invited to the Autodrome to watch one of the works 250 F. Maseratis being tested. I took an instant liking to the over-all appearance of the car. In action its acceleration was terrific and the handling very steady.

When Bertocchi asked me if I would like to drive a new prototype they had at the Autodrome that morning I politely but fi mly refused.

"I am only a mechanic," I told him, "and shall not be able to drive it fast enough."

I could not have said anything worse for Head Mechanic Bertocchi is as good a driver as some of the best *pilotes*. He took rather a dim view of my refusal but I had no intention of taking out this very potent piece of Grand Prix machinery and spinning it for their amusement. I could see no reason why I should be the star turn at the Modena Autodrome only thirty-six hours after my arrival.

Bertocchi then showed me the 250 F. in detail and I was particularly interested in the gearbox, which was a combined unit incorporating the back axle and a very nice piece of engineering work. It struck me that if the box on the G.P. Alta had been modified to operate as a combined unit it would have been very similar to the 250 F. layout. As a matter of interest, and bearing in mind the gearbox failures I had experienced on other cars, the Maserati box never gave any trouble at all in a series of over twenty races.

On Saturday I invited Bertocchi, the Secretary, the Chief Engineer, and a few of the senior mechanics to dine with me. I invited the mechanics because it was apparent that in the Maserati organization they were treated as professional men with a career rather than as artisans with a trade. This is so with Ferrari as well as with all the continental *equipes* and I wish it were more the case in this country.

From what I have seen it appears that British racing mechanics are often regarded as the chaps who hammer a knock-on wheel into position or pour a churn of fuel into a funnel. Few people realize their true worth and when a race meeting is over and the cars are loaded into lorries there are only a handful of people who are interested in the chaps who work on the cars behind the scenes.

The continentals have the right idea. Drivers, mechanics, team manager and patron all get together after a race. They are a team before, during and after the Meeting and that is the way I think it should be.

Bertocchi and the Maserati boys were obviously well known in the famous restaurant in Castelfranco where we dined for we were shown to the best table and given every attention. It was my first introduction to

Lambrusco, the renowned sparkling red wine of Modena. To please everyone I said it was just wonderful, but would have preferred a nice bottle of Burgundy. This was my first public relations move. I realized that I should be living and working with these people for a long time and the quicker we all became good friends the better for our Maserati.

We had a very quiet party, in rather a staid atmosphere, as Bertocchi does not loosen up at all and is always very serious and business-like. When he is around, then everyone else behaves. When I wore my rain-coat inside out on leaving the restaurant, to show my appreciation of the Lambrusco, Bertocchi was not amused.

To me he is more intelligent than many of the drivers I have met. He is not only a mechanic but very much a professional man and leads a strict catholic life. He paid me a great compliment after I had been in Modena a few days by inviting me to his home for the evening where I met his charming wife. I would describe him as typical of a London businessman. With an umbrella and bowler hat he would not be out of place in any city office and is the most conservative of all the Italians I know.

Bertocchi is shrewd and deliberate. There must be some point in everything he says and does and no time is wasted with a smile and small talk unless it is strictly necessary. He is completely wrapped up in his work and I do not think he has ever done anything else other than look after racing cars.

He is a first-rate driver of fast machinery and could have made a fortune as a driver ; but he is not interested and prefers to work behind the scenes.

" I go motor-racing as Head Mechanic of Maserati," says Bertocchi, " and it is my ambition every season to make it possible for my cars to win the World Championship."

I believe that, because of his relationship with Signor Orsi, Bertocchi could have a much higher position with Maserati if he wished, but prefers to remain where he is. People have said to me that Bertocchi is no different from some other mechanics, that he can be bribed. This is not so ; he is as straight as a die and would punch anyone on the nose who tried to bribe him.

On Wednesday I booked a call to Stirling after midnight for I knew he would be anxiously awaiting news of the 250 F. He fired a broadside of questions and I had to tell him the car had not been commenced. Naturally he was upset, but I pointed out that the " works " were only forty-eight hours behind schedule which is not too bad for the Italians. Stirling saw my point and our conversation ended with him telling me to find out whether the car would be ready for Pau on April 19th, in less than three weeks' time.

I tackled Signor Orsi next day and he confirmed that the first chassis tubes had not been prepared.

" It is rather difficult for me to commit myself," he said, " and you will appreciate that with a racing car it is impossible to guarantee a definite date at this stage."

I did not argue, but sympathized with his " difficulties," as I was anxious to gain his friendship. I could see the car would not be ready to race at Pau unless it was treated as a rush job and I did not want another Cooper-Alta effort—a G.P. challenger built in a fortnight. I was determined to have a racing car this time that had been thoroughly prepared throughout the whole range of its building.

A day or so later a major crisis developed. I had already found that it was easy to offend the Maserati people when I told them we would supply the paint for the car.

" We have any colour you want," they said. " Our paints are very good, you know."

I knew they would feel happier if they used their own paint and that is why the Maserati raced in that rather peculiar, sickly shade of Adriatic sea green.

An embarrassing situation arose over the pedals for the works were not at all anxious to alter their position. Stirling likes to have the throttle pedal on the right-hand side of the brake pedal, as on British cars, whereas the Italians have them the opposite way round. My insistence on the pedals being fitted our way shook the entire works and I could foresee major troubles arising if I insisted on too many things being altered to our liking. It was as though I had attempted to topple the structure of the Maserati organization. How dare I make such a suggestion !

"I do not know who you people think you are," Bertocchi said to me. " We have been building racing cars for over thirty-five years and surely we know what is best for the drivers. Is Mr. Moss so different from the champions of the world ? What is good enough for them is surely good enough for him."

He went on to explain that heeling and toeing is much easier with the throttle on the inside because the natural manner of relaxing the foot is to point the toe outwards.

" It is therefore an easy matter," said Bertocchi, " for a driver to find the throttle by turning his heel inwards when heeling and toeing. With your system a driver has to twist his leg outwards in an unnatural fashion."

He was quite right but it did not alter the fact that in this country, as well as driving on the " wrong " side of the road, we fit our normal production and racing cars with the brake pedal on the inside and that is where a driver instinctively puts his foot in an emergency.

" You will make unnecessary dangers for Stirling Moss," I told Bertocchi, " if you insist on the pedals being fitted your way."

Eventually he agreed to have the throttle altered to suit Stirling and after that particular argument I reckoned I had earned a week's wages in one day.

I thought to myself that I might as well be hung for a sheep as a lamb and raised the question of the seating position. Stirling likes to sit well back, with his arms outstretched, but Italian seating positions are very upright and the driver might almost be sitting in a London bus.

To my surprise Bertocchi was quite sympathetic and agreed to have a special seat made that was inclined slightly more to the rear, and thus better placed for a more relaxed drive. It was almost a major operation and meant altering the design of the cockpit by moving the cross member.

Whilst at the Maserati works I learned a lot about the 250 F. engine. I watched them being assembled and tested on the bench and have never seen such meticulous, painstaking preparation. The Italians go to absolute extremes with checks and rechecks before an engine is put on the test bed. For many years I have worked on engines but I would not have the patience of the Italians. I admire them for it but would reckon to do the job in three-quarters of the time taken by them.

Strangely enough, as jigs of alignment they used rather old-fashioned gauges, and did not use their special, highly sensitive micrometers. They even had a specially constructed jig so as to ensure a precise alignment of the crankcase and crankshaft bearings. The outside journals of the bearings were made such a close fit that the Vandervell thinwall bearings went in as a perfect assembly in the first instance. It was a closer fit than with old-fashioned pre-war engines where one used to fit the journals by scraping them.

The aluminium casing, cylinder head and camshaft alignment were treated with similar meticulous care and the engines were also assembled and checked for internal porous leaks, by using as much as 190 lb. pressure per square inch. I do not believe checks of this sort, at such high pressure, are made in this country.

I watched Salvadori's engine being tested on the bench and, according to the amount of weight it was lifting, 240 b.h.p. was being produced at 7,250 revs. The brake was a normal Heenan and Froud and I had no suspicions concerning its accuracy or any doubts about its readings. It was far more b.h.p. than I had ever extracted, and it was really something to watch this engine turning over at more than 7,000 revs per minute. I had never seen a power unit on a bench at such high speeds and yet it was perfectly smooth.

As we were under contract to Shell and B.P. I asked Bertocchi, who was in charge of the Test Bed, whether he would mind if we tried Shell fuel. He was quite agreeable and we found Shell better than the local Italian fuel. The readings appeared more stable, the power developed was slightly higher and the engine seemed to retain its power for much longer periods.

A few days later, I went over to the Autodrome and watched Salvadori trying his car. He certainly made it motor in a most impressive fashion, and then Bertocchi fairly streaked round the circuit in 1 minute 5 seconds, which is very fast indeed for Modena. I wrote in my diary that night " Seems the thing really goes."

The days were passing and I was beginning to get rather bored. Admittedly I did not have financial worries, as Stirling had given me a generous allowance, but apart from the odd driver passing through Modena and staying for a night at the Reali I had no one as a companion. My Italian was improving, but I could not carry on a conversation without the interpreter and I did not want him around all the time.

CHAPTER 28

OUT ON A LIMB

Divided loyalties—A violent argument about tyres—An oil bath for Francis—
Testing the " Maser."—En route to Bordeaux—I learn a lesson about tyres.

At the end of my second week in Modena I was bored and rather fed
up for the Modenese are hard-working and take a serious view of life.
Friendly as they are, Modena is not exactly the right place for a celebration
or night out. It would have been better had Tony been with me for then
I could have discussed what line to take with such matters as the pedals
and seating position. I would have liked someone in Modena to share
my problems.

I was in a difficult position and my loyalties were, so to speak, divided.
I knew it was my responsibility to have the car completed exactly as Stirling
wanted but, at the same time, I dared not upset the Maserati people too
much. I realized that if I was not too persistent about having things done
our way, I should make friends in the works and that would mean a great
deal once our season started. To the works staff our car was just another
Maserati—whether painted red, green, blue or yellow—and a good relationship between them and *Equipe* Moss was vitally important. I tried to build
up a friendly association so that I could introduce Stirling under the most
favourable circumstances.

Eighteen days after my arrival in Modena I was told that assembly of
our engine was about to start and decided to ask the two fitters who would
be doing the job to join me for a meal that evening. I had already established
a close friendship with the body-builder, Fantuzzi, in a similar manner ;
to date he was the only man in the works who did not argue with me.

Over a good meal and a bottle of wine I learned a great deal about the
250 F. engine and confirmed what Bertocchi had previously told me ; we
could use 7,800 r.p.m. instead of the normal 7,600 but it would mean changing the big-end bearings after every race, whereas if only 7,600 was used it
would be possible to complete at least two races without a change.

The picture of our race strategy was beginning to form and perhaps more
people will now understand why we kept down the engine revs of the
Maserati during the first few races, and before the works stepped in with
an offer which I will describe later.

I could see that, with the least possible delay, we should have to find
the most suitable rev range for our purpose. It meant finishing a race
of full Grand Prix length, a genuine three hundred miles at a steady,
previously agreed engine speed before we could determine our race strategy.
It was, in fact, a sensible approach and there was no thought of winning
races in those early days with the Maserati. We were more concerned with

finishing so as to learn something about the car, and of finding a way of reducing the penalty of 200 revs by the most advantageous use of back axle ratio, tyres and engine revolutions.

Stirling put through one of his periodic telephone calls that night. He was not very pleased about progress on the car and still annoyed that it could not have been completed for Pau.

" Well," I said, " you can safely enter for Bordeaux on May 9th. The car will be ready by then. Let's make up our minds that this will be our first race."

Whether he liked it or not there was no alternative but to accept the situation for he was eight hundred miles away. I was pleased not to be with him at that particular time for he was, understandably, getting frustrated. On the other hand he had left me out on a limb and it was a dangerous limb on which to sit.

Actually, I was not at all sure the car would be ready for Bordeaux but even so was not prepared to push the Maserati people. I thought to myself, after Stirling had rung off : " Whether you like it or not, this car is going to be finished in its own time and it's going to be *the* Maserati. We may miss one race but we shall do all the better in the next ! "

The following day I had a violent argument with the Chief Engineer, Ballentani, about tyres and would certainly have liked Stirling's support on that particular morning. As we were signed up with Dunlop I naturally wanted to try a set of their tyres on a similar car to our own. I went along to Ballentani's office to ask for the loan of four wheels so that I could fit one of the Maserati test cars with Dunlop and try it around the Autodrome but he would not hear of it.

" It's good enough for us to run on Pirelli," he grumbled, " with the most famous drivers in the world. Why should your Mr. Moss want anything different?"

" Look," I replied, " surely we can run the car on what tyres we like; that is our business. All I require is four spare wheels. Are you or are you not going to let me have them ? "

" No, I am not," replied Ballentani, " and I shall be obliged if you will kindly leave my office without further argument."

I was very angry but decided that discretion was the better part of valour and withdrew. I could see that I should not be able to try Dunlop tyres until we arrived in Bordeaux.

A few days later Stirling telephoned again to say he would be in Modena after Easter with his sister, Pat. He was worried about Salvadori who was apparently going to be supported by the works.

" Syd Green has been appointed Maserati agent for England," said Stirling, " and the works have even arranged that Salvadori will have an Italian mechanic to look after the car. Seems to me I shall be fighting a losing battle as a private owner."

I was not worried and told Stirling that, with the contacts I had built up in the works, we were going to have a good season, perhaps even beat the factory cars on occasions.

" I have fostered a lot of goodwill with my public relations," I explained " and we shall be better placed at the works than Salvadori can ever hope to be. He can advertise the fact that he is works supported but it will be our car that really gets the backing."

Stirling was not convinced but then he did not know all the facts. This Salvadori scare did not bother me at all.

I booked two rooms at the Europa, and the proprietor was so delighted that I think I could have eaten " on the house " from then on had I asked. I was already getting a free breakfast most mornings because of a conversation with the proprietor a few days after my arrival in Modena. He asked me why I did not park the Commer outside the hotel.

" Why should I ? " was my reply. " It is much safer in the works and I have the Vespa to run around the town."

" Don't worry about it getting damaged," said the Italian. " It will be quite O.K. as Bruni is on duty all night. Besides it will give us good publicity."

" Well," I replied, " if you want publicity, that costs money."

Eventually it was arranged that when the Commer was left for the night outside the hotel he would give me breakfast free of charge ; consequently it was often parked outside the Europa in exchange for coffee, rolls and jam.

Stirling arrived in Modena with one very much thrashed Jaguar Mk. VII. It had one of those comic hydramatic self-change gearboxes and I used to pull his leg about it for I take a very dim view of a racing driver who uses this sort of gear change. It's fine for old ladies and Americans !

Stirling complained about oil leaks from the torque converter and, although I knew nothing about its mechanism, he insisted that we strip it down. Admittedly, from the prestige point of view the green and cream Jaguar was an embarrassment, for it would refuse to move off from traffic lights which of course delighted the characters in the Fiat 600s and 1100s.

We tackled the job outside the Maserati works. To the unconcealed surprise of the Italian personnel, we put on overalls and set to work on the gearbox, whilst Pat sat in the back of the Jaguar with a pile of magazines.

The Italians could not understand why a famous racing driver like Stirling Moss, who could afford to spend nearly £6,000 on a Maserati, should want to work on his private car in a dusty, oily roadway instead of taking it to a garage and spending £3 to have the gearbox stripped down.

I started off underneath, whilst Stirling worked from the inside, and we changed over from time to time ; but I was underneath when we eventually removed the gearbox, having forgotten to drain the oil ! With the jointing disconnected, we manœuvred the gearbox to the rear and two gallons of oil gushed out and smothered me. I dare not let go of the gearbox otherwise it would have collapsed on top of me, and I just lay there— saturated in oil.

When I eventually got out from under the car I looked like a nigger minstrel and there was a roar of laughter from the bystanders. I had to use three packets of Tide to clean myself and, when Pat Moss was out of earshot, I swore loud and long about the hydramatic. We never cured the gearbox trouble in Modena, although it was taken out on two further occasions, and it was not until twelve months later that it was eventually put right.

Tony Robinson came out to Modena a week after Stirling and, although his arrival at the station at 4 o'clock in the afternoon meant that I missed Ascari—who won the Mille Miglia that year—on his way through Modena, I was more than pleased to see him.   At last I should be able to talk to someone in English and without worrying about public relations.

There was another reason why I was so delighted to see Tony.   During my motor-racing career I have never had a better assistant.   He was easy to get on with, very conscientious, and if I gave him a job to do—no matter what—I could rely on him doing it properly.   He did not need supervision and because of this was absolutely invaluable.   There was never any risk, with Tony Robinson, of a car going on to the grid without any oil in the gearbox or back axle.

The day after his arrival we saw the 250 F. in its completed orm.   The Maserati looked very businesslike and absolutely " right."   I felt, even without handling the car, that here was something superlative in its own class, a car that had been built by men who knew their job and whose conscientiousness backed their ability.

Next day we took the Maser. to the Autodrome where there was the usual polite conversation on the lines of : "After you, Mr. Francis ; no, after you, Mr. Bertocchi."   After fifteen minutes of restrained argument and discussion it was decided that I would do five slow laps and Bertocchi would put in five fast ones.

I was delighted with the feel of the car and as I trundled round the Autodrome (my careful progress can only be described as such) I felt that this was a racing car I could handle, a thoroughbred but with none of the vices so often associated with them.

To me it seemed no more difficult than driving the Mark VII Jaguar ; whether travelling at high or low speeds, the Maser. was entirely different in its handling characteristics from any other racing car I had ever driven. I would not mind racing such a car myself.   I would feel confident enough to do so although I did not have such confidence with cars I handled in earlier years.   They seemed highly strung whereas the Maserati gave me a feeling of security.

When Stirling tested the car next day he climbed into the cockpit, settled himself down in the seat and looked up with a smile as I gave the thumbs up sign.   He put in twenty or so fast laps and I could see that already he was absolutely at home in the green Maserati.   When he came in the Italians knew at once that he was more than satisfied with its performance and this pleased them no end.

This was it.   At last we were ready to move off and on Wednesday, May 5th, exactly six weeks after my arrival in Modena, we left the Maserati works on our way to Bordeaux.   It was midnight as we pulled away from the Europa and, three-and-a-half hours later with a hundred miles of the fast but dangerous Via Emilia behind us, we were in Milan.   At night this is a frightening road, with long distance lorries and coaches fairly streaking along in the sixties and flashing their lights continuously.   We had decided to complete the journey with no night stops, as we were due in Bordeaux on Friday morning, so pressed on through Milan and Turin, arriving in Susa six-and-a-half hours after leaving Modena.

From there, it was an uneventful run over the Mt. Cenis Pass through

Modane and down to St. Jean de Maurienne, where we had a cup of strong French coffee for breakfast, as opposed to the sickly, sweet Modena beverage.

Driving in shifts of three hours, we passed through Grenoble on Thursday night and at 10.30 a.m. on Friday arrived in Bordeaux where we met Stirling. Tony and I were exhausted, after thirty-five hours of non-stop driving, but Stirling was so obviously relieved and pleased that we had arrived safely and in such good time that everything seemed worth while. The weariness wore off. We had a new car, our first race was in forty-eight hours and the Maser. was really going to motor. Morale in *Equipe Moss* was high.

After lunch, we took the car on to the short, twisting street circuit and Stirling put in a few laps. He was not too happy about carburation which was, in fact, being affected by our use of axle ratio. We had fitted a slightly higher ratio than the other Maseratis for we had decided to restrict revs to 7,200, but by using this ratio the power curve was appreciably altered.

On the 250 F. the torque comes in at 4,800 revs and stays until 7,200. In our case the use of higher back axle gearing meant that the torque would be required to come in below 4,800, but in order to achieve this we had to alter the carburation. We therefore tuned the carburetters, using smaller jets and chokes, and succeeded in getting more torque between 4,500 and 4,800 revs. The car then handled very well indeed.

We had a discussion with Stirling about strategy, for this first race was vitally important and would be our yardstick of performance. We had to finish, and to do this with a new car first time out is not easy, for the driver is naturally anxious to test its potential. However, Stirling is a sensible, careful driver and readily appreciated that the Maserati would have to be treated comparatively gently so that we could find out, from the point of view of operation and maintenance under race conditions, how to treat it.

Our job was not to learn how a prototype could be improved, as had been the case with H.W.M., but to learn how to race a car that was in production and had been designed by some of the best brains in the world.

Ballentani had been right about the tyres as we were to find out. We had fitted Dunlops before leaving Modena and, as it looked as though there would be rain during the race, the tyres were well scrubbed. In fact, we had them properly cut by the Dunlop people.

Proudly Tony and I wheeled the green Maserati on to the grid. I had fixed Stirling's horseshoe on the offside of the cockpit body panel and the car also carried two small Union Jack transfers, supplied by Stirling. He was insistent that he would not drive the Maserati until they were in position.

We were on the third row of the grid, as in practice Stirling had wisely not tried to join the fierce duel between the Ferraris of Gonzalez and Trintignant and the Gordini of Behra. There were no works Maseratis but Schell was being given factory support.

As soon as the flag dropped I could see that Stirling was having difficulty in keeping the car straight under acceleration on a track already damp from a shower of rain just before the start. For twelve laps Gonzalez, Behra and Trintignant duelled for the lead whilst he took things quietly.

Soon afterwards it started to rain fairly heavily and as Stirling came down the straight towards the pits at the end of each lap it was obvious to me that when he put his foot down the car snaked on acceleration.   He was finding it difficult to stay on the wet road and, unable to use maximum power, was dropping farther and farther back.

A quick decision was needed for I knew the fault was not with the car or driver but with the tyres.   I told Tony to look after the pit and went along to the Pirelli people.

" Look," I said, " I want to buy four tyres right now."

Within a few minutes the tyres were fitted on four of our spare wheels and I put out the signal for Stirling to come in.   He had no idea what was going on but obeyed without question.   It was a fine example of race discipline.

Almost before he had stopped, the front end was up and the wheels being changed.   Then the back.   Only two people were allowed to work on the car and Stirling stood by whilst Tony and I replaced four wheels in a little over two minutes.   Naturally, the Dunlop people did not like it but what was the alternative !   We had to see whether the Maserati would behave better on the Pirelli treads.

When Stirling got away, the car was much steadier and he went like a bomb, although never exceeding our agreed rev limit of 7,200.   By the time the circuit dried out, three-quarters of the 123-lap race had been completed and he went even faster, delighting the crowds with his handling of the car.   We must have lost at least three laps during the early stages before the pit stop yet Stirling recovered two of them and finished fourth, the only Maserati to complete the distance.

If the race, which was won by Gonzalez, had continued for another ten laps, I guarantee he would have recovered another lap and beaten Trintignant for third place.

It was incredible what a difference the change of tyres made and it taught me a lesson ; the right type of tyre on a car is of vital importance. I was fully prepared to apologize to my friend, Ballentani, and did so.

The car had behaved itself impeccably and Stirling had not strained the engine.   He reported that the oil pressure had not dropped at all, which indicated that the engine was in good shape, so we did not strip down to examine the big-ends.   In any case there was not much time as the Maserati was due to race at Silverstone on the following Saturday in the *Daily Express International Trophy*.

After our routine Monday conference we left Bordeaux and, driving non-stop for five hundred miles, arrived in Calais twenty-four hours later. That night I spent at home in Woolwich whilst Tony went home to Neasden. By lunch-time on Wednesday we were in Brackley where I always prepare my cars in Alcock's Garage.   The proprietor, a very keen racing man himself, is always very helpful.

I wanted to work on the car at Brackley rather than Bordeaux, which was one reason for the non-stop drive to Calais and our first job was to change the axle ratio.   On the Maserati, if we had to change the reduction gears, as was the case at Brackley, it was a twelve-hour job.   It meant removing the oil tank, fuel tank, disconnecting the drive shafts and the propeller-shaft and also partly removing the de Dion tube   Only then was it possible to take out the entire gearbox and back axle assembly so that the ratio of the reduction gears could be changed.

If it was only a matter of changing the pinion ratio we were able to cope in three hours because by working underneath the car it was only necessary to disconnect part of the axle housing, remove the driving and driven pinions and fit replacement pinions.   We had to pay particular attention to the meshing of the gears, then we reassembled.

At Brackley I had second thoughts about the big-ends and dropped the sump to have a look at them.   As I had expected they were O.K.

CHAPTER 29

INTO BATTLE

The Plan of Campaign—Signals, job cards and data sheets—
De Dion trouble at Silverstone—Aintree, our first major victory—
More teething troubles in Rome—Fisticuffs at Spa.

A plan of campaign was worked out before the 1954 season commenced. We were determined to race in the most efficient manner, incorporating all the lessons I had learned since my first motor-race in 1948. It was not a matter of " we will have a go and let's hope to do well " as it had been in the past. This time we *had* to do well.

With Stirling I designed a special signal board which he made up after I left for Modena. Having decided not to use any of the normal motor-racing codes, which are based on a system of arrows, we invented our own code. The top of the board was designed to carry any one of four removable coloured strips, three inches deep ; either red, amber, white with blue stripes or white only.

The red strip meant " danger " and was used as a warning that someone was closing on the driver or that he was losing time to the man in front.

The amber strip meant " slow down " and indicated that there was no risk of being overtaken or that the man in front was too fast to catch. It meant " Why strain the motor ? Keep to a safe speed."

The white strip with blue stripes meant "Keep going as you are " ; the white strip on its own indicated a false signal and warned the driver not to take any notice of what was displayed on the board.

Underneath the removable strips the board was divided in three further sections. I used the top one to tell the driver how many seconds he was behind the man in front, the middle one to show his lap speed and the third one to indicate how many seconds he was ahead of the man following. Underneath the board small discs were suspended, indicating the number of laps still to be completed.

Thus I was able with one signal to pass the driver all the information required. However, it was quite a lot to digest when travelling really fast such as at Rheims and Monza, or arriving at the pits suddenly as at Silverstone, and eventually I stopped putting the lap times in the middle, as Stirling was not really interested. He was only concerned with how far he was behind the man in front.

Occasionally I interrupted the routine signals and put on the board the names of the first three drivers so that Stirling was kept informed what was going on at the head of the field when he was not there himself. I used to work it like this. I would show him the board with the first three placings, and next time round he would get P. for place and a number to indicate his position. Finally, on the next round, I would show him how much he was behind the man in front. Thus he was able to work out himself whether, in the time available, he had any chance of catching the man in front and/or getting in the first three.

So far as the mechanical preparation of the car was concerned we used job cards. Immediately after a Meeting, when certain jobs on the Maserati had been carried out, the person concerned (either Tony or myself) had to initial the card which was absolutely complete from the preparation and maintenance point of view. Provided all the jobs were done, nothing important was left out. It was more than anything else a valuable reminder, and also served as a maintenance and replacement of parts record as well.

These job cards were most useful in another way because we filed them after a race and, by referring to them when we next visited a particular circuit, a comment in the " Remarks " column often told us some peculiarity of racing on the circuit.

I also had data sheets which were a check on the performance of the car at each Meeting. I arranged with Stirling that he would keep his own set of sheets, whilst I kept mine, and they would not be compared until the end of the season. When we started to race the Maserati in 1954 there was every intention of carrying on as private entrants in 1955, and we intended to compare the data sheets of driver and mechanic at the end of the year so that we could organize ourselves more efficiently for the next season.

Our pit routine was quite straightforward. During the race I was responsible for the overall management, and looked after the signal board as well whilst Tony kept the lap chart. There was invariably someone else with us—sometimes an enthusiast, sometimes a friend—and when Stirling came in for any reason Tony handed the lap chart over to the third man and was free to help me.

At refuelling stops I halted the car and put the funnel in the filler whilst Tony stood ready with the first five-gallon churn of fuel. As soon as he started pouring, I picked up a second churn and stood ready. Then, when I had poured in my five gallons as well, it was Tony who closed the filler cap, then helped me to give a push start.

When it was a matter of changing a rear wheel, I stopped the car, Tony put the jack under the axle and I knocked off the wheel. Meanwhile, Tony rolled out the replacement, put it on the hub and hammered it fast and I let down the jack and pushed the driver on his way.

We worked out the routine pit stops so that neither of us ever completed a particular task. One of us would start the job, the other would continue and the first one would probably finish it. I always insisted on looking after the signal board and stopping the car, and as it was I who brought the Maserati into the pits I always found myself working on the outside. Tony always remained between the pits and car. He was never allowed to work on the same side as myself and consequently we avoided those time-losing, embarrassing collisions in the heat of the moment which one sees so often.

On Thursday we took the Maserati from Brackley to Silverstone and were very pleased with our practice time of 1 minute 51 seconds, next fastest to Gonzalez (Ferrari) who went round in 1-48. We had a nice quiet, restful night.

On Friday it was raining and the times much slower. There was no sense in pushing the car too hard, as it would not be possible in the wet to improve on the times set the previous day. However, the car suffered from lack of brakes and Stirling decided to change the Italian Frendo linings, fitted at the Maserati works, for a set of Ferodo.

It was a tedious, long job and meant working all Friday night. The first enthusiasts were already cooking breakfast in the enclosures by the time we had finished. I felt worn out but the brakes still had to be bedded in so I took the car out of the paddock and ran backwards and forwards on one of the inner concrete runways. The Maserati handled beautifully under heavy braking and I thought to myself : " This really is some motor-car."

In Heat 1 of the Trophy race Stirling finished third. He did not try to push the car too hard and it may have seemed to spectators that Moss was trying unsuccessfully to fight it out with Rolt on Rob Walker's Connaught before Rolt spun at Stowe. The fact is that Moss was much more interested in nursing the Maserati through the heat into the final than becoming involved in a duel. We had a lot to learn about the car and our maxim was still " finish not bust."

In the final a similar situation prevailed. We knew there was a tough programme of races ahead—at Aintree, Rome and Spa—and although Stirling drove faster, the rev limit of 7,200 still applied.

" What a fine race," is the description in my diary. From the third row of the grid he had moved up into third place by the end of the first lap. After five laps he was second, then Behra on a Gordini " took " him, only for Stirling to retake second place at fifteen laps. There he stayed, sensibly within his rev limit and behind Gonzalez, until the twenty-fifth lap when the de Dion tube broke. It was bad luck, with only ten laps remaining, for our car was certainly the fastest of the three Maseratis (Bira, Salvadori and Mieres), and Moss should have finished second to Gonzalez for there was no one anywhere near him when the tube broke. The Maserati works personnel at Silverstone thought a lot of his driving that day.

The broken de Dion tube can be put down to a development snag ; teething trouble if you like. After all, these 250 F. Maseratis were brand new cars designed for the 1954 season.

After Silverstone, we took the Maserati back to Tring and stripped down the engine. I had a look at the big-ends and mains and made an entry in the diary. " Since changing the oil they look worse."

Let me explain this oil business. When the Maserati was nearing completion, Bertocchi told me that although they were signed up with a particular company, the oils were not suitable for the hard work the engine had to do. They found some oil from a competitor which was more suitable for the Maserati engine so they purchased some and used it in our new car. I did not want to make a change for the Bordeaux race and, on checking the big-ends and journals in Brackley before Silverstone, I found them in first-class condition.

However, we refilled for Silverstone, but on checking the big-end and main bearings, the crankshaft journals, camshaft and cam followers I came to the conclusion that the oil was not suitable for our particular type of engine. In my opinion the oil used by Maserati would have suited us better. Hence the entry in my diary.

From my point of view as a mechanic, I cannot agree that it is a good thing to sign up with a particular fuel company in exchange for financial sponsorship. Their product may be quite satisfactory for one type of engine but equally unsatisfactory for another, and the whole thing becomes a business proposition, a ridiculous one to my mind in those cases where an engine would give a better performance on a different oil.

Quite apart from anything else I do not think sponsorship is in keeping with motor-racing in its basic form as a sport, Ideally, from the point of view of maximum efficiency an *equipe* should be free to use the most suitable oils and not be bound by sponsorship contracts.

Having said this I am the first to admit that without the fuel companies, motor-racing could not continue in its present form, Their sponsorship of racing car manufacturers largely enables cars to reach the " grid," while their bonuses on the result of a race often supplement to a considerable extent the prize money awarded by the organizers.

We finished the assembly of the engine by the end of the week and also had the carburetters to pieces when we found two injection passages blocked and cleared them. Then we modified the return springs on the butterflies, as previously they had broken and jammed the throttles, which was dangerous. Then we cut new clutch plates, which were turned for us by Weldangrind, and fitted them.

Whilst we were at Tring the de Dion tube was mended. I took it to the Weldangrind people and they made strengthening pieces, afterwards coming down to Tring and fitting the tube. It was my idea to put in reinforcement pieces as I considered the torsional stress should be equally spread over the whole tube, rather than all the stress being taken in one corner which had resulted in the Silverstone trouble. Weldangrind made a very good job of it and the reinforced tube was as good as new—and stronger.

As we did not have any jigs, and it was necessary to keep the tube straight, we fitted it in the chassis, carefully set—aligned the wheels and welded it in position. The chassis was also modified and welded in one particular place as it showed signs of weakening on the engine support members.

I did not get in touch with Maserati about the de Dion as I decided to do this job according to my own ideas and to show the works that we could deal with this sort of problem on our own.

Our next race was at Aintree, when the new circuit was used for the first time and the cars raced anti-clockwise. This led to a lot of argument amongst the drivers as to the speeds that were possible. I was sure that running the race anti-clockwise would have very little effect on the lap times, but Stirling was equally convinced that speeds would be increased and that Aintree would be the fastest circuit in the country. He insisted on the 45/15 and 13/20 axle ratio and we spent twelve hours at Brackley changing the reduction gear and pinion ratio. I was annoyed because I felt that at least we could have waited until reaching Aintree.

Sure enough at practice on Friday the axle ratio was too high. The best Stirling could manage was 2 minutes 12 seconds in the dry against the fastest practice lap, put up by Peter Collins in the Thinwall Special, of 2 minutes 5.8 seconds.   It meant changing to the Silverstone ratio again and, starting work at half-past five in the afternoon, we worked all night and eventually finished the job at 6 o'clock next morning.   Even then we could not be sure our choice of 46/14 and 14/21 was the most suitable ratio, but there was no time to make another change.   Snatching an hour's sleep we then had breakfast and went out to the circuit.

The car did not go too well in the first heat of the Aintree 200 and finished third.   We had not altered the choke and jet sizes since experimenting for the Bordeaux race and, whilst the Maserati had run quite well on these settings at Silverstone, it was not at all happy on the Aintree Circuit. The torque was too low at the top end.

We could have experimented with different chokes and jets in practice but it rained so hard most of the time that it was not practicable to do so. We took a chance after the heat, fitted larger chokes and jets, tuned the carburetters to compensate for the reduced rush of air through the chokes and just finished working on the car in time for the final.

Stirling finished first, after a most exciting race, and chalked up his first major victory with the Maserati.   The car never missed a beat and our decision to alter the chokes and carburation paid rich dividends.   The performance at the top end was improved to such a marked extent that it was a comparatively easy matter for Stirling to win from Parnell by no less than 48 seconds.

It was the first time a car prepared by me had won a fairly large event and I was very proud.   Admittedly there were no " works " Ferraris or Maseratis but the opposition was quite considerable and included two B.R.M.s., Parnell's Ferrari, our old sparring partner Salvadori in the sister car to our own and Collins in the fast but unreliable Thinwall Special. This was the second occasion that we had vanquished Salvadori's Maserati with its " works " mechanics.

The next race was the Rome Grand Prix, over 60 laps of the 4-mile Castelfusano Circuit, and it was decided that as soon as the final at Aintree had been run, and whether or not our car finished, Tony Robinson and I had got to leave for Crewe and the London train.   Since we had worked throughout Friday night the train journey would enable us to relax and we should arrive at Euston in time to have Saturday night at home.   The Commer would be driven to London for us and handed over on Sunday morning.   It was a thoughtful move on the part of Stirling and both Tony and I were very grateful.

Stirling is good in this way.   I have always said that, with his genuine concern for the people who work for him, he would have made a good officer and leader of men.   No one was more disappointed than he was when, at the age of seventeen, he volunteered for National Service (he wanted to fly in the R.A.F.) but was turned down and classified Grade 3 because of kidney trouble.

We were disappointed that we had to leave Aintree so soon after the race for there was not even time to congratulate Stirling on his victory. As soon as he received the chequered flag and started on his lap of honour

Tony and I were already on our way out of the circuit gates in a Standard Vanguard driven by a friend of Ken Gregory. He took us to Crewe where we caught the London train ; it was all rather flat. However, that is motor-racing. With one race finished it is time to think about and plan for the next, and sleep was more important to us than the celebrations in Liverpool.

Early on Sunday morning the Commer arrived at Woolwich and at 8.30 a.m. we set off for Dover. Five hours later we were clear of Calais and, by driving non-stop and taking our usual two-hour spells at the wheel, reached Dijon at 6 a.m. Monday and Turin at 11 o'clock that night, having covered 656 miles from Calais in 34 hours. We slept in the Commer, parked in a Turin street, and left next morning for Rome via our usual route ; Alessandria, Genoa, the Bracco Pass then La Spezia, and Civitavecchia. On Thursday morning we met Stirling in Rome.

The new Castelfusano Circuit is much faster than the old Caracalla one and it was obvious during practice that lap speeds were going to be in excess of a hundred miles an hour. When Stirling went out for his first run on Friday, I realized we should have to use a different ratio and working all night we changed over to 13/18 and 45/15.

On Saturday Stirling was lapping in 2 minutes 17 seconds as against Marimon's 2 minutes 15.4 seconds in a works Maserati, which was fastest practice time. That night we changed the ratio once more, and when the car was wheeled on to the front row of the grid at 5 o'clock on Sunday afternoon we were using 14/20 and 45/15. It was no use asking Maserati for the correct ratio because they were using trial and error as we were. It was a brand new circuit.

During the race Stirling put up a very good show. He was content to sit back in second place, whilst Marimon held the lead, for we were still keeping to the rev limit agreed at the beginning of the season and this was the fourth consecutive race with the same engine. We had, in fact decided that it would suit us very well to continue the season as we had started. There was no sense in pushing the car unnecessarily for, with such a rev. limit, we could not possibly beat the works cars.

However, fate was against us at Castelfusano. Eight laps from the end, Stirling coasted up to the finish line with the final drive gone, and waited patiently so that he could push the car over the line and thus be classified as having completed the race. A pinion gear in the back axle had broken.

It was another teething trouble. Maserati used helical type pinion gears and they had not proved very successful. From then onwards the reliability of the cars was improved by altering the design to straight cut gears. It was a radical change and, on the surface, may seem an odd way of dealing with the problem but it was the most practical way—and it worked. After the Rome race, Bertocchi—who was most impressed with the way Stirling had driven—told me that there was a modified type of gear on the stocks.

" Go down to Modena," he said, " before the Belgian Grand Prix and we will fix you up with a set."

We had fourteen days before the race, first round in Europe of the 1954

World Championship series, so we said *au revoir* to Stirling and set off for Modena. He was never in the least bit worried about our ability to arrive on time for the next race. He left everything to us and was confident that when he used the Maserati again it would be as near perfect as we could make it. Generally, there was a hurried conversation after a race on the lines of : " Got plenty of money ? When do you want me for practice ? " and he would be off. It is reassuring when your boss has such confidence in you and Tony and I tried to repay Stirling by not letting him down.

In Modena we wasted our time—apart from making a thorough check of the engine—because the new type pinion and drive was not ready ; so we stripped the damaged gears, repaired the damaged axle housing and reassembled with the old type pinion and drive.

We finished working on the car at 3 a.m. Wednesday, left Modena at 9.30 a.m. and arrived that evening outside Munich where we pulled off the Autobahn on to a laybye and slept for three hours. At 8.30 p.m. Thursday we were in Spa, having covered 435 miles from Munich in a little over sixteen hours. Even when there were two weeks between races we still had to drive around Europe flat-out.

We practised on Friday and Stirling recorded 4 minutes 46 seconds on the very fast Ardennes Circuit. It was a slow time when compared with the works cars, particularly the one driven by Fangio, who was making his first European appearance of 1954. He put in a fantastic lap of 4 minutes 22.1 seconds, not only fastest in practice but better than his own circuit record set with the 159 Alfa-Romeo in 1951. He really thrashed that motor-car and I later found that the needle of the rev counter had registered 8,100, no less than 900 revs more than we had been advised to use.

After the session, I had a talk with Bertocchi for I was not satisfied with the performance of our car.

" Well," he said, " you are on the wrong tyres again. Why don't you change to Pirelli. I can lend you a set for practice to-morrow."

He was quite right. We found that, with Pirelli fitted, Stirling was able to cut six seconds off his previous lap times without using any more revs. It amazed me.

Soon after the practice finished, the new type pinion and drive arrived from Modena and we worked all night, stripping and reassembling the back axle as well as modifying the rear drive housing. In the early hours of Sunday morning we were still working on the car but as the race was not until 3 p.m. we were able to snatch a few hours' sleep.

It was necessary to be careful during the Spa race for the engine had already covered a considerable number of racing miles and was not only showing signs of tiredness but using oil fairly heavily. We knew that a stop for oil would be necessary, as we dared not run on less than half a tank because of oil surge, and that put us at a disadvantage with the works cars ; their engines would not call for such a pit stop.

It was a most exciting race and the Moss *equipe* was on its toes for Mike Hawthorn was driving a Ferrari and there was a small matter of the Churchill Challenge Trophy. Mike had won it on two previous occasions and if he did so again in 1954 the Trophy would be his property.

When Marimon came in and retired his car after only three laps of the

36-lap race Mr. Orsi sent the Maserati competition manager to ask me whether I would agree to call in Stirling so that the Argentine driver could take over. Admittedly, Stirling was in pain with a boil under his arm but that was not sufficient reason for me to " recognize " in public that he was not as good as Marimon—for that is what such an action would have meant. I bluntly refused.

" Even with a boil, Stirling Moss is as good as Marimon," I said.

The Maserati pit staff were most annoyed and we were " on our own " for the rest of the race. However, I soon forgot the incident, being far too concerned about the stop for oil to bother about anything else. I estimated that we should need to replenish with exactly two gallons to finish the 316-mile race. At three-quarter distance—with Stirling lying third behind Fangio and Trintignant, and Mike Hawthorn out of the race having been poisoned by fumes—I called Stirling into the pits. There was no time to waste. Gonzalez had taken over Hawthorn's car, after repairs to the exhaust, and was going like the wind to make up for lost time.

I deputized Tony to do the job with a quick-filling oil replenisher, but it was not a pressurized supply and one of the Maserati mechanics—who did not realize we needed as much as two gallons—tried to snatch the oil out of Tony's hand and slam the filler shut after only a gallon had been put in.

There was no time for explanation. I stepped forward and caught him a beauty right on the point of the jaw ; he went out like a light. Tony finished his job in 21 seconds and Stirling went away, still in third place and ahead of Gonzalez. We finished that way and also won the Churchill Trophy although it was a hollow victory after Mike's misfortune.

As soon as the race finished, Mr. Orsi came to see me whilst Stirling was collecting his winnings.

" I cannot understand," he said, " why you should hit one of my mechanics. He was only trying to help and you had no right to deal with him so severely."

Orsi was very angry and continued before I had a chance to explain :
" He used to think you were a friend of his but is not so sure now. He is at the back of our pit, still in tears about the incident."

I explained to Orsi that I could not have dealt with the emergency in any other way.

" We had to put in exactly two gallons of oil," I told him, " to be sure of finishing the race."

Orsi, always fair and reasonable when he knows the facts, saw my point of view and a few minutes later I went to the Maserati pit. Whilst Stirling was being feted I was apologizing to the mechanic for punching him on the jaw so that we could finish " in the money."

CHAPTER 30

THE OFFENSIVE CONTINUES

Filming for " The Racers "—A complete " strip down "—
Villoresi borrows our car for Rheims—Preparing for the British Grand Prix.

Tony and I collected fifty dollars each after the Spa race for a few hours work as " extras " with Twentieth Century Fox. The film company was making " The Racers " and their intention was to follow the Grand Prix circus around Europe, filming special incidents to fit in with the race shots of a particular meeting.

Stirling had put up such a good performance that they asked whether he would be prepared to stay on at Spa so that he and the Maserati could be used for some sequences. It was a financially sound proposition, at a hundred dollars a day for Stirling Moss Limited, so that although Stirling was not interested he asked me to deputize.

We had a very easy time (at fifteen dollars a day) during the first two days, sitting around and doing nothing, whilst technicians built a balsa wood fence so that it could be knocked down. On the third day I drove the Maserati and scared myself stiff. It was a beautiful, sunny day and the film boys decided to " shoot " a crash on one of the fast bends that Fangio normally takes at 150 m.p.h. We were supposed to approach the corner from the opposite direction, as it suited the film people better, at something like 120 m.p.h. There were four of us in the scene ; de Graffenried, John Fitch, a Belgian driver and myself.

I represented Moss, closing on the others as we neared the bend and about to lap them. It was planned that de Graffenried, with John Fitch on his tail, would overtake the Belgian actually on the bend then hit the artificial fence on his way out and go off the road. I was supposed to pass all three cars immediately afterwards.

We made our first run. It was not good enough. The producer directing the sequence had a very strong amplifier which could be heard above the noise of the engines and even though we wore crash helmets— " Can't you go any faster," he shouted. " It's just a procession."

After the run he called us over to his stand.

" I want more competition, more hard work," he said.

" Well," replied de Graffenried, " why not speed up the film. We can act as if we are working harder."

" I don't want artificial stuff," fumed the film man, " I want to see you boys really working hard. There must be real action in the first place. I can speed up the film later on if necessary."

We made another run but the film people were not satisfied and this was scrapped as well. At the third attempt we pulled back some distance so that it would be possible to get up plenty of speed. De Graffenried set the pace and we approached the corner very fast indeed, much faster than I thought I could ever handle a racing car. I had to keep up with the other three, as there was no question of falling back, but I sat in the cockpit as we approached the bend thinking to myself : " I don't know how you are going to do this. It is much too fast for you."

Then it struck me that if Fitch and de Graffenried could do it in older type Maseratis than the one I was driving, I ought to be able to keep up with them ; so I pressed the throttle, gritted my teeth and went into the bend on their tails.

As soon as he left the corner de Graffenried hit the balsa fence with too much gusto. His front wheels ran into soft ground and John Fitch, on the outside, did not know whether to go through or wait and see whether de Graffenried spun.

At the very last moment the Swiss managed to get out of the soft patch and, with wood flying in all directions, shot down a side road away from the circuit whilst Fitch and I swept through.

It had been a very dicey few seconds because we could not overtake de Graffenried until he ran off the road and we just sat there, not knowing what to do. We were so close together that if he had spun there would have been a nasty pile up.

The film people were delighted for they had got a real action shot, with all of us worried stiff and working hard. The incident brought home to me how situations, over which drivers have no control, can arise suddenly during a race. I realized the risks they have to accept which can only be described as the " unknown factor." There is often no way out and we had been very, very lucky.

The producer thanked us and we were paid by the cashier. That night in Spa we had a hectic party with some of the film boys and most of the dollars were " blued."

Before leaving Spa Stirling made it quite clear that he wanted the Maserati thoroughly checked, tested and prepared for the British Grand Prix, and Bertocchi agreed to give us every assistance at Modena. By now the entire " works " organization was most impressed with Stirling's handling of the green 250 F. and, I think, with the efficiency of the small, three-man outfit. As a team we were a perfect partnership and I have never known better.

As soon as we arrived in Modena the 250 F. was taken straight into the main workshop, usually reserved for the team cars, and the engine stripped down completely. After covering the full distance of 315 miles in the Belgian classic, as well as considerable mileage in previous races, the car required a great deal of attention, particularly the engine which was obviously tired and using a lot of oil.

We knew that because of trouble experienced with engine bearings Maserati had produced a new type of crankshaft. It had modified connecting rods, which were slightly wider and gave a larger bearing area, and Stirling had asked for one to be fitted in our car. We also knew that the oil tank for the dry sump engine had been moved to the rear of the "works" cars in view of the fact that the original tank—fitted alongside the engine—

carried only a limited amount of oil ; this was another modification we were anxious to have. Finally I wanted the back axle examined for we had worked all night at Spa, modifying the housing for the new parts, and I was anxious to have my handiwork checked.

We had to sub-contract various jobs to the " works " personnel as otherwise we could not have coped in the time available. For instance, it would have taken Tony and I at least twelve days to strip down and rebuild the engine, even working fourteen hours a day. I had a plan by which we looked after the back axle and chassis whilst Maserati dealt with the engine, cylinder head and gearbox. There was no question at this time of Sig. Orsi doing anything free of charge.

After several days of hard work on the car I was asked to step along and see Ballentani. He enquired whether I was well looked after in the works and how I liked racing the Maserati. Then he asked a rather pointed question :

" Why does Stirling Moss not go more quickly ? "

" Well," I replied, " we have very good reasons. The Maserati is the private property of Stirling Moss and whether we continue to race or not depends on how much we win as place money and how often starting money can be collected."

Ballentani nodded.

" Please go on."

" Well," I continued, " we have worked out a programme of racing for almost every week-end—a much more crowded programme than your works cars—but at the same time our revs have to be restricted. From experience in the races run so far we have come to the conclusion that if the revs are kept down it should be possible to cover three or four races without a major overhaul. On the other hand if Stirling tries harder and we use a higher range of revs then I doubt very much whether the car will do more than one Meeting without an overhaul."

" I can see," said Ballentani with a smile, " that we must not compare your 250 F. with our ' works ' cars because quite obviously it has to be driven much more delicately."

I rather thought that he was " taking the mickey."

" Stirling gives your ' works ' cars at least 400 revs in every race, you know," I continued. " It is quite a lot to give away, yet he keeps up with them. He does so by cornering technique, not engine power, and your ' works ' cars would see the rear end of our Maserati much more frequently if we did not have to restrict our engine revs."

On this note the interview ended. A few days later I had another summons. This time Signor Orsi, Jnr., wanted to see me and when I went along to his office he asked whether Maserati could borrow our car and use it in the French Grand Prix as a factory entry for Villoresi.

He explained that as Fangio would be driving for Mercedes at Rheims he had invited Ascari and Villoresi to handle Maseratis, thus committing himself to provide two motor-cars at short notice in first-class shape.

" We Italians are very anxious to put up a good show against the Germans" he said, " and I felt you might like to help us."

" I am sorry," I told him, " I cannot take such a responsibility on my shoulders. I must first confirm with Stirling Moss."

In my own mind I had already decided that somehow or other I had got to persuade Stirling to lend Maserati the car. I thought, having a continental outlook myself in this way, that if I could get them under an obligation I should have the whole place at my disposal, and that it would no longer be such an expensive proposition to have work carried out there. That was my idea and as soon as Orsi asked whether he could borrow our car I felt like agreeing without consulting Stirling.

I telephoned London and, having got through to Stirling, I thought he was going to cut me off the line. He did not like the idea at all and was most annoyed about Orsi's suggestion. However, when I explained that it would do us a lot of good if we were helpful, and a lot of harm if we were not, Stirling eventually agreed—but on one condition.

" You must take everything off the car," he said. " Let them use their own gearbox and engine."

Next day I told Orsi, who was, of course, delighted with our decision, that Stirling Moss was honoured that the Maserati works should want to borrow his car. However, there were not enough gearboxes or engines in the works to replace the units on our Maserati and I told Orsi of Stirling's stipulation.

" Don't worry," he assured me, " if we use your engine I promise we will take full responsibility. Whatever happens, when the car comes back you will have a Maserati that is as good as new."

I agreed, without getting in touch with London, for I knew Orsi would keep his word and I could see a brand new engine coming up.

Stirling did not drive in the French Grand Prix because of his commitment with Jaguar in the Rheims 12-hour event. We had a discussion after the Spa race, when he mentioned that he would definitely like to enter the Maserati for the Grand Prix but I told him it was no use.

" You will have to be satisfied with one race. You will not do justice to the Maserati if you drive in the twelve-hour race first and then, two hours later, in a full length Grand Prix on a fast circuit like Rheims."

A wealthy American motor-racing enthusiast, festooned with cameras and light meters, took me from Modena to Rheims in his Simca so that I could watch the " form " in this return of the German cars. I had met him at Spa and discovered that he was on a month's holiday in Europe and anxious to see as much motor-racing as possible. I told him to follow us from circuit to circuit and, as a first step, he came to Modena with us after Spa.

When we arrived at Rheims, Stirling was naturally surprised but quickly recovered and ticked me off for letting Maserati use his car with our engine and gearbox. However, when I explained the problem he saw my point of view.

"After all," I said, " if Villoresi blows up the engine then we shall get a brand new one, so why worry. Of one thing you can be certain, we shall get all the help we need from Maserati from now onwards. In fact we will seek their help as the season progresses because otherwise the money bags are going to run rather low."

Alfred Moss was most disappointed that Stirling did not drive in the Grand Prix. After the race he said to me : " If Villoresi can finish fifth, then we could have finished too, and I think he was in the money. We should have raced ourselves, with Stirling driving."

Personally I don't think Stirling would have bettered Villoresi's placing, or even finished fifth, for he would have been too tired. I saw him after the twelve-hour race and it had definitely taken a lot out of him. Although he did not win, the car was in the lead for practically the whole race and Stirling drove remarkably well during the night to the extent that he was absolutely whacked. It would have been crazy for him to drive in the Grand Prix.

Sometimes I think that, in his enthusiasm, Alfred Moss expects too much of Stirling. There is a limit to what any man can do and, physically and mentally fit as he is, Stirling is no superman.

My American friend had to return to the States when his father died suddenly and I was given a lift to Modena by Bob Said and Luigi Chinetti. Said had to go via Paris as he had some business to finish there, and had one of those moving platforms the Americans call shooting brakes, which are so large inside that it is almost possible to take exercise whilst the vehicle is on the move.

We took it in turns to drive and Chinetti insisted that no one exceeded sixty miles an hour. We were all afraid of each other's driving and I thought this a very good idea. We changed every three hours and covered the 470 miles from Paris to Turin in just under fourteen hours.

Said is a good friend of Moss and thinks a lot of him. He is a typical American racing driver, who knows a lot about the game but does not succeed in making much of a mark ; one of those types who suddenly appear and just as suddenly vanish from the scene without leaving a lasting mark in the record book.

In Modena, Maserati were already working on our car. Bertocchi told me that everything would be stripped down, including the wishbones and front and rear suspension. The engine would be dismantled and reassembled with the latest type cylinder head which was producing a little more power. Signor Orsi was leaving no stone unturned, determined that the car would go to the British Grand Prix in tip-top condition.

I was on my own, for Tony had returned to England with Stirling after the French Grand Prix, but it did not matter for I was not allowed to touch the Maserati.

"It is our responsibility," said Bertocchi, " and we are going to do it. There will be no question of any charge."

Bertocchi agreed to modify the gearbox as we wanted a slightly lower first gear. Stirling had been experiencing difficulty taking off from the Start Line and we reached the conclusion that as first gear is not used very often it would be preferable to have a lower ratio for quick get-aways, rather than one more suitable on slow corners. Maserati had a special gear cut for us and the ratio was then very similar to first gear on the Grand Prix Alta, i.e. 2.5 to 1.

Our rear fuel tankage was modified as well in that a new type of riveted tank was used in place of the aluminium one, and a new oil tank fitted at the rear to replace the one we had fixed up ourselves in rather a hurry for the Belgian Grand Prix.

Meanwhile, I went to Pirelli in Milan and bought a set of tyres for the British Grand Prix. The Bordeaux and Spa races had convinced Stirling that Pirellis were the most suitable tyre for our particular racing car and I tried to use them whenever possible. A set of four Pirelli cost 65,000 lire—over £30—and as we did not reckon to do more than the practice session and a race on each set it was an expensive proposition with sixteen races in the 1954 season alone.

CHAPTER 31

EUROPEAN MERRY-GO-ROUND (1)

A tremendous development—The Moss-Hawthorn duel in the British G.P.—Disappointment at Caen—The tragedy of Onofre Marimon—Lost cause at the Nurburgring.

The day the car was finally finished, reassembled and painted once more in its Adriatic sea green, I was asked to Ballentani's office. On this occasion he did not waste time with preliminaries and came straight to the point.

" Would Stirling Moss go faster," he said, " if the factory helped you with the maintenance of the car."

This was a tremendous development for it meant that the vast Maserati organization was prepared to back a private entry.

" He will certainly go faster," I replied, " much faster. If Maserati are going to take the responsibility, and Stirling can risk a blow-up by running his engine at the absolute peak, then we will show you something."

Ballentani continued : "Actually, I was thinking that as the Silverstone race is your national classic it would be good for us and good for Stirling Moss if Maserati could win that race. It would give us great pleasure."

" It will give us even greater pleasure," I replied, " because as private entrants we have not been able to try for a win in any race so far."

" O.K." said Ballentani, " when you get to England tell Mr. Moss that Maserati will take the full responsibility for a ' blow up ' and please tell him to go quick."

In the Commer on the way to Calais, alone with my thoughts, I had plenty of time to consider the implications of what Ballentani had said. The one outstanding thought in my mind was that Stirling Moss had reached full world championship status and I could not help feeling that, if Stirling did well at Silverstone, there was every chance he would be invited to join Maserati as a " works " driver.

It was obvious that Maserati would not like to be beaten too often by a private owner, even with works backing, and our task was to put up such a good performance in the British G.P. that Maserati would not be able to delay their offer. I knew that at this time they only had Marimon and Mieres as regular drivers and did not have a full factory team signed up.

I also knew that Ascari and Villoresi were going to be loaned to Maserati by Lancia for the British G.P. and with these two in similar cars to our Maserati, and with Stirling " off the leash " as it were, I was determined that we would prove to the British public that Stirling Moss was as good as either of them.

There was also the Mercedes " bogey " and Juan Manuel Fangio. There had been a lot of talk about the phenomenal return to power of

Mercedes-Benz and most people forecast that future races would be a Neubauer benefit with the Mercs. finishing " One, Two, Three " ; then, three laps behind, would come the remainder of the field. I refused to accept this, even though Mercedes-Benz had shattered the opposition at Rheims, because I was sure the Germans had built these cars specially for Rheims so that they could make a sensational return on a circuit which provided the best opportunity of showing off their superior speed.

I honestly believed that at Silverstone, with Stirling at the wheel of a car he knew was equal to the team cars and could be used as though it were a team car, we were going to show the British public that Moss could keep up with Mercedes. There was also a long awaited duel that had to be fought with Mike Hawthorn who would be handling a Ferrari.

On Wednesday evening at 9 o'clock, having left Modena at 7.30 p.m. on Monday, I arrived home at Woolwich. I had driven flat out, only stopping for the odd swig of brandy every now and then or a cup of coffee. On Thursday morning, Tony and Stirling were waiting for me at Silverstone. When I passed on Ballentani's message Stirling was dubious.

" Do you really think they will stick to what they say ? "

" Of course they will," I replied. " Look how they have worked on the Maserati—without charging us a penny—for the Silverstone race. I am sure Ballentani will not let me down. If he does, I will never let him forget it. Seriously, Stirling," I added, " if you go quick they will back you up, and in this race you have got to prove your worth. This may well be the turning point of your motor-racing career."

In the practice sessions our Maserati went very well indeed. On Thursday the weather conditions were shocking and Hawthorn made fastest time in his Ferrari in 2 minutes 3 seconds. Next day, on a dry circuit, three people shook Mercedes-Benz. They were Gonzalez and Hawthorn with 1 minute 46 seconds and Moss with 1 minute 47 seconds. Finally, that master of practice sessions, Fangio—carrying only the minimum amount of fuel—went out in a Mercedes and streaked round in 1 minute 45 seconds. It was the first time an average of over a hundred miles an hour had been recorded at Silverstone with a 2½-litre car.

On Saturday, just before midday, the cars were wheeled out of the paddock on to the grid. There were four on the front row, one of which was our Maserati, and I was very proud—as head mechanic of a small independent *equipe*—that a green car prepared by me shared the grid with Fangio, Gonzalez and Hawthorn. There were twenty-seven cars behind us, including the Maserati team which had arrived late and only been able to practise unofficially.

In the weekly magazine *Autosport*, the Editor—Gregor Grant—wrote : " Moss's drive will long be talked about and on present form he must be reckoned as being an absolute top-liner."

When the flag dropped the new first-gear ratio enabled Stirling to make a terrific get-away and he was hard on the heels of Gonzalez as the field accelerated towards Copse Corner. However, he took things calmly at the start and after ten laps Gonzalez was still in the lead, followed by Fangio, and Hawthorn—in third place and one second ahead of Moss.

When I saw him close behind Hawthorn I thought to myself : " Very wise thing to do."

It may surprise people to learn that we rarely discussed policy before a race, sometimes referred to as race track strategy and tactics ; I call it plain common-sense for most of the time. We never had a preliminary discussion because we knew each other so well, and the game so well from the inside, that there was no need for us—as a singleton entry—to plan anything. After all, it was not as though I had several cars and drivers to control.

We thought on the same lines and many times Stirling would make a move whilst I was still planning it. We were, I think, telepathic and without communicating knew more or less what the other would be thinking at any given time.

With half the race distance almost run I thought to myself : " Let's show the British enthusiasts who is best—Moss or Hawthorn." For more than thirty laps it had been real cut and thrust between Stirling and Mike, with first one in the lead then the other ; the Ferrari and Maserati were never more than a second or so apart.

It was no use playing this game any longer and I put the red colour at the top of the signal board. Immediately the intensity of the " dice " increased as Stirling gave the Maserati engine all it had, secure in the knowledge that he could mete out the full treatment, up to 7,800 revs if necessary.

The way he handled the Maserati was masterly and he definitely proved —to me at any rate—that he could be every bit as good as Fangio and Gonzalez. Slowly he drew away from Hawthorn but for several laps I kept the red colour on the board. There was no retreat now. We had got to stay ahead. Mike fought back grimly and Stirling did not find it easy to maintain his slender lead as he gained a fraction of a second each lap.

As soon as Mike had dropped three or four seconds he must have realized it was no use continuing the chase, as it would probably result in his motor blowing up, and at forty-five laps—half distance—Stirling was ten seconds ahead. Ten laps later, to the delight of the huge crowd of ninety thousand massed around the Silverstone Circuit, Moss " took " Fangio. The Argentine driver was not at all happy with the streamlined Mercedes and it says a lot for his phenomenal powers of determination that he was able to press on as fast as he did.

Neither Moss nor I had any intention of trying to wrest the lead from Gonzalez. We were quite content to stay where we were but as the race was of full Grand Prix distance—ninety laps—there was still a long way to go, and anything could happen to take that hard-won second place away. In previous races we had so often suffered misfortune in the last ten laps that I could not help thinking to myself : " Is it going to happen again ? " At the back of my mind during that 1954 season was always the spectre of the final ten laps.

Sure enough, with only nine laps to complete, the Maserati was missing as the leading cars came through Woodcote. There was Gonzalez, then a large gap of almost a minute, then Hawthorn, but no sign of Moss.

Shortly afterwards he arrived at the pits, having abandoned the car out on the circuit.

" Something must have gone in the back axle," said Stirling, " because there is no more drive. The engine just goes on and nothing happens."

It seemed to me that something had broken either in the gearbox or input shafts but I was not too disappointed. Admittedly, we had not finished the race but Stirling had proved himself worthy of the motor-car and of a place in the " works " team. The result gave both of us terrific confidence and I knew the next step was not so very far away. There was no doubt that we had beaten Hawthorn fairly and squarely and now there were only three other challenges to meet—from Ascari, Fangio and Gonzalez. We could hardly wait until the next major event.

After the race we towed in the Maserati. It had been put out of the running by a silly fault, not a broken drive shaft as reported at the time. One of the reduction gears came loose and slipped off its splined shaft. After a time these shafts develop slight play and in this case the gear had been excessively tightened down by a nut with a locking washer.

Due to the play in the spline, on acceleration and the overrun, the gear had a tendency to rock slightly on the shaft and finally tore the locking washer out of its seating. The nut slowly unscrewed, over those exciting eighty-one laps, and eventually the gear slid off the shaft and there was no more drive. It fell to the bottom of the housing and lay there until we stripped down the gearbox.

If the nut had been left loose it would have rocked on the washer for many hundreds of racing miles before the washer wore out. This was the first time a Maserati had suffered this particular trouble and it had to be us ! It is uncanny how often Stirling is the driver who first experiences a par-ticular weakness. It is not that he thrashes cars because I know better than anyone that he does not. It is just his wretched luck.

There was only a week before our next race, the Formula 1 Grand Prix of Caen, but we stayed on at Alcock's garage, Brackley, to repair the final drive. There was no damage of any sort and the job was quickly completed. It was simply a matter of putting the gear back and improvising a temporary locking device.

As a matter of fact we were not looking for work because the Maserati had been entered in races at Caen, Nurburgring, Oulton Park, Pescara and Berne—in that order and on successive week-ends—that meant a round trip of well over 3,000 miles through five countries. It was a difficult enough proposition without hitches and turned out to be just about the five most fantastic weeks of my life, so crowded, busy and eventful that I hardly had time to scribble my usual terse notes in the diary.

The main opposition at Caen was Trintignant on a Ferrari, a very potent one and a " works " entry. There was a terrific " dice " between Trintignant and Behra's Gordini for pole position, which the former eventually won by recording 1 minute 26 seconds, whilst Moss and Behra both went round in 1 minute 26.4 seconds.

The road is very narrow at Caen and the grid organized on a 2/1, 2/1 basis. After the practice it was decided that Moss would share the front row as he had put up his fastest time before Behra, but I am sure the organizers would have put Moss next to Trintignant in any case because after the British Grand Prix Stirling was definitely ranked as one of the top flight drivers.

There was very little to do after the practice sessions, for the engine was still in perfect trim after the Silverstone race, and Tony and I spent the evenings in Caen with Stirling, putting on a local hazard course. It is a pastime he enjoys very much and seems to find it relaxing.

We stayed at the same hotel as Denis Jenkinson, the bearded Continental Correspondent of *Motor Sport*, and had some fun on the day of the race by smuggling a straw bale from the circuit into the hotel and putting it in Jenkinson's bed. When he returned after the race he had quite a struggle to remove the four foot by two foot bale, and next morning had just as much difficulty explaining to the management what it was doing in his room.

I have known Denis Jenkinson since my early days with H.W.M. We get on well together and I particularly admire him because, when he started as a motor-racing journalist, he used to travel from circuit to circuit in a rather derelict old Fiat 1500. Invariably, somewhere along the route to every Grand Prix, I would come across "Jenks" with just his feet protruding from underneath the Fiat and a thumb held out to indicate that he could mend it without our help. Every scrap merchant dealer on the continent knew "Jenks" in those days.

It took real guts for him to travel with Moss in the Mille Miglia in 1955, yet when I spoke to him about the race and put forward the view that he must have been scared stiff on dozens of occasions, his reply surprised me :

" It's funny, but I wasn't all that scared. All I know is that I was sick once."

I don't believe it for every human being has a certain amount of fear in his make-up and " Jenks " is no exception. A thousand miles at an average of nearly one hundred miles an hour through towns, villages and over mountains would terrify me even with a driver like Stirling.

I was bitterly disappointed at Caen, probably because Stirling had done so well at Silverstone, when Trintignant beat him. At the end of the first lap Stirling came round in the lead and stayed there for two-thirds of the race distance, forty out of sixty laps. He looked so secure that I was sure of victory if only he could maintain his eight-second lead. The Maserati sounded very healthy indeed and morale was high in our pit where Tony and I were the sole occupants, the plane carrying Mr. and Mrs. Moss and Ken Gregory having been grounded by bad weather.

However, Trintignant was never very far behind, and not slow to take advantage of the situation when it rained and forced Stirling to slow down. We were not racing on Pirelli at Caen, having decided to keep them for the most important events, and there is no doubt that although the wet circuit slowed down Stirling it had little or no effect on Trintignant, who took the lead on lap 46.

Admittedly Stirling passed him again six laps later but was only able to hold off the Ferrari temporarily and the Frenchman eventually won by three seconds. I considered that, with a lead of eight seconds before it rained, Stirling should have been able to keep the Frenchman at bay.

Stirling, I think, felt that he should have done better because when he pulled in after the race the first thing he said to me was :

" That's the best I could do, Alf.   I am sorry but I could not do any better.   If the rain had held off I could have kept the lead."

I could see that he was absolutely exhausted and that the race must have been a terrific mental strain.   With its short straights, much too short to be able to relax, Caen is a tough circuit requiring plenty of concentration to deal with a variety of corners, some fast and some slow.

However, I consider it was bad strategy that lost the race.   Stirling should not have taken the lead at the start but should have been as wise as Trintignant, who allowed his opponent to stay in front and wear himself out.   It is not easy to lead a race with a driver like Trintignant sitting on your tail and pushing, pushing all the time whilst still conserving his engine.

I made an entry in the diary: "No good blaming this on tyres or fading brakes.   I think Stirling should have let Trintignant go ahead.   We could have won, even in the rain, if he had played a waiting game.   Stirling looks absolutely tired out."

He had, in fact, used race tactics that are sound enough in a 500 c.c. race but which do not always pay off in a Grand Prix car.   He was perhaps over-confident, following his drive at Silverstone, probably thinking that he would have a " dice " for two or three laps at the beginning and then Trintigant would give in.   However, the Frenchman drove a terrific race ; frankly I think he was better than Stirling.

There was no time to waste after Caen ; we left almost at once for the Nurburgring and the German Grand Prix.   The Maserati was a little tired by now after a hard struggle at Silverstone and Caen but there was no time to return to Modena for a new engine.   Our only hope was that the Maserati factory team would be able to give us a reconditioned engine for the race.

Our first job on arrival at the " Ring " was to modify the suspension to suit the German circuit.   The " works " drivers had already discovered that when they " hit " the Karusel Curve at high speed the sump grounded, and it was necessary to lift the entire chassis and thus raise the sump.

I recruited the help of one of my friends in the Shell Mobile Workshop, one of several in Germany that are remarkably well equipped with a lathe, welding apparatus and almost everything one requires for servicing and maintenance.   Unfortunately they do not operate in this country.

The ever-helpful Shell technical boys readily agreed to modify the suspension and turned some packing pieces on the lathe so that I was able to pack the springs and lift the chassis.   On Friday the privately owned Maserati in British racing green lapped the dangerous, fatiguing Nurburgring at a speed that caused consternation in the pits of both Italian and German " works " teams.

I felt very proud as I stood outside our private entry pit and timed Stirling.   With an impeccable display of driving he put up fastest time of the day (10 minutes .05 seconds) and not only beat Gonzalez, Hawthorn and Marimon but was only eight seconds slower than the course record set the previous year by Ascari in a Ferrari.

The Maserati works " Box " was alongside ours in the paddock and I could see the mechanics were as pleased with Stirling's performance as if he had been a team driver. They could not do enough to help us and it was obvious that the entire outfit was taking a keen interest in the British Maserati and its youthful driver. That evening the Team Manager took Stirling aside. There was a short conversation and Stirling came back to our " Box."

"Alf," he said, "I want to talk to you. Let's sit in the Jaguar." He lost no time coming to the point. " They have just offered me a place in the ' works ' team. The car will be repainted red ; they will take full responsibility and look after it and are prepared to give me reasonable terms."

" Well," I said, " you had better accept their offer. So far as I can see the engine is worn out. You know this as well as I do. It's never going to finish the race."

" That's not the point," replied Stirling, " what are you going to do."

" Why worry about me," I replied. " In the first place you set out to become a professional racing driver and lately to win the World Championship, which you should be aiming at now. You have won the Gold Star so often that I am bored stiff with it. Aim higher than that. Have a crack at Fangio and Gonzalez."

" Don't talk nonsense," replied Stirling irritably. " I shall never do that for the simple reason that I am not as good as they are."

" You can be if you like," I replied, " and don't worry about me or Tony. We will find some other job. We shall not mind leaving under these conditions."

" Well," said Stirling, " I am not going to do it that way. I won't join the Maserati Works unless you come with me."

" That's O.K. with me," I said, " and thank you very much."

I have not forgotten that conversation in the Jaguar at the Nurburgring and I am sure that if I had said to Stirling : " You have your own outfit, your lorry and two mechanics and you cannot leave us high and dry in the middle of the season," he would have turned down the Maserati offer there and then. When he eventually reaches the very top of the ladder, as I am sure he will do one day, there will be few, if any at all, who can complain that he pushed them aside in his anxiety to get there.

It was finally agreed by the Maserati Manager that for the German Grand Prix the "works" mechanics would look after the car. After the race there would be a discussion to decide how Tony and I could be incorporated in the official team.

That night as we worked on the car, taking the body apart so that it could be hand-painted in red, Marimon suddenly appeared in the " Box." Although he only spoke a little English I was able to understand the gist of what he was saying. He was with us for half-an-hour or so and, after chatting about various points connected with the Maserati, talked about the difference between himself and Stirling.

"It seems to me," he said, " that you know the motor-car inside out and Moss knows the car just as thoroughly from the point of view of driving. The two of you are very close and it is a wonderful combination. I don't think I shall ever be able to beat Stirling for there is no relationship like that between me and my own mechanics."

I sympathized with Marimon, for he was a likeable young man and popular with drivers, officials and spectators, and told him that he was worrying about things unduly. After all, he had not had the experience of Moss and, on a circuit like the "Ring," it was understandable that Stirling should have gone round faster, particularly as that was our intention.

We wanted to put up a really fast time and impress the "works" for we knew the car would never last the race distance. Nevertheless, Marimon was upset and I think it was because a private entry had put up a better time than the No. 1 driver in the Maserati team. He was worried as well because, as a protege of his great friend Fangio, he had not done better.

On Saturday Stirling and Marimon went out on the circuit at the same time. In the pits we laughed and joked, little realizing that in this practice session tragedy was going to precede the Grand Prix of Europe. With the conversation of the previous night still fresh in my mind, I could see that the young Argentine driver was trying to "hold" Moss on that tricky circuit and that he could not do it.

Marimon lost ground from the time the cars went away from the pits and on the third lap there was no sign of him. Seconds passed and became minutes. Then we knew the worst. His Maserati had failed to take a bend and careered off the road. I wonder whether it was, in fact, pride that killed him ; the pride of a man who could feel his pedestal toppling ?

The three Argentine drivers, Fangio, Gonzalez and Marimon, had been great friends, and it was a terrible thing to see a big, burly man like Gonzalez with tears streaming down his face. Even the inscrutable Fangio was visibly distressed. As a result of the accident the second "works" car, which was to have been driven by Villoresi, was withdrawn from the race.

However, the Maserati concern wanted to have at least one car in the European Grand Prix so Stirling was released from official sponsorship and our "Maser" became a private entry again. Bertocchi said to me :

"You go home and get some sleep, Alphons. We will finish the car for you."

The Maserati mechanics worked all night fitting a different type cylinder head but were unable to install a new engine, and it was obvious to me that we were not going to get very far in the race. Actually, Stirling had over-revved the engine in practice and bent the valves and the mechanics had their work cut out to finish the job in time. When I arrived in the morning they were just tightening down the head.

Stirling said very little about the Marimon tragedy but this does not mean that he is harsh and unsympathetic. I would not say that he is much affected by what happens to other drivers, unless closely connected with them in some way, but any accident worries Stirling and he will be one of the first visitors at the hospital if a driver is injured. I noticed at Monte Carlo, when Ascari went into the harbour, that Stirling made a special point of seeing Ascari in hospital immediately after the race.

On Sunday it was wonderful to see the Moss Maserati on the front row of the grid for this vitally important championship event. Even though the car had been painted red, I had left the nose in British racing green and put the Union Jacks on as well.   There was a Mercedes, a Maserati and Hawthorn's Ferrari on the front row and the atmosphere was terrific, particularly as this was the first time the Germans had seen their own cars in action.   As the field roared away I walked to our pit with my heart hammering.   It was so damned exciting and almost frightening.

Stirling was lying third when the cars came past at the end of the first of twenty-one gruelling laps and there was excited comment in the pits and grandstand.   Was this young Englishman, this comparative new-comer to the front row of the grid, going to vanquish Mercedes-Benz ?

The massed German spectators around the " Ring " need not have worried for Tony and I knew there was no hope and that the engine would never last ; that in two or three laps at the most the big-ends would run out.   It happened sooner than we expected, just after the field had swept by after the first lap.   The red Maserati did not come round a second time for the big ends had gone nd a valve as well.

I was not sorry in one way that we were out of the Grosser Pries von Europa for I lived a lifetime every race with the Maserati.   We raced a very full season with Stirling driving this potent piece of Grand Prix machinery and it was the responsibility of Tony and myself to see that the car was properly looked after.   It was my job as well to control Stirling from the pit, and between the time the flag fell until the car came in again I was absolutely tensed up.   I worried myself stiff.   After all, it is a dangerous game and one never knows what may happen.

I am not so much worried about losing a race or breaking down but the anxiety that an accident may occur becomes so great that by the time the race is finished I am worn out ; I just cannot help it.   When I stand in front of the pits with my stop-watch I may look calm but am inwardly all churned up, mentally hurrying the race along so that it will finish sooner. I work out roughly how long it will last and then keep looking at my watch. How many more minutes before the damn thing finishes ?

In races on small circuits such as Goodwood, Oulton Park—even Rheims—I do not worry too much because the cars pass the pits at very short intervals, but at the " Ring " they disappear for ten minutes on every lap.   In that time a lot of thoughts pass through my mind and I worry more at the " Ring " than anywhere else.

The actual start of a race, even at Monaco where there is always a terrific scramble to get to the hairpin first, does not worry me too much as in the championship races and major Grand Prix the drivers know what they are doing.   It is the unknown factor that worries me, such as a driver rounding a corner flat out and finding a spinning car in the way or a dog running across the circuit.

This business of dogs being allowed on circuits should be stopped and every organizer should take as strong a line about it as the British Auto-mobile Racing Club.   Organizers should be much tougher and if anyone is found inside a circuit with a dog they should be thrown out.

I shall always remember a ridiculous sight at Oulton Park during one Meeting when a poodle was being paraded around the paddock with a Paddock Transfer attached to its collar !

CHAPTER 32

EUROPEAN MERRY-GO-ROUND (2)

*Brake failure in the Eifel Mountains—Modena to Oulton Park non-stop—
A field day for Moss—The gremlin at Pescara.*

Stirling had already arranged before the German classic to race at
Oulton Park the following Saturday, which left only five days to replace
the wrecked engine and get the car to the North of England. Before we
set off for the Nurburgring I had laughed at the possibility of running at
Oulton after Silverstone, Caen and the " Ring." However I did not say
anything to Stirling for it is better to sympathize with a driver in these
circumstances, and to try to work things out in the most satisfactory way,
otherwise one does not last very long as a mechanic.

Let me put it like this. You have to try and help not hinder—try and
humour a driver to a certain extent. You must not say : " Don't be silly,
we can never do it." You must say instead : " I don't know ; it's going
to be a bit tricky but we'll find some way of doing it." That is my outlook.

After the race Stirling went to the Maserati Manager, who had stayed
on as a spectator with the rest of the team, and had another discussion
about joining the " works." It was finally arranged that he would become
a team driver and use his own car, but that whilst it was being reconditioned
at Modena for the Pescara race, Maserati would supply us with another
car for Oulton Park.

It was entirely a question of whether we could get our own 250 F.
down to the factory and collect the new one in the time available. From the
" Ring " to Modena is a long way and I knew we should have to work on
the replacement car at the factory. The pedals would have to be altered
to suit Stirling and the axle ratio changed, and there was no one at Modena
to do it for all the racing mechanics had travelled with the *equipe* to
Germany.

Stirling promised to help all he could from his end and arranged to have
a lorry driver from James Edwards Limited of Chester waiting for us at
Dover to take the Commer to Oulton Park whilst we travelled north to
Crewe in a sleeper on the night train.

It was the longest run we had ever attempted in such a short time
(the " Ring "—Modena—Oulton Park—Modena) and when the Manager of
Maserati came to me with Stirling and suggested that we leave on Sunday
night, I said :

" No, we are going to stop here and have a good night's sleep. I shall
set off to-morrow morning."

The Italian thought I was crazy and not very co-operative but Stirling
knew me well enough not to argue.

"O.K., Alf," he said. "I leave it entirely with you. It's your responsibility."

We loaded the lorry, bedded down immediately and set off at 9 o'clock after a good breakfast. Going through the Eifel Mountains, where descents and uphill climbs follow each other with monotonous regularity, I had to use the brakes rather harshly as there was no time to hang about.

During one descent, trying to go as quickly as possible, I started to brake on the approach to a corner and discovered, to my horror, that nothing was happening in the braking department. The pedal was flat on the boards and there were horrible crunching noises underneath the cab which I could not identify at the time.

"The brakes have gone," I shouted to Tony. "We may have to jump."

What little hair I have stood on end as I changed down from top to third, then to second, and finally to first in an attempt to slow down the Commer by using the gearbox. The engine screamed its head off but at last the lorry stopped, some twenty yards from the corner and a flimsy wooden fence on the edge of a ravine. I straightened up, as Tony uncovered his eyes, and gave him a sickly smile.

"O.K." I said, "let's see what's happened to the brakes."

One of the front drums had split! By applying the brakes so hard and so frequently on that downhill descent the pressure on the shoes had broken the drum into three separate pieces. There was virtually no drum, only the severed end of the hydraulic pipeline! We carried no spare drums and for a few minutes I did not know what to do.

It was no use telephoning Rootes for a replacement because it would never reach us in time but we had to do something. As a last resort I decided to cut out the front brakes completely and run the transporter only on the rear ones; so we disconnected the piping, plugged the affected unions, bled the back brakes and continued on our way.

It was a dicey journey and it would not have been possible to make an emergency stop, for the back brakes were doing hardly any work at all. The front brakes had been fitted with two leading shoes and were fairly efficient, whereas those at the back were normal, standard "one trailing one leading shoe" type and proved practically useless. I cannot understand why, when the adhesion of the lorry at the rear end was much greater because of the twin wheels, the least powerful brakes were fitted on the back.

We pressed on and soon reached the Frankfurt Autobahn, pushing the Commer as fast as she would go and hoping that nothing would cross our bows without warning.

For the first time since leaving the "Ring," and with Tony driving, I was able to think about what had happened in the last few days and told myself that I had accomplished the job I had set out to do.

Stirling Moss was firmly established in the top flight but I knew that sooner or later—maybe in weeks, maybe in months—with Stirling a regular "works" driver there would no longer be that close relationship between us. It was no use being sentimental; better to accept the fact that *Equipe* Moss was finished. Moss, contender for the World Championship, had arrived.

There was another possibility and one that might easily result in the termination of our partnership. I had an idea even at this early stage that Mercedes would be after Moss for the 1955 season. I knew that I would never agree to work with the Germans even if Moss—and Mercedes—wanted me to do so.

It was a pity in many ways that we could not have continued on the basis of independents but I had to admit to myself that I had been absolutely wrong in my outlook about private owners. Even with a driver of World Championship calibre like Moss you cannot fight the " works " teams and get away with it. I never realized how difficult it is to fight the " big boys " until 1954 when we had the best opportunity ever of doing so.

A car can be prepared with one hundred per cent. enthusiasm and efficiency but you cannot race a whole season as private owners and be successful. The cost, the knowledge, the factory modifications ; it all makes a picture and the private owner never has all the answers at the same time. I had wanted to help Stirling Moss win the World Championship as a private owner but I realize now that I was trying for something that circumstances would never allow me to achieve. My efforts had only resulted in him being snaffled as a "works" driver. "Well," I thought to myself, "that's another ambition gone west."

I should explain that when I first started motor-racing it was my ambition to get across to the United States and to prepare and race a car at Indianapolis. I very soon realized in my first season with John Heath that the idea would never materialize, and that particular ambition was relegated to the background.

My rather melancholy deliberations were brought to a sudden end when the headlights went out, followed by a frightening noise underneath the floorboards of the driving cab. Tony had been fairly quiet since leaving the " Ring," particularly after the incident with the brake drum, and I think he was pleased that something had happened to put a stop to our suicidal progress. With a resigned note in his voice he turned to me :

" That's it," he said, " we shall *have* to stop now and wait until the morning."

My immediate reaction was one of anger. I was really annoyed, not only with Tony but with the transporter as well.

" Not on your ruddy life," was my reply. " I am prepared to accept the challenge even if you are not."

I crawled underneath the cab and found that one of the ball races in the dynamo had packed up. It is forbidden to stop on the Autobahn without lights so I removed the fan belt and we continued, with sidelights working from the battery. I thought that perhaps the engine might manage quite a large mileage before running dangerously hot but within ten miles she was boiling merrily. We should never get to Modena that way.

It was necessary to get the water pump working again, and that meant driving it from the dynamo, so there was no alternative but to repair the dynamo. We pulled off the Autobahn, drove a kilometre or so down a minor road and then swung off into a large farmyard. We stripped down the dynamo on our bench in the back of the lorry, where there was an emergency lighting system, and to my surprise I found that a spare ball race from the Maserati timing gears fitted exactly that particular dynamo. What a break ! Whistling cheerily I dropped in the ball race, added a bit of grease and we were on our way again with the dynamo and water pump in perfect working order.

On the Autobahn once more, I put my foot down and kept it there. The speedo' needle rarely dropped below the 60 m.p.h. mark and as we approached the Austrian Customs I turned to Tony : "I will take her through all the frontiers and then you can take over. You know the way once we are over the Pass."

I thought to myself : "Without brakes he is not going to have a very pleasant drive, and I don't like handing over, but what can I do ? If I don't close my eyes soon I shall drop off in the cab."

Having gone through the frontiers I made myself comfortable in my sleeping bag on the work bench. I had no intention of being next to the accident if one did occur and, after taking a good pull from a bottle of wine, fell asleep with a nagging doubt in my mind about giving such a responsibility to Tony. The Brenner can be treacherous in places, because although it does not have a succession of what I describe as serpentine corners some of the downhill stretches are very fast indeed. Nevertheless I slept soundly for several hours and only woke when the lorry stopped suddenly ; then there was silence. I could not make out what had happened or why the engine had been switched off.

I climbed out of the back and found Tony smoking a cigarette by the side of the road.

"What happened ? " I asked. " Is anything wrong ? "

" No," he replied. "I just scared myself so much on the last corner that I had to stop and have a cigarette."

He was as white as a sheet, his hands shaking. I looked back towards a sharp corner with a sheer drop on the outside.

" Thanks for telling me," I said.

It was now daylight and we changed over. Whilst Tony bedded down on the bench I drove the rest of the way to Modena and the first thing I did on arrival at the works was to request help with the fractured drum. We searched Modena but could not find one to fit the Commer and it was eventually suggested that the three broken sections should be riveted together and held in one piece by a steel ring similar to the type used to hold the wooden spokes of a cart wheel in position.

It was a good idea and, having shrunk a half-inch steel ring on to the drum, we connected up the brake system and found everything in order. At least, with a steel ring clasping the drum I could press the brake pedal as hard as I liked !

Then we turned our attention to the new car, for time was short, and worked the whole of Tuesday night and all day Wednesday completing its preparation, changing the axle ratio and altering the pedal positions. It was not until the late evening that the Maserati was loaded in the Commer. We had no illusions. The target was Oulton Park by Saturday morning, 1,100 miles away.

We had a bath at the Europa, changed into a clean suit of clothes, had a meal at the Giardinetto and precisely at midnight Wednesday/Thursday set off for Milan.

"We don't stop for anything," I told Tony. "We just have to go flat."

It will give you some idea how we pressed on in that wonderful Commer transporter for we arrived at Calais in time to catch an earlier boat on Friday than the one which had been booked, and had to wait six hours in Dover for the lorry driver from Chester. How we could have used those six hours for sleep during that thirty-two hour non-stop " blind " from Modena to Calais.

Alan Collinson of Ferodo and Denis Done, the Manager of James Edwards Limited, met us at Crewe on Saturday morning and took us to a restaurant for a really good English breakfast. By mid-morning we were at Oulton Park ; there was the left-hand drive Commer, standing undamaged behind the pits. The driver from James Edwards had looked after it very well.

We were soon in trouble. Reg Tanner of Esso, an old and valued friend, warned me that if Stirling won the race he would insist on samples of our oil being taken. He knew that Maserati did not use Shell oil in Modena and assumed, probably quite rightly, that this " works " car was not running on Shell.

I did not blame Reg Tanner ; far from it. After all it is his job to watch over the interests of Esso and in fact he did us a good turn, warning me before the race.

In front of the Esso paddock stand, where Reg Tanner and his boys could see us, we drained the sump, gearbox and back axle. Then we opened sealed cans of Shell X100 and, having flushed out the engine to take the detergent oil, replenished. It took us an hour or so and I could have used that time to far better advantage.

"Seems to me," I said to Tony, " that even when we have a brand new car and no work to do someone will find something to keep us busy."

Two minutes before the start I was " bulldozed " off the grid by a rather officious pit-marshal. I resented this *polizei* attitude because I knew very well that I should have to get off the grid when the one-minute signal went and was quite prepared to do so. As I walked away I noticed that the starter had a chequered flag in his hand instead of the usual Union Jack. I turned to the nearest marshal.

"One of your pals just pushed me off the grid," I said, "but your people don't even know which flag is the right one to start a race."

The marshal shouted to the starter and all was well. With a roar the field got away, Stirling streaking towards Old Hall Corner and passing several cars before he reached there. The Maserati, which had not practised and been relegated to the back row of the grid, went like a scalded cat and I gave up trying to pass signals to Stirling in the early stages. Every time the Maserati went by the pits he was in a different place as he rocketed through the field overtaking car after car.

I said to Tony : " It's no good ; we can do nothing until he is in the lead ; this is a jigsaw."

We did not have long to wait for by the end of the fourth lap Stirling had passed Parnell's Ferrari and was leading.   It was an easy victory and, having put up fastest lap at 85.11 m.p.h., he then proceeded to win the Formula Libre event with the same car, breaking his own lap record in the process and recording 85.40 m.p.h.   Gregor Grant in *Autosport* wrote : " Stirling Moss had a field day."   How right he was.

We stayed in Chester for the night and drove down to London on Sunday in the Commer, accompanied by a feature writer from *Everybody's*, who was " ghosting " a story for me in the magazine about Moss.   He nterviewed me in the cab during the journey to London whilst Tony drove. By Wednesday lunch-time we were in Modena again.   Our friends at the Maserati works were delighted to see us ; following Oulton Park, the Moss star was in the ascendency.   They were, however, just as impressed with our marathon run.   Inside a week we had driven from Modena to Calais, raced a car at Oulton Park, and returned to Modena ; a distance of some 4,500 miles in all.

There was very little time to waste, as we were due at Pescara on the Adriatic coast within forty-eight hours, and as soon as the " works " car had been unloaded we were told to get some sleep at the Europa whilst Stirling's own car was loaded in the Commer.   On Thursday morning we set off for Pescara and Moss was practising on Friday and putting up fastest time of the day over the very lengthy, triangular road circuit which is nearly sixteen miles in length, starting on the Adriatic coast road and running inland to the Abruzzi Mountains, then returning to the coast.

Stirling recorded 10 minutes 23 seconds, twenty-three seconds quicker than the fastest lap in the race which was put up by Bira on a Maserati.

I was rather bucked at Pescara because although Stirling was now the official No. 1 for Maserati he was not controlled by the " works " pit.   There was a gentleman's agreement that we would race from the same pit but that I would control Moss.   It meant that I could take advantage of the Maserati lap-scoring chart and ask for advice when I wanted it without having to account for my actions to Bertocchi or anyone else during a race. I appreciated the Maserati outlook and it emphasized once again the efficiency of our small three-man outfit.

The Moss Gremlin was at work again on the Pescara circuit.   It was wretched luck, for Stirling went so well during the first few laps that he should have chalked up a walk-over victory.   However, as well as changing the axle ratio at the factory the Maserati mechanics had fitted a new system of oil supply (a modification following the German G.P.) to the top reduction gear in the axle, which also contains the Z.F. differential.

The pipes from the oil pump leading upwards to the top of the back axle housing were of steel—and perhaps too rigid—for one of them broke on the fourth lap at Pescara.   Fortunately the legendary Moss sixth sense told him that something was wrong, and when he felt oil spraying into the cockpit he pulled off the circuit at once without doing any damage to the car.   It could have been a very nasty back axle seizure.

CHAPTER 33

EUROPEAN MERRY-GO-ROUND (3)

A challenge from Fangio at Berne—Drama on the St. Gotthard Pass—
Fast practice lappery at Monza—Harsh words with Officine Maserati—
Moral victory in the Italian G.P.

I hoped to see Stirling put up a really good performance in the Swiss Grand Prix at Berne, following the Pescara race, for I knew that he would be given maximum support by the factory. As a matter of fact Bertocchi planned to have Harry Schell's Maserati running, with the pedals adapted and the seating position altered to suit Stirling just in case his own car broke down. We had come a long way—in a comparatively short time—since my argument with Bertocchi about the pedal positions earlier in the season.

On arrival in Modena I was loaned six Italian mechanics and we went to work on the car raced at the "Ring." The engine was stripped down, in spite of the fact that this had been done after the German Grand Prix, the back axle rebuilt and the body checked and mended where necessary by my friend, Fantuzzi.

The car was virtually taken to pieces and put together again. Tony and I found ourselves working twelve to fourteen hours a day but the Maserati mechanics worked even harder for they were always there when we left at night and again next morning when we arrived after an early breakfast. They worked like beavers and could not have had more than two or three hours' sleep each night ; in fact there was an air of urgency about the whole works as Maserati prepared for the race.

As soon as the car was ready, complete with its nose cowling in British racing green and the Union Jacks, we set off for Switzerland in the Commer independently of the main "works" convoy. The Maserati lorries used the Simplon tunnel, which is too low for the Commer, and I had to work my way through the St. Gotthard and Furka Passes.

We were all anxious to have another crack at Mercedes-Benz, and Juan Manuel in particular, after the encouraging result of the British Grand Prix ; we were after Ferrari as well. I soon realized, talking to the Maserati mechanics, that they were convinced Moss—who was universally popular with the whole outfit—was the boy to beat Mercedes and Ferrari.

The Team Manager paid me a great compliment by suggesting that, during the race, I run my own signal pit on a different part of the circuit, but in telephone communication with the main block of maintenance and repair pits where the Maserati mechanics would look after such things as refuelling and tyre changes.

"They must have a high opinion of us," I said to Tony, "allowing the No. 1 'works' driver to be guided by his own mechanics.''

I took the Berne race very seriously for having settled an old score with Mike Hawthorn it was time to have a real crack at Fangio and Gonzalez. I wanted to prove to the crowd in this championship race on the difficult and dangerous, drivers' circuit of the Bremgarten that Moss could beat these two " aces " or at least race on equal terms with them.

Stirling himself was not so sure about his chances in spite of the fact that on the second day of practice he made fastest time on a wet circuit and delighted the crowds with an immaculate display of wet weather technique. Nevertheless, at the first practice session Fangio and Gonzalez had put up quicker times on a dry track, and Stirling was finally classified as third fastest.

We worked very late Saturday night on the final preparation of the car and it was well after midnight when Tony and I arrived at our hotel—the Volkhaus in Berne. There was Stirling with Denis Done and I was angry that he should still be up at such a late hour.

Tony and I had worked very hard on the car, convinced that this was going to be the most exciting race of the season so far for us—Maserati versus Mercedes and Moss *contra* Fangio—and yet instead of preparing himself for the race there was our driver having a good time, with the Swiss Grand Prix only a few hours away.

" Could I have a word with you privately," I said to Stirling.

" You can speak to me here if you like," he replied.

" Well, what I have to say I can't say in front of other people," I said. " This is a private matter."

" O.K." he said, " let's go into one of the lounges."

In the privacy of a lounge I said what was on my mind.

" Look, Stirling, we have worked hard on the car and one thing is sure ; to-morrow you are supposed to have a crack at Gonzalez and Fangio. The whole works organization is waiting for the flag to fall and is solidly behind you. What are you doing at this hour of the morning ? I honestly thought you were fast asleep."

" Don't talk nonsense," said Stirling. " I shall never beat Fangio or Gonzalez."

"It is you who is talking nonsense," I replied angrily. " If you have enough confidence to have a try then you definitely will beat them."

Stirling looked doubtful and I rammed home my argument.

"At least promise to have a try. You cannot disappoint the Maserati boys. They all believe you can do it, including Bertocchi and the Competition Director."

" Well," said Stirling, " I will do my best but don't worry about me. I know it is late and I am sorry but there is plenty of time ; I can sleep until 10 o'clock.

In his favour I must point out that Stirling finds it difficult to get to sleep at an early hour. He cannot settle down, and relaxes far more quickly in the cockpit of a racing car than in bed. However, I was fed up at Berne because I felt he should have taken the pre-race period more seriously.

On Sunday, having carried our signalling equipment and lap charts to a group of special pits between Forsthaus Corner and the starting line, we walked back to the paddock and wheeled the Maserati on to the grid. With a practice time of 2 minutes 41.4 seconds, as against Gonzalez at 2 minutes 39.5 seconds and Fangio at 2 minutes 39.7 seconds, Stirling was on the front row.   I could not help thinking, as I trundled out the electric starter and manœuvred it into position, of that memorable occasion some years previously when I had started the Grand Prix Alta on that same grid with a handle !

It was at Berne that Fangio acknowledged the challenge of Stirling Moss. A few minutes before the start the World Champion walked across to where we were standing and said in Italian : "Andiamo piano."   Then, without waiting for a reply, he turned and walked away.

" What did he say ? " asked Stirling.

" He was telling you ' we go slowly,' " I replied.

Stirling laughed.

" Don't stand there," he said, " tell him we have no intention of going slowly."

However, Fangio was now in the Mercedes, adjusting his crash hat, and in any case had been using a peculiar type of phrase common on the Continent and would not have understood Stirling's reply.   This saying was, in fact, a gauntlet thrown down for Stirling to pick up.

Because of his display of driving in the wet during practice, Stirling had caused consternation in the Mercedes and Ferrari camps.   In the wet it is skill that counts not speed, and by returning the fastest time of the day he had challenged the skill of Fangio at top level.   Fangio's expression used at that time actually meant : " I am going to have a crack at you," because if you say to a driver on the continent "I hope you break your neck and legs," you actually wish him the opposite.   Fangio intended to go quickly—not slowly.

It would have taken hours to explain this to Stirling, and we had only three minutes, but it was a challenge and a compliment at the same time for Fangio was convinced that he and Stirling were going to fight out that particular race at the head of the field.   Fangio saw him as one of the two main adversaries at Berne ; he and Moss would set the pace, together with Gonzalez.   I was delighted at the turn of events, for this placed Stirling fairly and squarely in the top class.

As soon as the flag had dropped I made my way to the signalling pit, and organized things so that Tony lap-scored whilst I looked after the signals with Alfred Moss as assistant.   I had to accept the fact that he would be present there and was not prepared to argue the matter.   After all it was the Swiss Grand Prix and no one was going to stop Alfred Moss seeing this race from whatever vantage point he chose.

We were sandwiched between the Mercedes and Ferrari pits and it was not a good position for signals because these pits at Forsthaus are just after a corner which forces drivers to use the inside of the circuit, almost hitting the pavement in order to get on the right line for the bend in front of the grandstand which is usually taken flat out.

At the beginning of the race Stirling was lying third behind Fangio and Gonzalez, and the distance between the three cars was so little that it was very difficult to pass signals.   I had to put out my board whilst Fangio was travelling under it and Gonzalez was about to do so.   As soon as he had passed I quickly lowered it for a second, then lifted it again as Stirling went underneath. It did occur to me once or twice that if I dropped the board someone would get badly hurt, and I consider the Forsthaus signal pits are very dangerously situated.

During the race Stirling definitely proved he could do his stuff. Very early on he overtook Gonzalez and settled down to a comfortable six seconds behind Fangio. He continued like this—never more, never less than six seconds behind the Argentine for seventeen laps—until Hawthorn moved up into second place.

During this period Neubauer tried on several occasions to get Fangio clear of Stirling, and at one stage there was great excitement in the Mercedes pit when Stirling gained two-tenths of a second. Next lap, out went the "faster" signal, and Fangio responded by knocking off what Stirling had gained. However, nothing that Neubauer did with his little flags and signals could increase the 6-second gap that separated Fangio and Moss for so many laps.

It was obvious that Fangio was trying hard and that Moss was not going to give him an inch. This was the stuff! Holding Fangio securely on a circuit like the Bremgarten. However, once Hawthorn had passed, Gonzalez followed suit. With twenty-one laps completed Stirling pulled into the pits without any oil pressure. As the Maserati was wheeled away he prepared to take over from Harry Schell but soon afterwards Schell coasted into the pits with a dead engine and no oil pressure. That was the end of the Moss challenge at Berne.

A silly thing had ruined our chances. As I have described earlier Maserati modified the oil tanks before the British Grand Prix by fitting them at the back instead of alongside the engine, with filler caps of a new type incorporating a small nut to hold the spring-loaded collar. The nut had come undone, dropped in the oil tank, travelled slowly through the oil passages into the pump and finally destroyed it. A similar fate befell the Maserati driven by Schell.

For his performance in the race and during practice Stirling was acclaimed the driver of the day in Berne. In countless bars after the race enthusiasts talked of his bad luck for there would have been a terrific scrap between Fangio and Moss. I felt the same as they did for I had expected great things of Stirling after those first twenty-one laps. He had gone so well in second place that I had wanted to see more and his brief spell had not been long enough for me really to enjoy it. I was depressed for another reason ; Tony, who did not get on too well with the Maserati mechanics, went back to England after the Swiss Grand Prix and left me on my own again.

Stirling was given a large roll of cheese, weighing about two hundred-weight, by the organizers of the race and he promptly offered it to the Maserati *equipe*. It was cut by Bertocchi into equal shares and I received a piece, which I am afraid I never ate because I put it in the Commer and forgot all about it. When it eventually made its presence known by its powerful smell I threw it away.

I almost wrecked the Commer and killed myself on the return journey to Modena over the St. Gotthard Pass. Having reached the top quite safely I found that a snowstorm had been raging but nevertheless pressed on down the other side.   On almost every corner the Commer would slide, right itself and slide again, the tyres unable to retain a firm grip on the snow-covered granite bricks.

There was one particular corner, with a very steep approach, where I knew it would be necessary to reverse.   From previous experience I was well aware I should not get round on one lock and as I neared the corner I became more and more apprehensive.   Should I be able to bring the Commer to a full stop ?

I was, of course, descending the Pass in first gear and taking it very gently, but I dared not put much pressure on the brakes and when the hairpin corner came into view I gently applied them.   Nothing happened, apart from the fact that the wheels locked and, with terrifying precision, the Commer slid towards the hairpin and a small, utterly inadequate protective wall.

I could feel the veins standing out on my neck as, panic-stricken, I forced the gear lever into reverse.   There was a horrible grinding of teeth but it did the trick and the wheels spun backwards sufficiently for me to slide the tail round the corner, straighten up and continue down the Pass. Once clear of the hairpin I gingerly pulled up and lit a cigarette.   For a few seconds, with only a flimsy wall between me and a drop of thousands of feet, I had known real fear.

In Modena the Maserati was prepared by the " works " mechanics for the Italian Grand Prix at Monza on September 5th.   There was quite a lot of work to do, because the engine had been damaged when the oil pump ceased to function, and Schell's car was in a similar state.   It was decided that our car would be taken to Monza on Friday and that Stirling would drive one of the practice cars during the unofficial session on Thursday.

Keen competition between Fangio and Moss—Mercedes and Maserati— was expected at Monza and the entire works more or less shelved everything else to get the factory cars, particularly the one belonging to Stirling, pre-pared for the race.   The oil tanks were modified, for no one wanted a repeat performance of the Berne debacle, and the contractor changed. Entirely new oil and fuel tanks were supplied from another source, of riveted construction and made by people who specialize in aluminium aircraft tanks.

It was decided at this stage that a new type of oil pipe would be used but just before the design was finished and accepted I complained to the Competition Manager.

" The joints in the oil pipe lines are not flexible enough," I pointed out, " with the two ends of the piping almost joined together."

He told me that I was worrying unduly, and that the joints were satis-factory, but events during the race were to prove him wrong.

On Thursday, having lunch at the Giardinetto, I received a telephone call from the Autodrome : " How long would it take me to get from Modena to Monza."

" Well," I replied, " normally it takes four hours to get to Milan ; it is over a hundred miles and a very busy road as you know."

" That's no good," said the voice at the other end.   " We must get your car to the circuit this afternoon before the track is closed because both the practice cars have blown up. Stirling Moss has not yet had a drive."

Mention of Stirling was sufficient and, leaving an unfinished meal of tagliatelle—the tasty speciality of Modena—I rode back to the factory on the Vespa and within half-an-hour the Maserati was loaded and I was on my way. An Italian mechanic accompanied me on what proved to be a record-breaking journey for we left the works at 2 p.m. and arrived at Monza at 5.30 p.m., having covered one hundred and twenty miles in three-and-a-half hours.

I drove on the limit all the time, swearing like a trooper when other lorries did not get out of the way and muttering to myself : " Why don't they open their bloody eyes or look in the mirror."

The Italian took it all in and when we eventually managed to pass these lorries he leaned out of the window as we drew level, shook his fist and shouted : " Open bloody eyes." Then, with a huge grin, he proudly relaxed again and prepared to deal with the next offender. They were the only words he used during the entire journey.

Most of the lorry drivers were very good. When I blew the horn and they looked in the mirror and saw " Stirling Moss " across the front of the Commer, they lost no time pulling over and blew a fanfare on their hooters as we passed. They knew the Italian Grand Prix was on Sunday and Moss was reckoned a safe bet after his performance at Berne.

At Monza, after our hectic dash, the car was unloaded but Stirling did not practise. It had been decided, after I left Modena, that as he knew the circuit fairly well there was no sense in risking the car until the session on Friday, particularly as Maserati were so short of cars.

On Friday Fangio turned in a lap at 1 minute 59 seconds, whilst Stirling recorded 2 minutes 0.8 seconds, Gonzalez (Ferrari) 2 minutes exactly, Ascari (Ferrari) 2 minutes 0.2 seconds and Villoresi (Maserati) 2 minutes 0.2 seconds. It was, however, on Saturday that the fur really flew. The sun was very hot and only Mercedes went out in the early afternoon. Then, at 4 o'clock, Ascari delighted the Italian spectators by turning in a lap at 1 minute 59.9 seconds. Stirling came over to where I was sitting on the pit counter : " I would like to have a go now," he said, " I think I can do better than that."

" Well," I replied, " it's no use going now. Let's wait until the sun settles down and the weather is cooler. You will get better performance out of the engine and feel better yourself."

Stirling agreed and we sat on the pit counter discussing the relative merits of an ever-moving parade of blondes, brunettes—and one or two red-heads—who were " circulating " in the paddock area.

The official practice finished at six. At five twenty-five I called on one of the Maserati mechanics to give me a hand and we started up the engine and warmed it on soft plugs. Then the hard plugs went in and Stirling was away. I told him to do only five laps ; two slow warming-up ones, followed by the third, fourth and fifth as fast as possible.

On his third lap he put up best time of the day at 1 minute 59.3 seconds although we actually made it 1 minute 59.2 seconds. As soon as the announcement came over the loud-speakers, Ascari jumped into the cockpit of his Ferrari and went away in a blare of sound, determined to do better.

Only eight minutes of the practice session remained, and Ascari went like a bomb, eventually reducing Stirling's time by one-tenth of a second on the very last practice lap of the day. This gave him fastest time but Fangio still retained pole position with his lap in 1 minute 59 seconds on the Friday.

Everyone congratulated Moss, including Signor Orsi, who was convinced—as we were—that he had gone as fast as Ascari. Still, the timekeeper's decision is final and we were credited with third fastest time of the sessions. It had been a most exciting half-hour.

Within ten minutes of the end of the practice the Maserati mechanics started to strip down our car. I could see no reason for this sudden activity because the engine had behaved perfectly. The car had only covered fifteen laps and the revolution counter needle showed it had not been over-revved. To make matters worse the tyres were removed from our car, put on the one Villoresi was to drive and replaced with partly-worn ones. I was furious, and buttonholed Bertocchi.

" I do not think it is a very good idea to strip down the engine," I said to him, " when there is no need for it, because assembling in this sort of workshop may do more harm than good. And why have you changed our tyres ? "

Bertocchi was quick to answer :

" It is my responsibility," he said, " and I shall do what I think is right."

"Well, so far as I am concerned that is not the case," I replied. " I have been accepted into your team as mechanic to Stirling Moss and it was agreed that I should have the responsibility for his car."

Within seconds civil war had broken out in a manner of speaking and Bertocchi and I were bawling at each other like a couple of fish-wives. Alfieri, the Competition Director, then joined the fray.

" You have no idea what is going on," he told me. "As Villoresi is going for the battle with Fangio he will need better tyres than Moss."

This annoyed me even more for I knew Stirling was No. 1, even though Villoresi had gone very well indeed in practice, and it seemed to me that unfair favouritism was being shown.

" Unless I get my tyres back," I said to Alfieri and Bertocchi, " I shall tell Moss what is going on and you can explain your actions to him."

I stormed out of the " box " and walked over to the restaurant bar, wondering whether to telephone Stirling at his hotel and explain the situation. Over a cup of coffee I decided not to do so, as it might upset and worry him during the night. I have seen drivers looking absolutely washed out and in no fit state to handle their cars because of an argument with someone or other on the night before a race, and I had no intention of upsetting Stirling on the eve of what might well prove to be his greatest triumph.

I need not have worried for when I returned to the " box " I found that the original tyres had been fitted on our Maserati and the engine had been left for me to assemble. As I stood there Bertocchi came over and, smiling in a very friendly but rather embarrassed fashion, told me that I could choose any one of the Maserati mechanics as my assistant.

It seemed I had won the day but there was no time to lose and I started at once on the reassembly of the engine. The job was finished in the early hours of Sunday morning and I then noticed that the auxiliary petrol tank was leaking. It was taken out and soldered, by which time it was daybreak and I was tired out. I returned to the hotel in Monza, slumped down in a chair in the entrance hall and went to sleep for a couple of hours.

The argument and ensuing work on the engine had put all thoughts about the flexibility of the oil pipes out of my mind. Had I not been otherwise engaged I would have removed the aluminium piping and substituted rubber tubing for part of the run, thus allowing greater flexibility. The existing tubing was some eighteen inches long in the vicinity of the joints but the piping itself inside the rubber was too close and the joints, therefore, too rigid.

The start of the Italian Grand Prix was at 3 o'clock, and I felt prouder than ever before as, with a works mechanic helping me, I wheeled the Moss Maserati on to the front row of the starting grid, alongside Fangio and Ascari. " This," I thought to myself, " is where Stirling must show the world that as a driver he is second to none."

The atmosphere, as always at Monza for the Grand Prix, was terrific, and eighty thousand people waited tensely for the sort of " flat out, win or bust " duel one usually sees at this stage of the season on the famous autodrome.

With an earsplitting roar the field got away and at the end of the first lap, following an excellent start, Stirling was already engaged in a terrific scrap for third place with Ascari and Gonzalez, behind the Mercedes of Kling and Fangio.

The way in which Stirling kept his own engine in one piece whilst Ascari, Gonzalez and Villoresi all blew up is to me one of the finest examples of restraint in the very thick of the fight and the best answer I know to people who say that Stirling breaks cars. He certainly does not and never has done ; the way in which he refused to be drawn into that monumental " dice " in the early stages of the race was masterly and showed him in true championship colours.

Blue and white (stay as you are) remained on my signal board the whole time whilst Fangio and Ascari fought for the lead and Stirling held back, calmly waiting his chance to move up when one or both of the leading cars blew up.

Just before half distance, with Ascari leading Fangio and Moss (Gonzalez was well back, having blown up his first car), I noticed from my stop-watch that Villoresi was gaining a second a lap on Moss and immediately went to the official Maserati pit to investigate the reason. I was operating my own pit at Monza, with a works mechanic to help me, whilst Ken Gregory looked after the lap chart.

My enquiry about Villoresi was received rather coldly.

" We are trying to send him into the battle," explained Bertocchi.

" Well," I replied, " you told me definitely at Modena that Stirling

Moss was your Number 1 and if you speed up Villoresi I shall speed up Moss."

This had the effect of forcing Bertocchi to put all his cards on the table.

" We definitely consider Villoresi our Number 1, and we should like him to win."

" O.K." I replied, " if that is how you feel, and seeing that you mis-informed me, I shall run the rest of the race as I want for Stirling Moss— not according to your wishes."

I was angry because I knew, as did the Maserati people, that Stirling was racing with some cards still up his sleeve, and could not understand the logic of speeding up Villoresi to a dangerous degree when Stirling was holding the fort for Maserati. With half the race still to be run it would surely have been better if the Italian had been held back to support Moss.

What happened came as no surprise to me. Villoresi passed Moss (who looked a little taken aback by this piece of works strategy, but wisely refrained from contesting the challenge), and two laps later passed Fangio into second place. It was a short-lived triumph for soon afterwards he came in with a bent propeller shaft and that was the end of his Grand Prix.

All eyes in the Maserati pit were on us but no one tried to interfere as I kept Moss in the picture, telling him every lap how many seconds he was behind Fangio and Ascari and thinking to myself that the time could not be far off when these two would wear themselves out.

" This battle cannot go on for ever," I said to Ken Gregory.

When Stirling eventually took the lead, it was not because I speeded him up but because Ascari and Fangio slowed. Approaching the Curva Grande, Stirling found himself going faster than these two and very quickly " took " first Fangio, then Ascari. The Italian fought back and regained the lead for two laps before coming into the pits with a wrecked engine— one of the valves having dropped into its cylinder.

The following lap Moss was four seconds in the lead and gaining three to four seconds a lap. He is very regular, and if not speeded up will lap consistently at the same speed, so that without actually going any faster he not only passed Ascari and Fangio but increased his lead.

There was great excitement in the Maserati pit and Sig. Orsi came along and asked me to slow down Stirling.

" I never speeded him up," I replied. " We are not going all that quick, just keeping our regular times."

However, Orsi wanted Stirling slowed, and as he came round on the next lap I held out the appropriate signal.

Even though his lap times decreased by two seconds he was still gaining on Fangio, who was absolutely whacked, and the " slower " signal was permanently on my board from then on. Nevertheless, Stirling built up a tremendous lead (for a race that had been so close) of twenty seconds.

Twelve laps from the end the Moss Gremlin went into action. As I was converting the prize money from lire into pounds sterling and making tentative plans for a celebration in Milan that night, one of the Maserati mechanics warned me that he had seen a haze trailing behind the car as it approached the Curva Grande. Next lap we saw it ourselves and knew something was wrong.

When Stirling came round again he pointed over his shoulder in the direction of the oil tank ; it was obvious he was losing oil and we were fully prepared for the pit stop. He took on three gallons, which was syringed under pressure into the tank in a matter of seconds, but as soon as he accelerated away we could see that two of the three gallons had been left behind on the track. By the time he reached the Curva Grande he was out of oil and there was no pressure.

Desperately Stirling tried to continue, although he must have known it was a hopeless task, and on the South Curve the engine seized solid. As the car started to free-wheel, he jumped out and pushed. I ran to meet him and from somewhere he found a tired grin to greet me.

" Hard luck, Alf," he said, " the thing just went damned solid."

Only those few words ; nothing else.

There was no despair and I could see Stirling was inwardly elated at the way he had beaten them all—Gonzalez, Ascari, Fangio, Hawthorn. He saw the race in its true light, a race in which he proved to himself and the world of motor-racing that he was as good as the men at the top. Many people said at the time that he must have been bitterly disappointed and angry but this was definitely not the case.

As we approached the finish line I could see that the effort of pushing the car nearly half-a-mile had almost exhausted him. It would have worn out any normal driver, even if he had not driven a Grand Prix, and I marvelled at his fitness and sheer guts. He managed another smile when Neubauer walked out from the Mercedes pit and patted him on the shoulder. I leaned over.

" I can't help you, Stirling," I said, " we are being watched but I'll go and get you a drink."

I passed him a bottle of Coca Cola as the Maserati came to rest a few yards short of the finish line, and Stirling sat on the tail and waited for Fangio to complete the last few laps so that he could push the car over the line and qualify as a finisher.

He was the first to congratulate Fangio after he had received the chequered flag and completed his lap of honour. The World Champion, looking very much the worse for wear after the gruelling race, turned to Stirling. " It is for me to congratulate you," he said. " You are the moral victor."

This was not only the view of Fangio, but of most other people as well including the Competition Director of Pirelli Tyres who decided to pay Stirling Moss a bonus on the strength of his moral victory.

That night, just before undressing, I wrote in the diary : " Stirling drove a marvellous race. Fate plays strange tricks. The oil pipe would not have broken if I had modified it, and I did not do so—indirectly— because of an argument with the people who would have given anything to win the race and beat Mercedes."

CHAPTER 34

EUROPEAN MERRY-GO-ROUND (4)

" Maser " versus Vanwall at Goodwood—Brake linings and Stirling Moss—
A 4 a.m. incident in Liverpool—An easy win at Aintree—En vacance—
A terrifying journey—Anti-climax at Barcelona—Home again.

At Modena after the Monza race we took the engine out of the chassis. It was almost impossible to disconnect the clutch bellhousing due to the fact that the whole unit (bellhousing and drive shaft to the clutch) had seized solid. The engine had been completely wrecked and the crankshaft was not only blued but oxidized to such an extent that no one at Maserati —in twenty-five years of motor-racing—had ever seen a blowup like it.

It meant building a complete new engine, with the exception of the crankcase, for the September Goodwood Meeting. Nothing else was usable—even the crankcase had been slightly distorted due to overheating— and we settled down to a complete rebuild in the Maserati works.

Incidentally, after Monza, Ballentani agreed that I had been right about the flexibility of the piping and modifications were made to all the cars.

I had arranged with Stirling some weeks previously that I would have a holiday after the Goodwood and Aintree meetings and before the Spanish Grand Prix at Barcelona on Sunday, October 24th. When we had dinner together in Milan after his superb drive in the Italian classic he told me he had brought the Mark VII Jaguar out to Italy so that I could use it. " She has been reconditioned by Jaguars," said Stirling, " so you will have a really good motor-car for your holiday."

He was always very thoughtful in this way and although to some people he appears preoccupied and perhaps a little selfish, this is far from the case. He gets a lot of pleasure out of springing a surprise on the lines of his very welcome offer of the Jaguar, and I was delighted for it would now be possible for me to take my wife on her first continental holiday.

Stirling in fact treated me very fairly the whole time I was with him. Even when I was working at Tring he used to pay me a food allowance of 10s. a day. There was never any argument about money and I was never criticized for being too extravagant. As soon as I joined him he was quick to make a point about expenses. " One thing I do not want to do Alf," he said, " is to leave you short of money as you so often were with H.W.M."

Incidentally, there was no arrangement between Stirling and myself during the 1954 season that I would have a proportion of the winnings and I was not on a percentage basis. However, I had no cause to complain for he was more than generous when things went in our favour.

It may seem strange that the driver who persuaded H.W.M. to give the mechanics a cut of the prize money did not do so with his own *equipe*, but the Maserati was a considerable expense in the first place and undoubtedly the most expensive car he had ever had to maintain. It was simply a matter of running at a profit and there was not sufficient spare cash available to give me a regular percentage of the winnings. Anyway, I was quite happy with my basic salary of £11, a personal expense allowance of £3 a week to entertain trade contacts and an adequate travel allowance.

Just before leaving Modena for England Ballentani asked me to step into his office and told me that I was travelling in the capacity of technical adviser to the Maserati team. " Tell Stirling Moss," he said, " that whatever happens at Goodwood and Aintree we must either collect the lap record or come first. If you can get them both, then so much the better. We want you to control the movements of the car during the two races as you always have done," he continued, " but there is no need for you to do anything. We are sending four mechanics and they can do all the work : it's about time you had a rest."

We set off in convoy. I drove the Jaguar, whilst the Maserati boys travelled in a very rapid Fiat lorry with our car and another Maserati for Mantovani to drive at Aintree. I had decided to leave the Mark VII in Calais so that I could pick it up for our holiday after the races in England. It did not matter how hard I " pushed" the Mark VII from Modena to Turin—clocking 60 or 70 most of the time—I could not shake off the lorry. Those Maserati " works " mechanics sure could drive and I parted company with them at St. Jean de Maurienne.

I recollect asking two of the mechanics to travel with me as I thought it would be more comfortable for them. This was the head mechanic's answer, " None of us can travel with you," he said, " because if we have an accident the insurance will not cover us. So long as we have our accidents in our own lorry we are O.K. Thank you very much."

The last meeting of the season at Goodwood was an interesting one i only for the " dice " Stirling had with Mike. We were using the Monza car, the original 250 F., and before leaving Modena I was asked to suggest ratios for the two meetings. I was sure the Goodwood race would be won at a much faster average than previous events in 1954 and I suggested that we use the Silverstone ratio ; this was a slightly higher one than I would have used earlier in the season.

When we arrived at Goodwood on the Saturday morning Stirling was there and set off on a practice lap as soon as the car had been unloaded and checked over.

When he came in he did not seem too happy. " What axle ratio are you using Alf ? " he asked.

" The same as when we were here last time," I replied untruthfully.

"Well," said Stirling, " I reckon I am 200 revs down on the straight."

" Why worry ? " I told him. " Our time is already four seconds faster than Peter Collins in the new Vanwall but if I drop the axle ratio we may lose that four seconds."

I think this would have been the case because Stirling lapped Goodwood in 1 minute 32.6 seconds, which was very quick indeed and 1/5th of a second faster than Ken Wharton in the B.R.M. Afterwards there was very little to do to the car, which was almost brand new in any case, except make a routine check in the paddock stall.

On the starting grid next day for the Formula 1 Goodwood Trophy I repeated my orders from Modena. " If you cannot win then for goodness sake establish a new lap record otherwise I shall be in trouble." Stirling took it seriously although I had only been joking. "All I can do Alf," he said, " is to try."

" Well," I said, " you had better try hard because otherwise it is me who will be carrying the can."

He certainly did try hard and was not only leading the field by the end of the first lap in the twenty-one lap race, but putting a respectably safe distance between the Maserati and its chief challenger, the $2\frac{1}{2}$-litre Vanwall of Peter Collins. Stirling stayed in the lead until the end of the race and won by twenty seconds from Collins.

In the Formula Libre race Mike Hawthorn drove the Vanwall and had a tremendous " dice " with Moss. Collins drove the big Thinwall special to victory followed by Wharton in a B.R.M., but it was the Moss/Hawthorn duel that had the crowd on its feet for the entire ten-lap race. It was almost heart-stopping to see them both streaking down Lavant Straight, almost wheel to wheel, and into the chicane together. They were so close that I fully expected Mike to " pip " Stirling out of the chicane on each of the ten laps.

The difference between the red and green car was so little that I could not time it. I just did not know what to do for the red strip had been on my signal board the whole time. Finally, I chalked HAW in big letters on the board, held it out for Moss to see and pointed at my back to indicate that Mike was practically driving on Stirling's fuel tank. Stirling knew this in any case but I was so excited at the prospect of beating both Mike and the Vanwall that I signalled the obvious.

However, it had a very satisfactory effect for Mike was so amused at my antics, particularly my latest effort with his name, that he roared with laughter and gave me the V sign as the two cars streaked past the pits. It was then my turn to laugh because in taking his attention from the track to give me the sign he lost a second, and there was a wider gap from then onwards. Stirling succeeded in retaining his slender lead and finished third not more than six feet ahead of the Vanwall.

The rivalry between Moss and Hawthorn, which became more intense after the British Grand Prix, was good natured and very sporting. There was nothing remotely vicious about it and they fought a very clean battle with no dirty work on either side. At Goodwood, Stirling gave Mike every opportunity to pass (if he could) and at Silverstone Mike did the same for Stirling.

The Maserati mechanics were delighted with our success at Goodwood and in high spirits we set off for Blakes Garage, Liverpool, in the Fiat lorry.

We found on stripping down the car for a pre-race check over that the brakes would have to be relined. The twenty-one lap race for the Trophy, the ten-lap Formula Libre race and six or seven practice laps had worn away a quarter-of-an-inch of the lining. There was very little else remaining inside the drums, other than rivets !

The linings had worn far more at Goodwood than in the British Grand Prix at Silverstone, which is understandable because Goodwood calls for heavier braking. Nevertheless in 1954 Stirling used a lot of brakes and did not learn to do with less until he joined Mercedes-Benz and went around behind Fangio.

In my opinion he was hard on brakes during the season and this fact was brought home to me at the Maserati works after the Belgian G.P. at Spa, when Bertocchi made a comparison between the World Champion and Moss.

Each driver covered approximately the same distance but when we returned to Modena after the race, it was only the linings on our car that had to be changed. " You see," said Bertocchi in answer to my complaint about the quality of the linings, " Juan Fangio is not so hard on brakes. You will have to make this point to Stirling Moss."

It is not a quick job relining the brakes on a Maserati because it is a hand-made car and the shoes are not interchangeable. They are machined in such a way that they will only fit either top or bottom on one particular wheel and there is no question of switching shoes.

Before Stirling went out for the first practice session at Aintree a new set of linings was fitted but after only fifteen laps, during which he put up the fastest practice time of 2 minutes 3.6 seconds, the linings had been very badly worn and it took us all Friday night to reline again. I did most of the work, as well as checking the engine, in view of the fact that Stirling had asked me to do so rather than supervise the preparation of the 250 F. as Ballentani had suggested.

Light relief at Aintree was provided by the mechanics working on Mantovani's Maserati which had not gone at all well in practice and would not respond to their tuning. During Friday night, whilst I was busy on our car they took off the cylinder head and had the carburetters to pieces. Then, at 4 o'clock in the morning—just as I had finished my tappings of the linings—the Head Mechanic decided to push-start the car.

Can you imagine trying to start a racing-car at that hour of the morning not very far from the Adelphi Hotel ? I thought to myself, " This will mean a question in Parliament at the very least."

However, the Italians brushed aside my protest and I could not persuade them that there are certain laws in this country that one has to obey.

" We can start or drive a racing-car any time of the day or night in Monza or Milan so why not Liverpool ? " argued the Head Mechanic.

" O.K." I said, " but I am on my way."

Fortunately they were unable to start the car because the mechanic who sat in the driving seat was either short sighted or tired out. Almost as soon as they began pushing it down the hill from Blake's Garage they ran full tilt into the back of a parked Ford Prefect !

There was a long and colourful argument next morning between the owner of the Ford and the Italian mechanics during which I acted as interpreter and eventually the Ford owner very sportingly settled for £10 in cash. Had the police been called in we should have had to explain why we had attempted to start an unregistered racing-car on the Queen's highway ; and I don't think the Liverpool magistrates would have appreciated our point of view.

In the *Daily Telegraph* Trophy, Stirling shared the front row of the grid with Behra's Gordini, Hawthorn's Vanwall and Schell's Maserati. It was not a very interesting race for he took the lead from the start and won by the comfortable margin of fourteen seconds from Hawthorn who fought a terrific battle with Schell for second place. After being presented with the trophy Stirling congratulated Mike on his driving and Mr. Vandervell on his motor-car, a sporting gesture made in all sincerity.

I knew we could never win the Formula Libre race if we had to rely on the brake linings lasting, particularly as the opposition included the new Mark II B.R.M.s which were very fast and the potent Thinwall Special in the hands of Peter Collins. With 4½ litres against our 2½, the Thinwall was more than a match for the Maserati.

Stirling had used the brakes heavily in the Formula 1 race and on examining them in the paddock afterwards I estimated—from the rate of consumption of linings—that by the time he had finished ten laps of the seventeen lap Formula Libre race he would have no linings left. The shoes would be bare.

On the starting grid, where he had pole position again, I leaned over and explained the situation : " Whatever happens," I said, " you have only enough brakes for ten laps. I suggest the lap record at the beginning to please Ballentani and then just look after your brakes and don't worry about winning the race.

Wharton and Flockhart had B.R.M.s on the front row, together with Collins in the Thinwall, and when the flag fell it was Flockhart who got away first but Collins who led at the end of the first lap with Stirling not far behind. I could see that all was not well with the Thinwall and recalled that the Vandervell car had suffered a lot of carburation trouble in practice. It was obvious that more trouble was on the way and I was fairly certain that the Thinwall would never finish the race.

The problem of whether or not Stirling should try for the lead was solved on the seventh lap when the Thinwall started to misfire badly and Stirling automatically moved up into first place. By this time most of the opposition had disappeared ; Schell and Wharton—on Maserati and B.R.M. respectively—had collided, whilst Mike Hawthorn had retired with the Vanwall.

From then onwards Stirling stayed in the lead and just for good measure established a new absolute circuit record of 2 minutes 0.6 seconds, thus giving Ballentani a British " double." Stirling came home eleven seconds ahead of Mantovani, making it a nice " works " finish, and as soon as he arrived after his lap of honour and pulled up in the pit area I ran over to congratulate him. He smiled as I patted him on the back and then—with obvious glee—said, "And Alf I've still got some brakes."

Stirling was not kidding. He still had some brakes and definitely had not used them so heavily in the Formula Libre race. In the *Daily Telegraph* Trophy he had worn away two-thirds of the linings and started the second race with only a third, yet when I examined the linings in the paddock they still had almost a third intact. To my knowledge that was the last time he ever used a lot of brakes so that it is true to say that Stirling Moss was still learning about this particular aspect of motor-racing as late as the end of the 1954 season.

After the race we set off from Aintree in high spirits and, having called for my wife at Woolwich, drove down to Dover in the Fiat lorry. The Maserati mechanics disliked driving in England so much that they asked me to handle the lorry on the journey to Aintree and back, preferring to risk a crash with me at the wheel—and all the insurance complications—rather than drive themselves.

Each time I handed over to the Italians they complained about the narrow roads, the slow drivers and—at night—the inadequate street lighting and " the silly law that allows old cars to dip one headlight and drive on the other one." Everything about England was wrong and I used to lose my temper. "At least," I told them on one occasion, " we don't have scores of cyclists without lights of any sort riding on our main roads at night as you have in Italy."

" It is easy to avoid them," replied the Head Mechanic, "if you keep your eyes open and your thumb on the horn button."

However, I should not grumble too much about the Maserati organization for the Head Mechanic paid the passage money on the cross-channel steamer for my wife and, before setting off for Modena, satisfied himself that the Jaguar was in the garage where I had left it. Then, thanks to Stirling, Sylvia and I had our first continental holiday. From Calais we drove to Rheims and Monte Carlo, spending a few days with my friends at the Diodato. Then it was Rome, Florence and Venice in the green and cream Jaguar that excited comment wherever we went.

The fourteen days passed all too quickly and from Venice we returned to Modena where the factory personnel were waiting to finally assemble the Maserati for the Spanish Grand Prix, the last championship event of the 1954 season.

I started work on the 250 F. without delay—on the Sunday morning in fact—and with a team of Maserati mechanics worked all day and most of the night as well, finally completing the assembly of the car at 2 o'clock on Monday morning. I had a few hours sleep and at 7 o'clock we were out on the Autodrome testing the car.

Imagine the panic when a piston was burned during this test and we had to return to the works and strip down the engine. It was a faulty piston and nothing to do with the mixture, and the odds are that the piston was too tight ; it just packed up.

It took thirty-six hours, working almost non-stop, to fit another engine in the chassis and we were not ready to leave Modena until Tuesday afternoon. The Maserati " works " lorries had already left with the other team cars, including a spare for Stirling to use on the first day of practice. I made the journey without an assistant to help out with the driving, but Sylvia came with me and learned at first hand about the sort of journeys I had described so often in my letters home.

We reached Susa on Tuesday night and left at 6 o'clock next morning, and it was a shocking drive as the Mt. Cenis is closed at this time of year and I had to take the Commer over Mt. Genevre. As on previous journeys the narrow road over the Pass was very slippery and treacherous and I can recollect several occasions when my wife screamed and covered her eyes. She was sure we were about to go off the road and over the side.

It was a terrible descent to Briancon but we eventually arrived there safely and went on as far as Narbonne, close to the Spanish frontier, having covered 350 miles in one day. We arrived in Barcelona at 3 o'clock on Thursday afternoon—only forty-eight hours after leaving Modena and with nearly eight hundred miles on the speedometer.

" I hope we do not have to try and break our necks on the way back to Modena," said Sylvia. " That was the most terrifying journey I have ever made."

Using my normal procedure I made my way to the Automobile Club, as I had never been to Barcelona and did not know the location of the circuit or the whereabouts of the Maserati garage, but on arrival at the Club I got precisely nowhere. My Italian did not work wonders and I could neither understand Spanish nor make them understand me so I gave it up as a bad job, went outside, cocked my ear and listened for the sound of cars practising. It was then a matter of following my nose as it were and I drove in the general direction of the noise, eventually arriving on the Pedrables street circuit which is on the outskirts of Barcelona and utilizes part of the main entry roads.

However, it was impossible to get the Commer on to the circuit, as it was closed for practice, so I left Sylvia in the cab and made my way across the track to the paddock area. There I met Stirling, looking very depressed and in a rather belligerent mood. He even ticked me off for arriving late for practice.

" Look," I said, " I am a day early, not a day late. They told me at the works that I need not arrive until Friday and that you could use the spare car."

" What was the use of that ! " replied Stirling. " I went off the road : the pedals were in the wrong place."

My answer was not a very sympathetic one. " It just shows that you need a father always to remind you where the pedals are. You should have taken things easy to-day and not tried to go fast. After all there are two more days of practice."

I knew I had " needled " Stirling when he snapped back, " Why don't you get the damned car out so that I can have a go with it."

However, following our *tete-a-tete* it was too late for Stirling to practise with our 250 F. and we had to wait until the following day. I could sense that he was not very happy about the car when he practised on Friday, and my fears were confirmed when he pulled into the pits after a few laps and switched off angrily. " It's no damned good at all," he said. " I don't feel like going very fast because it is not right."

I could not understand it for the car had been completely rebuilt after Monza. It seemed to me that the " prang " on Thursday had put him off his stroke. Mind you he was not alone, for Hawthorn and Collins both spun on the same corner as Moss in that first practice session.

" Well," I replied, " if you say it is not right I will speak to Bertocchi and perhaps he will give you a different car."

When I discussed the matter with the Italian a few minutes later he was quick to point out that there was absolutely no difference between the factory cars and Stirling's own car.

" Well," I replied, " you know how people are. No one is going to convince Stirling of that. Why not give him one of the other team cars and let him convince himself."

" O.K. Alphons," agreed Bertocchi with a smile, " there are six motor-cars here. Ask your Mr. Moss which one he would like to try."

When I passed on Bertocchi's message Stirling was not sure which one to take out first and I suggested Mantovani's car. Stirling sat in the cockpit, whilst the wealthy and very likeable Italian driver looked rather annoyed, then took it round the circuit for a few laps. He was still not at all happy and told me when he came in again.

" The car I went off the road in felt good to me."

Away he went again, this time in Musso's car, and once more came into the pits complaining that it was not as good as the one he had " pranged." " So far as I can see," said Stirling, "I might as well drive my own Maser."

I made an entry in my diary after the practice, " Seems that no car is right for S.M., but I think his ' prang ' is the real trouble. Am not looking forward to the race."

That night axle ratios were changed on all the Maseratis as during practice it had been found that the " works " cars had not been geared properly and were too low for a circuit with such a long straight. We worked until 4 a.m. and I then snatched some sleep and was woken by a Maserati mechanic two hours later so that I could finish the job.

I broke my rule on this occasion of not turning in until the car was absolutely ready but I was dog tired. It had been quite a week, with hardly any sleep in Modena after my holiday, a flat-out drive to Barcelona and very little sleep since arriving in the city. All in all, I have never felt more unsettled before a race.

On Sunday, not very long before the cars were due to go on the grid, Alfieri—the Competition Director—asked Stirling if he would break up the opposition. The Italian was more worried about the Lancia-Ferraris, which had clocked fastest time of the day in practice, than the Mercedes.

Stirling bluntly refused : " I don't feel much like driving anyway," he told Alfieri, " and under no circumstances am I going to go with half a tankfull to break up the opposition. I am going to try and finish the race," continued Stirling, " whatever my final placing."

Alfieri then asked Schell, who was driving a semi-private " works " entry, whether he would set the pace.

" O.K." agreed Schell, " I will certainly do it for you as there is nothing I would like more than to have a crack at Ascari and Hawthorn."

The fuel tank of the Franco-American's car was half-filled and Schell was told to go like a bomb from the drop of the flag and to continue that way as long as the engine would stand it. Alfieri reckoned that if Schell could keep up these tactics for a third of the race distance the Lancia-Ferraris would blow up.

Things did not work out that way for although Harry fairly rocketed around the Pedrables Circuit, and led the race for eleven of the first twenty-nine laps, there was no one to carry on the fight for Maserati when he retired. I remember him coasting into the pits with a car that was virtually a wreck. "And where is the second man now," he asked. " I have done my job. Ascari is out and Hawthorn has had to drive damned hard to hold on to me."

Unfortunately there was no second man for while Schell had been engaged in his meteoric drive, Stirling had retired with a faulty scavenge oil pump. As a matter of fact I was not sorry for I could see that he was not at all happy on the Pedrables Circuit. There is no doubt in my mind that the spin in practice put him off form, although Hawthorn was un-affected by his gyration at the same place. Neither do I think Stirling was very pleased with his position on the second row of the grid, particularly after his wonderful performance at Monza.

Although Stirling is not a temperamental driver I feel sure he was not in the right mood for motor-racing at Barcelona. There was no fire in his driving and I imagine he was as pleased to get out of the race as I was to have him out of it. This was the first time he had raced on the Spanish circuit but I don't think this had anything to do with his performance because it is not a particularly tricky one ; in any case I have never known him badly put off form by the characteristics of a circuit.

It could be that, having convinced himself at Silverstone, Berne and Monza of his capabilities, the spin gave him an inferiority complex ; this, together with a place on the second row of the grid, perhaps upset his pride. Whatever the cause, by my reckoning he was hardly in the same class at Barcelona as Fangio, Villoresi, Ascari and Hawthorn ; he certainly could not match their times.

There is a possibility that he had some personal problem before the race for it is a fact that a driver's personal problems and worries during the week preceding a meeting are a very important factor. Perhaps there was something in the background, about which I knew nothing, that had upset him ?

This question of mental fitness is vital and Moss himself reckons it to be the most important factor in a driver's makeup for no driver can give his best unless his mental approach is absolutely unworried and " right " for the job in hand. After all, it is mental concentration in the main that wins motor-races.

Neubauer has investigators watching the drivers. He knows if one of them has any personal troubles and will insist—much earlier than any other team manager would do under similar circumstances—that the man in question joins the factory well before the race. He likes to keep a careful eye on his drivers and establish the atmosphere of competition. It is a psychological weapon and pays great dividends.

Frankly I was disappointed that Stirling had put up such a mediocre performance in the practice sessions and in the race itself. I felt that we had been bounced back almost to the beginning of the season and that it would be necessary for us to fight all over again to regain our lost prestige. We had climbed fast and dropped just as quickly ; it was an anti-climax and, in addition, Mike Hawthorn had won the race in a superb fashion, soundly turned the tables and given us a good trouncing. It was a depress-ing and unspectacular end to that wonderful 1954 season.

After the Barcelona race, endeavouring unsuccessfully to follow the

Mercedes convoy as it fairly streaked through the narrow streets of towns and villages, my wife asked me to sum up my feelings about the season.

"Well," I told her, " I feel proud that Stirling has got where he has because after all I have prepared the car. I have helped him to achieve a certain position—where he wants to be and deserves to be—but at the same time I can see that I shall have to start thinking about my future. We shall not be able to retain our close association in a " works " set-up ; we have been a small but happy family as a private *equipe* and all that will go by the board."

On the other hand, I had established such a good relationship with Maserati that it was agreed I should carry out my own development schemes on the car in England during the closed season before joining them again for 1955. They were quite willing for me to make fuel injection experiments with SU, whilst they experimented in Modena with Italian fuel injection systems, and it was agreed that the most satisfactory one would be chosen, developed and used in 1955. At that time it was an accepted fact that Stirling would drive for Maserati again although no firm arrangements had been made.

I spoke my thoughts aloud to Sylvia as the Commer hummed along towards the frontier—the German lorries having disappeared from sight. " I am going to really concentrate in England on this development work, with disc brakes as well as fuel injection, so that I become just as indispensable in my own way to the works as Stirling, for I do not want to be a passenger in the set-up."

I was looking forward to the winter months when I would prove to Maserati that with our development facilities in England and their co-operation we could achieve great success in 1955. I felt confident that with the right approach we could pip Mercedes-Benz and nothing would have given me greater pleasure ; I should have achieved a life ambition for I have always striven to prove that there are other people who can be just as superior in the field of motor-racing as the Germans.

Sylvia and I spent several weeks in Modena whilst the car was being completely rebuilt before being handed back to Stirling as his private property. Maserati intended to return the car as they had received it but in fact we got it back in much better condition. When they took the 250 F. "on the strength" at the Nurburgring it was finished but when the car was returned to us it was almost a brand new one, painted green and complete with the horseshoe ; it had stayed on even when it carried the Italian colours of red because I made it myself and no one dared take it off.

Stirling likes horseshoes. When I arrived in Italy to assist in the building of the Maserati I riveted one on to the body, using brake lining rivets to show seven nails in the horseshoe. Stirling was delighted ; his lucky number is seven and the Standard, Jaguar and Commer transporter all had sevens in their registration numbers.

Two days after arriving back in England Tony and I were stripping down the 250 F. in the Jaguar works at Coventry. Sir William Lyons and his technicians were anxious to study the Italian car from the point of view of design whilst we were delighted with the facilities put at our disposal by Jaguar. With the full co-operation of Maserati the plan was to take out the engine and hand it over to the S.U. factory experts for fuel injection experiments whilst Dunlop worked on the disc brakes. We planned to run the car with fuel injection and disc brakes at the first Goodwood meeting of 1955.

It was arranged, before I returned to London and the Annual Dinner of the British Racing Mechanics, that S.U. would notify me as soon as the necessary fittings and drives had been made, also the manifold, so that I could take part in the experiments. It was the same with the disc brakes ; the Dunlop people would make all the necessary brackets and fittings, then contact us before starting tests.

CHAPTER 35

1955 : HAPPY NEW YEAR ?

Ken Gregory drops a bombshell—Moss, Mercedes and Maserati—
Fuel injection and disc brakes on the 250 F.—
Difference of opinion at Goodwood—Moss versus Behra at Bordeaux—
A " seize up " at Silverstone.

It was Ken Gregory who dropped the bombshell about Stirling joining Mercedes-Benz. When he told me, in the offices of Stirling Moss Limited, I thought to myself, " That's the end. I had better look for another job." I felt bitterly disappointed at that moment ; I loathed motor-racing and everything to do with it and was sorry I had ever gone to Walton for the interview in 1948. With Stirling joining the German team I was not sure that I had anything left for which to fight. That vital incentive to win had been destroyed.

My own small world was toppled by this startling news. I had looked forward so much to racing with Stirling in 1955, within the framework of the Maserati works set-up and against Mercedes-Benz. My feelings were mixed. Partly I was upset because I could not continue my own personal scrap with the Germans—a scrap dating back to the day my country was invaded by their armoured columns—and partly I was bitterly disappointed because I wanted so much to see Stirling beat them as a driver. Let's face it ; I consider that Neubauer signed up Stirling because he was a danger to the German team not because he wanted him as No. 2 to Fangio.

Gregory could see I was upset. " If Stirling and Mercedes want you to do so," he said, " will you join them as technical interpreter and liase between Stirling and the ' works ' personnel ? "

" Well," I replied, " I am working for Stirling and will do what he asks but I would prefer not to work for the Germans."

Gregory did not pursue the topic of Mercedes-Benz but quickly pointed out that, whatever happened, Stirling wanted me to stay on and look after the Maserati. It was his intention to race the car throughout the season, sometimes driving it himself when Mercedes-Benz commitments allowed him to do so, sometimes engaging other drivers to handle it.

It was typical of Stirling that having signed this lucrative contract with Mercedes he should have given some thought to my position in 1955. After all a professional racing driver can never earn sufficient in the limited time he is in the top flight to safeguard his future, and by keeping me on the pay roll with the Maserati, Stirling was committing himself to an expenditure of several thousand pounds during the season with no guarantee of returns.

At home in Woolwich that night I sat staring into the fire and wondering whether I had been too sentimental about motor-racing, whether I should have treated the sport as a straightforward business proposition as Stirling was doing. I realized that it had been a mistake to allow a sentimental ambition to guide me ; here I was, high and dry, with my driver contracted to another team and with nothing for which to fight.

I thought to myself that if other people can treat motor-racing as a strictly business proposition it is about time that I started to think in similar terms.

At the B.R.D.C. Dinner early in December we had a short sharp conversation about the Mercedes contract. " Look Stirling," I said, " I never will approve of this move to Mercedes-Benz. I can co-operate with any other nation but not the Germans."

He knew that I disapproved very strongly about what he had done and we never discussed the matter again. At the same time I had to admit that had I been in Stirling's shoes I would have done exactly as he did.

The Maserati people were just as disappointed as I was. There was no one of the same calibre to replace him. The morale of the whole works —and I know how they felt because I was there early in 1955—from Orsi down to the lowest paid mechanic or floor-sweeper reached a low level and stayed there for the entire season.

In 1954 when there had been work to do in the evenings or at night the Italians never grumbled, and often they worked all night. Moss was tremendously popular but I could see when I went back in 1955 that no one had taken his place in their affections. There was just no more interest in the sport ; Maserati were racing as I used to do with H.W.M., to collect the starting money. When that sort of atmosphere sets in at the works then you might just as well pack up and give the current season a miss.

In my opinion, what Stirling did had far-reaching consequences. Had he stayed with Maserati during 1955 I am convinced there would have been a very different approach to the sport that season by Signor Orsi. He might even have produced the V8 but naturally an organization like Maserati is not going to spend a lot of money on development of such a power unit unless there is someone to drive the car.

People in the Maserati works used to tell me that Stirling joined Mercedes because the Germans had more money and a much larger organization but this was not the case. It was not simply that Neubauer bought out a competitor ; admittedly he was willing to pay a lot of money to obtain the services of Stirling so that he could not compete against the German team, but so far as Stirling was concerned I am sure he went to Mercedes with one object in mind—to gain experience and thus strengthen his chances of one day winning the Championship of the World on a British car. I go so far as to say that, with this patriotic motive to the fore, Stirling " used " Mercedes just as much in 1955 as they " used " him.

After the contract had been signed, Maserati forthwith lost all interest in our experiments with disc brakes and fuel injection. However, towards the end of January, Dunlop and S.U. were ready and I went to the S.U. factory whilst Tony went to Jaguars with the intention of finishing the assembly of the master cylinder for the disc brakes, modifying the bulkhead and painting the chassis. Over at the S.U. factory I made provision for a new rev-counter drive, finished the assembly of the camshafts, fitted a new oil tank and installed the three Weber carburetters in preparation for bench tests.

With the 250 F. engine on the bench we first of all made a run on carburetters, as it was necessary to have some basis of readings for future reference. When I put the engine on normal settings (as it was when I received it from Maserati) it developed only 212 b.h.p.—uncorrected readings—at 7,000 r.p.m. and " pulled " 84 lb. with an exhaust system that was not exactly perfect.

When we made a new manifold to take the fuel injection, the power increase was fantastic ; we pushed up the brake horse-power by as much as 50. It was a most successful experiment but we had no inkling of the troubles we were going to experience with it due to a considerable time-lag as the power came in. It used to do so always at the wrong time.

As a matter of interest the power—with the shop exhaust and two open pipes, and carburetters was as follows :

R.P.M.	LBS.	B.H.P.
2,500	71	63.5
3,000	73	78.5
3,500	78	97.5
4,000	75	107
4,500	84	135
5,000	91	162.5
5,500	95	186.8
6,000	95	203.5
6,500	89	207
7,000	84	210

The tests were carried out with Weber carburetters having choke tubes of 36 millimetres, air bleed jets of 175 and a main jet of 200. The plugs used were 52s, oil pressure was 6 kilograms, oil temperature 90 degrees, water temperature 65 to 90 degrees and the barometer 29.48.

The subsequent tests at S.U. continued throughout February with Tony and me commuting between London and Birmingham. On March 10th the engine was fitted in the chassis at Jaguar and a day or so later we took the car over to the Dunlop factory at Coventry where the final adjustments of the disc brake settings were made. Our next stop was Silverstone where we carried out the first test run of the 1955 season.

I did most of the driving as there was no one else available at that particular time and found the engine very powerful indeed. The entry in my diary tells the story of that first test. " Fuel injection gives fantastic power and disc brakes are amazing, but pedal pressure is too low."

A week later, having returned from his season in the southern hemisphere, Stirling took the car out at Silverstone. He lapped consistently at 1-52 (with a best time of 1-51) and completed 45 laps ; he was delighted with the performance of the car. I could not help thinking what a wonderful season Stirling could have had in 1955 with this fuel injection system and disc brakes on a "works" car.

At Goodwood, on the first day of practice for the Easter Monday

Meeting, Stirling was both pleased with the car and yet dissatisfied. With a similar axle ratio to the one used at the previous Goodwood meeting, in October, 1954, where he had lapped in practice at 1 minute 32.6 seconds, he was getting more than 7,800 revs down Lavant Straight as against 7,200 in October.

This gain of 600 revs was roughly equivalent to 15 m.p.h. down the straight but in spite of the increase in power his lap times dropped to 1 minute 33 seconds. " The car oversteers very badly," he told me irritably, " and does not want to travel in a straight line on the corners ; it goes absolutely haywire."

I was certain that we had too much power and that it was coming in " with a bang " each time he pressed the throttle, for it was extremely difficult to control the car on acceleration through and out of the corners. When I put forward this point of view I was told by Alfred Moss not to be ridiculous. " How can you in effect accuse Stirling of not being able to handle a powerful motor-car ? " he asked. " Is the Maserati any more powerful than the B.R.M. he tried at Monza in 1951.

The argument intensified when Alfred Moss and Stirling suggested that I had altered the track when modifying the chassis at Dunlops to take the disc brakes. Stirling even went so far as to tell me I must have shortened the wheelbase. This was just plain nonsense and I spent hours in the paddock at Goodwood, measuring and checking the dimensions of all the other 250 F. Maseratis. There was, of course, no difference in track or wheelbase but Stirling and his father were still convinced that I had spoiled the handling by some error with my modifications during the winter.

The argument continued at the Fleece Inn, Chichester, where our hosts John and Dorothy Brierley are old friends of Stirling Moss and myself. I am afraid I went to bed in the early hours of the morning still not having convinced Stirling.

In the Formula Libre race, which Peter Collins won with the B.R.M., the Maserati was a real handful and Stirling was unable to keep Salvadori's 250 F. Maserati at bay. Roy was in any case well and truly on form and, on the second lap he " took " Stirling to the undisguised delight of Syd Green and his boys. We finished in third place.

The S.U. fuel injection system relies entirely on atmospheric pressure with metal diaphragms controlling the supply of fuel, and in the twenty-one lap Richmond Trophy—the main event of the day—when one of these diaphragms developed a leak the mixture became weaker and weaker until eventually the engine died completely through lack of fuel.

Undoubtedly the Maserati was tremendously powerful and very difficult to handle. Whatever Stirling was gaining down the straight he was losing on the corners—where he usually excels—because the fuel injection completely altered the handling characteristics of the car. It just went from one extreme to the other, from rather bad understeer to a very positive and dangerous oversteer.

It proves that the torque of an engine can entirely alter the handling of a motor-car. A designer or mechanic can go round and round in circles trying to cure bad handling and blaming the chassis when the fault is not there at all. I knew nothing had been done to the 250 F. and that there was nothing wrong with the chassis, track or wheelbase ; it was obvious to me that the engine was at the root of the trouble.

After the race I was determined to convince Stirling. " Look Stirling," I said, " I'll give you my week's wages if I am wrong. Let's put the carburetters on to-morrow and I will prove it to you."

I won my bet for he was able to lap the Sussex circuit in 1 minute 31 seconds on carburetters as against 1.33 with fuel injection. If carburetters had been used for the race we probably would have won.

It was at Goodwood that Stirling asked me who should drive the Maserati for the 1955 season. I at once suggested Lance Macklin for I knew him well—both as a driver and as a person. " It would be pleasant to work with Lance again," I said, " and I reckon he ought to be able to handle the Maserati without difficulty."

Stirling agreed and it was arranged that Lance would drive the car at Monaco in the first World Championship event of the season.

After Goodwood, Tony and I took the Maserati over to Bordeaux in the Commer transporter, which had been checked over by the Rootes Group and was as good as new. We arrived at Dover at 9.30 p.m. on Tuesday, April 19th, and immediately ran into a host of difficulties with the Customs and Excise. They were very awkward indeed and I wondered, as midnight drew near, whether we should ever get aboard the Night Ferry. However, the various problems were eventually ironed out and by 4 a.m. Wednesday we were clear of Dunkirk. Having spent one night in Paris we arrived in Bordeaux early Thursday evening.

Stirling joined the Mercedes-Benz outfit after the Goodwood meeting, for the Mille Miglia practice sessions, but it was agreed that he could fly back to Bordeaux for the Formula 1 race, and I met him at the airport on Friday. He told me as we drove into town that he would have to return to Italy immediately after the race on Sunday and I could almost see Neubauer issuing a leave pass for 72 hours to the new boy in the team.

Stirling was no longer his own master and it seemed to me that he was more intense, perhaps a little more worried than he had been when we were a singleton outfit. He did not appear to have very much time for anything else other than Mercedes-Benz and I suppose this is understandable. He was obviously preoccupied with the Mille Miglia, which he was to win so brilliantly with " Jenks " of *Motor Sport* as his passenger.

I remember telling myself as I worked on the 250 F. that the 1955 races were going to be dull ones when Stirling was not available to drive and just as dull when he was able to do so. I hoped that, with the scene dominated by Mercedes-Benz, he would make this the first and last race with the Maserati for it was obvious that he did not have a great deal of interest in the car.

During the race, on the twisty Bordeaux street circuit which we knew so well by this time, the Moss Gremlin struck again. Stirling drove remarkably well, harrying the works car of Behra until half distance when one of the fuel tank straps broke. The Maserati team manager must have breathed a sigh of relief when Stirling pulled into the pits, for the last thing he wanted was for Moss the independent—in between commitments with Mercedes-Benz—trouncing the " works " cars.

It took four minutes to make the strap safe but once Stirling got away from the pits he went like a bomb and pulled up to fourth place, only twenty-four seconds behind Behra. He drove at a terrific pace, establishing a new lap record in the process and proving beyond doubt that like most drivers he can go faster when he is not winning.

Stirling is the first to admit this and has always said nothing is more difficult than trying to go fast under the handicap of a comfortable lead. " I like to have something to aim at," he maintains.

We had bad luck again at Silverstone, the second race of that disasterous 1955 season with the green Maserati, when the engine seized solid after only ten laps of the sixty-lap *Daily Express* International Trophy. It was a bitter disappointment for Stirling—and the British public as well—after his epic victory in the Mille Miglia.

He had been given a terrific welcome in England on his return from Brescia and was anxious to cap his success by winning this important Silverstone race ; I think he would have done so if the engine had not over-heated on the first day of practice and dropped a cylinder liner by two-thousandths of an inch.

Naturally we did not appreciate at the time what had happened, for the necessary precision instruments were not available to carry out a check. We knew only that the water system was being pressurized and that it was in some way due to the combustion chamber. There were no water leaks in the chamber but it was nevertheless acting under pressure, pumping air into the water system and forcing water out of the radiator cooling system. The engine ran hotter and hotter and we could not fathom the cause.

Three times during the days preceding the race we had the cylinder head off and carefully lapped it (there is no jointing provided) fully con-vinced that the head was warped. However, the real cause of the trouble was No. 5 cylinder—fractionally lower than the others—but we did not discover this until after the race.

We could not have rectified the trouble before Silverstone, even if we had known what it was ; I could only keep my fingers crossed and hope that we might be able to finish the race, even though running the engine hot and losing water. It was not to be.

The Maserati lost water at a faster rate than I had estimated and it was a waste of time to replenish at the pits at intervals of five laps or so. The engine was forcing out water under pressure at such a rate that there was nothing we could do.

When the car seized up, Stirling abandoned it and walked back to the pits. He was understandably disappointed and I was downright miserable for there is nothing more depressing than knowing a car is not right and being ignorant of the cause. " I am sorry," I said to Stirling, " we did our best but I just don't know what's the matter with the car."

On Sunday night we were on our way to Modena, crossing on the Night Ferry and pushing on, flat out, through Belgium, Germany, Austria and the Brenner. There was only one way to put the trouble right ; a visit to the Maserati works with all the embarrassment it was obviously going to cause on both sides. I knew as soon as we arrived soon after lunch on Wednesday that we should no longer be treated as friends but as customers and on a strictly business basis. The Italians were not hostile, far from it, but they made it clear to me that they were bitterly disappointed at the turn of events.

They gave us full co-operation but we were definitely treated as clients and no longer as independents with factory support. I felt very uncomfortable for I knew that officially the factory did not want to have anything to do with us. Quite frankly we worked there on sufferance and very largely on the friendships I had built up with these Italians when I lived in Modena whilst the 250 F. was being built.

However, both Orsi and Bertocchi told me that if ever Moss drove for them again they would be delighted to have me in the works " set-up." This was good news for there was always the chance that Mercedes would not race in 1956.

We stripped the engine down immediately, had it checked with special precision instruments and found the discrepancy of two-thousandths of an inch. By Wednesday—seven days after our arrival in Modena—the engine was ready for bench testing and having run it in for several hours we set about fitting it in the chassis during the late evening.

With an Italian fitter to help us we worked all night, finally completing the job at 5 a.m. and then snatching three hours sleep before leaving for the Ventimiglia Frontier. Tony drove the Commer and a few kilometres outside Modena I made an entry in my diary, " Tip to engine fitter for working all night 3,000 lires ; bottle of brandy and box of cigars for Mont-calieri 4,200 lire." Do you see what I mean about an expense allowance ? A mechanic must have one.

CHAPTER 36

A TALE OF WOE

Red faces at Monaco—Uhlenhaut tries the disc brakes—
Shattered hopes at Albi—A blow-up at Spa.

At Monaco, with Lance Macklin handling the green Maserati for the first time, we did not even qualify ! On the first day of practice Lance was rather slow, partly due to an unsuitable axle ratio which restricted engine revs to 6,400. His best time was only 2 minutes 1 second as against the fast boys who were lapping in between 1 minute 41.1 seconds (Fangio, Mercedes), and 1 minute 44.9 seconds (Musso, Maserati) ; this did not please the organizers very much. Monaco is, of course, a circuit where the number of starters is restricted and in 1955 there was a field of only twenty cars.

The sad story of the Maserati at Monaco was more or less concluded on Saturday at the final practice session when Macklin revved a cold engine rather too enthusiastically on the way out of the pits. The high oil pressure forced one of the return oil pipes to burst and the circuit was smothered in oil. Sufficient to say that the incident caused a delay of over an hour whilst the oil was being cleared, and this did not please the organizers or Alfred Neubauer for that matter who had been ready since 5 a.m. with his stop-watches and little flags.

When the practice finally started Macklin managed to get down to 1 minute 48.8 seconds, but the Frenchman Pollet, with a Gordini, recorded this time before Lance and was therefore classified as the twentieth starter. The Moss Maserati was undoubtedly in disgrace with the officials of the European Grand Prix.

Nevertheless the car did put in some fast practice laps when Rudolf Uhlenhaut took it round the circuit. Our pit was next door to Mercedes and Stirling pointed out to Uhlenhaut that we had disc brakes on our Maserati ; would he like to drive the car.

The German was delighted for, apart from Hawthorn's Vanwall, no other car was using disc brakes at Monaco.

It was a pleasure to watch Uhlenhaut in action as he went round the tricky street circuit and it convinced me that he is every bit as good in a racing car (or a sports car for that matter) as many of the best *pilotes*. As he pulled into the pits I had to admit to myself that he is a superb driver which is unusual for a man who is also reckoned the finest automotive engineer in the world.

Although I only spoke to him on rare occasions throughout the season he always appeared very reasonable and with a pleasant personality. There is nothing " high hat " about Uhlenhaut and he will always find the time to speak to or give advice to anybody.

I watched the European Grand Prix as a spectator and standing next to me in our pit was the personal mechanic of Fangio, an Argentine of Italian descent who travels round the circuits with the World Champion. I don't think Mercedes paid him anything and he probably drew his salary from Fangio.

I believe Nuvolari, Farina and Sommer all had personal mechanics, engaged for the psychological effect by the *equipe* concerned. On the Continent there is a very strong feeling that a mechanic who starts with a driver and watches his climb to fame should stay with him wherever he goes. This was a point of view put to me by Bertocchi when I arrived in Modena after the Silverstone race. But, as I explained to him, even if the Germans would allow an ex-Pole to join them I would never agree to do so—unless Moss absolutely insisted ; then I would go because he was my boss.

I had to have some interest in the Monaco race so kept a stopwatch on Stirling. He was running very close to Fangio—only a few seconds separating the two German cars—and I decided to have some fun at the expense of Fangio's man. On several occasions I turned to him and said, " Fangio will have to watch out if he does not want Moss to pass him."

Then, after Moss had turned in one very fast lap : " Stirling gained a little there you know, not much—just a tenth-of-a-second."

The poor mechanic looked dubiously at his stop-watch and I could see he was really worried. He kept waving at Fangio to go faster and Stirling must have noticed him doing this, for after the race when I told him what I had done he said at once, " That was the chap who was always waving him on ; I never could make out who it was, especially coming from your pit."

I believe that this mechanic does in fact control Fangio to a certain extent, irrespective of signals given by team managers, and I am told that when the pace is really hot and Fangio is in danger of being beaten, the great Argentine driver takes more notice of the signals from his mechanic than of those from the pit staff. Fangio certainly seemed to speed up in the Monaco race when as a result of my leg-pulling the mechanic urged him on.

I learned a little about Mercedes team discipline when I tried to get in touch with Stirling at his hotel one evening. The hotel had been fully booked by Mercedes-Benz and all calls had to be vetted by Neubauer otherwise the receptionist refused to put them through. Finally I succeeded in contacting Stirling but before I had a chance to tell him who it was he spoke quickly into the receiver : " I am just going off to bed—right now." It was 10.30 and he must have thought it was Neubauer or Uhlenhaut on the other end of the line.

I thought his driving at Monaco was immaculate. I was not surprised for I had expected that it would be so, and if he had been handling a " works " Maserati I reckon he would have passed Fangio. I felt this throughout the season ; had he driven as No. 1 for Signor Orsi in 1955 I am sure he would have had a brilliant year although it must be admitted that he would not have gained such valuable experience. As No. 2 to Fangio he learned a great deal as did Peter Collins the following year. Nevertheless I am sure there would have been certain races during the season that Stirling could have won for Maserati.

Stirling was naturally disappointed that our car had not even qualified at Monaco especially after its mediocre performance earlier in the season. It had been a particularly expensive business having the engine repaired after Silverstone, and taking all things into consideration Tony and I were just as fed up about it as was Stirling.

From Monaco we moved on to Albi for the Formula 1 Grand Prix. Macklin practised on Friday and lapped in 1 minute 20.2 seconds, only one-tenth of a second slower than Louis Rosier who put up fastest practice time. The organizers decided to use only part of the Albi Circuit and lap speeds worked out very closely to Silverstone. We therefore decided to change the axle ratio to 12/18 and 46/14 and having done this felt fairly confident about the outcome of the race.

A plan of campaign was worked out with Macklin on the lines that he would get into position behind the leader as soon as possible and stay there until the last few laps before moving up to challenge. The plan worked quite well and Macklin was second for part of the race until he suddenly noticed the engine overheating and called in at the pits, afraid to continue in case of a blow-up. To our dismay we found one of the three engine-bearers had broken off ; the engine was more or less hanging from the two remaining ones !

The breakage had been caused by misalignment at the factory. Every Maserati engine is different because the machining is not carried out in jigs and there are certain discrepancies in assembly. In our case, as the engine had seized solid at Silverstone it was decided at Modena that we should have a different crankcase, but unfortunately there was not sufficient time available between races to give careful consideration to the question of alignment.

When the engine was fitted in the chassis for Monaco we found that it was straining one of the bearers but it was no use worrying ; there was no time to change the housing and we just had to hope for the best. There was no indication of trouble at Monaco but at Albi the electron cracked, and once the housing had broken Macklin lost all the oil and ran some of the big-ends as well, which unfortunately we did not notice at the time.

Macklin drove very well at Albi although at times he appeared to be a little slow. He had not lost any of his skill since the H.W.M. days and I felt inclined to agree with the French enthusiasts who, as far back as 1951, argued that Macklin had a better style of driving than Stirling Moss.

I am sure that if Macklin had really tried hard in those days he could have equalled Moss on almost any circuit ; the difference was very little. He had never had an opportunity of racing a Formula 1 car prior to 1955 and I was hoping for a good season with him. However, luck was against us for the car was never right when he drove it and, of course, there was the Mercedes accident at Le Mans in which Macklin was involved.

His wife summed up his driving very well after the Albi race. "All he needs is a bit of pepper because he has got the style, knows how to drive and is very safe."

Actually, I think Macklin played it perhaps a little too safe at Monaco and Albi. He had not taken into account the considerable increase in speeds since his races for H.W.M., in so much as no driver these days can play it as safe as he would like if he wants to be successful. The margin is narrowing every day and drivers who have been in the game a number of years have got to appreciate this vital factor.

A week after Albi we were due to race the Maserati in the Belgian Grand Prix at Spa. It had been arranged with the organizers that a Belgian would drive the car and our old friend Johnny Claes was engaged. We set off for Spa as soon as possible because I had decided to do all the repairs to the engine there, hoping to borrow spares from the works organization.

When Tony and I got the engine out we found several big-ends gone whilst one of the connecting rods, which must have been running very hot, had blued. I had spare bearings but no connecting rods and unfortunately Maserati were unable to help when they arrived with the " works " cars. However, when I showed the blued con. rod to Bertocchi he did not seem very concerned.

" That's perfectly O.K." he said, " all you do is just polish it and clean out the blue. By polishing it you will relieve the stresses again."

I did as he suggested and we managed to assemble the car in time for the second day of practice. I was able to arrange for Claes, who had never previously driven a Maserati, to " run in " the car soon after day-break and get used to it at the same time.

I drove round the Spa circuit twice at a reasonable speed to give it the basic " run-in " and then asked Claes to continue. He lapped three or four times at quite comfortable speeds but never completed the fifth lap and we found him on the back leg of the circuit with a big pool of oil under the car. The con. rod, which had become brittle at Albi, overheated and broke like glass. The whole bottom end then fell out and that was the end of our race. The material must have hardened, for it just packed up.

I enjoyed watching the Belgian Grand Prix, the second championship event with Fangio and Moss in the same team, and it was a pleasure to see them going round, no more and no less than four or five seconds apart. It was the Monaco story all over again and how I wished Moss had been leading the " works " Maseratis.

The 1955 season must have cost Stirling a fortune with the green 250 F. Nevertheless he was always very reasonable on those occasions when we met, sometimes before and sometimes after a big race but rarely for more than a few minutes. He treated me as team manager for his own *equipe* and it was embarrassing to say the least that I had to ask him for more and more funds every time we met.

Spa was the second blow-up. What a season ! Trying to finish Silverstone and blowing up, not even getting the starting money at Monaco or Spa, not finishing at Albi—and blowing the engine up at Spa as well. He was really very good about our misfortunes. After all, apart from the cost of repairs, it takes on an average about £70 to cover the travelling expenses of two mechanics, and petrol for the lorry, to move from circuit to circuit. I have found over the years that this estimate has not varied much. Stirling took it all in a most understanding way and never lost his temper.

CHAPTER 37

SAME CAR—DIFFERENT DRIVERS

A spin for Macklin at Aintree—Hawthorn drives the 250 F. to victory at the Crystal Palace—Gerard excels at Charterhall—Wrong ratio loses Snetterton race—Moss versus Parnell at Aintree—In American colours.

We had our work cut out to get the 250 F. ready for the British Grand Prix at Aintree. The Maserati people were very helpful and as misfortune followed misfortune they became more and more sympathetic. At Spa, just before Claes took the car out on the circuit, the Head Mechanic—who knew I was not at all happy about the con. rod—said to me, " If we finish to-day's practice without trouble, we may be able to lend you a spare engine for the race." Fate was, however, against us for not only did we blow-up, but Behra blew up a factory car and had to be given the spare engine.

At Modena, in the works once again, we stripped the 250 F. and fitted a replacement engine. As the Moss Maserati was dealt with on a strictly business basis, Tony and I did practically all the work ourselves in order to save expense. In any case Maserati could not have helped for they only had a limited number of first-class fitters and these chaps were busy on the "works" cars, preparing them for the British classic.

Eventually the Maserati was ready and we left for England and our home base at Tring, where Alfred Moss suggested we changed the colour of the car. "After three blow-ups," he said, "it is about time we had some other colour than green."

I suggested red and white, the Polish national colours, and Stirling quite liked the idea but Alfred Moss insisted on grey. Perhaps he thought that in the colours of a battleship we might be able to bulldoze our way through to victory !

When it had been painted in a ghastly shade of grey, John Morgan, the Secretary of the British Automobile Racing Club, was so horrified that he asked us to repaint it in some shade of green for the British Grand Prix. And so, with more than enough work to do anyway, I spent three hours after the final Aintree practice session slapping green distemper all over the car, having paid a local garage hand £1 to help me.

During practice I was rather disappointed at the time of 2 minutes 9.8 seconds recorded by Macklin, for the car was well known on the northern circuit and Moss held the lap record of 2 minutes 0.6 seconds, recorded in October, 1954. As a matter of fact neither Moss nor Fangio, driving for Mercedes, could better this and it was not until the second day of practice that Moss was able to beat the old record (by only two-tenths of a second) and Fangio to equal it. Macklin was able to get down to

2 minutes 8.4 seconds but in my opinion had been badly shaken by his shocking experience at Le Mans and was right off form.

In the actual race the fastest lap of 2 minutes 0.4 seconds was recorded by Moss—two-tenths of a second better than his 1954 best—and I reckon he could have done as well with the " works " Maserati on this Aintree circuit. In fact had he been driving a " works " car I cannot help feeling that he would still have beaten Fangio and probably by a larger margin. This was one of the 1955 races that he could and should have won as No. 1 driver for Maserati.

Our 250 F., resplendent in its green distemper, finished eighth after an excursion into the straw bales at Tatts Corner. At the time Macklin was travelling comfortably in seventh position, which was not too bad, and the odds were that we should finish fifth or sixth because cars were packing up left, right and centre. However, in a car that held the lap record, he was not going quickly enough for me and in agreement with Ken Gregory I decided to give him the faster signal.

As Macklin passed the pits I held out the board with the red strip at the top but he never completed the lap. He ran out of road at Tatts, clouted the straw bales and then walked to the pits in a leisurely fashion. When he arrived some minutes later he complained that I should not have speeded him up.

" Well, there is no point in arguing," I said, and then to Ken Gregory, " Can you look up the regulations ? Are we allowed to give assistance and push-start the car outside the starting area ? "

Apparently we could, so I shouted to Macklin, " Come on Lance, we can argue the question afterwards. We want to get you moving."

Macklin, Tony and I sprinted to the car and we were already pushing it as Macklin settled in the cockpit. He rejoined the race and came home eighth, eleven laps behind the leader, which is where he would probably have finished if I had not speeded him up and he had not run out of road. We must have lost a good ten minutes whilst he walked to the pits from Tatts after his incident to tell me how stupid I was.

The car finished in an immaculate state ; there was not a spot of oil or dirt anywhere. Driving back to Tring on Sunday I thought to myself what a crying shame it was that Stirling had not handled the car and given Mercedes something to think about.

I must admit that 1955 was a miserable season for me. There was not the same incentive to win, the same target to aim at, that had been the driving force of *Equipe* Moss. Whilst appreciating that Stirling could not have done any different and fully aware of the fact that I had advised him to join a " works " team as far back as August, 1954, I felt more and more, as the season progressed, that I had been abandoned in mid-stream.

As soon as the Mercedes-Benz contract was signed I was pushed into the background and there was no longer that close relationship between Stirling and myself, a relationship that had developed over the years since I met him for the first time at Odiham airfield. It was understandable that if I would not, or could not, go with him to Mercedes-Benz I should become a back-number but I was not very happy about it.

I should of course have parted company with Stirling at the end of the 1954 season rather than continue to race the green Maserati, for I knew what it was costing him to run the car and this knowledge made me feel uncomfortable. It would not have been so bad if the 250 F. had put up a better performance especially during a season when all of us wanted so much to humble Neubauer and Mercedes-Benz.

It was a strange coincidence that our old rival Mike Hawthorn should give the green Maserati its first victory in 1955. A few days before the Crystal Palace meeting on Saturday, July 30th, Ken Gregory telephoned me : " Mike Hawthorn is driving the Maser. at the Palace ; give him all the help you can."

I was delighted for the " Farnham Flyer " would certainly get the best out of the car and, quite apart from this, I should be able to carry my feud with Tony Vandervell into the enemy camp. I have always enjoyed " dicing " as an independent with the Vandervell outfit but don't ask me why. Maybe it is because the Vanwalls have a millionaire behind them and it is always fun as it were to twist the tail of the lion.

At practice on Friday, Harry Schell in the Vanwall was one-and-a-half seconds faster than Mike and this is quite a big margin on a small circuit like the Palace. I spoke to Mike after the practice and asked him whether he could go any quicker.

" The car is going perfectly well," he replied, " and that's the best I can do ; I just don't know how it would be possible to knock off that deficit."

We followed up the conversation with a conference in the back of the Commer when I asked him questions about the circuit. I wanted to find out exactly how many gear-changes he was making on each lap and where he was making them, for I had the germ of an idea that might topple the ever-confident and irritatingly over-confident Vanwall outfit. " Is it O.K. with you ? " I asked, " if I lower the axle ratio and also take one leaf out of the rear spring, thus altering the handling characteristics of the car."

Mike was intrigued. " What's the idea ? " he questioned.

" Well," I explained, " I reckon we can run this race with only five gallons of fuel in the tank instead of the normal load of twenty gallons but the car will not handle unless I take a leaf out of the cantilever. The soft-ness of the springing should compensate for lack of weight at the rear end. Then if the axle ratio is dropped you can use second gear for the start and then only third and top for the rest of the race."

I could see that Mike was with me. " You will have to watch the revs coming down the hill to the grandstands to avoid over-revving and you might even have to lift your foot," I continued, " but if it comes to it, then use 200 revs more than normal and go to 7,800. I am not going to give in easily to Harry Schell and the Vanwall."

Mike smiled. " I know how you feel, Alf," he said. " You change the ratio and do all the other things you want to do and I will do my best."

He won the first heat by 1.6 seconds from Salvadori (Maserati) which delighted me as much as it surprised the Vanwall outfit, especially as our Maserati also set up the fastest lap in 1 minute 42 seconds. However, Schell won the second heat quite easily and I could see that he and Tony Vandervell were confident of victory in the final.

Stirling was the starter and when he dropped the flag Mike fairly rocketed off the line in second gear and left the rest of the field, including Schell, in his exhaust smoke.   He went round Ramp Bend first and no one ever caught him.   Try as he might, Schell could not close a gap of just under two seconds although he certainly tried hard.   I was delighted when Mike won by 1.6 seconds and established a new circuit record, this time of 1 minute 3.4 seconds (78.93 m.p.h.).   Gregor Grant had some nice things to say about us in *Autosport* the following Friday :—

" Hawthorn's immense skill together with a well prepared car had defeated the much fancied Schell-Vanwall combination."

When Mike had completed his lap of honour he was presented with a large silver trophy which was immediately filled with champagne and just as quickly emptied over the bonnet of the Maserati.   The trophy was then filled again and Mike handed it to me so that I could have the first drink. It was a very thoughtful gesture on his part and I consider it one of the nicest compliments paid to me in nearly ten years of motor-racing.   We left Crystal Palace in the best of moods.

So far as I am concerned Mike Hawthorn is one of the best, once you get to know him, and the Crystal Palace incident proved to me that he has an unselfish nature.   I think I could work with him as well as I used to do with Stirling Moss and it would be an enjoyable partnership.

I noticed during practice that he was rather a happy-go-lucky sort of person and quite resigned to finishing second in the race—although his practice laps were faster than the best times previously recorded by Stirling with the same car.

As with Stirling it is possible to discuss with Mike Hawthorn where a fraction of a second can be knocked off on this corner, another fraction on that.   His willingness to talk about the Crystal Palace problem convinced me that I could co-operate with him and go places ; on the other hand, he would never have suggested to me all the work involved in altering the axle ratio and modifying the springing.

The Palace race emphasized how a car can be altered for a particular circuit and how it can make all the difference between winning or losing. Over two years I got to know that Maserati and what sort of tricks I could play with it ; the Palace race was a simple instance of success as the result of a driver and mechanic discussing the problem and resolving completely to alter the handling characteristics of a car.   It meant taking quite a risk but Hawthorn trusted me and was confident that I could do the job without endangering him.   It does show how important is that close co-operation and mutual trust between driver and mechanic.   However, what had given me the most satisfaction at the Palace was beating the Vandervell outfit.

A week later the Maserati was entered at Charterhall with Bob Gerard as driver.   I was pleased to have the opportunity of working with yet another new *pilote*, particularly one of the calibre of Gerard.   I had, of course, seen and spoken to him around the circuits and knew him as a fast but steady driver always game in the face of heavy odds.   Having watched his B.R.M.–baiting tactics on several occasions I classified him as above average but never credited him as a potential top flight championship driver.

It was the Charterhall meeting that changed my opinion and I am fully

Monte Carlo, 1955. Outside the Diodato at Rocquebrun, Alf Francis modified the Commer to the extent of making a stand to support the runners so as to have plenty of elbow room underneath the 250 F. It should be noted that at this time Dunlop disc brakes and wheels are fitted to the car.

The 'works' of the 250 F. showing the interesting layout of the front suspension, engine and chassis where simplicity is the keynote. Compared with the other cars on which he has worked the 250 F. Maserati is a firm favourite with Alf Francis. He modified the engine successfully in 1954, having experienced heavy wear on the camshaft and cam followers, by hardchroming the cam followers (adding 2/1000-of-an-inch of hard chrome) and modifying the delivery of oil to the points of contact on the camshaft and cam followers. Undue wear was never experienced again whereas previously a new camshaft and cam followers had been necessary after every race of full G.P. distance.

Lucozade tastes just as good in New Zealand as anywhere else. Moss has just won the 1956 New Zealand G.P. in spite of a leaking fuel line and Alf insisted on Stirling having a soft drink rather than the champagne produced by the organizers. Says Alf. " Champagne and petrol fumes don't mix and anyway Stirling is teetotal."

Equipe Francis. Mrs. Sylvia Francis, who designed and painted the cover for this book, rarely visits a motor race. Here, with Alf's daughter Krysia (a name which is a Polish abbreviation of Christine) she is at the Crystal Palace. Says Alf, " Few people can have had such an understanding wife. For nine years she has been a motor-racing widow."

convinced—even to-day—that if Bob Gerard did not persist in driving a British car and bought himself a Maserati or Ferrari we should see him as a challenger in the World Championship series as was Moss in 1954.

I learned from his mechanics that he refuses to buy a foreign car, that he either drives British or nothing, but if he was given the same opportunity as Moss and Hawthorn I am sure he could establish himself in their class in a very short space of time. It was a pity that so few people (the crowd was little more than ten thousand) saw Gerard in action with a Formula 1 G.P. car. It should have been Silverstone or Goodwood.

The practice times proved to me that once he was in the car and the axle ratio was right he could really go places. In making the fastest time of 1 minute 23.8 seconds he unofficially beat the circuit record of 1 minute 24 seconds established by Wharton in the 16 cylinder B.R.M. Although the Bourne car was not reliable it went very quickly when it did go, and it was really something to watch Gerard going just as fast on his first outing with the Moss Maserati. He looked perfectly at home and in fact took to the Maserati like a duck takes to water.

During the heat and final of the *Daily Record* International Trophy, Gerard was more than satisfied with the 250 F. and thought it handled remarkably well. He won both races, setting up a new circuit record in the final—which he shared with Louis Rosier (Maserati)—of 1 minute 23.5 seconds (85.92 m.p.h.), half a second better than the previous best by Wharton in the B.R.M.

Unfortunately the very bumpy circuit caused one of the shock-absorber brackets to break off in the final but even with this handicap Gerard still managed to win from Horace Gould, also driving a 250 F. Maserati, by quite a handsome margin. Without wishing to belittle the performance of Gould in any way I must make the point that whilst Horace had driven his 250 F. on several occasions, Gerard had never handled one previously. Gould was considered quite a fast driver but Gerard just left him standing.

At Leicester, in Bob Gerard's garage, we prepared the Maserati for Stirling to drive at Snetterton the following week-end. There was a slight radiator leak caused by the roughness of the Scottish circuit that had to be repaired and we had a spot of trouble with the clutch. On examination we found one of the plates broken, quite a common occurrence with the 250 F.

As Stirling had not driven the car since Silverstone he wanted to practise as much as possible, so on Thursday we had our own session on the bumpy Snetterton Circuit. The handling characteristics of the Mercedes and Maserati are very different, the former having considerable understeer and the latter tending to oversteer. From the driver's point of view this extreme difference can be dangerous and Stirling lapped consistently at 1 minute 47 seconds which was rather on the slow side. I was hoping he would put up a better time in the official practice session on Friday.

However, he could only manage third fastest, behind the Vanwalls of Schell and Wharton, and this worried me for I was anxious to have another go at Tony Vandervell. Our best time was two seconds faster than the previous day but still slower than Wharton (1-43.8) and Schell (1-44.0).

After the practice I had a chat with Stirling and we decided to change the axle ratio for a higher one and to fit 46/14 and 11/16. We both agreed that this should give an improvement in speed where it was needed—at the top end. It meant working all night and dismantling the entire back axle, for the reduction gears had to be changed as well as the pinion gears. We had no garage or pit at Snetterton and had to use the Commer. I can tell you I was pretty well whacked by the time the job was completed in the early hours of the morning.

During the 25-lap Formula 1 race, which Harry Schell won for Vandervell, Stirling was rather slow and found himself having to fight a terrific duel with Jack Brabham's Cooper-Bristol for third place. The Australian "diced" with Stirling until four laps from the end when the rear-engined Cooper spun off at the hairpin and Stirling went through to finish third, behind Wharton's Vanwall.

There was nothing wrong with the Maserati engine and the car put up a mediocre performance simply because the wrong axle ratio had been fitted. I am afraid the only occasion we raced together in months as *Equipe* Moss ended on an unhappy note. Both the Vanwalls had trounced us and my face was very red as I drove away from Snetterton and the jubilant Vandervell outfit just as soon as I could get the Maserati securely stowed in the Commer.

The only consolation was that Stirling had put up fastest lap during his "dice" with Brabham and it does underline the driving skill of Moss. Even with the wrong axle ratio he was faster round that bumpy circuit than either of the Vanwalls.

We tried again with the Maserati at Aintree on September 3rd and it was a most exciting race. In practice Reg Parnell in the aerodynamic "works" Connaught made fastest time and Stirling could only manage second fastest. His best lap, in 2 minutes 5.8 seconds, was no less than five seconds slower than his record time with that same car on this circuit, and only four seconds faster than Macklin's best at the British Grand Prix Meeting.

I do not consider that Stirling was a formidable opponent either at Snetterton or Aintree simply because it was not a feasible proposition for him to change cars, from Mercedes to Maserati, and then expect to drive the Italian car as he had done in the past. As I have explained they were entirely different in their handling characteristics and there was a considerable variation in the torque of the two engines. It just did not pay off when Stirling tried to go really fast in the Maserati.

Nevertheless, he had a terrific "do" with Parnell who went into the lead with the Connaught as soon as the flag fell. Reg went like a dingbat—in my opinion few people can go better than the Derby man when he is on form—and held Moss at bay for thirteen close-fought laps. Then, with only four laps to go, the Maserati went out of the race in a cloud of smoke : we had burned a piston ! This let Roy Salvadori through with his 250 F. into second place and, with only two laps remaining, the unfortunate Parnell ran a big-end and a surprised Salvadori was the winner.

We left Aintree immediately after the race for I intended to catch the Night Ferry from Dover on Sunday. Stirling had promised John Fitch that he could drive the Maserati in the Italian Grand Prix the following week-end and we had precisely five days in which to reach Modena, repair the engine, then get the car to Monza for the Friday practice session.

An entry that I made in my diary after the Aintree race is an interesting sidelight on the expense of racing a G.P. car. " Received from S.M. 200,000 lire to pay Maserati ; also 100,000 lire to pay expenses." At the rate of exchange current at the time it represented £175.

Once clear of the Night Ferry, and thank goodness we had no trouble with the Customs, we thrashed the Commer until I thought she would blow up. I think Tony and I, taking turns, drove the transporter harder than ever before and if the Rootes Group knew half of what that engine went through they would never believe it. We drove all day Monday and all night as well reaching St. Jean du Maurienne at 8 a.m. Tuesday and Turin by lunch-time. That evening we were in Modena, a little over 36 hours after clearing the customs at Dunkirk.

We had only two-and-a-half days to work on the car, so after a bath and a shave at the Europa, Tony and I set about taking the engine to pieces that night. We were fighting a losing battle because Maserati were so busy getting their own cars ready for the Italian classic that they could not even lend us one mechanic to help. Even had they done so it would have been a physical impossibility to get out the engine, rebore it and then fit new pistons in the time available. Nevertheless we still had a real problem on our hands for when the piston burned at Aintree a big groove had been cut in the cylinder liner. There was only one solution ; improvise and bodge up.

We found another piston with an equivalent compression ratio, and using a scraper I cleaned out the sharp edges of the groove and reassembled the engine. By the time we had completed the job and painted the car white and blue so that Fitch could race under the American national colours it was Thursday night. As we turned in at the Europa I reminded Tony that the last time we had slept a full night was before the Aintree race, over a week previously.

" You don't have to tell me," he replied, " I reckon we must be lunatics actually to enjoy motor-racing."

The funny thing is that people do enjoy motor-racing and the tougher it gets the more they like it. As I have said before there is tremendous satisfaction in meeting and overcoming a challenge and the more challenges there are the more we like it even though we may moan about it at the time.

On Friday afternoon John Fitch took the white and blue Maserati out on the Monza autodrome. We knew the circuit from A to Z by now and no time was wasted fitting the correct axle ratio ; with 44/16 and 12/17, Fitch was going up to 7,300 revs on the fast stretches. However, he was not very happy because he felt he was sticking out of the car too much in the air-stream. He is a big chap and insisted on me fitting a larger wind-screen which I did on Friday night.

On Saturday we practised again but I did not expect Fitch to record any startling times ; in fact we were resigned to finishing the race rather than challenging any of the really fast boys. After all, we could not hope to beat the German or Italian factory cars unless they all blew up.

By this stage of the season the Moss Maserati was sadly lacking in development. Throughout the year, whilst the " works " cars had been developed and modified, we had remained stationary. Not one single modification had been made to the car whereas the previous year Signor Orsi had ensured that our 250 F. progressed at the same rate as the " works " cars.

It does prove my point that it is really a waste of time to race against the factory with a view to winning races. You can start and you can finish, with maybe place money every now and then to supplement the starting money, but your chances of ever winning a major event are practically nil.

However, Fitch did not put up the slowest practice time by any means, for Horace Gould (Maserati) and Lucas (Gordini) were behind him on the starting grid. As a matter of interest our best time was 3 minutes 3.1 seconds as against the best time by a " works " Maserati, driven by Behra, of 2 minutes 50.1 seconds.

Horace Gould asked me to run his pit as well as mine and after a conference my suggestion was agreed that we raced the two Maseratis with only a half tank of fuel. It meant making a refuelling stop but this was preferable to running the hazard of a terrific bump on the surface of one of the bankings where the de Dion tubes and rear axles of all the cars were taking a hammering. I reckoned it was better to accept the delay of a pit stop rather than run the risk of being put out of the race by circumstances beyond our control.

Gould drove remarkably well and enjoyed himself immensely, as of course he always does in the cockpit of a racing car. He is another Harry Schell, always ready for a spot of clowning, but on this occasion treated the Italian classic with due respect and impressed a lot of people with his handling of the car. Unfortunately, soon after he had made his refuelling stop, part of the concrete banking broke up and Gould ran over this section immediately afterwards and took off the entire base of the sump. That was the end of his Italian Grand Prix.

John Fitch finished ninth after two pit stops, one for fuel and the other for tyres. The car went very well and it was a great satisfaction to Tony and I that after such a series of misfortunes we were classified as finishers in this last big race of the 1955 season.

Fitch was quite happy with his placing, four laps behind the leaders, but I consider him a better sports car driver than a Grand Prix one. He is a very nice person and could almost be described as the American Peter Whitehead. He does not push himself or the car too hard and is one of those sensible drivers who know their limitations and do not try to exceed them.

CHAPTER 38

NEW ZEALAND INTERLUDE

It amazed me that the Maserati had finished the Italian Grand Prix because the piston slap was about 20 thou. ! Back in Modena once again new cylinder liners were fitted, as well as a new and stronger type crankshaft, and new type bearings. Having stripped down the car I found the gearbox housing cracked and this also had to be replaced. Generally speaking the 250 F. was completely rebuilt ; gearbox, suspension links, engine, bodywork. Nothing was overlooked.

By the end of September I had returned to our home base at Tring and a few days later Stirling put an interesting proposition to me. " Would you like to go to New Zealand ? " he asked. " They want me to race at Auckland after Christmas. If you like the idea I think I can make it a paying proposition."

" Well," I replied, " it sounds very nice but I shall have to ask my wife whether she minds me being away from home for such a long period."

That night I told Sylvia about the proposed trip and she did not object so I telephoned Stirling next morning.

" Good," he said, " I am pleased to hear it. It will make a pleasant change for both of us."

I was looking forward to racing again, just the two of us, as we had done so often in 1953 and 1954 with *Equipe* Moss. I could not think of any more pleasant way of finishing the 1955 season, which had been rather depressing and miserable in more ways than one.

However, I could not see the Auckland race re-establishing a close partnership between Stirling and myself. Although I knew Mercedes were not racing again in 1956 I felt that my work for Stirling was finished and quite frankly could see no earthly reason why he should keep me on the pay-roll for another season.

He would certainly join one of the Italian "works'" teams, probably Maserati, for there was no sense in his racing our own 250 F. which by the start of the 1956 season would be hopelessly obsolete. By the same argument there would not be much object in racing it—with different drivers— as we had done in 1955.

If Stirling joined Maserati there would still be no place for me, even though Orsi and Bertocchi had made it clear they would like to have me back. The trouble was that whereas it would, I think, have been possible for me to prepare Stirling's car within the framework of the works' organization in 1955 it was no longer possible in 1956.

We had seen very little of each other during the 1955 season and our relationship had not been a very close one, but I knew that if he joined Maserati we should have to work together very closely indeed if I was to look after the car in my way, which on occasions would probably upset

Bertocchi ; and I knew very well that neither Stirling nor Orsi would want this.

Let me put it like this ; in 1955 Stirling and I would have presented a united front but in 1956 I should have been on my own. So I decided that if he went to Maserati it would be without me. Furthermore, I must confess that I can only work happily if I have full responsibility for a particular project. This had been the case during the 1954 season, with Stirling an " independent," but it would not be like that within the framework of the works set up. My insistance on wanting to run the show, in the case of Stirling's car, would have caused too much trouble.

Taking all the above factors into consideration I had no doubt in my own mind before I left for Auckland that 1956 would sooner or later see the end of our association.

Early in October, having crated the spares and sent them separately, I took the 250 F. to the Albert Docks in London and saw her loaded aboard a ship for New Zealand. The Maser. was stowed on the deck with several private cars. If one crates a car one expects to find it turned upside-down, whereas if it is stored upright without any form of protective covering the body may be dented but that is about all.

I sailed for Wellington, via Curacao and the Panama Canal, on November 25th on R.M.S. *Rangitata* and when I tell you that my old friend Stan Ellsworth was on board (Peter Whitehead having also been invited to race at Auckland) you will understand why I had an uneasy feeling that the trip might be a disasterous one from the point of view of finance. It was. We had a wonderful time on the *Rangitata* even though we travelled tourist class, four to a cabin and next to a laundry that could not exactly be described as " the silent service."

Our cabin was about 8 ft. x 8 ft. and there was one wash basin. In the morning while one of us dressed the second man washed whilst the third and fourth stayed in bed. Nevertheless we had five exciting and restful weeks, with drinks and cigarettes ridiculously cheap, the poker dice always available at the bar and a generous expense account from Stirling Moss and Peter Whitehead respectively.

We arrived in Wellington at the end of December and left the same night for Auckland, some four hundred miles away. On arrival the President of the Automobile Club of New Zealand drove us to our hotel and the following day there was a cocktail party given by the Press where we were introduced to several competitors and mechanics who had already arrived from different parts of the world.

The New Zealanders are friendly, hospitable people and they have a lovely country. If ever I emigrate that is where I shall settle, for they are modern without going to extremes and the standard of living is high. After the Auckland Grand Prix I would willingly have retired from motor-racing and settled down in New Zealand with a small business built around a petrol pump station. My wife would have been delighted for I should have stopped travelling and become a normal human being once again.

I was prevented from doing so by the lack of ready cash, which is the penalty of becoming a motor-racing mechanic. I have never been able to save anything in spite of the fact that I do not smoke or drink heavily and have yet to meet a mechanic who can put a reasonable amount aside each week with an eye to the future.

Perhaps we ought to have a Mechanics Union to protect our interests in a sport which has become such a strictly business proposition. Starting money, place money, contributions from oil and tyre companies ; it has always been so but it seems to me that slowly but surely the old sporting atmosphere is going by the board, although I should like to think I am wrong.

The Maserati had already arrived in Auckland but to my consternation there was no sign of the spares or tools ; I did not even have any sparking plugs. We were signed with Lodge and as Whitehead and Gaze were racing on Champion there was no question of borrowing from them.

As the day of the race drew near I became more and more worried, particularly as Stirling was due in Auckland by air only a day prior to the commencement of official practice. When he arrived, with Parnell and Whitehead, I met him at the airport and drove him to the Tasman Hotel. In the car I broke the sad news. " We have no spares at all," I said. " We shall have to do the race with one set of wheels, no tools, plugs or jacks."

Stirling took it remarkably calmly and having got this piece of bad news off my chest I felt better. However, a motor-cycling enthusiast had read in the local paper of my predicament, and he brought a suitcase full of old plugs to the hotel. To my surprise several of them were absolutely O.K. Sufficient to say the car went well enough in practice to put up fastest time and win pole position on the front row of the grid.

As soon as the flag dropped in the 210 mile New Zealand Grand Prix, Tony Gaze went into the lead with his Ferrari but Stirling overtook him on the first lap and from then onwards just pressed on. By half distance he had already lapped everyone, including the second man, and as the race drew to a close was lapping them for a second time.

As we always experienced bad luck during the final nine laps I kept my fingers crossed for the outcome of this race in the Southern Hemisphere and was not entirely surprised when the Gremlin caught up with us.

There were frantic signals from Stirling as he went past the pits and I knew it was fuel trouble for he was pointing backwards at the tank. I also knew that I did not have any equipment for refuelling and asked Stan Ellsworth, who was looking after Tony Gaze's car as well as Peter White-head's Ferrari, if he would lend me some churns. Quite rightly Stan refused, " Sorry Alf, I dare not in case one of my cars has to come in for the same reason."

However, I had already made good friends in Auckland and I gave the wink to one of them who was helping me. He quickly nipped behind the pits whilst Stan was otherwise engaged and pinched a couple of churns which we filled with our fuel Then I put a signal out for Stirling.

I was not sure whether or not he wanted fuel but when the car came in and I had a look at a leakage which had developed in the fuel line (a broken suction pipe) it was obvious the Maserati could not have continued for more than eight or ten minutes. Fuel was spraying out of the fracture at such a rate that I estimated a replenishment of ten gallons would be required.

Eight laps, at an average of 1 minute 30.5 seconds per lap remained, and

I knew that for ten gallons to escape through the fracture would take longer than twelve minutes.

Stirling went away after a thirty second pit stop, and although he had lost a considerable part of his lead, he still finished twenty-three seconds ahead of Tony Gaze's Ferrari. It was an incredible performance by Stirling who never used more than 7,200 revs during the entire race, won at an average speed of 78.9 m.p.h. and established a new lap record of 1 minute 28 seconds. I was delighted that we had beaten the nine-lap bogie and that *Ecurie* Moss had won such a convincing victory.

I had practically no time at all with Stirling at Auckland and the only occasion I saw him was during the hours of practice. I did endeavour to have a talk with him at a dinner-dance after the race but it was just hopeless to try and get anywhere near him. However, I knew he was thinking of disposing of the 250 F. and cornered him in his room at the Tasman Hotel at 11 o'clock next morning. Jack Brabham was there, trying to buy the car, and I came in just as Stirling was telling Brabham, "Alf knows all about it, contact him after I have gone."

A few minutes later Brabham left and we went downstairs to the restaurant for an early lunch but no sooner had Stirling found a table than an attractive middle-aged woman came over to us. " Do you mind if I join you," she asked. We could not very well refuse and once again I was prevented from asking about the car. Then, immediately after lunch, a B.P. Director and his wife called to take Stirling to the airport and on arrival there I saw my chance.

" I'm just going in here," said Stirling pointing towards the gent's toilet.

" That's fine," I replied, " I'll come with you."

Inside I tackled him, " What do you want me to do with the Maserati ? "

" Do anything you like," he replied, " just sell it. See what you can do here—if not take it back to England. Don't let it go for less than £3,500."

As the plane climbed and turned away from Auckland Airport I thought to myself that if I had not achieved anything else I had at least gained the complete confidence of Stirling over the years we had spent together. It was a nice thought that he was prepared to let me deal entirely with the sale of a motor-car worth nearly £4,000.

CHAPTER 39

1956 : THE WRITING ON THE WALL

A memorable Goodwood—The Cooper-Climax project—
A battle of wits with B.R.M.—The mixture as before—
Off to Webers again—I lose a good friend.

It came as no surprise to me when Stirling Moss joined Maserati for
1956. I consider he was quite right in deciding to " drive foreign " for yet
another season rather than chance his luck with one or other of the three
British marques. Apparently any ill feeling between Stirling and the
works had been pushed aside in an endeavour to present a strong Maserati
challenge.

Early in March, a few days after my arrival at Tilbury from New
Zealand, I saw Stirling in the office for a few minutes before he rushed off
somewhere or other in his usual manner. That evening I had dinner with
Alfred Moss.

There was no suggestion either from Stirling or his father that I should
join the Maserati works with the express object of looking after the car that
Stirling was to drive, and from what I could make out my immediate task
was to remove the disc brakes from our own 250 F. and replace them with
drum brakes so that the car could be sold. From this you will gather that
I was not able to dispose of the car in New Zealand either to Jack Brabham
or to anyone else.

Can you wonder that as I drove back to Woolwich that evening I told
myself that the 1956 season was going to be an even more frustrating one
than 1955, particularly if there was not even going to be a Formula 1 car
for me to look after. What really upset me was that for the first time in
years I should not be racing at Goodwood on Easter Monday, the opening
meeting of the season.

However, I did go to Goodwood and it was a memorable meeting in
more ways than one for it was there that Stirling decided to buy a Cooper-
Climax, a decision that was to have far-reaching consequences.

Over at Tring I had almost finished working on the 250 F. and had
replaced the drum brakes when Alfred Moss asked me to go down to
Goodwood for the practice sessions. " Maserati are sending over one
of their latest fuel injection cars for Stirling to drive," he told me, " it
would be nice if we could go down there together and be on hand just in
case we are wanted."

I readily agreed because I was naturally interested to see this latest product
from the Modena factory. I knew the car was fitted with a Bosch pump
on an injection system designed and fitted by Maserati themselves and I
wanted to see how the performance compared with our own efforts the
previous season with petrol injection.

The " works " car did not handle at all well during the practice session on Easter Saturday and the lap times recorded were disappointingly slow when compared with those set by our own 250 F. Maserati, running on normal Weber carburetters, the previous year.   The fault with the handling was, to a certain extent, similar to the trouble we had experienced in 1955; it was the old story of too much power coming in at unusable parts of the rev range.

The fuel injection system was not the only problem that faced Alfieri and his two Italian mechanics, for the pistons seized during practice ! The seizure may have been due to some fault with the injection system in that the mixture was far too weak at certain periods in the rev range, prob-ably caused by an air leak.

Maserati asked me to help and I was delighted to do so, as pleased as a substitute who has been called on at the last minute to play in a team. I knew we should have our work cut out to get the car ready for Monday and suggested to Alfieri that I take the " works " lorry to Tring and collect our own 250 F. " We can try out both cars early on Easter Monday," I told him, " and decide which one has the best performance.   In any case," I added, " if the fuel injection proves troublesome on your car then we can fall back on ours."

Alfieri was quick to see my point and I set off for Tring in high spirits, collected our own car—still in its battleship grey—and returned to Chichester.   There I joined the Italian mechanics who were already hard at work.

During Saturday night, Sunday and Sunday night we built an entirely new engine with parts taken from the power unit in the " works " car and a spare that had been brought over from Modena.   We had to strip down completely two engines in order to make up one new one, for the cylinder head and pistons from the engine of the " works " car had to be removed and fitted on the spare and all that we used of the spare engine was the crankcase and crankshaft.

The job was finished in the early hours of Easter Monday and when, later on, Stirling tried the two Maseratis it was decided to use the " works " car because—with its fuel injection—it was two-tenths of a second faster than ours.

I must say our old 250 F. went very well indeed.   It was a wonderful motor-car and stood up to some very hard motor-racing miles over two busy seasons.

Actually I think the "works" car would have been used at Goodwood in any case, unless hopelessly slow, for Maserati would not have been very happy about sending over a 250 F. and then having it pushed aside whilst Stirling Moss raced in something that was virtually obsolete.   There was also the matter of fuel injection ; Alfieri had brought a development engineer with him and naturally both he and his colleague were anxious to see how the injection system on the factory car behaved under race conditions.

During the Richmond Trophy, the main event of the day, which Stirling won after a terrific scrap with Scott-Brown's Connaught, I had nothing whatsoever to do with the control of the car from the pits.   It was entirely a works' responsibility and I felt very much an outsider with Stirling driving a familiar Maserati once again, after his season with the Germans, and with me in the role of spectator.

Alfieri and the Maserati mechanics were of course delighted when Stirling not only won the 32 lap race but established a new lap record as well at 95.79 m.p.h., but I could not help noticing that the Italians were not so enthusiastic about working with Stirling as they had been in 1954. I think they still resented very much the fact that he had joined Mercedes-Benz and there was not the same personal regard for Moss that previously had almost amounted to devotion.

It was at Goodwood during the Saturday practice session that Stirling decided to buy a Cooper-Climax, a car that I can only describe as a bone of contention between us. He was asked by John Cooper to try Salvadori's 1460-c.c. works car and was so impressed with the way it handled that I believe he placed an order on the spot. "Alf," he said to me afterwards, " by modifying the suspension and using our own ideas, and with you tuning the engine, I think we are really going to make this motor."

We had quite a long talk about the Cooper-Climax but I found it impossible to get enthusiastic about the project. I remembered only too well the disappointing results of previous ventures with Coopers, for my association with the Surbiton works had always meant long hours and hard work, first with the Ray Martin Cooper-Alta, then with our own Cooper-Alta.

After two seasons of looking after a Formula 1 car like the 250 F. Maserati, when very little work in the nature of design modification was required, I did not relish the idea of shouldering the responsibility of racing a car that would probably involve me in hours of extra work as had been the case with Coopers previously and also with H.W.M. It was not that John Cooper was unco-operative, for he is one of the most helpful and co-operative people with whom I have ever worked ; it was just that I *knew* we would have snags.

In 1954 and 1955 with the Maserati I had been spared the anxiety of design snags and quite frankly was not at all happy about another project centred around a new British car which was not even a World Championship contender, but a small capacity sports car.

Shortly after my discussion with Stirling about the Cooper-Climax I remember telling Sylvia, " One thing is sure, I shall never last the season out just trundling around to sports car races with this new Cooper-Climax. I shall be going backwards instead of forwards in motor-racing and this is not for me."

For another reason I was fed up. We had no proper workshop in England and I was more or less living on the charity of people like our old friend Geoffrey Taylor of the Alta Car Company or John Cooper ; I never had a workshop of my own where I could sit down quietly and really think around a problem. In 1954, and 1955 as well to a certain extent, my base had been the works at Modena, but in England I had no firm base unless Alfred Moss's garage at White Cloud Farm, Tring, can be described as such.

A few days before the Aintree Meeting on April 21st, Ken Gregory telephoned and told me that Stirling's own Maserati had been entered for him to drive in the Aintree International 200. " There will be no Italian ' works' cars," he said, " but B.R.M. and Connaught will be there."

I was worried, for after the tough 1955 season followed by the race in Auckland the 250 F. should have been thoroughly prepared. However, there was no time at all to do anything with the car and it was taken to the northern circuit more or less on the off-chance that it would behave itself, particularly in the braking department.

The best practice time put up by Stirling of 2 minutes 6.6 seconds was disappointingly slow when compared to his time of 2 minutes 0.6 seconds recorded with this same car in 1954, or his even better time with the Mercedes in 1955 when he got down to 2 minutes 0.4 seconds.

The car was slower partly due to the fact that disc brakes were no longer fitted but mainly because it was a very tired motor-car. A highly developed engine such as the 250 F. requires constant attention to keep it in a proper state of tune.

No one was more surprised than I when Stirling Moss won the race, particularly when it is appreciated that Scott-Brown in practice recorded 2 minutes 3.8 seconds in the Connaught, nearly three seconds better than Stirling's fastest practice lap. If the Maserati " works " cars had been there we should not have stood a chance.

Stirling won the race partly due to the rugged reliability of the grey Maserati and partly due to my pit control in the later stages. It was a battle of wits between myself and the B.R.M. people which I eventually won. I had no discussion with Stirling about tactics before the start but we both knew B.R.M. and Connaught would be out to break each other in the two hundred mile race, and it was just plain common-sense for us to stay within striking distance and watch points.

As soon as the flag dropped and the B.R.M.s and Connaughts went at it hammer and tongs, I could see that we should have to play a waiting game. To my mind a terrific dice between the British cars at such an early stage was quite unnecessary and I was not at all surprised that before quarter distance had been reached both Hawthorn in the B.R.M. and Scott-Brown in the Connaught were out of the running. At 20 laps the race order was Brooks (B.R.M.), followed by Stirling a long, long way behind ; the gap was as much as 27 seconds at one time.

It was at 40 laps that a combination of failing brakes on the B.R.M. and a little canniness on my part altered the whole race picture. As soon as I realized that the B.R.M. was falling back and we were gaining, even though it was such a very small amount each lap, I knew that the race was ours ; it was the beginning of the end.

One must not, however, inform the opposition of a gain of this nature until it increases and becomes more than a second a lap. Then is the time to notify your driver because he will be so encouraged that he will probably save another second himself without being pushed any more, whilst it is so disappointing to his rival that the odds are he will run out of road by trying too hard.

Stirling had been gaining slightly on Brooks for several laps prior to the fortieth, and when I discontinued my pit signals this caused a heated argument between Alfred Moss and myself. " Stirling is asking for times and you are not giving any," he fumed. " Why not ? "

"I want to keep Brooks and B.R.M. in the dark about my intentions," I replied. " I will give Stirling a signal when the time is ripe."

A few laps later I showed Stirling his time as well as giving him the " faster " signal and, as he began to narrow the gap even more rapidly, the B.R.M. pit suddenly realized what was happening and Mike Hawthorn himself tried to speed up Brooks by giving the most urgent " hurry up " signs. Suddenly he pulled into the pits and there was an excited exchange of words between the two B.R.M. drivers before Brooks got away again. However, by then Stirling had taken the lead and there he stayed.

Admittedly the B.R.M. was in trouble with its brakes but nothing was done to the car in the pits and it seems to me it was an unnecessary stop that only resulted in them losing the race. Undoubtedly the B.R.M. pit had been thrown off balance when I stopped signalling and I consider this one of our best victories with the 250 F. for it was a race won entirely on judgment.

As always at a race meeting Rob Walker, the patron of the Pippbrook Garage *equipe*, was enjoying himself immensely and, after his Connaught retired, offered to give us a hand. I remember him coming over, "Alf do you want me to time anybody or do anything for you ? " I like to think it was probably the Aintree Meeting that prompted Rob Walker to contact me a few weeks later when I was out of a job.

It was at Aintree that Stirling drove the Cooper-Climax for the first time but the car proved a great disappointment. After Goodwood I had assisted in the ccnstruction of the chassis at Surbiton and John Cooper installed one of his own 1460-c.c. engines so that Stirling could race at Aintree. On the first day of practice it was obvious to both of us that the Cooper was a handful and did not behave anything like as well as the car he had borrowed from Salvadori at Goodwood or the one he had driven in the British Empire Trophy, at Oulton Park, which he won so con- vincingly.

The car was very difficult to control and understeered to an alarming degree ; each time Stirling went into a corner it just refused to continue on the line selected by the driver and it was my impression that the trans- verse leaf spring at the front end was somewhere at fault.

I therefore decided to remove one of the spring leaves and this undoubt- edly improved matters to such an extent that Stirling managed 2 minutes 13.8 seconds as against Hawthorn's Lotus at 2 minutes 13.2 seconds and Salvadori's Cooper at 2 minutes 10.6 seconds. However, the car was far from right and Stirling could only manage fifth place in the sports car race in the 1100-c.c.—2,000-c.c. class. He was really having to work hard to control the car and in the hands of a lesser driver the outcome might have been serious.

He was naturally very disappointed indeed with the performance of the Cooper-Climax and I was no less fed-up about it. However, whereas he had been enthusiastic about the project in the first place I never reckoned we should set the world on fire with this car. I knew one thing; it was going to take a lot of hard work to put it right, even when the cause of the trouble was finally located. It was " the mixture as before."

The handling was a problem for John Cooper and the car went back to Surbiton whilst I went to Coventry, picked up our own Climax engine which was ready by this time and set off in the brand new Standard Vanguard van of *Equipe* Moss for Bologna and the Weber factory. It was Stirling who originally suggested Italian carburetters on the Climax engine and we were both agreed that they should give us reliability from the point of view of carburation, and more power out of the engine even if the handling was not right—or so we thought. Unfortunately events proved otherwise.

Actually, Stirling had agreed that I visit Webers at the end of April so that I could see the Mille Miglia. On my way through Modena to the Weber works in Bologna I called at Maserati, as I planned to take my friend Fantuzzi, the body builder, to see the race with me.

On arrival I found the entire works an absolute hive of activity with Stirling Moss and Denis Jenkinson in the middle of it all. It was rather an embarrassing situation for, after all, I had a job of work to do at Webers' and did not want to upset Stirling by wandering around the factory like a visiting dignitary greeting various acquaintances. I just said a quiet " hello " to Signor Orsi and Montcalieri, the secretary, and went on my way.

On arrival at Webers I found that the Maserati works had been trying to get me. " Will you ring Stirling Moss as soon as you can," I was told.

Naturally I lost no time, thinking that perhaps Stirling wanted me to help with the preparation of his Mille Miglia car. However, when I got through it was an entirely different problem that he had on his mind. " You had better come back here," he said, " and shake hands with all your friends. They are most upset that you just put your head round the door and then pushed off."

The Italians are funny people in this way and are very hurt if you visit anywhere within a hundred miles and do not call and see them or telephone so I returned to Modena at once. I really felt quite honoured that my old friendships had stood the test of time. They are a decent crowd at Maserati and I have never met nicer or more sincere people in all my years of motor-racing.

That evening I had dinner with Moss and " Jenks " at the Reali. They were not very hopeful of their chances, for the car had been prepared very hastily at the works, and I could see that they had no great confidence in even finishing the course let alone winning.

Fantuzzi and I watched the first part of the race in the vicinity of Rimini on the Adriatic coast and from there made a cross-country dash to the Raticosa Pass. It was really remarkable how easily we were able to reach a good vantage point on the Pass. The van, with the name of Stirling Moss in large letters on the side more or less gave us *carte blanche* to " steam " up narrow mountain roads on the outside of a long, slowly winding queue of assorted vehicles carrying spectators. On one occasion an elderly Italian in a topolino Fiat ran off the road in his anxiety to get out of our way. People cheered and clapped as soon as they saw Stirling's name on the van.

Unfortunately he did not get as far as the Raticosa and we learned from the wireless in the Vanguard that he had crashed and not even reached the Rome Control. I felt fairly certain, having talked with them the previous night, that neither he nor " Jenks " would be sorry to be out of the race.

A rendezvous had been arranged at Modena in case of trouble and on arrival at the Europa I received a telephone call asking me to pick up Stirling from Bologna railway station. I could see the funny side of it when he and " Jenks " stepped off the train, with Stirling wearing a hastily obtained suit which was by no means a good fit and poor, bearded Jenkinson looking very tired and dishevelled.

From Bologna I drove them both to Brescia and on Monday morning Stirling caught a plane from Malpensa. After I had dropped him at the airport I returned to my hotel in Bologna with the intention of starting work on the engine at Webers, but I knew John Heath had crashed in the H.W.M. and decided to go and see him in hospital at Ravenna. The receptionist at the hotel telephoned the hospital to find out the visiting hours and passed on their message, "Any time you like to call it will be O.K."

I drove the 45 miles to Ravenna at a fairly leisurely pace, stopping on the way to buy fruit and cigarettes for John Heath, and arrived at the hospital in the late afternoon. I cannot tell you how deeply shocked I was when the Matron met me in the entrance hall. " I am afraid," she said, " that Mr. Heath died a few minutes ago."

I was stunned by this news. As the Matron led me to the mortuary I told myself that motor-racing had lost one of its staunchest and most sincere supporters and I had lost a good and respected friend.

If I could have obtained permission I would gladly have carried his body back to England in the Vanguard of Stirling Moss Limited. I think John Heath would have liked it that way ; one last journey across Europe in a racing van with all the paraphernalia of engines and spares and against the clock. Of course there is sentiment in motor-racing and I am the first to admit it.

CHAPTER 40

THE BONE OF CONTENTION

A fruitless visit to Modena—More power for the Climax—Too many cooks— Paul Emery almost beats the " Maser."

It was a fruitless, frustrating visit to the Weber factory. Ken Gregory's letter to their Milan office had not been forwarded to Bologna and consequently no one there knew anything about the proposed visit. On arrival I found there was no spare test bench on which to run the Climax engine so as to compare the S.U. and Weber readings. The carburetters were in fact only fitted on a trial and error basis and it was all very unsatisfactory, and very different from my previous visit with Peter Whitehead's Cooper-Alta when we had achieved such remarkable results.

I could understand the point of view of my old friends Gallini and Galletti. "We have a schedule of work to maintain," said the latter, " and much as we should like to do so, I cannot release a test bed for you inside three weeks." Nevertheless we still had seven days at Weber's—as a new manifold had to be fabricated—and the time was not entirely wasted.

On my way back from Bologna to Dunkirk I called at the Maserati factory and was asked to go along to the Board Room where a Directors' Conference was in session. I have never seen so many long faces, for the Mille Miglia had been a real disaster for Maserati ; twenty-two cars were entered but only two finished and Signor Orsi asked me whether I would like to express an opinion.

" Well," I said, " I think your Design Department needs a little refreshment so far as sports cars are concerned ; you should send your people round to various works and let them have a look at other motor-cars. If a designer makes a tour he is bound to come back with some new ideas."

This scheme did not appeal to Signor Orsi or his directors and he asked whether I had any other ideas.

" Well," I replied, " large factories buy other motor-cars for their designers to study ; why don't you do the same thing ? "

" Why not approach Colin Chapman," I continued, " because he is the one who goes to extremes with power to weight ratios ; it may give you some ideas for your future models."

The idea was approved and Signor Orsi asked me to make the necessary arrangements through Ken Gregory with Colin Chapman. Within a little over four weeks Maserati took delivery of a Lotus and so far as I know it is still in the works at Modena.

On arrival back in England, after a fast journey in twenty-one-and-a-half hours' running time from Modena to Dunkirk in the Vanguard, I put the Cooper-Climax engine on the bench at Geoffrey Taylor's, and although

Rob Walker's Cooper-Climax during a pit stop for oil and water in the 1957 Syracuse G.P. After Alf Francis had spent the entire winter improving the power output of the engine by no less than 15%, Jack Brabham drove the car in a race of full G.P. distance at Syracuse and finished 6th. Rob Walker, sleeves rolled up, is talking to Brabham and Alf Francis, whilst Horace Gould is watching Alf's 1957 apprentice, Michael Redgrove, fastening the bonnet cover.

When Jack Brabham ran out of road during practice for the 1957 Monaco G.P. he almost went through the back door of the Casino. The chassis of the car, completed only two days previously, was wrecked. After weeks of hard work and anxiety this was a disappointing debut for an exciting new 2-litre car specially built for the Monaco race where the circuit is eminently suitable. Eventually the engine was used in another chassis and Brabham finished 6th.

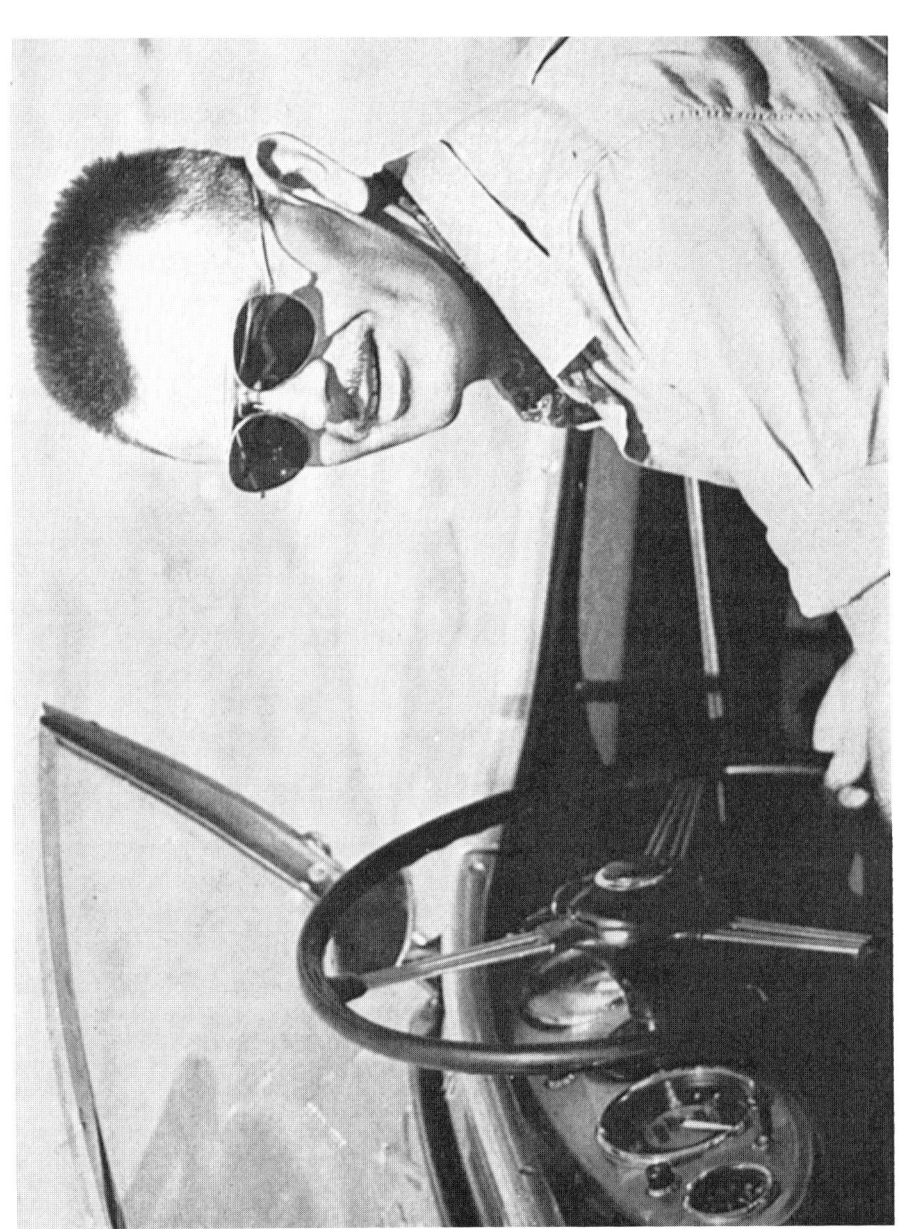

there was an improvement in brake horse-power with the Weber's over and above the S.U. readings, it was only 4 b.h.p., and I decided to have the cylinder head off. I modified the ports and cleaned them out and also modified the water circulation passages, so that the original Coventry-Climax design of the cylinder head was altered slightly, and this resulted in another 3 b.h.p.

Once I had completed my work on the head, the engine was able to develop more power and we finished with a figure in the region of 103 b.h.p. at 6,000 r.p.m., having started with 94 at 6,000.

While running the engine on the bench I noticed that at very high revs —over 5,800—there was a sudden loss of power which I attributed to inadequate fuel supply. Weber carburetters require a much higher pressure of fuel delivery than other types, something in the region of 6 lb. per square inch, whereas the two S.U. electrical pumps were only supplying 2 lb. per square inch at the most. Neither did the S.U.s prime too well ; they were reluctant to pick up fuel unless actually submerged.

I made up my mind that on my next trip to Italy I would buy a Tipo Mona fuel pump, a very reliable unit manufactured by an aircraft concern in Milan. For two seasons, using one on the 250 F. Maserati, I never had any trouble at all and was able to practically ignore its existence.

Although the new engine was installed in the Cooper-Climax for the Crystal Palace Meeting at Whitsun there was no opportunity for either Stirling or myself to try the car before the Meeting. The engine was still on the bench at Alta Engineering on Tuesday and I had my work cut out to finish the preparation of the car and get it to the Palace circuit by Saturday morning for the official practice session.

Stirling was bitterly disappointed with the car. "After all this time," he said to me, " the handling has not been improved at all and I take a pretty dim view of it."

It seemed to me that he reckoned I was not doing very much work on the car, which was definitely not the case for I was concentrating on getting more power out of the engine whilst John Cooper tried to find the cause of the bad handling.

"After all," I argued, " they built the car and it is up to them to sort out the handling difficulties."

Unfortunately, although John Cooper and his boys had gone over the chassis with a fine tooth comb between the Aintree and Crystal Palace meetings, they had not been able to cure the understeer and eventually the blame was laid at my door.

It happened this way. When Stirling complained to Charles Cooper, after his first run at the Palace, Charles bluntly told him and his father that the car was all over the place because I had fitted Weber carburetters and raised the b.h.p., thus altering the torque of the engine and spoiling the handling.

Charles Cooper's theory, with which Alfred Moss was inclined to agree, did not make sense to me because how on earth can anyone alter the handling of a car that weighs seven or eight hundredweight to such an extent by increasing the power of the engine by so few b.h.p. at certain revs ? The increase was so little that I doubt very much whether Stirling even noticed it and most drivers would be hard put to notice a difference of 10 b.h.p. on a racing-car.

I was beginning to have a real dislike for this motor-car, because no one would listen to me and I was on my own. In the old days of *Equipe Moss*, Stirling would have quietly discussed the matter and probably accepted my advice. Now there were too many cooks—Alfred Moss, Charles Cooper, John Cooper and several others as well—ready to express their views and condemn me at the same time ; unfortunately no one was the *chef* with the answer.

I found out during the discussion about engine torque that I had been blamed for the bad handling of the car at Aintree when it had an engine on loan from John Cooper. The father and son partnership reckoned that when I polished the front spring I altered the rate, and John Cooper insisted on fitting a standard spring for the Crystal Palace meeting. It made very little difference to the handling of the car, and I never expected that it would do so. When I polished the spring at Aintree I merely removed the oxidization and this could not possibly have affected the handling.

There was absolutely no doubt in my mind that the Cooper was very different from the " works " car that Moss had tried at Goodwood on Easter Monday. At a later date, as you will see, we found the real reason for the trouble and I was exonerated from all blame.

The car was eventually raced at the Crystal Palace on S.U. carburetters because Stirling insisted on having them ; to please him I did what was wanted although I personally felt pretty browned off about the whole situation.

The car was second to Les Leston in the Anerley Trophy after Leston went into the lead and stayed there in spite of all Stirling's efforts to pass him. In the Norbury Trophy Stirling just managed to squeeze by into the first corner and there he stayed, building up quite a considerable lead which was at times as much as three or four seconds and eventually winning by 1.2 seconds and setting a new sports car record for the circuit of 77.22 m.p.h.

As I watched the car I told myself that it would see the end of me ; it was a " bag of nails " so far as I was concerned. I had been dealing with the Maserati and Moss in the World Championship field and here I was being accused of altering the torque and upsetting the handling of a sports car.

I can tell you I was worried stiff about whether it would go off the road ; it looked really dangerous and there was no doubt that Stirling was having to drive on the limit. He was not trying all that hard to win the race or break the lap record but just to hold off Leston and stay on the road at the same time. I have rarely seen him work harder at the wheel of a car.

As soon as the race finished I buttonholed him and asked what he wanted me to do with the Cooper. His reply was short and to the point, " Sell it."

It became crystal clear to me at that moment that he was just as fed up with the car as I was. It was a gloomy outlook but I refused to be beaten by this troublesome sports car and took it to Brands Hatch the week after the Palace meeting with Jack Brabham as test driver. It was here, at £2 a day for the hire of the circuit and after many experiments and trial runs, that we discovered the bad handling of the car was all tied up with the front spring as I had thought.

The rebound of the spring was not sufficient, due to the fact that it was bottoming on the shock-absorbers brackets. It was easy to understand why, when I had taken a leaf out of the front spring at Aintree, thus giving another 3/16th of an inch clearance, the handling had been slightly improved.

At Brands Hatch I took the leaf out again but did not, as at Aintree, put packing pieces underneath ; in other words the spring was lifted by a quarter-of-an-inch. There was an immediate improvement in handling and Brabham reckoned the Cooper-Climax was as good as his own car. On one occasion, towards the end of our week of testing, he went round the Kentish circuit in 1 minute, which was good going in May, 1956.

When we returned to Coopers and discussed the problem, John Cooper agreed that our theory must be right. As soon as the spring was lifted high up without more clearance being given, the car handled perfectly well. A faulty welding jig during the construction of the chassis had caused all the trouble in the first place, but a fault of such small degree that its effect on the handling was very difficult to trace. It does show how a tiny error of this nature, during the construction stage, can cause all sorts of problems, troubles and unnecessary arguments.

The Maserati behaved very well in both heats of the big race at the Palace, the London Trophy, and this was pleasing because it was the last appearance of the 250 F. before I took it over to Modena so that it could be stored.

In the first heat Rob Walker's Connaught, formidable opposition in the hands of Reg Parnell, went off the road and Stirling was harried by Paul Emery in the Emeryson and Bob Gerard in the Cooper-Bristol ; actually Emery, who always goes like a bomb and a half at the Palace, took the lead on two occasions but Stirling eventually won by three seconds.

In the second heat it was more or less the same story, with Emery driving very fast and very well but with Stirling nevertheless comfortably within his limits.

" We must make a close race of it," Stirling told me just before the car was pushed on to the grid, " otherwise the spectators are going to be dis-appointed. What I want you to do is keep a careful watch on the lap record because I would like to collect that as well." (Remember it was Hawthorn in this same car who established the record the previous year and Stirling was anxious to put that matter right !) " I want to do the lap record," he said, " during the first four laps of this heat, because if I wait until later I may pull too big a lead over Emery. If I do it early on I can then have a 'dice' with Emery and the public will be happy."

I at once made arrangements with the Timekeeper's Box that as soon as the record had been broken someone would give me the thumbs up signal so that I could slow down Stirling.

In practice our plan almost failed. Stirling led for four laps and during this time established a new absolute circuit record of 79.94 m.p.h., but Emery—driving most impressively—took the lead soon afterwards and quite an exciting dice developed, with Stirling going ahead again towards the end of the race.

However, he was baulked by a tail-ender at the start of the last lap and Emery slammed through into the lead. Stirling just managed to catch and pass him on that final lap to win by only 3/5th of a second. He had cut things a bit too fine, Emery had driven even better than in the first heat and we nearly lost the London Trophy!

The faithful old Maserati went very well indeed and was no trouble at all. We were geared as with Hawthorn the previous year and I also removed a spring leaf and cut down the fuel load to five gallons. Conditions were therefore exactly the same as when Mike handled the car, and Stirling was delighted to beat Mike's speed of 78.93 m.p.h. by such a handsome margin. As a matter of fact I am sure that the main reason he drove at the Palace Meeting was to prove to himself that he could get round the circuit just as quickly as Mike had done.

CHAPTER 41

THE SHOWDOWN

The day after I arrived back from Modena, having taken the Maserati there on the trailer, I started to strip down the Cooper-Climax so that I could learn more about this very rapid yet troublesome sports car. If I cannot build a chassis from the start I can at least take it to pieces and rebuild again. This is in line with my policy of getting to know all I possibly can about a motor-car on which I have to work and which my driver has to handle.

I did not start on the car at Cooper's until fairly late in the afternoon— having completed a 480 mile " blind " in just under 12 hours with the Vanguard and trailer from Chambery to Calais the previous day—and was hard at work when the telephone rang just after 4 o'clock. It was Ken Gregory. " Can you get the car over to Rheims right away," he said, " so that Stirling can get in some practice to-morrow afternoon for the 12 Hour Race."

" That's practically impossible," I replied, " the car is in pieces now."

" Well, do what you can," Ken insisted. " You must try hard. They are paying us a lot of starting money."

" Well," I countered, " even if I get there, I cannot guarantee that the car is going to stay in one piece. There is no time to prepare it for such a long distance race."

As soon as he had rung off, I put the problem to John Cooper and as always he came to the rescue. John is one of these people who look at you blankly if you talk about a 48 hour week or every other Saturday off ; he is a seven-day-a-week man for fifty-two weeks a year and not afraid of hard work.

With his pipe—usually unlighted—gripped belligerently between his teeth John Cooper can tackle any job in the Surbiton works and do it just as well as his experts. The men who work for him think a lot of him and so do I. With his help the car was reassembled during the night and the axle ratio changed to a more suitable one for the fast Rheims circuit. The car was in fact fitted with the 3.7 ratio.

On Thursday morning, exactly forty-eight hours after arriving in London from Modena, I drove the car to Ferryfield, its wheels still wet as my first job the previous day had been to paint them in Stirling's off white colours. The Cooper-Climax was driven aboard a " Silver City " freighter, much to the interest of holidaymakers en route for France with less potent machinery, and at 10 o'clock we were in the air. An hour later the car was off loaded at Calais

I collected the Vanguard which had been left in a Calais garage when I returned from Modena, so that it was ready for me to pick up en route to the Rouen Meeting, a week after Rheims. I, of course, had no idea we should be racing at Rheims.

The Cooper-Climax was loaded on the trailer and at teatime, after a flat-out run in the best traditions of the old days with the Commer transporter I was in Rheims. I think I left Calais just before 2 o'clock and soon after 5 o'clock was in the cathedral city. I really thrashed the Vanguard, clocking 75 and 80 in places, with the Cooper firmly secured on the trailer.

Stirling practised that evening and made fastest time of the day for cars up to 1,500-c.c., maximum capacity for entries in the first Rheims 12 Hour Race ; even so he complained that the engine was missing over 5,800 revs. " It just does not pull over five-eight," he said, " it has no power at all."

My immediate reaction was to blame the power loss on lack of fuel supply but Stirling would not agree. " It is because of the Webers," he argued, " that is why the car will not go over five-eight. If we use S.U.s then it will go to six-five."

It seemed that the Cooper-Climax had its own gremlin, quite apart from the one that accompanied Stirling around the circuits and I thought to myself, " This car will never be right. We have cured the bad handling and now we have a problem with the engine."

Unfortunately I had not brought a Tipo Mona pump back from Modena and there was nothing I could do to improve the rate of fuel supply ; that was the real trouble, not the Webers. Nevertheless I worked until 3 a.m. on the car, preparing it as best I could for the race.

On Friday Stirling practised again and although he put up fastest time of the day in 2 minutes 47 seconds, even quicker than his time on Thursday, he still complained of lack of power over 5,800 revs. Actually I could not see that it mattered because he was still four or five seconds faster than anyone else. " Why not leave the Webers," I argued.

However, he insisted on twin S.U.s and once again, with no one to help me, I worked all night on the car. In the morning can you imagine how furious I was when I had to change back to Webers again for the simple reason that the throttle linkage, as originally modified and shortened by me to fit the Webers, was not long enough for the S.U.s?

I could have kicked myself, for there was nothing I could improvise on Saturday morning before the start of the race at 10 a.m. that would stand up to twelve hours of hard driving. I had no alternative but to replace the Webers.

At 5 o'clock in the morning I made a start and completed the job by 9 a.m. I said nothing to Stirling about it, because there was nothing he could do in any case, but I did mention it to Alfred Moss who was most sympathetic.

When I arrived on the circuit it was with Webers again and naturally Stirling was disappointed and annoyed as well. However that was not the end of my troubles at Rheims by any means. On the start area in front of the pits the entire automatic voltage control mechanism, complete with coils, fell off the chassis !

Having sorted out this particular problem I was then giving the car a final check over some thirty minutes before the start when I notice a spongy feeling about the brake pedal. A quick investigation showed that one of the hydraulic pipes leading from one shoe cylinder to the other had fractured and was leaking. This meant another panic operation, and I just managed to fit a new length of piping in time for the start ; I was almost on my knees by the time the flag dropped.

I put down all these troubles to the fact that I had been told to replace the carburetters when I should have been preparing the car properly for the race. I would much rather have left the Webers in position in the first place, even though the engine was missing over 5,800, because according to our practice times we were considerably faster than anyone else and there was no need to try and extract the last ounce of power out of the engine.

It was at Rheims, where we came to loggerheads over the policy of how to prepare the Cooper-Climax, that I definitely decided that it was almost the last—if not the last—meeting I should attend with Stirling Moss. I knew that I would have to get back somehow into the Grand Prix field and pack up these fiddling little races with sports cars where there are a hundred and one technical advisers.

In the race itself Stirling kept going extremely well for half an hour or so and went faster than I had ever seen him drive the Cooper previously. He was at least five seconds quicker than anyone else in spite of the Webers and lack of power at the top end, but an early pit stop soon after 10.30 was the first of many and when he came in for fuel later in the morning we could not restart the engine for some time because of an air lock in the fuel lines.

To make matters worse the engine became rougher and rougher until eventually Stirling handed over to Phill Hill who was forced to retire soon afterwards due to overheating caused by lack of fuel supply. The engine had been running on a weak mixture at high speed, and at Rheims—a very fast circuit indeed where very little overrun is used—the cars are always going hard on the engine. Due to the heat generated in the combustion chambers, the engine overheated (although the pistons were not burned) and a considerable amount of water was lost.

Once the Cooper-Climax started to lose water the cylinder head studs stretched because of the heat and in the end we had a water leak into the combustion chamber which caused our final retirement. The only consolation was fastest lap in 2 minutes 45.8 seconds, particularly as the Porsche that won the race could not get anywhere near this time.

At Rheims, on Sunday, I watched the French Grand Prix but did not enjoy it, largely because I was just a spectator, and unable to look after Stirling. Nevertheless, it was a most exciting race and wonderful to see how the British Vanwall driven by Harry Schell got in amongst the Ferraris.

Next day I started work on the Cooper-Climax. Stirling had told me not to change the Webers as Peter Jopp was due to drive the car at Rouen. Stirling was contracted to Aston-Martin and they naturally would not release him.

When I asked how the engine had behaved during the race he told me that it had given no trouble until the overheating started. This was encouraging but even so the cylinder head had been damaged by overheating and required removal. I had a fairly easy day, only working until 9 p.m., and finished off the head next morning but it was some job changing all the studs.   Having altered the axle ratio to 4.1 in preparation for the Rouen race, I took the Cooper-Climax for a test run on the Rheims circuit, by this time open to normal traffic again.

I had only completed half a mile or so when I noticed the needle of the oil pressure gauge fluctuating violently and stopped the car at once.   It was well that I did so for on arrival at Rouen next day I took the sump off and found the big-ends gone !   Fortunately I was able to get replacement bearings from Mike Hawthorn—who was driving a Lotus at Rouen—and working most of the night and next morning as well I fitted new big-ends. Unfortunately Jopp had to miss the Friday practice session because I was busy on the car and what with one thing and another Stirling, Jopp and I were all rather fed-up about the Cooper-Climax.

On Saturday, Peter Jopp was not putting up very fast times in practice and whether Stirling thought the twin Webers were to blame I do not know but the fact remains that after lunch he told me to fit the S.U.s.

I walked off on my own for a few minutes, trying to calm down ; it was no use.   This was the showdown at last.   I went over to where Stirling was sitting in his 220 Mercedes with Judy Noot, his secretary.   " I am terribly sorry Stirling," I said, " but I would like to resign."

I think he expected something of this nature and was perhaps relieved that at last matters had come to a head.   " That suits me fine Alf," he replied.

In the race next day Jopp overtook Mike Hawthorn, immediately after the start and just before the first corner.   He went into the bend too fast and overturned the Cooper-Climax without hurting himself badly.   However the car was wrecked.

A lot of nonsense has been talked about ill-feeling between Stirling Moss and myself ; the true facts are that in London a few days after the Rheims race Stirling handed me a cheque for £100 and thanked me very much for all the work I had done for him.   " I am sorry you have to leave Alf," he said, " and if ever you need any help or assistance don't forget that I am still your friend."

CHAPTER 42

EQUIPE ROB WALKER

The F.2 Cooper-Climax—With Tony Brooks at Oulton Park—
Success at Brands Hatch—Tuning the Climax engine—
We cause a stir at Syracuse—Single or twin camshafts ?—
A resounding victory at Goodwood.

Naturally it felt very strange to be unemployed after so many years of hard work but I was determined not to find myself a new job too quickly and took my wife and daughter for a short seaside holiday. We talked a lot about the future and I had to admit that I was fed up with motor-racing. "Nevertheless," I told Sylvia, "I want to remain connected with motor-cars in some way, maybe in the Design Department of one of the large manufacturers like Rootes or B.M.C."

A few days after returning to Woolwich from our holiday I went over to the Cooper factory at Surbiton. I wanted to have a mooch round and keep myself in the picture. On arrival I was told there had been a telephone call from Pippbrook Garage, Dorking, and would I please telephone a Mr. Jolliffe the manager. I knew this was one of Rob Walker's garages but must admit I was surprised when Jolliffe asked me over the telephone whether I would like to take charge of Rob Walker's Competition Section based on Pippbrook.

"Well," I replied, "actually I have other plans and I don't think I want the job."

"O.K." he said, "but if you ever change your mind be sure and let me know."

I told my wife about the proposition that night in Woolwich.

"Well," she said, "Dorking is a very nice place and after all you will have to start thinking about a job ; the money is getting rather short."

After another week or so of being "on ice" I decided to call at Pippbrook and find out more about the job. The complicated and lengthy pre-liminaries of joining an organization such as Rootes are rather different from saying "yes" over a pint of beer, and after a month I was still out of a job ; my limited resources were running short.

At Pippbrook I was made most welcome both by Rob Walker and Stan Jolliffe. It was only necessary for me to make up my mind and I could start right away. There was only one thing that was really worrying me, "Dorking is too far away from Woolwich," I told Jolliffe, "and I definitely am not going to work as I used to do with Stirling Moss ; living in digs and cafes when I am in this country. I want some home life on those rare occasions when I am in England."

"Well," replied Jolliffe, "we might even be able to fix that."

And fix it they did. Rob Walker found a delightfully situated country cottage for me on the outskirts of Dorking. It used to be a pub—the Old Barley Mow—and Sylvia and I knew the moment we saw it that the cottage was just what we wanted.

At the end of August, seven weeks after leaving Stirling Moss Ltd., I joined Pippbrook Garage, Dorking, but could not help feeling that in going back to motor-racing I had made a big mistake. It seemed that I would never learn my lesson and that whilst there was a wall available I should continue to bang my head against it. However, I knew very well that I had been forced back into motor-racing because I could not afford to wait whilst my application for a much more stable and secure type of job in the motor industry went through the usual channels. Strictly speaking there had been no alternative.

I soon found myself caught up in the old crazy whirl but this time it was different ; within a few weeks of joining Rob Walker I realized that for the first time in nine years of motor-racing I had authority as well as responsibility. It all added up to what I had wanted for so long and Sylvia had a home in the country which she had always wanted.

It came as a surprise to me—and a great encouragement as well— when I learned that Rob Walker had bought a Formula 2 Cooper-Climax with the object of entering it for the Gold Cup Race at Oulton Park. So far as I could ascertain at the time there were no plans for racing the car afterwards and the main objective was to try and cover the purchase price of the Cooper by winning the £1,000 prize money.

Rob Walker was not setting his sights too high by any means for C. A. S. Brooks had agreed to drive the new car and to many of us in September, 1956, young Tony Brooks was already well on his way up the ladder.

This new F.2 project was really something that I could get my teeth into ; I felt that given a chance with the Coventry-Climax engine (which I knew so well yet which had been the " final straw " in *Equipe* Moss) I could prove that it would stand up to considerable development without the handling qualities of the car being upset. At Pippbrook no one would object to my ideas or my way of working things out.

Once the order for the chassis had been placed I lost no time in getting in touch with John Cooper and asking him to deliver the power unit to me as soon as possible so that I could start " modding " it whilst the chassis was being finished. Unfortunately there was some hold up and Coopers were unable to meet my request which meant that our car went to Oulton Park more or less in standard form whereas the works Coopers were " given the treatment."

Naturally the last thing John Cooper or his father wanted was for us to give the " works " cars a trouncing, so they decided to risk raising the compression ratio by a considerable margin. By increasing to 11 : 1—as I found out later—they must have given their engines another 6 or 7 b.h.p.

However I was able to spend almost two weeks at Surbiton helping with the assembly of the Cooper, following my own doctrines of being with a car from the start and thus building reliability into it. There was, of course, the usual panic ; the engine did not arrive from Coventry until a few days before the Gold Cup Meeting and the final assembly was not completed until the evening of September 19th. We left for Oulton Park that night, an untried, untested car in the transporter, with the intention of running in the engine and bedding down the brakes at the Thursday practice session. One of these days—perhaps when I retire—I am going to take my time over building a racing car.

In practice Tony Brooks was the fastest driver on the circuit at 1 minute 52.2 seconds with Salvadori on a " works " car next best at 1 minute 55.6 seconds. We could have won the Gold Cup and the £1,000 as well if I had not made a major error, mainly due to my lack of knowledge of the handling qualities of the car. I fitted new tyres, hardly scrubbed at all, for the race instead of running on part worn ones ! The new tyres upset the handling of the car to such an extent that when Brooks took up his position on the starting grid after the warming-up lap he was understandably upset.

" What have you done ? " he asked. " What's wrong with the car ? "

" Well," I replied, "All I have done is fit four brand new tyres."

This conversation took place only a few minutes before the start and there was no time to do anything about the tyres. I knew then that we had lost the race and as the field streaked away towards Old Hall Corner I sat on the pit counter and told myself "Alphons you still have a lot to learn about motor-racing."

It was a bitter pill to swallow for even during the second and third practice sessions, with the tyres half worn, Brooks had gone better than Salvadori—who well deserved his win and led Brooks over the line by 25.2 seconds as well as recording fastest lap at 84.95 m.p.h. For a long ime Brooks " diced " with Jack Brabham on another " works " Cooper for second place until the Australian had fuel pump trouble and dropped right back. I made a note in the diary " This Brabham sure can go."

After Oulton Park there was the Brands Hatch Meeting on Sunday, October 14th, and bearing in mind the lesson I had been taught about the tyres I did not make the same mistake a second time. We raced at Brands with worn tyres and I also cut the weight of the Cooper to the barest minimum by making very careful calculations in connection with fuel consumption. When the blue car went on the grid it was certainly not carrying any unnecessary weight.

There was unfortunately very little time to do anything about the engine. However, I did fit a Tipo Mona mechanical fuel pump—which I had meant to do on Stirling's car—and this definitely improved perform-ance. Where previously the power had dropped off at 5,800 revs per minute it now kept on going up to 6,500 and over. This was according to Brooks who is the last person in the world to mislead or exaggerate.

The car went like a bomb at Brands whilst Brooks drove like a master, leading the 12-lap race from start to finish. This time we beat the " works " Coopers—although not for a £1,000—but even so Brabham on the " works " car put up fastest lap at 75.15 m.p.h.

With the " long winter of discontent " ahead of me I made up my mind to really go to work on this new F.2 Cooper. By now I was highly enthusiastic about the car and convinced that development of the power unit would open the eyes of a lot of people in 1957. I must admit that I was not quite sure from which angle to approach the project of tuning the engine. However, first things first, and I set out to find what the engine needed ; what it lacked in fact.

It took me about three weeks—running the engine on a bench in the Alta works under precisely the same conditions as if it were on the car— to really get to know it.

I went over to the Alta works simply because I knew I should be left absolutely alone there. Geoffrey Taylor does not like people to bother him and consequently makes a point of not bothering other people. He has been a staunch friend to me throughout the whole of my motor-racing career and I shall always be grateful for the help and advice he has given me over the years.

I set the engine on a bench, using the same tanks and fuel pumps, and then tried to run it to destruction. I soon learned that there was a lack of fuel supply which I had previously suspected. After all an engine running at a certain absolute torque requires a certain minimum supply of fuel per hour and I came to the conclusion that the flow was insufficient on the engine as originally installed by Coopers.

The first thing I did therefore was to ensure that the engine received as much fuel as it wanted as and when required. The resultant improvement in flow not only increased the peak revs from 6,500 r.p.m. to 7,000 r.p.m. but it was possible to keep at 7,000 for five minutes. It also improved performance to the extent that I found another 3 b.h.p.

My next step in the search for power was to experiment with the induction manifolds. I eventually decided to use one of 10 degrees semi-downdraught—slightly slanting the horizontal Weber carburetter to this new angle—and this gave a few more b.h.p. I also increased the compression ratio from 9.6 to 1 to 10.1 to 1, until finally the engine gave a figure of 113 b.h.p.

Coopers had of course increased the compression ratio for Oulton Park but in my opinion they went to extremes, running at 11 to 1 which naturally caused the engine to overheat badly. To my mind it was more by luck than design that Salvadori finished the Gold Cup race.

Before settling for 113 b.h.p. I tried the engine on different fuels and discovered that by using certain mixtures I could gain something like another 5 b.h.p. It was obvious that we should have to enter the car whenever possible in races where the fuel limitations were not strict and allowed the use of such mixtures.

Highly delighted with my experiments I then abandoned further tuning of the engine and concentrated on modifying the chassis. My main object was to lighten it and with this in mind I discarded the battery and employed a magneto which not only helped to lessen the weight but gave me another 1 or 2 b.h.p.

Coopers do not like using magnetos because they always experience a lot of timing gear trouble. They argue that a magneto imposes far too great a load and puts too much stress on the timing gears. However I took a chance and made a start by driving the fuel pump off the first reduction timing gear. It worked quite satisfactorily and in my opinion this form of drive actually preserves a gear from destruction. To my mind the damage Coopers have experienced has been caused by the gear pitching and causing vibration. By putting a load on the gears I stopped the pitch. My experience convinced me that if I put an even heavier load on the gears I should achieve even more reliability, so I put on the magneto and from that time we have had no trouble.

Admittedly since then I have fitted a modified type of gear but only because it was on the market and easily obtainable ; it was not really necessary.

Taking away the battery and using a magneto cut out a lot of weight and I then made an alteration to the general chassis lay-out, altering the driver's position so that it was more forward and comfortable whilst at the same time giving him what I describe as " a more competition-like feeling." To cut a long story short I worked very hard indeed on the F.2 Cooper-Climax during the winter months and expected great things of both car and driver when we set off for Sicily on Tuesday, March 26th.

With £10 in cash, £80 in travellers cheques, 11,000 French Francs, 230 Deutschmarks and 160,000 Italian Lire—totalling £210 in all—two of us set off in the van of *Equipe* Walker for the Syracuse Grand Prix, the first race of the 1957 season. Needless to say there was the usual panic (explained somewhat because we took Rob Walker's 1956 Formula 1 Connaught as well) and I was my usual surprised self to find that we were actually on the boat with the transporter when it sailed from Dover.

We got to Syracuse in very good time and having left Dunkirk at 3 a.m. on the 27th arrived at 10 p.m. on the 2nd—a distance of 1,900 miles in 6 days 19 hours. Briefly this was our timetable.

March 27th—Arrived Cologne 6 p.m.
March 28th—Depart Cologne 10 a.m.—arrive Munich 9.30 p.m.
March 29th—Depart Munich 9 a.m.—arrive Trentino 8.30 p.m.
March 30th—Trentino to Ancona.
March 31st—Ancona to Foggia (stopped to have powerful horns fitted
    at cost of 28,000 lire. Well worth it).
April 1st—Depart Foggia 8 a.m.—arrive Crotone 7 p.m.
April 2nd—Depart Crotone 9 a.m.—arrive Villa St. Giovanni, 3 p.m.
Crossed by ferry to Sicily. Arrived Syracuse 10 p.m.

You can see that we were not hanging about anywhere and in fact we arrived in Syracuse with plenty of time to spare. The situation was, how-ever, soon back to normal. During the Friday practice session Peter Walker had a piston seize up on the F.1 Connaught due to a water leak and that meant an all night session in the nearby Fiat garage.

As we started to take the Connaught engine to pieces I observed ruefully to my apprentice, Michael Redgrove, that it was a pity the first practice session had not been on Wednesday.

"At least," I said, " we should have had more time to rebuild the engine. We could have made a start last night instead of doing a round of the cafes."

We did not finally finish the car until 10.30 p.m. on Saturday night after 18 hours of almost non-stop work and I was more than relieved to get to bed. Fortunately we had no trouble with the little Cooper ; it fairly rocketed round the tricky Sicilian circuit in practice and although we knew the car did not stand an even chance against the pukka Formula 1 machines we, all of us in the Pippbrook *Equipe*, were sure the Cooper-Climax/Brabham combination was going to make the Italians sit up and take notice. It did. They could not understand how a 1½-litre car with a little known driver could stand the pace for 70 laps of the 3½ mile Syracuse circuit ; laps that demand the best from driver and car.

Brabham kept the Cooper going until the end and came home sixth, five laps behind the " works " Connaught of Bueb. From the point of view of reliability it was a good day for Pippbrook because Peter Walker brought home the Formula 1 car in eighth place. Incidentally we used a 3.7 : 1 axle ratio on the Formula 2 Cooper.

We were back in England with the two cars on April 16th—having left Syracuse on the morning of the 9th—and there was very little time to get the Cooper ready for its next duel with the " works " cars and the new Formula 2 machinery from the Lotus stable. The Coopers and Allison's Lotus all had the new twin camshaft engine whilst we only had the single camshaft, but this did not worry me because I prefer the single cam engine.

It all comes down to a question of torque and the mechanical efficiency of an engine. The single cam unit does not require so much painstaking attention in the tuning and preparation stage as does the twin cam one. Furthermore, the torque of my single cam engine at 3,000 revs per minute is almost as great as the twin cam version at 4,800 and there is a point—around 3,500—where my gain over the twin cam is as much as 36 b.h.p.

The single cam engine was developed entirely with the object of producing a lot of power in the lower rev ranges. By concentrating on developing still more the basic design it gives me a continuous upward surge over a range of revs from 3,000 to 6,500 whereas with the twin cam engine—even though it goes up to 7,500—it only has really useful power from 5,000 upwards. It stands to reason that the twin cam cars only have a usable range extending over 2,500 revs whereas I can get results with the single cam over a range of 3,500.

With the extended rev range the gears can be spaced wider apart and one result of this is that it is not necessary to make such careful calculations in gearing or axle ratios. In addition the single cam car accelerates at lower speeds much more rapidly than the twin cam one, even though the latter engine develops more ultimate power.

We had our usual panic at Goodwood when Jack Fairman in the F 1 Connaught charged the chicane in practice on Saturday and damaged a track rod as well as making a considerable dent in the nose. Fairman was more or less mesmerized by a wildly spinning B.R.M. on the far side of the chicane and as the sizeable crowd in the stand rose to its feet as one man he found himself put completely off line by this new diversion.

We were the fastest people in practice with the Formula 2 car which naturally upset Coopers, and the father and son partnership was even more upset when on race day Stirling Moss wagered Charles Cooper half-a-crown that Brooks would beat the " works " cars of Salvadori and Brabham. Charles Cooper could not very well refuse the bet.

Following so close on the Syracuse race the little Cooper behaved wonderfully well. There were no difficulties of any sort and this was indeed a change for the first Goodwood meeting of the season. I was so sure about the car that for the only time in years I did not bother to carry out the final preparation. It was very slack of me and a bad example to my apprentice but I had a feeling that Brooks would " walk it." He was just as delighted with the car as I was.

There were eight runners in the race and when the flag fell Brooks fairly rocketed off the line ; actually he jumped the start, due in my opinion to faulty flag timing by the starter, and I knew at once that he would be penalized or disqualified.

I kept him going fast whilst I asked one of the officials if he could find out the majority view of the Stewards and Judges. I was more than relieved when he came back and told me that in his opinion my driver would be penalized but not disqualified. " If they penalize," he added, " it should not be more than fifteen seconds."

Meanwhile Brooks got right out in front and stayed there, strengthening his position immensely when on the fourth lap both Salvadori (Cooper) and Allison (F.2 Lotus)) retired, leaving a grim Brabham to try and catch the flying Pippbrook car. I kept Brooks going so fast that he eventually built up a lead of eighteen seconds over the Australian and once he was securely established with this safety margin we relaxed, positive that the race was ours. He finally won the 12-lap race by 18.2 seconds from Brabham and was penalized five seconds.

So far as Brooks as a driver is concerned I think he is in the top flight with Moss, Collins and Hawthorn. He is one of these few people—like Fangio—who appear on the motor-racing scene, sit in a motor-car and walk away with an important race (like Brooks did in the Syracuse Grand Prix of 1955) to the utter amazement of everyone. Fangio was the same in his early days with the Simca-Gordini. He only had to sit in the car to look like a race winner.

Brooks is a " natural." With very little Grand Prix experience, and here again he is so like Fangio, he races effortlessly against drivers who have been in the game for years.

After the 1957 Monaco race, when I was discussing motor-racing at the Maserati works with Signor Orsi and Guerino Bertocchi (two men who have been connected with the sport all their lives) they both maintained that Brooks will be the next man to win the Championship. Bertocchi has more opportunities than most people of talking to Fangio, and after Monaco the great Argentine driver told him that Brooks would be the next World Champion. Bertocchi does not tell old wives tales and I have no reason to doubt the authenticity of his story.

Although I have had very little to do with Brooks (I only met him for the first time at Oulton Park for the Gold Cup race) I certainly agree with Orsi and Bertocchi. Tony Brooks does not strike me as a man who has to study motor-racing or try particularly hard. He is a man who settles himself down confidently in the cockpit of a racing car, wins the race and brings back the car in perfect condition. When you have a look at the engine it does not look as though it has ever done a race.

How he goes so quickly can only be explained by the fact that he is a born racing driver. He is remarkably easy to get on with and never tries to excuse his own performance by, for instance, complaining that the gear ratios are 100 revs out or anything like that. He is also a perfect driver with whom to work, a driver who is prepared to leave the preparation of the car entirely to his mechanics.

He never grumbles but does insist on one thing : for the race the car must be exactly as it was during practice. If he is satisfied with the car in practice then that is how he wants it for the race and no alterations of any sort must be made to tyre pressures or suchlike. This is a very sensible outlook and it is easy to see why he was so upset when the car handled badly at Oulton Park after I had put on the new tyres.

CHAPTER 43

TO BE CONTINUED . . .

*An Idea is Born—Maximum co-operation from Coventry-Climax—
Working against the clock—Brabham crashes at Monaco—Action stations—
Alarm and despondency—A superb drive.*

The idea of a larger engine in the successful Formula 2 chassis—like so many ideas—was born during a trial session at Goodwood. Rob Walker had arranged for Salvadori to try our F.1 Connaught and F.2 Cooper on the Sussex track, prior to the Syracuse G.P., and we were all very pleased with the results. After the initial warming up lap Salvadori was clocking 1 minute 32 seconds regularly with the F.1 car—faster than it had ever gone before at Goodwood—whilst with the smaller F.2 car he was lapping in 1 minute 36 seconds, which compared very favourably with the times of the new twin O.H.C. Climax-engined Coopers. We were naturally delighted with the progress we had made with development during the winter months.

Just before we were due to leave Goodwood, Salvadori asked me to step along to the Pippbrook lorry. John Cooper was there together with Rob Walker, and as soon as we arrived Salvadori asked me what would be my reaction to a scheme for putting a 2,000-c.c. engine into the existing F.2 chassis to replace the 1,460 c.c. unit.

" Well," I replied, " for a start it would probably win the Monaco G.P., but where are we going to find an engine of this size to fit the car ? "

John Cooper quickly answered my query. "I reckon it is possible to modify one of the existing twin cam engines by having a special crankshaft made, together with new liners and pistons. I have already discussed the idea with one of the Coventry-Climax draughtsmen and it seems it would work."

John Cooper continued, " Someone will have to take the responsibility of ordering the crankshaft, liners and pistons. We cannot do it ourselves as we are far too busy—but I have drawings ready which I can supply."

The idea sounded a good one to me. With an oversquare engine, a dry weight of 7½ cwt. and power in the region of 180 b.h.p., a 2,000-c.c. Cooper-Climax should be faster (in theory at least) than any other car on any circuit.

I summed up my feelings. " If that is how Coventry-Climax feel," I said, " then a 2,000-c.c. engine is the answer. We can enter the car in Formula 1 races on short, twisty circuits and definitely we are going to make a lot of people sit up and take notice. One thing is sure ; if we do not try it now someone else is bound to do so."

It was at this stage that Rob Walker joined in the discussion. One of the great satisfactions of working with him is that he gets tremendously enthusiastic about any scheme which means " having a go " at the big boys, and it was Rob Walker who took the full responsibility for this new project. He placed an order there and then with John Cooper for the chassis and engine.

Enthusiasts who have followed the fortunes of this first car and others developed from it would do well to remember that it was Rob Walker who put the larger capacity Coopers on the map for it is a fact that the Cooper Car Company was not anxious to risk the financial outlay for that first guinea pig car. It was a risk that could have ended in failure—like so many projects connected with motor-racing—but instead it has been reasonably successful. It certainly has not failed.

John Cooper agreed to arrange for the special crankshaft to be made, so that the stroke of the engine could be lengthened, and then placed an order with Coventry-Climax to supply the remainder of the engine on condition that I supervised its final assembly. We hoped that the eventual capacity would be over 2 litres but in the event Coventry-Climax considered it a practical impossibility to exceed 2 litres and restricted the cubic capacity to 1,960-c.c.

Once the order had been placed with John Cooper and we had all agreed that Monaco on May 19th (the F.1 championship event) would be the ideal race in which to try out the car against the Ferraris and Maseratis we got down to the detail work. I spent a great deal of time over at Coopers discussing such matters as fuel tanks, gearing, the fire-proof screen and modifications to the body and tankage so that the new car would conform more closely to Formula 1 regulations.

Our next problem concerned fuel. After making enquiries from Coventry-Climax I learned that the estimated compression ratio was 12 to 1 and therefore decided to use a large proportion of petrol to ensure economical consumption, a vital necessity with such a small lightweight car where tankage would have to be kept to the minimum. I knew that it would only be possible to carry something in the region of 25 gallons.

I finally decided to try 65% of 100 octane with 35% alcohol even though this would reduce the power output slightly and our next problem was where to carry the fuel. We finally settled for tanks along the side chassis members which meant widening the body but nothing about this project was too difficult for John Cooper—who was bubbling over with enthusiasm from start to finish—and no sooner had the decision been made than drawings were prepared and the fuel tanks ordered.

I then gave some thought to the carburation and chose Webers, the most reliable carburetters to my mind so long as people understand fully how to tune them. This meant a trip to Modena where I saw my old friend Mr. Galletti at Webers and asked his advice concerning the carburation of the Climax engine. He suggested a choke bore of 42 mm. and this led to the next question. How could we ensure a fuel pressure of 4 to 5 lb. a square inch ? The answer was my old favourite, the Tipo Mona pump.

Meanwhile Coventry-Climax had been busy with the engine. All of us—Coventry-Climax, Coopers and myself on behalf of Rob Walker— worked perfectly as a team ; it was a wonderful effort on the part of the

Coventry firm and the amount of enthusiastic support their technicians gave the project was terrific. Many people do not realize that Coventry-Climax is a very large organization, by no means in existence solely for turning out a handful of engines for racing cars each year. Their whole attitude over the project was most helpful and refreshingly unselfish.

On my return from Modena I asked John Cooper to arrange with Coventry-Climax to have the Tipo Mona pump fitted and to ensure that the pump should be partly submerged. Coventry-Climax readily agreed and made the necessary modifications so that the pump could be incorporated in this way. No mechanical pump is self priming and if it is partly submerged then the risk of an air lock is considerably lessened.

As soon as the special crankshaft of stronger quality steel was ready I left with it for Coventry. In the back of a new Morris Minor 1000 van I also carried a 50 gallon drum containing my special mixture of 100 octane Esso and alcohol. It meant working flat out at Coventry for three days and most of the nights as well and the engine was ready to put on the test bench at Friday midnight, little more than 60 hours before we were due to leave Surbiton for Monte Carlo. Coventry-Climax made the necessary arrangements for the engine to be run in the early hours of Saturday morning and anxiously we waited to see what its potential would be in lb. feet or b.h.p.

To my delight—and to the delight as well of Mr. Hassan and Mr. Spears of Coventry-Climax—the figures exceeded our expectations and joyfully we took the engine off the bench and loaded it in the Minor 1000. It was Saturday May 11th, just eight days prior to the Monaco race.

I drove the Minor 1000 " flat " to Surbiton and within minutes of my arrival the engine was being installed in the Cooper chassis. We worked all Saturday night and during Sunday as well and it was yet another job that " started five minutes before midnight "—midnight being the time of departure for the motor race. John Cooper, in shirt sleeves and pulling away at an empty pipe was on the job with us all the time, together with Jack Brabham, the Australian, who had been signed up to drive the Cooper at Monte Carlo, as our original choice—Salvadori—was under contract to B.R.M. and required by the Bourne concern for the " round the houses race." Naturally Jack Brabham put all his enthusiasm into the project (no one will ever be able to call him " Idle Jack " for he works like a beaver) and he " lived " the 1960 c.c. Cooper together with the rest of us.

I wondered as we struggled to complete the assembly of the car, working against time in no uncertain fashion, whether I should telephone Rob Walker and tell him I could not possibly guarantee to prepare the car well enough for it to qualify at Monaco. Had I done so I know he would have been terribly disappointed but nevertheless his reply would have been on these lines :

" Well, Alf, I think you know best."

However, I was determined that somehow or other we would get the new Cooper to the starting line at Monaco in good trim. There was no question of trying out the car at Goodwood for we were booked on the ferry for Monday night and all Jack Brabham was able to do was to get a little of the " feel " of the car on the roads adjoining the Cooper works and on the by-pass. It was more in the nature of a proving run to ascertain whether the fuel pump, gear selector lever, foot pedals, etc., were working properly.

We finally left Surbiton at 4.30 p.m. on Monday and having cleared Dunkirk by 5 a.m. Tuesday arrived in Valence at 9.30 p.m. that evening, having covered 485 miles. We made a stop in Dijon of at least two hours for the inevitable leisurely French lunch and our actual running time was 14½ hours.

Next morning we set off at 7.30 a.m. for Monte Carlo where we arrived exactly twelve hours later. I was just about all-in. having driven solo on both days as Michael had no previous experience of driving on the Continent, and I think this must be the fastest two-day run I have ever made with a transporter.

Rob Walker and most of the *Equipe* were already in Monte Carlo but of Jack Brabham, the driver, there was no sign. He had previously told me not to worry if he did not arrive on Wednesday as he would probably stay a few miles outside Monte Carlo and have a good night's rest before the first practice session, at 6 a.m. on Thursday morning.

However, there was no sign of the Australian next morning when we went out on the circuit and whilst Rob Walker was naturally anxious to try out his new motor-car I insisted that the first person to drive it in practice should be the man chosen to handle it in the race.

Like every other sport, motor-racing has a certain amount of old ladies' gossip circulating around the pits and paddock and if another driver handled the car first time out, so many views and reasons would be put forward by the uninformed that Brabham would get nothing but a distorted picture of what had really happened.

I wanted to prevent anything of this nature occurring and was quite prepared not to practice at all on the first day. After all there was still Friday and Saturday. However, Rob Walker arranged for Roy Salvadori and Peter Collins to drive the car for a few laps and all I could do was to buttonhole the two drivers and insist that they did not exceed a certain rev limit. I knew that if they tried to go quickly and Brabham was unable to equal their times when he eventually arrived it would not only dishearten him but perhaps force him to go faster than he should.

Both Peter Collins and Salvadori played the game by taking things very easily and although the car went very well, neither driver was able to make any worthwhile comment about its handling. The lap times were fairly slow with Collins going round in 1 minute 55 seconds. However, this was the way I wanted it.

After the practice as we were taking the Cooper back to the Diodato garage just before 10 o'clock, I saw Brabham's Borgward ; at least he was in Monte Carlo and I felt both relieved and angry. I thought to myself, " You will have to be taught a lesson," so I stopped the lorry as the Borgward drew level on the other side of the road and called over :

" How did you enjoy your sightseeing tour ? I thought we came down here to go motor-racing."

I don't think Brabham liked it but I had to say something to let off the steam that had been building up inside me during three hours of anxiety at the practice session. I don't know what made Brabham late.

At 6 a.m. next morning the Pippbrook Cooper with Brabham at the wheel was put through its paces. Before he went away from the pits I told him that although it was necessary for the car to put up an acceptable qualifying time he should take things easy. As he went off on his first lap I had a sickening feeling in my stomach that something disasterous was going to happen.

Sure enough an enthusiastic Brabham—delighted with the performance and handling of the car—overlooked the fact that the ratio between front and rear brakes had not been finally adjusted and came into the corner near the Casino too fast for the brakes. He went off the road and that was the end of our challenge at Monaco with a Cooper in the Formula 1 Class. When I heard the news I turned to Michael : " If you get off on the wrong foot," I said, " something always goes wrong."

It was no use crying over spilt milk and fortunately there was a way out. Although it was not possible to repair the Formula 1 Cooper in time for the race we could switch the Pippbrook engine to the Formula 2 Cooper which we had taken to Monaco as second string. Les Leston had been entered as the driver of this car but had blown it up in practice on Friday. It was the works' Cooper that Brabham had driven at the Goodwood Easter meeting.

It was a question of action stations with a vengeance for whatever happened we had got to qualify at the Saturday session or we should not even be in the race. We loaded the two Coopers into the transporter and drove to the nearest garage where we divided ourselves into teams—one from Pippbrook and one from Coopers. It was 10 o'clock in the morning.

Our team consisted of Michael, Stan Jolliffe (our manager), a friend of Rob Walker's from Dorking—Mr. P. Windibank, an auctioneer— who was on holiday in Monte Carlo at the time and myself. Mr. Windibank had never seen a motor race until Monaco and found himself more or less pressganged into service. He was a great help.

In the Cooper team there was John Cooper, Jack Brabham and an Australian friend of Brabham who had travelled down with him in the Borgward. Whilst they took the engine out of Leston's car we removed the 1960-c.c. power unit from the Pippbrook car. We worked throughout the day without a break—eight hours in all—and once the new engine had been installed in the chassis of the " works " Cooper it was then only a matter of preparing the car finally for the practice session.

Whilst Michael and I started on the old familiar checking routine the others packed up and wisely left us to finish the job. When we had completed the preparation I made a final check of the joints for tightness, made sure there was sufficient fuel for the practice session, and then loaded the car in the transporter.

We had no illusions on the Saturday morning. This was the final practice session where we had *got* to qualify the car for the starting grid. If it had been raining that morning we should never have been able to get round quickly enough to qualify, bearing in mind the times that other drivers had already recorded on a dry road.

Fortunately the weather was ideal and Brabham succeeded in recording 1 minute 49.4 seconds. He was in fact going faster with the second string car than with the F.1 Cooper ; he seemed to have more confidence— perhaps because it was the car he had driven at Goodwood. Anyway he knew precisely how the car handled and was completely at home in it. There is a lot to be said for driving a car you know well.

In my opinion Jack Brabham can put out quite a potent challenge as was proved at Monaco. He has made rapid progress since the start of the 1957 season and must not be underestimated. I know a lot of people will agree with me when I say that he will become very much a force to be reckoned with. He is that unusual combination of a first-class engineer and a first-rate driver, so rarely found in motor-racing.

There have been occasions when I have been a little short with Jack Brabham simply because I prepare the car and he drives it but I must admit that he knows what he is talking about as an engineer. The snag is that he gets just as enthusiastic about preparing the car as driving it and is not always content to leave its preparation to me.

We had no trouble at all during the practice session and packed up after ten laps, hoping that we had qualified. The results and final acceptances were not notified until the official practice finished and we were, of course, delighted to find that the Cooper had put up the thirteenth fastest time in a field restricted to sixteen starters. Having checked carburation, temperatures, tyre pressures and fuel consumption we loaded the Cooper into the transporter and returned to the Diodato garage.

The car was not handling entirely to Brabham's satisfaction and I was convinced that here was another case of the tyres being too new. It was my view that with well-worn tyres on the driving wheels Brabham should be able to knock one or even two seconds off his lap times. However, there was no question of using such tyres for the full distance on a circuit like Monaco which really gives tyres the treatment.

A compromise was the answer and it suddenly occurred to me that there was a set of slightly-worn tyres in the transporter that we had used at Goodwood for a few laps on the Pippbrook F.2 Cooper.

Before leaving for the Diodato I discussed the matter fully with Brabham —weighing up all the pros and cons—and he agreed that the tyres should be fitted for the race. They made a tremendous difference. Even with the larger tankage and carrying more fuel (and with more traffic on the road during the race itself) we were going 1½ seconds quicker every lap than we ever did in practice. It just goes to prove that if we had fitted these tyres during practice we should not have had to worry so much about qualifying. One is always learning in motor-racing.

Having completed the wheel change we went through the stages of a general checkover and actually finished working on the car at a reasonable hour, convinced that the Cooper was " right." It was a very different story on Sunday morning when we arrived at the Diodato garage soon after 8 o'clock for there was an ominous pool of oil underneath the gearbox housing.

I knew at once that we should have to remove the gearbox and make sure there was no internal damage. I could not see any visible cracks on the outside and wanted to convince myself there was no trouble inside, for gearboxes are a weakness of Cooper cars and I dared not take any chances.

We set to work within a few yards of the inviting blue waters of the Mediterranean. To my relief the trouble proved to be a bearing cap nut that had cracked and naturally loosened with vibration. Nevertheless, it took us an hour or so to replace the gearbox and it was mid-morning by the time we were through.

There was no time for us to sit back and relax for I wanted to practise a pit stop for fuel. The tankage of the Formula 2 chassis is slightly smaller than on the Formula 1 car and I knew that we should have to call in Brabham before the end of the race. It was a good job we tried out the drill, for Brabham's friend—who had offered to help us in the pits—upset most of the contents of a five-gallon churn over the nose of the car, due to the filler being too small.

We all set to work at once with rubbing down compound to remove the whiteness from the paintwork and get it back to a respectable shade of British racing green again. It was after midday by the time we had finished and I decided that before pushing off for lunch we would start the engine and check that everything was O.K. Michael and the Australian gave me a push start but no sooner was the car under way when I was horrified to find that there was no fuel pressure !

I could not understand what could possibly have gone wrong for the previous evening it had been O.K. Gloomily I climbed out of the cockpit and spoke my thoughts aloud.

" There's no damned fuel pressure, the race starts in less than three hours and I reckon this is a hoodoo car."

Having got this off my chest I removed the fuel pump and took it to pieces whilst Michael and the Australian looked on anxiously. So far as I could see there was nothing wrong so I replaced it. When I started up there was still no fuel pressure, so I had the pump off again and tried to adjust it by first increasing, then reducing the pressure setting. There was still no pressure and I finally came to the conclusion that it was probably the fuel gauge itself that was at fault.

I told Michael to fetch me a spare gauge from the transporter and by the time this had been fitted it was already 1 o'clock. Within an hour we should have to be on the circuit before they closed it.

Hopefully I settled down in the cockpit and the boys gave me a push start. The engine fired and I looked at the gauge. Still no damned pressure ! I dared not delay any longer and, shouting to Michael and the Australian to get down to the pits with the transporter, I set off with the Cooper.

On arrival at the circuit I had another look at the fuel pump and gauge. By now I had calmed down as there was nothing else that could be done in the time available and I had a careful look at the gauge. Suddenly out of the gloom came a ray of sunshine ; I recognized it as an old one that I had been carrying with me for years, a gauge that had never worked properly anyway.

Nevertheless we still did not know for sure whether there was any fuel pressure and, strictly speaking, the car went to the start without any. I just kept my fingers crossed and hoped that both gauges were dud, for without any pressure it was almost a waste of time to start in the race.

There was the usual heart-stopping scramble to reach the Gasometer Bend first after the flag had dropped (there are few more exciting sights than the start of the Monaco round-the-houses race) and Brabham was in there with the Ferraris, Maseratis and Vanwalls when the field streaked by at the end of the first lap.

When the car came by again on the second and third laps I thought to myself, " How clever he is to keep going without any fuel pressure." For although I assured Rob Walker that only the gauge was faulty, not the pump, I was far from convinced that this was the case.

What we did not know was that as soon as the flag dropped and Brabham got the car under way the gauge started to work and was showing a normal pressure of four pounds by the end of the first lap.   I wish we had known this in the pits for as each lap was completed we became even more anxious about the next one.

Mr. Windibank was worried for a very different reason.   When we changed over the engines I organized things in such a way that each member of the Pippbrook team had a specific job to do and Mr. Windibank was told to remove the exhaust manifold from our engine and to refit it in the F.2 chassis.   He is very conscientious and for lap after lap—as Brabham tore round the Monaco circuit—the auctioneer from Dorking sat on the pit counter with an expression of acute anxiety on his face ; would the manifold, which he had fitted with such loving care, remain firmly in position throughout the race ?

During that Monaco Grand Prix, his first motor-race, Mr. Windibank came closer to understanding the trials and tribulations of motor-racing than thousands of enthusiasts who have watched the sport on circuits all over Europe.

After ten laps, by which time the triple crash had eliminated Moss, Collins and Hawthorn—and Brabham was lying in sixth place ahead of Masten Gregory's Maserati, and Trintignant's Ferrari—the crowd in the grandstand was beginning to take an interest in this impudent little green car that had suddenly appeared from nowhere.

They cheered Brabham as the Australian " diced " successfully with Flockhart in the B.R.M. and after thirty laps it was Fangio (Maserati), Brooks (Vanwall), von Trips (Ferrari), and Jack Brabham—followed by Flockhart (B.R.M.), then Menditeguy, Masten Gregory and Scarlatti— all on Maseratis.   Then came Lewis-Evans (Connaught), Trintignant (Ferrari) and Bueb (Connaught).

I mention the placing at some length because it really was incredible how the flying Cooper was so well up in the field after thirty laps at Monaco against the cream of the world's Grand Prix cars and drivers.

And so it went on.   For another twenty laps a highly delighted Brabham tore round the Monaco circuit and at fifty laps the race order was Fangio, Brooks, Menditeguy, von Trips, Flockhart and Brabham. However, the Australian re-passed Flockhart shortly afterwards and it was at this stage that we started to think about the fuel stop.   It was Rob Walker who finally decided that we should stop Brabham at sixty laps instead of fifty as we had previously planned, so as to reduce the danger of being re-passed by the B.R.M.

To me and to most people it was absolutely incredible that our car was still running. Here we were holding our own with the " big boys " and quite frankly it was almost unbelievable to me that we had reached the stage of even discussing the possibility of bringing in the car at sixty laps, let alone actually doing so.

On the sixty-second lap Brabham pulled into the pits and we went through the refuelling drill as though we had been working together for years. Our enthusiasm was tremendous. Everything was done so quickly that when Brabham got out of the car and tried to have a few quick words—which he likes to do however hectic the race—he was banged on the shoulder and bundled back into the cockpit. He did not even have time to take a swig from the bottle of water on the pit counter.

With Brabham in the car I shouted " Contact " and pressed the electric starter, a special plug and solenoid switch with a pistol grip sort of arrangement ; to my dismay nothing happened. In desperation I pressed it again but still nothing happened. I could see through the aperture in the body panel that the starter was not turning and looking over my shoulder I shouted to John Cooper.

" The starter does not work. Pass me the quick lift jack so that we can get the rear wheels off the ground and start in gear by turning them."

Meanwhile Charles Cooper was getting so excited that I thought he would fall off the pit counter and eventually his enthusiasm exploded into the two words—repeated heatedly several times—" push it."

In the excitement he had forgotten all about the regulation forbidding a push start as had everyone else in the pit with the exception of myself. From then on everything happened far too quickly for me and I looked on helplessly as John Cooper, Michael and the Australian started pushing the car. Almost immediately the Cooper " fired " and streaked away from the pits, going like a bomb. Meanwhile the unfortunate Australian had caught his hand on the rear cantilever spring and returned to the pits in some considerable pain.

Personally I could have shot all three of them for I knew that this breach of the rules could easily end in disqualification of the car. The rules were most emphatic that no car could be push started. So far as I was concerned we were as good as out of the race and it was now a matter of seeing whether the Cooper could last the full race distance so that we could learn something from its behaviour over two hundred tough, exacting miles.

Charles and John Cooper were undismayed and immediately set about working out an alibi. " We can say that the car was started electrically," John pointed out, " but the Australian got hooked on the cantilever and we all had to chase after the car to get him free. As a matter of fact," continued John—warming to his theme—" we were not trying to push start the car but to stop it ! "

I knew very well that this story would not hold water if either Maserati or B.R.M.—whose pits were very close to ours—chose to lodge a protest.

However, nothing was said and this may be due to the fact that on the hundredth lap—with only five more to go—the Cooper packed up near the railway station when Brabham was lying third. Pluckily he pushed the car towards the finish line during which time Masten Gregory, Lewis-Evans and Trintignant passed him. The Cooper finished sixth and I cannot help wondering whether a protest would have been lodged if misfortune had not dropped us back three places.

What had happened was that the mounting of the fuel pump could not stand the fatigue and broke. The pump itself fell off and that was the end of our Monaco Grand Prix. But what a wonderful race it had been for *Equipe* Walker. The little Cooper was one of only six cars to finish out of sixteen starters and in spite of not getting that hard-won third place we were all delighted with its performance. After all we had achieved something and in motor-racing—like any other sport—an achievement is not necessarily measured in terms of victory or even a place in the first three.

So far as the future is concerned, I feel confident that *Equipe* Walker will go from strength to strength. So far as I personally am concerned I would like to put on record that Rob Walker and Pippbrook Garage have enabled me to get a kick out of motor-racing again and to enjoy it. I feel as enthusiastic about it all as when I started with John Heath in 1948 ; the wheel has turned full circle and I am back where I started in so far as my morale is as high as it has ever been and I am anxious once again to match British cars against the world as John Heath did so courageously with the H.W.M.s.

CHAPTER 44

CONTINUED WITH PRIDE

A bitter disappointment—Moss diced with
shredding tyres—Fangio fears for his crown—
The lonely winner

It must have been a bitter disappointment for Rob Walker and Alf Francis when their Walker-Cooper—driven by Jack Brabham and lying third in the 1957 Monaco Grand Prix with only five laps to go—retired with a broken fuel pump mounting.

Brabham had put up an incredible performance against the Ferraris, Maseratis and Vanwalls. The little 1960 c.c. Cooper was one of only six cars to finish out of sixteen starters when the Australian pluckily pushed the car over the finish line.

Eight months after the Monaco race—and eight weeks after this book was first published, in November 1957—*Equipe* Walker hit the jackpot when Stirling Moss drove the Cooper to victory in the 1958 Argentine Grand Prix and defeated the Ferraris and Maseratis with over half a litre more under their bonnets. It was a sensation, and gave Rob Walker and Alf Francis their first ever victory in a World Championship event.

What an achievement for *Equipe* Walker but more was to come. In the Monaco Grand Prix in May the Walker-Cooper—driven by Maurice Trintignant—gave Rob Walker and Alf Francis their second World Championship victory in a row.

At the time I was Motor-Racing Correspondent of *The Observer* and Alf gave me an exclusive story on each race. *The Observer* pieces have been recreated more-or-less as they appeared in 1958 and it is fitting that the final chapter in the Alf Francis story should highlight two such memorable victories for a British car.

PETER LEWIS

November 1991

Motor Racing

Moss Diced With Shredding Tyres

ALF FRANCIS, chief mechanic to R. R. C. Walker, owner of the winning Cooper-Climax, tells his story of the Argentine Grand Prix in an exclusive telephone call from Buenos Aires to PETER LEWIS in London.

I SHALL never forget this race, and the terrific gamble we took in running the Cooper-Climax right through to the end on the same set of tyres. If the race had gone on for another five laps, or even less, it would have finished us. The tyres would not have lasted out.

But our gamble was worthwhile. It enabled me to share with Stirling Moss a victory in a world championship event.

I remember only too well how hard we tried in 1954 with Moss's private 250F Maserati to bring off such a victory, but we never quite made it. Now we have done it at last—and with a British car.

Rob Walker's Cooper-Climax will go down in history as the first privately entered car to triumph over the works' teams. I only wish he had been here to see how this wonderful little car in the hands of Moss astounded the Argentine crowds.

For me it was a welcome and exhilarating return to working with Stirling 16 months after leaving *équipe* Moss and joining R. R. C. Walker. Without Moss at the wheel we could not have won.

Perfect Team

In fact with only Tim Wall (my Australian assistant) and myself in the pits, and Stirling out on the circuit, we had a most workable combination. There was perfect understanding and co-operation. I got a lot of pleasure out of the way we made the Maserati and Ferrari teams sit up during the practice sessions.

Incidentally, Guerino Bertocchi (head mechanic to Maserati) and three other Italian mechanics were there to look after all the Maserati entries. It seems that Maserati are still going motor racing even though they do not have an official works team.

Stirling was somewhat concerned about driving the Cooper-Climax. Except for a few practice laps at Goodwood last September he had never handled it. Nevertheless, he was next best to Fangio's fastest time of the day in the second practice session.

Eye Injury

The car went well on the new fuel and we were obviously getting the figure of 174 b.h.p. that I had obtained before leaving England. The Cooper-Climax compared favourably with the Ferraris (all Vee-sixes) and the Maseratis and was running better than it did when Jack Brabham drove it at Brands Hatch on Boxing Day.

This was mainly because of better preparations and modifications to help cool the cockpit. These modifications, which included airscoops and external oil and water pipes, really paid off. The heat was intense and the circuit a tiring one. A cool or relatively cool driver stood a better chance.

Unlike the usual pre-race panic, there was little to do on the car after the practice sessions, although the gearchange was inclined to be slow. We could not improve it much and it stayed this way for the race. Then, when Stirling was joking with his wife, Katie, in front of the pits she accidentally poked her finger in his eye. So Stirling drove on one eye in the qualifying trials, and could only manage seventh fastest time.

Nevertheless, the car was going well, and although I could not see us winning, I reckoned a place in the first three, if the damaged eye did not ruin our chances.

In the race, Moss got away to a terrific start, one of the best I have ever seen him make. Then it was a matter of taking things quietly and watching points. I knew from the practice sessions that our tyre wear would be terrific, and that we ought to call in the Cooper-Climax after 50 laps. Meanwhile, our strategy was to wait and see.

So we kept the car lapping regularly at 1 min. 44 sec. or 1 min. 44.5 sec. while Hawthorn and Behra scrapped for second place. On the twentieth lap we were up there with them. Collins was out of the running, having broken a half-shaft on the starting line.

On lap 35 we went into the lead when Fangio stopped for tyres. Stirling was driving a wonderful race, making up time on the slow corner as only he knows how. But I was getting more and more worried about those tyres.

Another Chance

After the sixtieth lap we slowed down the Cooper to rest the tyres. For the same reason we decided against going for fastest lap.

At 70 laps—10 from the finish—Moss was 29 sec. in the lead from Musso. At the finish he led the Italian over the line by only 2.7 sec.!

Those 10 laps, with the gap rapidly closing, were like 10 hours to Tim Wall and myself. But we had to take the risk—one of my biggest gambles in 10 years of motor racing. Had we stopped for tyres the Cooper-Climax could never have won.

Now we have the Buenos Aires Grand Prix next Sunday and there is very little that we have to do to the car. As this is a Formula Libre event, we will use alcohol fuel and I hope to do well. It is a slower circuit, and the race is run in heats, with half an hour between heats. New tyres are expected early in the week.

Stirling Moss is excited about the car and hopes to drive it again this season. I think he will, and there is nothing I would like better than to race with him and the Cooper-Climax at Monaco in the second world championship event of the 1958 season.

Motor Racing

Fangio Fears For His Crown

As told by Alf Francis to Peter Lewis

WHEN Stirling Moss asked me to fit a flask filled with orange squash in the cockpit of the Cooper-Climax a few hours before the start of the Argentine Grand Prix I knew he was going to make a non-stop run.

This worried me because tyre consumption tests had told us that, with new tyres just barely "scrubbed," we might manage to complete 50 laps of the 80-lap race. I have never been on a circuit where tyre wear is so heavy.

I fitted the flask behind closed doors, but even so two people found out about it; one was a TV commentator, the other a motoring correspondent. I do not know if they told our rivals, but in any case nobody believed it was humanly possible for Moss to make a non-stop run. Actually, Fangio did not consider us as a rival. He was more concerned about the Ferrari.

The bluff worked, and I even got out the quick-lift jack 30 laps from the end, pretending to prepare for a tyre change. However, it did not fool the TV commentator who, apparently, told his audience: "The mechanic is bluffing. Moss will not stop for tyres."

'Over the Hill?'

If Ferrari had known we were not going to stop, they would have speeded up Musso. The only reason the Italian closed up during the latter stages of the race was because Moss slowed at the rate of two seconds a lap for the last 15 laps.

I was not surprised that Fangio wore out his tyres so early in the race. The Argentine Press was critical of him, and one newspaper summed up the general feeling: "Is the old man over the hill?"

I am inclined to think he may be. He is not the confident Fangio we knew last season. There was anxiety in his eyes during the whole Argentine series, and the worried look of a man who wonders if his pedestal is toppling.

His practice times varied by as much as two seconds a lap and watching him on the corners it was obvious that he was pushing himself beyond the limit. I have never seen Fangio cornering like it. To my mind Behra was more polished.

Clutch Gone

The aviation petrol surprised me. The Formula I cars do not appear to have lost any power at all, and I do not think lap times will be slower than last year on the European circuits.

By the way we do not expect too much from our Cooper-Climax at Monaco. It does not have the legs of the Ferraris and Maseratis on a twisty circuit. The handling of the car has got to be improved, and the gearchange as well. It is too slow.

In the fourth lap of the Argentine Grand Prix Moss broke the hydraulic system operating the clutch mechanism when the gear jammed in second. For the rest of the race—76 laps—he changed gear without a clutch although he himself thought he was still operating it.

Bitter Anger

I was bitterly disappointed and angry about the accident that put us out of the Buenos Aires Grand Prix. It is ridiculous to allow cars like the one that rammed Moss to take part in major international events. Their roadholding is hopeless and, generally speaking, the skill of their drivers is appalling. Few of them even got to know the circuit properly.

The Chevrolet that rammed Moss hugged the inside of the circuit after leaving the start line, and just went straight on at the first corner, hitting Moss in the side as he went round on the outside.

I dread to think what would have happened if the Chevrolet had arrived a second or two later and got mixed up with the main pack.

═══ *Motor Racing* ═══

The Lonely Winner

ALF FRANCIS, chief mechanic to R. R. C. Walker, owner of the Cooper-Climax that has won two out of the three World Championship Grand Prix races this year, talks to PETER LEWIS.

WHEN Stirling Moss won the Argentine Grand Prix last January with a car prepared by me, I was naturally a very proud man, but I never dreamed that another one of our cars would win the Monaco Grand Prix on May 18.

To tell the truth I don't think a great deal about our chances of victory in any race. It's no good having pipe-dreams, for looking after a racing car is a strictly routine job of work, and my job as chief mechanic is to get the car on to the starting grid in the best possible trim. Usually I have so much on my mind that the outcome of the race is a secondary consideration.

After the Silverstone meeting on May 3 where our new two-litre Cooper-Climax was driven by Maurice Trintignant we went back to Pippbrook Garage, Dorking, where I prepare Rob Walker's racing cars with Tim Wall, an Australian and my assistant mechanic, and Michael Reach our 19-year-old apprentice. Apart from a bench drill, we have the normal facilities of a service station but nothing even remotely comparable with the Vanwall and B.R.M. set-up. People are amazed when they visit Dorking and find us in a workshop that is little larger than the car itself.

(Jane Bown)

Rob Walker...the winning owner.

*   *   *

Our main concern after Silverstone—apart from fitting a new cylinder head to cure a tendency to overheat—was to "tailor" the cockpit of the Cooper to fit Trintignant. He is a small wiry man with narrow hips and had been bounced about at Silverstone like a pea in a pod. This matter of the seating position is vitally important and there is no doubt that Trintignant can save a second a lap on most circuits if he is nicely fitted in the cockpit.

We had quite a lot of work to do before leaving for Monaco and it meant 10 days from 8.30 in the morning until nine or ten o'clock at night. These are quite normal working hours but when things get really hectic in motor-racing all-night sessions are commonplace. The engine, gearbox, suspension, chassis and body had to be checked; our spares list had to be worked out based on the number of Continental races which we intended to enter and had to include different back-axle ratios and types of tyres for the Monaco and Zandvoort circuits.

When I had made all the necessary arrangements for getting the Commer lorry across to the Continent, and collected sufficient travellers' cheques and cash for two

weeks, we left Dorking for Dover. Incidentally it cost nearly £60 to take the lorry across the Channel and back plus £50 for petrol whilst on the Continent and return plus £3 a day expenses for each of us. The 10-day trip to Monaco and Zandvoort cost Rob Walker well over £300.

We had a leisurely trip to Monte Carlo with Tim and I sharing the driving and having left Dunkirk at 6 p.m. pushed on to Rheims for the night. The next night we spent in Lyons, leaving there at 8.30 on the morning of the third day and arriving in Monte Carlo 10 hours later.

Trintignant practised on the Thursday morning and was very slow indeed, so much so that his best time of one minute 46 seconds would not have qualified us as starters for the Monaco Grand Prix. It suddenly occurred to me that perhaps I was using the wrong type of tyre: one designed for long-distance racing and long life as opposed to one with a more rapid rate of wear but better properties of adhesion. Sure enough when we changed the tyres Trintignant knocked four seconds off his lap times.

On the Friday morning, in the practice session that took place from 5.45 a.m. to 8.30 a.m., he was even better and got down to one minute 41.1 seconds. There is no doubt that the best time to qualify at Monaco is during this early morning session when tyre adhesion is at its best. When the sun has dried out the dampness it leaves a perfect surface but it takes some effort to get up at that time.

∗   ∗   ∗

Trintignant did not attempt to put up a better time at the Saturday practice session and our next task was to see how the twisty Monaco circuit had affected the car. It meant removing the body to check whether it or the chassis had been affected by lateral stresses, and particularly whether the flexibly mounted fuel tanks had been misplaced by side thrust and were touching the body, which could cause a leak.

All was well and having estimated that we should require 17 gallons of fuel at 11 miles per gallon the Cooper's tanks were filled up and the car was ready. Actually we carried 22 gallons, with five in reserve, and used 16 during the race. The Vanwalls with a petrol consumption of only six miles per gallon had to carry 40 gallons, which is quite a lot of extra weight.

On race day the three of us organised the pit with extra fuel, spares for the carburettors, magneto and ignition system, four wheels complete with tyres, oil, and all the usual motor-racing paraphernalia with enough wire to hold the body together in the event of the Cooper shaking anything loose. Then we were on the grid with Trintignant confidently settled in the cockpit and as happy as a sandboy.

Three—two—one minute to go. As always my heart stood still as the cars surged forward in a rapidly moving traffic jam towards the Gasometer Hairpin. I breathed a sigh of relief when Trintignant came round at the end of the first lap having emerged unscathed from the fray.

From then on I marvelled at the way the dapper little Frenchman tacked himself confidently on to the tail of Brabham in the new 2.2-litre Cooper-Climax and then, after ten laps, on to Stirling Moss's Vanwall. There was nothing that Stirling could do to lose the Cooper and there Trintignant stayed.

∗   ∗   ∗

When Stirling took the lead Trintignant moved up as well and when the Vanwall retired the Cooper took first place and held it to the end. To us in the pit Trintignant never looked as though he was having to push either himself or the car and was obviously enjoying his "Jack the Giant Killer" tactics.

There were two thoughts in my mind when the race was over and we had won. First of all I wanted to get far enough away from the pit to light a cigarette and secondly it was suddenly brought home to me that to start a lone entry in two successive world championship races and win them both against powerful team opposition was something that called for a celebration that evening. And believe me we sure celebrated.

EPILOGUE

Sadly, Alf Francis, that brilliant and talented man, died in Oklahoma in June 1983 at the age of 65. Our thanks to his daughter Krysia for compiling this brief summary of events between 1958 and 1983.

1958	Alf continues working for Rob Walker. Stirling Moss joins the team which has many successes in Formula 1 during the next three years.
1959	Alf works with Valerio Colotti on racing gearbox for Rob Walker's 2.2 litre Cooper, type FPF.
1961 (May)	In the Monaco G.P. – with Rob Walker's 1.5 litre Lotus-Climax 18 – Stirling Moss and Alf scored their greatest victory. There was panic on the grid when – with 30 gallons of fuel in the tanks – Alf welded a cracked chassis tube.
1961-62	Alf moves to Modena, Italy and joins Gears Speed Development, manufacturing Colotti Francis gearboxes.
1962 (April)	Stirling Moss crashes at Goodwood.
1963	Collapse of G.S.D. Alf works on Mario Cabrall's F.1 car at A.T.S. in Bologna.
1964	Alf works on F.2 Cooper at A.T.S. for Jo Siffert.
1965-70	Alf joins Serenissima as Development Engineer and designs a special prototype sports car for Count Volpi, building six Serenissimas.
1971	Alf moves to Classic Motors, Oklahoma City as Service Director to advise on restoration of classic cars for the Preservation Hall Auto Museum of Classic Motors. Also prepares cars for Wayne Horst Racing Team.
1975	Forms own company 'Alf Francis Inc. Scuderia' in Wichita, Kansas.
1981	Sets up European Classics Scuderia, Oklahoma, specialising in classic cars. Prepares Formula Ford with Phillip Rogers.
1983	Alf develops lung cancer.

Alf Francis outside European Classics Scuderia with a Formula Ford. This was the last car he worked on before his death.

POSTSCRIPT

From The Alf Francis Diary For Tuesday July 4th, 1950

What a life. Why on earth did I ever undertake such a job—it's worse than working in the salt mines of Siberia. We had snow and fog on the Mt. Cenis—it must have been the worst night ever on the Pass. I am absolutely worn out—must press on.

INDEX